ESSAY ON TRANSCENDENTAL PHILOSOPHY

Also available from Continuum:

Being and Event, Alain Badiou
Conditions, Alain Badiou
Infinite Thought, Alain Badiou
Logics of Worlds, Alain Badiou
Theoretical Writings, Alain Badiou
Theory of the Subject, Alain Badiou
Cinema I, Gilles Deleuze
Cinema II, Gilles Deleuze
Dialogues II, Gilles Deleuze
Difference and Repetition, Gilles Deleuze
The Fold, Gilles Deleuze
Foucault, Gilles Deleuze
Francis Bacon, Gilles Deleuze
Kant's Critical Philosophy, Gilles Deleuze
Logic of Sense, Gilles Deleuze
Nietzsche and Philosophy, Gilles Deleuze
Proust and Signs, Gilles Deleuze
Anti-Oedipus, Gilles Deleuze and Félix Guattari
A Thousand Plateaues, Gilles Deleuze and Félix Guattari
Seeing the Invisible, Michel Henry
After Finitude, Quentin Meillassoux
Time for Revolution, Antonio Negri
Politics of Aesthetics, Jacques Rancière
Of Habit, Félix Ravaisson
The Five Senses, Michel Serres
Art and Fear, Paul Virilio
Negative Horizon, Paul Virilio

ESSAY ON TRANSCENDENTAL PHILOSOPHY

Salomon Maimon

---

*Translated by Nick Midgley, Henry Somers-Hall,
Alistair Welchman and Merten Reglitz*

Introduction and Notes by Nick Midgley

Note on the Translation by Alistair Welchman

continuum

Continuum International Publishing Group
The Tower Building
11 York Road
London SE1 7NX

80 Maiden Lane
Suite 704
New York NY 10038

www.continuumbooks.com

Translation © Nick Midgley, Henry Somers-Hall, Alistair Welchman, Merten Reglitz, 2010

Introduction to the Translation © Nick Midgley, 2010

Note on the Translation © Alistair Welchman, 2010

All rights reserved. No part of this publication may be reproduced or transmitted in any form or by any means, electronic or mechanical, including photocopying, recording, or any information storage or retrieval system, without prior permission in writing from the publishers.

British Library Cataloguing-in-Publication Data
A catalogue record for this book is available from the British Library.

ISBN: HB: 978-1-4411-5476-7
  PB: 978-1-4411-1384-9

Library of Congress Cataloguing-in-Publication Data
Malmon, Salomon, 1754–1800.
  [Versuch über die Transzendentalphilosphie. English]
  Essay on transcendental philosophy/Salomon Maimon; translated by Nick Midgley ... [et. al].
    p. cm.
  Includes bibliographical references and index.
  ISBN-13: 978-1-4411-5476-7 (HB)
  ISBN-10: 1-4411-5476-0 (HB)
  ISBN-13: 978-1-4411-1384-9 (pbk.)
  ISBN-10: 1-4411-1384-3 (pbk.)
  1. Transcendentalism. 2. Kant, Immanuel, 1724–1804. I. Title.
  B3066.v413 2010
  181'.06–DC22

2009027559

Typeset by BookEns, Royston, Herts.
Printed and bound in Great Britain by the MPG Books Group.

Contents

The Translators — vii
Introduction to the Translation — ix
Note on the Translation — lvii
Note on page numbering, notes, references and typography — lxv
Acknowledgements — lxvii

Dedication — 1
Introduction — 5
Chapter 1 — 11
    Matter, Form of Cognition, Form of Sensibility,
    Form of Understanding, Time and Space
Chapter 2 — 19
    Sensibility, Imagination, Understanding,
    A Priori Concepts of the Understanding or Categories,
    Schemata, Answer to the Question *Quid Juris?*,
    Answer to the Question *Quid Facti?*, Doubts about the Latter
Chapter 3 — 44
    Ideas of the Understanding, Ideas of Reason, etc.
Chapter 4 — 49
    Subject and Predicate. The Determinable and the
    Determination
Chapter 5 — 56
    Thing, Possible, Necessary, Ground, Consequence, etc.

CONTENTS

Chapter 6	63
Identity, Difference, Opposition, Reality, Logical and Transcendental Negation	
Chapter 7	68
Magnitude	
Chapter 8	70
Alteration, Change, etc.	
Chapter 9	80
Truth, Subjective, Objective, Logical, Metaphysical	
Chapter 10	85
On the I, Materialism, Idealism, Dualism, etc.	
Short Overview of the Whole Work	90
My Ontology	126
On Symbolic Cognition and Philosophical Language	139
Notes and Clarifications on Some Passages of this Work whose Expression was Concise	173
Appendix I Letter from Maimon to Kant	228
Appendix II Letter from Kant to Herz	230
Appendix III Maimon's Article from the Berlin Journal for Enlightenment	238
Appendix IV Newton's Introduction to the Quadrature of Curves	250
Glossary of Philosophical Terms and their Translations	253
Bibliography	259
Index	263

The Translators

Nick Midgley is a philosopher and translator based in London. He co-translated Habermas's 'Dialectical Idealism in Transition to Materialism' in *The New Schelling*, ed. Judith Norman and Alistair Welchman (Continuum 2004).

Merten Reglitz is a PhD candidate in philosophy at the University of Warwick.

Henry Somers-Hall is Senior Lecturer in Philosophy at Manchester Metropolitan University. His primary research interests are German Idealism, phenomenology, and the philosophy of Gilles Deleuze.

Alistair Welchman is Assistant Professor of Philosophy at the University of Texas, San Antonio. He is the co-translator of Schopenhauer's *World as Will and Representation* (Cambridge University Press 2010) and has written widely on the instersections between German idealism, contemporary European thought and cognitive science.

Introduction to the Translation

Maimon's Life and Formation as a Philosopher

Maimon was born in 1753 in Lithuania in the kingdom of Poland, to whose monarch the *Essay on Transcendental Philosophy* is dedicated. He was thus twenty-nine years younger than Kant (born in 1724), but he lived only to the age of forty-seven, dying in 1800 four years before Kant.

He wrote an autobiography[1] which covers the period of his life up to approximately the time of the publication of the *Essay on Transcendental Philosophy* in 1790, and it is from this source that the following account of his early years is drawn.

He was born Shlomo or Salomon ben Joshua into a poor family in the village of Sukowiborg; he was, as he later puts it in the letter to Kant included in this volume, 'condemned at birth to live out the best years of my life in the forests of Lithuania, deprived of every assistance in acquiring knowledge' – this is not quite true for his father hopes he will become a rabbi or Talmudic scholar and he is sent away to school very young where he studies the Torah and Talmud. At the age of eleven a marriage is arranged for him as a way out of poverty, and he is a father by the age of fourteen. He lives with his wife until he is twenty-five, learns the Roman alphabet and studies the Kabbalah and Maimonides; he also reads books of natural science and earns some money practising medicine. He makes

---

[1] Salomon Maimon, *Salomon Maimons Lebensgeschichte*, ed. Zwi Batscha (Frankfurt: Insel Verlag 1984), trans. J. C. Murray as *The Autobiography of Salomon Maimon* (Chicago: University of Illinois Press, 2001).

contact with the Hassidim but breaks with them very strongly and devotes a chapter of his autobiography to criticising their irrationalism; it is the rationalism of Maimonides that attracts and inspires him.

Determined to pursue his study of the sciences he walks out of his marriage in 1777, setting off for Berlin, never to return. He has no money and sleeps rough or stays with rabbis who know his family or whom he is able to impress with his learning. When he arrives in Berlin he is carrying a copy of a commentary he has written in Hebrew on Maimonides *Guide to the Perplexed*. The entry of poor Jews to the city is controlled by its Jewish community, and fearing that his pursuit of rational enquiry poses a threat to orthodox religion, the Elders dismay Maimon by turning him away. He heads back east, travelling from place to place, at times living as a tramp and beggar but eventually has the good fortune to be taken in by the chief rabbi of Poznan, who finds him work as a private tutor. He remains here for two successful years before taking up again his project of scientific study in Berlin. Returning to Berlin, but this time arriving by coach, he avoids the vetting to which only the poor were subjected. He enters the circle of the so-called Berlin Aufklärer around Moses Mendelssohn, which includes Kant's former student and Mendelssohn's physician, Markus Herz; he reads Wolff, Locke and Spinoza. His time in Berlin is evidently not however just one of quiet study, for Mendelssohn has cause to question his dissolute behaviour and he leaves the city once again. He travels this time to the west, to Holland and Hamburg, and at his lowest point contemplates suicide in a Dutch canal. He is able to return to his studies when he obtains a scholarship to study for two years at the Gymnasium in Altona.[2] It is here that he adopts the name Maimon in homage to Maimonides, know in Hebrew as Moses ben Maimon. On finishing at the Gymnasium, rather than taking up residence again in Berlin, on Mendelssohn's suggestion he moves to Breslau where he translates Mendelssohn's recently published *Morgenstunden* into Hebrew and writes a Hebrew text on Newtonian physics. He takes courses in medicine with a view to a career as a doctor, and obtains more employment as a tutor.

He finally returns to Berlin after Mendelssohn's death in 1786, where he remains for the next nine years, and it is not until then that he reads

---

[2] Altona is now a bohemian district of Hamburg, but it was then under Danish control. It developed an important and lively Jewish community, because Jews could live there free of the onerous restrictions imposed by the city of Hamburg itself.

INTRODUCTION TO THE TRANSLATION

Kant's *Critique of Pure Reason* which had been first published in 1781 and whose second edition appeared in 1787. It is not known exactly when he first read it, but his page references in the *Essay* always refer to the first rather than the second edition, and though it is possible that his interest was sparked by discussion of the new edition, the *Critique* had in any case only become the centre of philosophical debate in Germany several years after it first appeared.[3] He describes his encounter with the *Critique* thus:

> The way I went about studying this work was very particular. At a first reading, I only arrived at an obscure idea of each part. I then tried to render it distinct by thinking it for myself, and thus tried to enter into the spirit of the author, what is properly called putting oneself in the author's place. As I had already appropriated the systems of Spinoza, Hume and Leibniz in the same way, it was natural that I sought to find a system agreeing with all these systems – a coalition-system. And in fact I found it and established it in the form of comments and explanations of the *Critique of Pure Reason* which finally gave birth to my *Essay on Transcendental Philosophy*.[4]

Maimon presented his manuscript to Markus Herz who forwarded it to Kant in April 1789. At this time Kant is at the height of his fame and since publishing the *Critique of Pure Reason* in 1781 he has been developing the whole system of the critical philosophy, publishing the *Prolegomena to Any Future Metaphysics* to popularize the *Critique* in 1783, the grounding of Newtonian physics on the *a priori* principles demonstrated in the *Critique* in the *Metaphysical Foundations of Natural Science* in 1786, a revised second edition of the *Critique* in 1787 and the consequences of the critical philosophy for morals in the *Critique of Practical Reason* in 1788. When he

---

[3] There is nevertheless evidence that Maimon's *Essay* is not based on the first edition of the *Critique* alone. Firstly the example of a synthetic *a priori* proposition to which he most frequently refers is: 'a straight line is the shortest between two points', an example which appears only in the 'Preamble' to *Prolegomena to Any Future Metaphysics* and the Introduction to the second edition of the *Critique*, but not in the first edition. Second he takes up Kant's question 'How are synthetic *a priori* propositions possible?' which Kant also brings to the fore in the 'Preamble' to *Prolegomena to any Future Metaphysics* and in the Introduction to the second edition of the *Critique* (B19–24), but which is less prominent in the first edition.

[4] Maimon, 'Lebensgeschichte', *Gesammelte Werke*, Vol. I, p. 557.

xi

INTRODUCTION TO THE TRANSLATION

received Maimon's manuscript he was working on the *Critique of Judgement* which will appear a few months after Maimon's essay in 1790. During this time Kant has tried to ignore the provocations of his critics and leave the defence of his philosophy to others, in order to devote all his energies to the enormous task of completing the critical system. So when he writes back to Herz two months later, he complains at Herz having asked him to read such a long and difficult manuscript. He has, he says, only managed to read the first two chapters,[5] but he goes on to shower praise on Maimon's *Essay*:

> just a glance at it was enough to make me recognize its excellence, and not only that none of my opponents has understood me and the principle question as well as Mr Maimon, but also that only a few people possess such an acute mind for such profound investigations.
> (Letter from Kant to Herz, May 26, 1789)[6]

Kant nevertheless considers it inappropriate for him to recommend the book to a publisher on the grounds that it is largely directed *against* him. Nevertheless there is no doubt that this praise increases Maimon's standing in Berlin and he finds a publisher for the *Essay*.

Kant's response to the *Essay* is limited to the criticisms and recommendations for revisions made in this one letter. Maimon writes to him several times over the next ten years seeking Kant's opinion of his subsequent publications but Kant never replies. Maimon is further frustrated that his *Essay* is never reviewed, he challenges Reinhold over this and Reinhold replies that he didn't feel he sufficiently understood him; Maimon himself sends a copy of the *Essay* to the *Allgemeine Literatur Zeitung*, which had become the leading journal of Kantian philosophy, but the editor informs him that three of the leading speculative thinkers of the time have turned down the invitation to review it on the basis that they could not grasp its depths. So there is a sense of Maimon both achieving recognition and still feeling unrecognized. Fichte, who was shortly to become famous after publishing his *Doctrine of Science* in 1794, wrote in a letter to Reinhold in 1795:

---

[5] In fact Kant's discussion of the *Essay* in this letter comprises the material of the first three chapters of the published version of the *Essay*.
[6] This letter is in the Appendices.

INTRODUCTION TO THE TRANSLATION

> My respect for Maimon's talent knows no bounds, I firmly believe, and I am ready to prove, that he has turned upside down the Kantian philosophy as it has been generally understood and as you yourself understand it. He has accomplished all of this without anyone noticing, whilst everyone looks down on him. I think that the centuries to come will mock us bitterly for this.[7]

In the ten years between the publication of the *Essay* in 1790 and his death in 1800 Maimon will publish eleven books, numerous articles and co-edit a journal of empirical psychology. Up until his death in 1793, the writer and educator Karl Phillip Moritz seems to have played an important role in Maimon's life.[8] They may have felt kindred spirits since both were outsiders who had struggled to reach where they were now with little formal education. Moritz had a life story as picaresque as Maimon's; from equally humble beginnings he too had spent time as a beggar and a tramp and attempted suicide before finally achieving success. He had risen to the rank of professor at a famous Berlin Gymnasium and was a close friend of Goethe who admired his autobiographical novel, and a member of the circle of Berlin *Aufklärer* around Mendelssohn. But Maimon remained an outsider in a way that Moritz no longer was, and the following passage from a letter to Goethe shows his vulnerability:

> My circumstances are quite well known. They are just as the circumstances of a man cannot otherwise be, who has no fortune, no profession, who practices no business or trade, who thoughtlessly fell in love with philosophy, wedded himself to it without first considering how he would support himself and philosophy ... I can also make no claim on any public teaching position. The novelty of the case in itself (since no one of my nation has yet ever held such a teaching position),[9] want of language and diction, an original way of thinking very different from the usual, and the love

---

[7] Daniel Breazeale, *Fichte's Early Philosophical Writings* (Ithaca, NY: Cornell University Press, 1988), pp. 383–84.
[8] See Mark Boulby, *Karl Phillip Moritz – At the Fringe of Genius* (Toronto: University of Toronto Press, 1979).
[9] Maimon is referring to the Jewish nation and the prohibition of Jews from occupying teaching positions.

INTRODUCTION TO THE TRANSLATION

of independence from everything that limits performance according to a particular norm put impediments enough in the way.[10]

With the help of Mendelssohn and Herz, Moritz had established the first German journal of empirical psychology *Magazin zur Erfahrungsseelenkunde* which appeared continuously from 1783 until 1793, the year of his death. He was celebrated for his 'autobiography', *Anton Reiser – ein psychologischer Roman*,[11] which appeared in instalments in the magazine between 1785 and 1790 and was likely the inspiration for Maimon's own autobiography which appeared in 1792 and 1793 under Moritz's editorship.

Maimon is acknowledged as co-editor of the final three volumes of the empirical psychology journal and indeed seems rather to have taken over the editorship, for in Volume 8 he publishes a new 'plan' for the journal. The journal's title *Gnothi seauton oder Magazin zur Erfahrungsseelenkunde als ein Lesebuch für Gelehrte und Ungelehrte* (Know yourself, or a magazine on empirical psychology as a reader for the learned and the unlearned) speaks of the Socratic ideal of self-knowledge and a desire to popularize, and shows that the journal sought to be educational rather than scientific or academic. It published accounts of mental illness, depression and paranoia, and although Maimon's editorship took it in a more philosophical and theoretical direction, his involvement in it bears witness to his continuous interest in empirical science.

He spent the final five years of his life on the country estate of an aristocrat, an admirer of his philosophy who became his patron, during which time he continued to write and publish. He died there at the age of only forty-seven in 1800.

Maimon's Other Writings

Although best known today for the *Essay* and his *Autobiography*, Maimon published prolifically in the 1790s; his books include a philosophical dictionary, essays on moral philosophy, proposals for the revision of

---

[10] Letter to Goethe, quoted in Freudenthal, 'A philosopher between two cultures', in *Salomon Maimon: Rational Dogmatist, Empirical Sceptic* (Dordrecht: Kluwer 2003), p. 2. (The letter can be found in Günter Schulz, 'Salomon Maimon und Goethe', Vierteljahresschrift der Goethe Gesellschaft, 16 (1954), pp. 272–88).

[11] Boulby (op. cit.) argues that the work is subtitled 'a psychological novel' not because Moritz wanted to deny that it was autobiographical but because it tells the story of a man who lead his life under the illusion that he was a character in a novel.

INTRODUCTION TO THE TRANSLATION

philosophical language and an annotated German translation of Henry Pemberton's *A View of Sir Isaac Newton's Principia*. However, in all these diverse works, Kant's critical philosophy is the common thread: the notes to Pemberton are his occasion for critically examining *Kant's Metaphysical Foundations of Natural Science*, his works on moral philosophy are reactions to Kant's moral philosophy, and no less than four of his books published after the *Essay* – *Incursions in the Domain of Philosophy* (1793), *Logic* (1794), *Categories of Aristotle* (1794) and *Critical Investigations* (1797) – contain extensive interpretations and rewritings of the *Critique of Pure Reason*.

An edition of his collected works that includes his philosophical correspondence was published in seven volumes between 1965–76, but the texts are unedited photographic reproductions of the original publications and the collection does not attempt to include all his works (for example it omits works written in Hebrew). His *Autobiography* was republished in German in 1911 and since then translations have appeared in English, Hebrew and French. Of his philosophical works only the *Essay on Transcendental Philosophy* has been translated – into Hebrew in 1941 and into French in 1989. Florian Ehrensperger of the University of Munich published a new German edition of the *Essay* in 2004 which includes editorial material, and he has also announced the project of producing a critical edition of the complete works.

The Structure of the Book

The structure of the book is complex and for this reason a brief account of what the different parts contain may be helpful. The *Essay* itself consists of an introduction and ten chapters; but four supplements were added to this, which together are longer than the *Essay* itself. These are: 'A Short Overview of the Whole Work', 'My Ontology', 'On Symbolic Cognition and Philosophical Language', and 'Notes and Clarifications'. In addition we have ourselves appended a number of texts discussing the *Essay* to the original publication: a letter from Maimon to Kant and one from Kant to Herz, a journal article on the *Essay* written by Maimon shortly after its publication and an extract from Isaac Newton's *Introduction to the Quadrature of Curves*.

The *Essay* itself does not follow the carefully elaborated structure of the *Critique of Pure Reason* at all closely. The first two chapters roughly deal with the matters covered by Kant's 'Transcendental Aesthetic' and 'Transcendental Logic' respectively, that is to say the first chapter deals with space and time as the forms of intuition and the second chapter with the question of our right to use pure concepts of the understanding of experience; it is in Maimon's view Kant's great merit to have raised the question *quid juris?*, the fundamental question of the *Critique*; but Maimon claims that the transcendental deduction and schematism of the categories have failed to provide a satisfactory answer. Chapter 2 ends by also raising the question *quid facti?*, that is to say Hume's sceptical doubt as to the actuality of natural necessity; in fact *in toto* this long chapter constitutes in itself almost a complete essay on the *Critique*.

In Chapter 3, Maimon moves on to the third of what one might call the elements of Kant's system: Chapter 1 deals with *intuitions*, Chapter 2 with *concepts* and Chapter 3 with *ideas*. Here he introduces his principal innovation which will provide his answer to the question *quid juris?*, the concept of ideas of the understanding as differentials. Unlike Kant (for whom reason and its ideas are consigned to the transcendental dialectic and do not play a part in the transcendental analytic which describes how metaphysical and mathematical knowledge is possible), Maimon gives ideas a constitutive role in knowledge.

Chapter 4 is also radically innovative with respect to Kant's system. Eberhard had argued that a fault in the *Critique* was its lack of a principle for synthetic *a priori* propositions analogous to the principle of contradiction that governs analytic propositions, to which Kant retorted that the principle was indeed there for all to see.[12] Maimon evidently agrees with Eberhard on this issue and in Chapter 4 he sets out to supplement Kant's account with a principle concerning the special nature of the relation of determination of subject by predicate in a synthetic *a priori* proposition.

Chapter 5 deals with modality, which in the *Critique* is principally dealt with in the 'Postulates of Empirical Thought'. Maimon analyses many different ways in which the possible, the actual and the necessary can be thought in relation to one another. Of particular importance to the central epistemological concern of the *Essay* is his discussion of the meaning of 'actual'. He rejects the rationalist (Wolffian) definition of it as something that is completely determined, regarding it as merely something that is perceived in empirical intuition. In this he is of course close

---

[12] Kant discusses this in his letter to Reinhold of 12 May 1789. An English translation can be found in I. Kant, *Philosophical Correspondence 1759–99*, trans. A. Zweig (Chicago: University of Chicago Press, 1967), p. 141.

INTRODUCTION TO THE TRANSLATION

to Kant's view, the difference lies in the fact that Maimon accords empirical intuition (and hence the actual) a lower cognitive status than Kant (throughout the *Essay* the actual is opposed to the real).

Chapter 6 deals with what Kant calls 'concepts of reflection', for example, identity and difference (A260ff/B316ff). These concepts play an important but – compared with the categories – rather hidden role in synthesis in the *Critique;* but in the *Essay,* the concept of difference in particular is quite fundamental.

While Chapters 4 to 6 turned from the analysis of the nature of cognition conducted in the first three chapters, to the clarification and definition of concepts, Chapter 7 returns to a consideration of the nature of sensible intuition, in a discussion of the difference between extensive and intensive magnitude.

Chapter 8 takes up from where Chapter 3 left off, discussing the necessary character of experience. Specifically, it looks at matters Kant discusses in the 'Analogies of Experience': substance and accident, persistence and alteration. It establishes an *a priori* 'principle of continuity', viz. that the objectivity of experience depends on alterations being continuous.

In Chapter 9 he returns to the definition of concepts, setting out the different kinds of truth. Finally, Chapter 10 concludes the *Essay* with an examination of the 'Paralogisms of Pure Reason' – Kant's critique of the metaphysical doctrine of the soul as a simple, numerically identical substance (A341ff/B399ff), against which Maimon argues that his theory of ideas allows one to conceive of the metaphysical 'I' as something one can approach ever closer to, although never reach; the chapter ends by clarifying Maimon's philosophical position with respect to Materialism, Idealism and Dualism.

Turning to the texts appended to the *Essay,* the 'Short Overview of the Whole Work', much of which is written in the form 'according to Kant ... , on the other hand according to me ..' greatly clarifies Maimon's differences from Kant, which are often hard to determine in the work itself; it also includes a discussion of the 'Antinomies of Pure Reason' (A405ff/B432ff) which the *Essay* itself had not covered. Since Kant's letter to Herz discussing the manuscript of the *Essay* suggests that the work would be improved if Maimon set out his position more systematically and added a discussion of the antinomies of pure reason, there is reason to think that the 'Short Overview' was composed only after Maimon read this letter.

The 'Notes and Clarifications' contain much important material on

INTRODUCTION TO THE TRANSLATION

topics that, as Maimon says, were 'dealt with too briefly in the work itself'. This part of the work is much more significant and philosophically substantial than an author's endnotes might customarily be expected to be; it ends with a Concluding Note in which Maimon compares different philosophical systems including his own, 'both with regard to the legitimacy or illegitimacy of their claims and to their advancement or obstruction of the interest of reason'.

It might be thought odd to find a chapter entitled 'My Ontology' in a book on Kant's *Critique of Pure Reason*, in the light of Kant's famous statement there that:

> ... the proud name of ontology, which presumes to offer synthetic *a priori* cognitions of things in general in a systematic doctrine (e.g., the principle of causality), must give way to the modest one of a mere analytic of the pure understanding.
>
> (A247/B303)

However, Kant's project can also be understood not as the attempt to *substitute* a new conception of philosophy (as critique or analysis) but rather to *reformulate* and *reorient* the traditional rationalist programme of metaphysics and ontology by redirecting them from things (as they may be regarded in themselves) to objects (of experience).[13] In the 'Architectonic of Pure Reason' section of the *Critique* for instance, Kant outlines a 'philosophy of pure reason' in which critique itself would play a preparatory role and whose substance would comprise a 'metaphysics' (A841/B869), a metaphysics of which 'ontology' would itself be a part (A845–6/B873–4). In addition, of course it was in his own university lectures on ontology that Kant presented the doctrine of the *Critique* to his students. These constituted the first part of his lectures on metaphysics, for which throughout his career Kant used Baumgarten's *Metaphysica* as the textbook, but used the opportunity to present his own ideas.[14]

---

[13] This interpretation of Kant was pioneered by Hans Friedrich Fulda, 'Ontologie nach Kant und Hegel' in *Metaphysik nach Kant?*, ed. Dieter Henrich and Rolf-Peter Horstmann (Stuttgart: Klett-Cotta, 1988), pp. 45–80 and has been recently taken up by Karin de Boer in 'The Dissolving Force of the Concept: Hegel's Ontological Logic' *Reivew of Metaphysics* 57.4 (June 2004), pp. 787–822.

[14] Student notes of different versions of these lectures have been published, and several versions of the lectures on ontology from the 1780s and 1790s can be found in English translation in Kant, *Lectures on Metaphysics* (Cambridge: Cambridge University Press, 1997).

INTRODUCTION TO THE TRANSLATION

Maimon uses Baumgarten in exactly the same way here, so 'My Ontology' should be understood not in the sense criticised by Kant, but rather in the sense endorsed by Kant: as Maimon states, with admirable clarity: 'for me ontology is not a science that is applicable to the thing in itself, but only to appearances' (p. 239).[15] Here Maimon presents his own critical take on certain of the categories dealt with in Baumgarten's 'Ontology'. 'My Ontology' contains further discussions of many of the concepts dealt with in Chapters 3 to 8, including an important discussion of a proposition that seems to contravene the principle of determinability (discussed in Chapter 4); it also contains a very clear formulation of Maimon's difference from Kant in regard to the role of the categories, stating that they are not, as they are for Kant, conditions of experience whose existence Maimon doubts, but 'conditions of perception in general, which no one can doubt' (p. 261).

Finally, the first part of the appendix 'On Symbolic Cognition and Philosophical Language' discusses the difference between intuitive and symbolic cognition and includes a critical discussion of his friend Lazarus Bendavid's book on the concept of infinity in mathematics. This constitutes a clarification of his position in the *Essay* with respect to the nature of mathematics and his critique of the role of pure intuition in mathematical cognition, as well as the claim that the new methods of the calculus are superior to classical geometrical methods. The latter part of the essay deals with an issue not discussed in the *Critique of Pure Reason*, that of the importance of language to knowledge. This issue had been raised by Locke in his *Essay on Human Understanding* and by Leibniz in his *New Essays on Human Understanding*, and Maimon refers to Leibniz's project of a 'universal characteristic' and to other schemes for the invention of a language that would accurately reflect the structure of thought and knowledge. He says he intends to pursue the project of inventing a true philosophical language in a future work, and this he does in part in his *Logic* of 1794.

We have also appended two letters, a journal article by Maimon and an extract from a work by Newton to the text of the *Essay*. The first letter was written by Maimon to accompany the manuscript of the *Essay* he sent

---

[15] Maimon adds that this conception on ontology is rather different from 'the concept usually associated with it' (p. 239). This fundamental change in the conception of ontology, and the ambiguity it introduces, has been historically very significant both in the development of classical German idealism and twentieth-century phenomenology.

to Kant, and it is interesting in particular for the way Maimon summarizes the innovations of the *Essay*. The second is Kant's letter addressed to Markus Herz but intended to be passed on to Maimon, which contains Kant's opinion of the *Essay*, and his criticisms and suggestions for improvements. The journal article, which was also included in Ehrensperger's 2004 German edition of the *Essay*, is Maimon's response to a request to clarify his position with respect to the different philosophical 'sects' of the day. Finally, a short extract from Newton's *Introduction to the Quadrature of Curves* has been included. We did not wish to encumber the *Essay* with unnecessary extraneous material but hope this text will be found useful in the following ways: (1) it provides a diagram that explains what Maimon is talking about in his example of how differentials cannot be presented in intuition in Chapter 2; (2) it provides an independent account of what Maimon means by a ratio being preserved even when infinitesimal; (3) it gives a glimpse of the scientific background to Maimon's descriptions of lines being generated from points, areas from lines, etc.

Style and Method of the Essay

Will readers of this first English translation of the *Essay* fulfil Fichte's expectation and look down on Maimon's contemporaries for failing to grasp either its meaning or its importance? Fichte's statement flatters every reader who approaches the *Essay* that they may redeem the stupidity of Maimon's contemporaries and finally give him his due. But human intelligence has not increased with the passing of time, and Reinhold and his contemporaries were not stupid.

Certainly the *Essay* is difficult and I want to briefly examine in what this difficulty consists. First it is very densely argued – for example, Chapter 2 crams an almost complete account of transcendental philosophy into 20 odd pages. Its principle concern is the very heart of Kant's argument in the *Critique*, that is the 'Transcendental Deduction' and 'Schematism of the Categories' sections, which are themselves the most difficult and densely argued parts of the *Critique*. In this respect the difficulty is largely just a result of the difficulty of the subject matter.

Second there is the problem that Kant's own presentation of transcendental philosophy varies between the first edition of the *Critique*, the *Prolegomena* and the second edition, but Maimon seldom gives specific references to Kant's works and himself nowhere acknowledges any

INTRODUCTION TO THE TRANSLATION

difference in Kant's views across these three publications. This means that, for example, his claim that for him the categories are necessary for perception whereas for Kant they are necessary for experience is valid if referring to the position Kant presents in the *Prolegomena*, but much more doubtful if referring to the position of the *Critique*.

Third, there is the problem of distinguishing Maimon's presentation of Kant from his presentation of his own theory. As I said above, these are counterposed in the 'Short Overview' but in the *Essay* itself it is often not immediately clear where Kant ends and Maimon begins. This raises some much more interesting questions about Maimon's style and method than the first two sources of difficulty. In discussing these questions I will be drawing on an essay by Gideon Freudenthal called 'A Philosopher Between Two Cultures'.[16] Freudenthal argues that Maimon 'philosophized in the form of commentaries' as was common in pre-modern philosophy. His commentary on Maimonides *Guide for the Perplexed* was indeed presented in the traditional way, printed in the margins with the text itself in the centre. Maimon thus stands between two cultures: the pre-modern culture of commentary and the modern culture of the systematic treatise that establishes itself on new foundations. And these are not only structural differences: the norms of good writing are also different. Maimonides states that he has deliberately disordered the *Guide* so that truths should be glimpsed and then disappear again from view, in order not to transgress against God's will in making them visible to all. So a reflection on the cultural relativity of critical norms is required before assessing Maimon's method. Of particular interest here is the question of Maimon's 'system'.

I mentioned above that Kant suggested he work up the *Essay* into his own system of transcendental philosophy, and that to an extent the 'Short Overview' responds to this task; but it does not do so by removing the commentary on Kant, instead it sets out Kant's views in opposition to his own. But it is interesting to note that in his correspondence with Reinhold, Maimon responds brusquely to what he regards as Reinhold's patronizing suggestion that he has yet to work out a system of his own: 'it is my innermost conviction that my system is as completely elaborated as any other'.[17] This suggests he regards it as the responsibility of his readers

[16] G. Freudenthal, 'A Philosopher Between two Cultures', in *Salomon Maimon: Rational Dogmatist, Empirical Sceptic* (Dordrecht: Kluwer, 2003).

[17] Letter to Reinhold, *GW*, IV, p. 241.

to discern his system from its context as commentary; earlier in this Introduction I quoted Maimon's description of how he went about writing the *Essay*: he described it as a 'coalition-system' of Spinoza, Hume, Leibniz and Kant, and 'established' in the form of comments and explanations of the *Critique*. But in spite of these references to his own 'system', Maimon also argues that truth has a higher value than systematicity, and this may be a further source of the difficulty of the *Essay*. In a letter to Reinhold he distinguishes their approaches to philosophy and questions the importance of Reinhold's attempt to establish the *Critique* on more fundamental principles than Kant[18] himself had done:

> We have chosen different philosophical methods. For you system, necessity and absolute universal validity are of paramount importance. Hence you ground your philosophy on facts that are most appropriate to this goal. For me truth is the most important even if it is demonstrated in a way that is less systematic, absolutely necessary and universally valid. Newton's *Principia*, which contribute so much to the extension of our knowledge of nature, are for me more important than every theory of the faculty of *a priori* cognition, which can only be used to deduce what is already known (although of course less rigorously), and which is itself grounded in undemonstrated propositions.
>
> (*GW* IV, p. 263)

This remark is highly interesting in itself for the low status it accords to transcendental philosophy in comparison with Newton's *Principia*, but I want rather to discuss the implication of putting truth above system. The *Essay* is exhilarating and frustrating to read in the same measure because Maimon seems to write as he thinks, and new thoughts, new questions constantly pop into his mind. This makes reading the *Essay* a rollercoaster ride in which as soon as you think you have reached a level of understanding you are thrown back down into puzzlement by a new thought or a new doubt that Maimon raises: the *Essay* promises the reader both delight and despair. But the great virtue of the *Essay* lies in the brilliance of its thought, and the loss of system may be worth the price.

---

[18] See Reinhold's *Essay on a New Theory of the Human Faculty of Representation* (*Versuch einer neuen Theorie des menschlichen Vorstellungsvermögen* (Prague: Widtman & Mauke, 1789).

INTRODUCTION TO THE TRANSLATION

I want to make one final point regarding Maimon's thought. The *Essay* develops the notion that only intuition has objects, not the understanding: the business of the understanding is thinking and to think or comprehend something is to grasp it as *flowing* or in terms of the way it arises [*Entstehungsart*].[19] Thought is active and spontaneous and does not fix what is fleeting, but rather the reverse. Transcendental philosophy releases thought from both subject and object towards the anonymous and the unconscious.[20] The restless thought of the *Essay*, despite the demands of his readers, is not necessarily Maimon's thought or anyone else's, and if it cannot be boxed into propositions of the form: 'Maimon thinks x' this may be just because it is exhibiting the very process of thinking.

Maimon's Transcendental Philosophy

I want to devote the rest of this Introduction to looking at some of the respects in which Maimon transforms Kant's transcendental philosophy. First, consider the question: what is 'transcendental philosophy'? In the letter from which I quoted above, Kant says that although Maimon's philosophy takes a very different path from his own, 'still he agrees with me that a reform must be undertaken, if the principles of metaphysics are to be made firm, and few men are willing to be convinced that this is necessary'.[21] Transcendental philosophy is the method of this philosophical reformation that will attempt to establish metaphysics on a new foundation and hence to show how it is possible and what its limits are. Hence transcendental philosophy is constituted in terms of a new problem as well as its solution. Maimon calls his book *Versuch über die Transzendentalphilosophie*, that is to say, an essay on transcendental philosophy, and as he points out in the Introduction, *Versuch* means 'attempt', it is his attempt at this new form of philosophy called 'transcendental':

---

[19] See Chapter 2, s.33.

[20] Concerning the 'subject' I am referring to Kant's critique of the Cartesian 'I' as thinking substance in the 'Paralogisms' as well as the difference between empirical and transcendental egos; concerning the 'unconscious' I am referring to Maimon's association of consciousness with intuition (which has objects) as opposed to thought (which does not) (see Chapter 2, s.81).

[21] See the letter from Kant to Herz included in the Appendices.

INTRODUCTION TO THE TRANSLATION

> The great Kant supplies a **complete idea** of transcendental philosophy (although not the whole science itself) in his immortal work the *Critique of Pure Reason*.[22] My aim in this enquiry is to bring out **the most important truths** of this science. And I am following in the footsteps of the aforementioned sharp-witted philosopher; but (as the unbiased reader will remark) I am not copying him. I try, as much as it is in my power, to explain him, although from time to time I also make some comments on him ... To what extent I am a Kantian, an anti-Kantian, both at the same time, or neither of the two, I leave to the judgement of the thoughtful reader. I have endeavoured, as much as I could, to avoid the difficulties of these opposed systems (something that I also wanted to show in my motto).[23] How far I have succeeded in this, others may decide.
>
> (Introduction, s.8–9)

In the *Essay* Maimon is not seeking to present an accurate account of the *Critique of Pure Reason*, nor is he going to attempt to complete the *system* of transcendental philosophy of which Kant presented the idea. Rather, he emphasizes, his aim is to uncover what is fundamental to transcendental philosophy, its most important truths. Hence his description of the *Essay* in his *Autobiography* as a 'coalition-system' is misleading if it is taken to mean a mere combination of different philosophies; rather, insights he has learned from different philosophers are brought to bear on the single problem of transcendental philosophy. That Maimon takes on the task of transcendental philosophy explains why Kant's response to him is completely different from his response to another of his 'opponents', Eberhard. For although some of Maimon's criticisms of Kant seem to come from a Leibnizian-Wolffian standpoint close to Eberhard's, it wasn't Eberhard's disagreement with his doctrine that infuriated Kant but Eberhard's claim that he had 'seen it all before'. Indeed Kant is so incensed by Eberhard's claim that all that was important in the *Critique* could already be found in Leibniz, that he broke his resolve to ignore criticism and keep to his task of completing the critical system to pen a 50-page polemic against Eberhard entitled 'On a

---

[22] Kant describes the *Critique* in this way in the Introduction (A13/B27).
[23] Maimon is referring to the quotation from Virgil on the title page.

INTRODUCTION TO THE TRANSLATION

Discovery According to which any New Critique of Pure Reason has been made Superfluous by an Earlier One',[24] which appeared shortly after Maimon's *Essay* was published in 1790. Kant judges Maimon differently because although he is an opponent he is one who acknowledges the necessity and importance of Kant's new approach to philosophy. Nevertheless Maimon's claim that he is not just copying Kant but 'from time to time I also make some comments on him' greatly understates the difference between Maimon's transcendental philosophy and that of Kant. I now want to sketch out in broad strokes how they differ.

The roles of the object and pure intuition in transcendental philosophy

In the *Prolegomena to any Future Metaphysics* Kant describes how the *Critique* was born from Hume's challenge to the concept of causation, that is to say, Hume's claim that we have no justification for using this concept to assert the existence of necessary connections in the world we experience. Kant's response broadened Hume's problem first into the general problem of our right to apply any *a priori* concept at all to experience and secondly to include the different problem of how mathematical knowledge was possible. The possibility of both mathematics and *a priori* knowledge of the empirical world (which Kant calls metaphysics) are thought by Kant to depend on the possibility of applying *a priori* concepts to intuitions, and this application he calls a 'synthetic *a priori* judgement'. Hence explaining the possibility of both these kinds of knowledge depends on answering the question 'how are synthetic *a priori* judgements possible?'.

The term Maimon likes to use to identify the core problem of transcendental philosophy is '*quid juris?*' the question of legitimacy, or of 'what right?'. This was the legal term Kant introduced to describe the demand to which his transcendental deduction of the categories responds: with what right do we apply *a priori* concepts to experience?[25] In the transcendental deduction and the schematism Kant seeks to demonstrate the legitimacy of the categories with respect to experience. Hence the question '*quid juris?*' refers to the possibility of

---

[24] See Henry E. Allison, *The Kant-Eberhard Controversy*, a translation with introduction and supplementary materials of Kant's 'On a Discovery According to which any New Critique of Pure Reason has been made Superfluous by an Earlier One' (Baltimore, MD: Johns Hopkins University Press, 1973).

[25] A84/B116.

metaphysics in particular rather than to the general question of transcendental philosophy, viz. 'how are synthetic *a priori* judgements in general possible?'.

There are two fundamental conceptual innovations that Kant introduces to solve the question '*quid juris?*': *pure intuition* and the *object*. The logic of how they both contribute to the solution is complex and they have a certain independence from one another. I cannot analyse this complexity at length here but I want to delineate the roles of pure intuition and the object clearly enough to bring the difference between Maimon and Kant into focus.

Let me first provide a summary of the roles these new concepts play in the *Critique*. Both mathematics and metaphysics are domains of synthetic *a priori* judgements and hence of *necessity*. For Kant what distinguishes a synthetic judgement from an analytic one is that it applies a concept to an intuition rather than remaining within the realm of concepts and simply explicating the concept. The problem is to explain how such an amplificatory judgement can nevertheless be necessary. Kant's solution invokes pure intuition and the object. In mathematics, *a priori* mathematical concepts are constructed in pure intuition (for example 'triangle' determines a figure in space). Because this pure intuition is *a priori* it is necessary and because it is pure rather than empirical there is no question as to the understanding's right to determine it in different ways. In metaphysics pure intuition plays a similar role, a metaphysical *a priori* concept (category), for example 'cause', does not determine empirical intuition directly (which would beg the question '*quid juris?*') but determines time (pure intuition). However, what are similar operations lead to radically different results because the categories work together to determine a structured world of *objects* in necessary relations, which Kant calls 'experience', whereas mathematics produces an imaginary world and only acquires objectivity at second hand, in so far as it is applicable to experience.[26] Hence the notion of objectivity distinguishes the domain of metaphysics from that of mathematics.

It is not an exaggeration to say that almost all the differences between Maimon's transcendental philosophy and that of Kant stem from

---

[26] See B146–47: 'The pure concepts of the understanding even if they are applied to *a priori* intuitions (as in mathematics), provide cognition only insofar as these *a priori* intuitions, and by means of them also the concepts of the understanding, can be applied to empirical intuitions'.

INTRODUCTION TO THE TRANSLATION

Maimon's rejection of Kant's notion of pure intuition. He claims that either there *is* no pure intuition, or to the extent that there is, it cannot fulfil the function Kant demands of it. With respect to Kant's other prime conceptual innovation, the concept of the object, we will see that the difference between Maimon and Kant is more complicated. Maimon reduces the status of objects of intuition to mere actualities lacking necessity, but also brings in the notion of the real object as a limit concept. Kant's letter commenting on the *Essay* ignores Maimon's attack on pure intuition and concentrates rather on what he sees as Maimon's failure to grasp the fundamental role of the object in answering the question '*quid juris?*'. Before looking at what Kant says, let us return to the role he gives to the object in solving the problem. Kant argues (against a radical empiricism such as Hume's) that our experience is structured: we are self-conscious subjects observing a world of objects (in so far as we are self-conscious we are, in part, objects to ourselves). Objects are constructed through the synthesis (transcendental deduction) and determination (schematism) of pure intuition (time) by the *a priori* concepts of the understanding or categories. In the letter, Kant insists to Maimon that this production of *objects* by *a priori* concepts is fundamental to the possibility of experience:

> No sense *data* for a possible cognition could ever represent objects without these conditions, nor indeed ever attain that unity of consciousness that is required for cognition of myself (as object of inner sense). I would not even ever be able to know that I had these sense *data*, consequently **for me** as a cognizing being they would be absolutely nothing. They could (if I imagine myself as an animal) still carry on their play in a regular way, as representations that would be connected according to an empirical law of association, even influencing my faculties of feeling and desire, yet unaware of my existence (assuming that I am conscious of each individual representation, but not of their relation to the unity of representation of their object, by means of the synthetic unity of their apperception), without me ever cognizing anything, not even my own state.
>
> (Letter from Kant to Herz)

On this account, the objective value of what is produced (objects of experience) does not derive either from what it is produced from or from how it is produced. Rather it is because they make objectivity possible that the *a priori* concepts or categories are legitimized. So Kant presents this as the core of transcendental philosophy that gives the structure of the answer to the question '*quid juris?*'. The theory of pure intuition is secondary: pure intuition only explains *how* the objective world is produced, viz. through the application of *a priori* concepts to pure intuition. Kant continues:

> ... even if we were capable of intellectual intuition (e.g. if the infinitely small elements of intuition were *noumena*), then such judgements could not achieve necessity (according to the nature of our understanding in which such concepts as necessity are to be found) because an [intellectual] intuition could only ever be a mere perception.
>
> (Letter from Kant to Herz)

He is here describing Maimon's theory which we shall discuss below, but for the present what I am interested in is Kant's point that the issue of the question '*quid juris?*' is not the gap between concept and reality. If we could somehow immediately understand reality with our concepts, so that the difference between reality and concept disappeared, nevertheless we would only experience this as a perception. It would be rather as if we took a drug and experienced a higher reality – in the end, whatever its quality this is still just a perception, but what Kant seeks to establish is objective validity. So from Kant's point of view a direct access to reality cannot be distinguished from a merely subjective perception, because such cognition lacks objectivity or in other words we have no means of distinguishing the real from the subjective, only for distinguishing the objective from the subjective. I don't think the *Essay* has an answer to this challenge from Kant, but the issue is rather whether Maimon succeeds in formulating transcendental philosophy in a new way so that this issue of objectivity is no longer central.

'Quid juris?' and 'quid facti?'

Before turning to the central theme of the *Essay*, the rejection of pure intuition and the new solution to the question '*quid juris?*', I want to look briefly at the relation of the question '*quid juris?*' to another question that Maimon calls '*quid facti?*' or question of fact. In the 'Concluding Note' to the *Essay*, Maimon describes his philosophical position as that of a 'rational dogmatist and empirical sceptic.' This refers to the fact that Maimon's

INTRODUCTION TO THE TRANSLATION

criticism of Kant is conducted on two flanks: an internal rejection of pure intuition involving a new solution to the *'quid juris?'*, and an external attack under the banner of Humean scepticism. This sceptical attack is upon what Maimon calls the 'fact'. The fact in question is the existence of what Kant calls 'experience', that is an empirical reality structured by the categories that consists of objects in necessary relations with one another; Maimon asserts that Hume is right: we cannot know that there is any necessity in the empirical world. Maimon calls himself a rational dogmatist because (as we shall see) his solution to the *'quid juris?'* is rationalist; but he is an empirical sceptic in denying the fact of experience. Now if the *'quid juris?'* is understood as seeking an explanation of how experience is possible, the importance of this question would seem to be radically undermined by doubt as to the very existence of experience. Every reader of the *Essay* faces the difficulty of understanding how Maimon can doubt the 'fact' without pulling down the whole edifice of transcendental philosophy that he has so painstakingly and brilliantly built up in constructing a new solution to the *'quid juris?'*; one can respect the honesty of his scepticism, but it is hard not to let one's faith in his task waver when he seems to countenance that it might actually all be for nothing. To understand how Maimon can separate these two questions, I want to look at how they are connected in Kant.

In the 'Short Overview of the Whole Work' Maimon characterizes the fundamental structure of Kant's argument with the following syllogism:

> If experience exists the categories must apply to it (they make it possible).
> But it does exist.
> Hence the categories are objectively valid.[27]

He accepts the first premise but rejects the second. So the Kantian philosophy has only hypothetical validity.[28] Does this syllogism accu-

---

[27] This is not a direct quotation, see 'Short Overview', s.186.
[28] This point is reinforced not contradicted when he says elsewhere that he believes that 'Kant's philosophy is in its own way as irrefutable as Euclid's' (Notes & Clarifications #3, s.338). For rather than taking the traditional view of Euclid's *Elements* as a paradigm of certain *a priori* knowledge, his view is that it falls short of metaphysical truth in exactly the same way as the critical philosophy – all the theorems proved therein are merely hypothetically true, i.e. true *if* the axioms are true. (See Chapter 9, s.148–49).

rately present the structure of Kant's argument? In fact this is how Kant presents his philosophy in the *Prolegomena*, but not in the *Critique* itself. The *Prolegomena*, says Kant, adopts an analytic approach in which the existence of mathematics and necessary truths about experience is first assumed and then analysed to show how it is possible. But the *Critique* is synthetic, that is, it seeks to produce synthetic *a priori* knowledge without presupposing its existence. In fact the place of experience in the *Critique* involves a hermeneutic circle: it is both presupposed and brought to light. That it is presupposed is revealed in the very first sentence of the Introduction to the first edition: 'Experience is without doubt the first product that our understanding brings forth as it works on the raw material of sensible sensations' (A1), and what is more the 'Transcendental Aesthetic' obtains its subject matter – the pure forms of intuition – by abstracting from experience, i.e. by removing from experience that which is contributed by concepts and by sensation. However, the true nature of experience is only revealed by showing how it is produced and this is what is done progressively in the 'Transcendental Analytic'. This means that the presupposition of the fact of experience and the demonstration of how it is possible are more entwined in the *Critique* than Maimon acknowledges.

A second complication in the relation between the question *'quid juris?'* and the question *'quid facti?'* arises from another difference between the *Prolegomena* and the *Critique*. This is the distinction between 'judgements of perception' and 'judgements of experience' that Kant introduces in the *Prolegomena* but which is not present in either edition of the *Critique*. On the account of the role of the categories in constituting objects of perception Kant provides in the letter to Herz, we would have no consciousness either of ourselves or of a world of objects without the categories: and this is in general the position of the *Critique*. But in the *Prolegomena* the role of the categories is apparently more modest: their use distinguishes experiential judgements (which assert necessity) from mere perceptual judgements. An example he gives of a perceptual judgement is 'when the sun shines on a stone it grows warm'. This he says contains no necessity because it merely associates two perceptions; but it is transformed into an experiential judgement when I say 'the sun warms the stone' because I then add an *a priori* concept of the understanding, namely, 'cause', and hence necessity, to the original judgement. On this account, unlike the first, it is quite possible to deny the categories this use, i.e. to deny the truth of metaphysical propositions that assert their application to experience, without destroying the coherence of perception itself. It seems to be this account that Maimon has in mind when he asserts that for him the categories are not, as they are for Kant, conditions of experience, whose existence Maimon doubts, but 'conditions of perception in general, which no one can doubt'.[29] Thus this provides a strategy for regarding Maimon's scepticism as more limited than it at first appears: Maimon is taken to agree with Kant that the categories construct the world we perceive, but to doubt that this is sufficient to determine necessary connections in this world. So a negative answer to the *'quid facti?'* does not undermine the solution to the question *'quid juris?'*, so long as this is interpreted as an explanation of the production of perception by the categories. To pursue this line would require further analysis of Maimon's understanding of the distinction between perception and experience and of the distinction between objectivity and necessity, which I cannot undertake here. But even if it is accepted that his scepticism is thus qualified on occasion, there are certainly other passages where he applies it not just to Kant's account of the application of the categories, but to his own:

> Kant assumes there is no doubt that we possess experiential propositions (that express necessity), and he proves their objective validity by showing that experience would be impossible without them; but on Kant's assumption, experience is possible because it is actual, and this is why these concepts have objective reality. But I doubt the fact itself, that is to say, I doubt whether we possess experiential propositions and so I cannot prove their objective validity the way Kant does; instead I prove only the possibility that they are objectively valid of the limits of objects of experience (which are determined as objects by reason in relation to their corresponding intuitions), not [that they are valid] of objects of experience themselves (which are determined in intuition). As a result, the question, *quid juris*? must fall aside (in as much as pure concepts are applied to ideas). So things *can* stand in this relation to one another; but whether they do so in fact is still in question.
>
> ('Short Overview', s.186–87, emphasis added)

---

[29] 'My Ontology', s.261. Maimon alludes to this example from Kant on a number of occasions.

INTRODUCTION TO THE TRANSLATION

In the final sentence Maimon states that he has successfully answered the question '*quid juris?*' by showing how *a priori* concepts *can* apply to the 'limits' of intuitions, but that nevertheless that they actually do so remains in doubt.

Maimon's critique of pure intuition

I want now to turn to a central theme of the *Essay*: Maimon's criticism of Kant's doctrine of pure intuition and of the role it plays in Kant's solution to the question '*quid juris?*', and to examine Maimon's alternative solution. After their respective Introductions, the *Critique* and the *Essay* both begin in the same way with an analysis of perception and with the claim that sensible intuitions can be analysed into matter and form. Their matter is sensation and this, Kant says, is how we are affected by objects and is therefore *a posteriori*; their form, however, which is the way we order sensation in space and time, is *a priori*. Kant writes:

> I call that in the appearance which corresponds to sensation its matter, but that which allows the manifold of experience to be intuited as ordered in certain relations I call the **form** of appearance.
>
> (A20/B34)

And Maimon writes:

> For instance, the colour red is given to the cognitive faculty (we say '**given**' because the cognitive faculty cannot produce the colour out of itself in a way that it itself prescribes, but behaves merely passively in relation to the colour). This colour is therefore the matter of the perceived object. But the way we perceive the red colour as well as other sensible objects is this: we order the manifold [that is] in them in **time and space**. These are the forms. For these ways of ordering the manifold do not have their ground in the red colour.
>
> (Chapter 1, s.13)

Thus far both appear to be Leibnizian accounts of space and time – space and time as ordering relations (e.g. A is to the left of B which is to the left of C; P is before Q, etc.). However there is more to space and time than

xxxii

mere ordering: they also have extension, and mere ordering does not create extension. Leibniz addressed this problem by offering separate theories of space and of extension, supplementing his relational theory of space and time with a theory of extended matter.[30] The different ways in which Kant and Maimon account for extension mark out a divergence between their theories. Indeed a close reading of the passage from Kant quoted above already reveals a slight difference from Maimon: Kant is not saying that space and time *are* orderings but that they '*allow* this ordering', making them conditions of the ordering rather than the ordering itself. In the paragraph that follows, Kant describes arriving at the pure form of space by abstraction in the following way:

> If I separate from the representation of a body that which the understanding thinks about it, such as substance, force, divisibility, etc., as well as that which belongs to sensation, such as impenetrability, hardness, colour, etc., something from this empirical intuition is still left for me, namely **extension and form**. These belong to the pure intuition, which occurs *a priori* ...
> (A20–21/B35, emphasis added)

Here 'form' probably means 'shape' and he is assigning the properties of both shape and extension to the pure intuition of space. A little further on again he says that space determines the 'form, magnitude and relation' of bodies to one another (A22/B37). Now although the 'Transcendental Aesthetic' is often read as a theory of space and time in its own right, and as such compared with the different theories of Leibniz and Newton, its place and purpose within the architectonic of the *Critique* is determined by the needs of the 'Transcendental Analytic'. It is because of the use to which the pure intuitions of space and time will be put in the 'Transcendental Analytic' that Kant needs to endow it with the properties of extension and magnitude in addition to relationality. Hence in a way rather different from the way that I described the hermeneutical circle of the presupposition of experience, pure intuition has to already possess properties that concepts will later determine in it (in particular extensive magnitude). A purely relational space and time are insufficient for this purpose.

---

[30] Passages from Leibniz setting out the theories of space and extension are provided as an Appendix to Russell's *Philosophy of Leibniz* (London: George Allen & Unwin, 1975), p. 239ff.

INTRODUCTION TO THE TRANSLATION

As we have seen, Kant arrives at pure intuition by abstraction from experience:

> We will isolate sensibility (1) by separating off what the understanding thinks through its concepts, so nothing but empirical intuition remains; (2) we will then detach from this everything that belongs to sensation, so that *nothing remains except pure intuition* and the mere form of appearances, which is all that sensibility can offer *a priori*.
>
> (A22/B36)

Maimon questions whether this act of abstraction is as straightforward as Kant makes it seem. Clearly on a Leibnizian view of space it is not possible, because if there are no objects, there are no relations and hence no space or time. This is precisely the objection that Maimon makes to Kant's theory: if one takes away the contents from space and time one is not left with some sort of invisible extended containers, one is left with nothing at all.[31] Kant can reply that because space and time are not merely relations but have extension, the abstraction is possible, but Maimon argues that form and material content cannot be separated because the material differentiation of sensation grounds the extension of space and time.

In Kant, pure intuition makes mathematical and metaphysical knowledge possible – it is a principle component in his answer to the question '*quid juris?*'. Kant's strategy is as follows. The problem is that of how *a priori* concepts can apply to *a posteriori* intuitions. Well, suppose that these *a posteriori* intuitions themselves are in part *a priori*, then there will be no problem in explaining how an *a priori* concept can apply to this *a priori* part of the *a posteriori* intuition and as long as there is no problem in how the *a priori* and *a posteriori* parts of intuition are themselves connected together, the problem is solved. This is why the *Critique* starts by establishing the existence of pure intuition in the 'Transcendental Aesthetic'. Once this has been established the 'Transcendental Deduction' and 'Schematism' show how *a priori* concepts are applied to it – that is to say how they synthesize and determine it into objects. The 'Schematism'

---

[31] Space as intuition is 'the image of the difference of things in general': the homogeneous empty space of Kant's theory cannot be imagined in itself, but only relative to some differentiated space. ('Notes & Clarifications', #9).

also shows how the pure sensible concepts of geometry (eg. triangle, circle, etc.) determine the pure intuition of space into geometrical figures. There is a particular reason why the pure intuitions bequeathed to the 'Transcendental Analytic' by the 'Transcendental Aesthetic' have to have extended magnitude. The possibility of geometry and of mathematical natural science depends on the ability of the categories to produce determinate measurable spaces and times – extensive magnitudes. In the 'Axioms of Intuition' Kant explains that an extensive magnitude is an aggregate of smaller parts. It is infinitely divisible so that every part in turn is made up of parts. This means that the synthesis of a determinate magnitude must be a synthesis from what is already extended (there are no simples). Now it might be thought that the 'Deduction' and 'Schematism' show how pure intuitions are *produced* through synthesis, thus showing the *production* of what the 'Transcendental Aesthetic' simply assumed as *given* (pure intuitions obtained by abstraction). For in the 'Schematism' Kant says 'I generate time itself in the apprehension of the intuition' (A143/B182) and 'I cannot represent to myself any line, no matter how small, without drawing it in thought, i.e. successively generating all its parts from one point' (A162/B203). But this picture is quite misleading; the true picture is on the contrary that the 'Transcendental Aesthetic' supplies the 'Transcendental Analytic' with pure intuition. For by its definition extension *cannot* be synthesized from what is not extended, and so its synthesis presupposes its pre-existence. All that synthesis can do is put together its indeterminate parts into determinate wholes.

So Kant's solution to the '*quid juris?*' is for the form of the concept not to apply directly to the matter of intuition but to its form, which becomes so to speak a second order matter for the form of the concept to determine. Another way that Kant expresses this is to say that space and time are not just forms of intuition, but are themselves (pure) intuitions, or as he says in the second edition deduction, space and time are not just 'forms of intuition' but themselves 'formal intuitions'.[32]

In the 'Transcendental Aesthetic' pure intuition is abstracted from sensation so that it can be examined alone, but if space and time are more than just orderings of sensation then the question remains to be

---

[32] B160, note. The complexity of the different meanings of pure intuition in the *Critique* is clearly presented in Henry E. Allison, *Kant's Transcendental Idealism* (New Haven, CT: Yale University Press, 1983), Chapter 5.

addressed of how they are *connected* to sensation. Kant finally addresses this in the 'Anticipations of Perception' in terms of the notion of 'filling': sensation *fills* time and space. But this filling (in spite of the picture that the word 'filling' might conjure up) is not extensive but 'intensive'; that is to say, each instant of time or point in space is 'filled' with sensation to a greater or lesser degree (greater or lesser intensity). So sensation has no extension of its own, it appears extended because it fills every point of space and time to a greater or lesser degree.[33] Thus Kant declares that sensation has intensive but not extensive magnitude: unlike extensive magnitude, intensive magnitude is not made up of parts.[34]

Having sketched out the role of pure intuition in Kant's theory I now turn to Maimon's discussion of space and time in the first chapter of the *Essay*. Maimon generally accepts Kant's claim that space and time are *a priori* forms of sensibility.[35] But he breaks with Kant in offering two different accounts of space and time: first as *concepts* and second as *intuitions*. As concepts, Maimon gives them an absolutely fundamental role as *conditions of consciousness of sensible objects*. He argues that the essential characteristic of thought is 'unity in the manifold':

> So if *A* and *B* are completely identical, there is in this case no manifold. There is therefore no comparison, and consequently no consciousness (and also no consciousness of identity). But if they are completely different, then there is no unity and, once again, no comparison, and consequently also no consciousness, not even consciousness of this difference, since, considered objectively,

---

[33] I note in passing that there is a problem with how space and time as extensive can be filled in this way, for if they have no smallest parts, *what* is it that is filled?

[34] See A167–68/B209–10. The apprehension of sensation fills only an instant, it 'is not a successive synthesis proceeding from the parts to the whole sensation, it therefore has no extensive magnitude I call that magnitude which can only be apprehended as a unity intensive magnitude'.

[35] The claim that for Maimon space and time are *a priori* forms has to be qualified because in an endnote to the first chapter he argues that this can ultimately only ever be a hypothesis: 'For example, I see a red object in space, I notice that space is to be found not only in the red object, but also in every other sensible object that I have perceived; by contrast, the red colour is to be found only in this object, and from this I conclude that the red colour must be grounded in the object itself but that space is grounded merely in the cognitive faculty in relation to every object in general. But why to every object in general? *Perhaps one day there will be an object that I perceive but not in space (or in time)*' ('Notes and Clarifications', #5, emphasis added).

difference is just a lack of identity (even though, considered subjectively, it is a unity, or relation of objects to one another). As a result, it cannot have objective validity. So space and time are these special forms by means of which unity in the manifold of sensible objects is possible, and hence by means of which these objects themselves are possible as objects of our consciousness.

(Chapter 1, s.16)

Without space and time we would have no consciousness of sensible objects. He further describes space regarded as a concept as 'the representation of the difference between things in general' and as the concept of the 'externality of things to one another' [*außer einander sein*] or their 'being-apart' [*Auseinandersein*]. The concepts of space and time are therefore not concepts of extension but of relation. Maimon explicitly argues that it is not possible to construct an extended space or time as pure intuitions from such concepts:

If I posit two points, *a* and *b*, that are separate, then neither of these points is yet a space, only their relation to one another is. So in this case there is no unity of the manifold of space, but rather an absolute unity of space, that is to say, it is not yet an intuition. Perhaps someone will say that, although it cannot be an intuition, it can be the element of an intuition if one assumes another point, *c*, besides *b*, so that the intuition of space will arise from the being-apart of *a* and *b*, and then of *b* and *c*? But this is to forget that when we describe relations and connections as separate, this only amounts to saying that they are different from one another (because a concept cannot be something outside another concept in time and space). But in themselves and abstracted from objects, these two relations are not different from one another. Consequently no intuition of space can arise from adding them together. And it is the same for time.

(Chapter 1, s.24–5)

As relations, space and time are likened to such *a priori* concepts of the understanding as cause. Such relational concepts are, he says, absolute unities or units (*Einheiten*), since their terms (left/right, before/after, cause/effect) cannot be separated without the concept being annulled. Since they can be neither divided nor added they are clearly not extensive quantities.

INTRODUCTION TO THE TRANSLATION

Nevertheless space and time do also exist as intuitions. But as such he says they are 'imaginary things' (Chapter 1, s.19) which the imagination produces by treating what is relative as absolute. In acting in this way he says the imagination is not guided by the understanding (which only recognizes relations of difference) but is acting illegitimately and its products, space or time as pure intuitions, are described as 'transcendent'. The argument is that space is the representation of difference, but pure intuition abstracted from any content is homogeneous, therefore pure intuitions are impossible (since they contradict the nature of space). Maimon argues that we can see that space is indeed correctly defined in terms of representing difference if we consider the representation of a homogeneous space. Imagine a completely homogeneous expanse of water; this is, he says, only extended relative to something else that is differentiated; if it were simply considered in itself it would have no determinate extension and could indeed be said to have no extension at all (he is perhaps thinking of it occupying the whole visual field). This argument seeks to establish that extensive magnitude depends on difference, and hence on intensive magnitude (which is intensive because, as a relation, it cannot be divided into parts).[36] Hence the homogeneous manifold (of space or of time), whose synthesis Kant describes in the 'Axioms of Intuition', is a fiction; as we saw in Maimon's demonstration that space as intuition cannot be synthesized from space as concept: without *difference*, synthesis is impossible to conceive. Although on the one hand Maimon seeks to demonstrate the impossibility of pure intuition, on the other hand he accepts that Kant is right to say that the pure formal geometry of Euclid is conducted by the imagination determining the fiction of absolute space in different ways to produce its objects in pure intuition. But he argues that all the necessity that geometry contains lies in the rules for producing these intuitions, *not* in the intuitions themselves. For figures produced in intuition are of completely arbitrary size and all that matters from a mathematical point of view is what is contained in their determinate concept, i.e. their inner nature and relations.[37] Maimon uses an example of a mathematical

---

[36] Russell states that Leibniz's relational theory of space caused him to attribute it intensive but not extensive magnitude. See Russell, op. cit., pp. 113–14.

[37] It is significant that Maimon never discusses the distinction Kant makes between a 'schema' and an 'image' (A140/B179ff.), and treats the terms synonymously (as meaning 'image'). For Kant the schema is, among other things, 'a general procedure for

synthetic *a priori* truth that Kant had introduced in the *Prolegomena*, 'the straight line is the shortest between two points'. He argues that imagining this line in pure intuition will not help to prove that it is the shortest:

> So, assuming that time and space are *a priori* intuitions, they are still only **intuitions** and not *a priori* **concepts**; they make only the terms of the relation intuitive for us, and by this means the relation itself, but not the truth and legitimacy of its use.
>
> (Chapter 2, s.60)

I want next to look at the consequences of Maimon tying space and time to difference.

The reality of difference

If extension depends on difference, if the extended world in space and time is a representation of differences, what are these differences? If there is no manifold in the pure forms of sensibility, space and time, it must lie in the matter of sensibility, in sensation. Maimon pursues this thought beyond the idea of differences between sensations to the thought of sensations *as* differences. To introduce this idea let us go back to Kant's idea of isolating pure space and time by abstracting from empirical intuition in which they are combined with sensation. This act of abstraction establishes space and time as pure intuitions, but at the same time it implies that once space and time are abstracted from empirical intuition, the sensation left behind is non-extensive. We have seen that Kant indeed treats it as non-extensive in the 'Anticipations of Perception'. Maimon addresses the nature of sensation abstracted from space and time, which he calls 'sensible representation in itself', at the beginning of Chapter 2:

> Considered in itself as a quality, every sensible representation must be abstracted from all quantity whether extensive or intensive. For example, the representation of the colour red must be thought without any finite extension, although not as a mathematical but

cont.
providing a concept with its image' rather than an individual image. This means that Kant could reply to Maimon's criticism by saying that for him pure geometry deals not with particular images, but with universal necessary schemata.

INTRODUCTION TO THE TRANSLATION

> rather as a physical point, or as the differential of an extension. It must further be thought without any finite degree of quality, but still as the differential of a finite degree. This finite extension or finite degree is necessary for consciousness of the representation, and is different for different representations according to the difference of their differentials; consequently sensible representations in themselves, considered as mere differentials, do not yet result in consciousness.
>
> (Chapter 2, s.28–9)

In a footnote he defends the introduction of the concept of the 'differential' from mathematics into philosophy on the grounds that Leibniz in fact originally developed the differential calculus within his philosophy of the *Monadology*, from where it was taken over into mathematics.[38] He adds in another footnote that these differentials are not 'absolute' unities as the *concepts* of space and time are, but 'determinate' unities or *units through whose addition a finite extensive or intensive sensation is produced*. He further boldly calls the differentials 'noumena':

> These differentials of objects are the so-called *noumena*; but the objects themselves arising from them are the *phenomena*. With respect to intuition = 0, the differential of any such object in itself is $dx = 0$, $dy = 0$ etc.; however their relations are not = 0, but can rather be given determinately in the intuitions arising from them.[39]

---

[38] I believe this claim is false, but cannot present evidence against it here. The reader is referred to the following collections of Leibniz's papers which also contain extensive editorial material: Leibniz, *The Labyrinth of the Continuum: Writings on the Continuum Problem, 1672–1686*, trans. with an introduction by Richard Arthur (New Haven, CT: Yale University Press, 2002); Leibniz, *Naissance du calcul différentiel*, ed. M. Parmentier ed. (Paris: Vrin, 1995).

[39] It is notable that Maimon here describes a differential as having no value on its own but only acquiring a value in relation to another differential. According to the so-called 'rigorous formulation' of the calculus developed by Cauchy and Weierstrass in the nineteenth century, the differentials are thought to have no meaning independently of the derivative – the function dx/dy. Hence talk of infinitesimals came to be condemned as lacking rigour, indeed as lacking any meaning (see C. Boyer, *The History of the Calculus* [New York: Dover, 1959]). This view has more recently been challenged by Abraham Robinson's rigorous definition of infinitesimal numbers as a special class of numbers with distinct properties – in so doing Robinson explicitly set out to restore the standing of Leibniz's approach to infinitesimals (see A. Robinson, *Non-standard Analysis* [Princeton, NJ: Princeton University Press, 1996]).

INTRODUCTION TO THE TRANSLATION

These *noumena* are ideas of reason serving as principles to explain how objects arise according to certain rules of the understanding.

(Chapter 2, s.32)

This means that extension is intrinsically material for Maimon, and in this respect there is a similarity between Maimon and Leibniz, because for Leibniz too only matter is extended while spatial relations are not. I argued above that according to Maimon, synthesis of the homogeneous is a contradiction in terms. However, he himself describes the syntheses of a sensation of a finite intensive and extensive quantity as syntheses of the homogeneous:

Consciousness first arises when the imagination takes together **several** homogeneous sensible representations, orders them according to its forms (succession in time and space), and forms an individual intuition out of them. Homogeneity [*Einartigkeit*] is necessary because otherwise there could be no connection within a single consciousness.

(Chapter 2, s.30)

Now according to what he has said before, ordering the sensible representations in time and space presupposes their difference, so how can the homogeneous be ordered in this way? In Chapter 1 he writes:

If there were only a uniform intuition, then we would not have any concept of space, and hence no intuition of space either since the latter presupposes the former. On the other hand, if there were nothing but different types of intuition, then we would have merely a concept, but not an intuition, of space. And it is the same for time.

(Chapter 1, s.18)

It seems to me that just as homogeneous extension can in fact only be thought in relation to difference, although Maimon does not say so, homogeneous synthesis must also take place in relation to difference. This could be thought in two ways, either (1) homogeneity is only relative not absolute likeness, so that it is the minimally different differentials that are brought together, and/or (2) homogeneous differentials are differentiated through the different differentials with which they are connected, for example a representation of red is made up of a set of differentials (of extension, of quality of colour, of intensity of colour, etc.) and these could each vary differently from representation to representation.

Having described how Maimon conceives of space and time as representations of difference, I want now to look at their role in Maimon's theory of knowledge, and examine how Maimon thinks the differentials resolve the question '*quid juris?*'. To answer the question 'how do *a priori* concepts apply to empirical intuitions?', Maimon and Kant adopt the same initial strategy. First they agree that it is impossible to justify the direct application of *a priori* concepts to empirical intuitions, secondly they analyse empirical intuitions and find something within them to which *a priori* concepts *can* be applied without problem. For Kant this is pure intuition as the form of empirical intuitions, for Maimon it is the differentials of sensation that precede the synthesis of empirical intuitions. I discussed above how for Kant the fact of the synthesis of objects is more important than the status of pure intuition or how pure intuition makes this possible (pure intuition derives its status from the object and not the reverse). So although objects are completely formal until their extension is filled with sensation, their objectivity and necessity are completely independent of this acquisition of materiality. In other words, the explanation of the relation of sensation to the pure forms of intuition that the 'Anticipations of Perception' provides is off to one side of the main line of argument. It is indeed presented in terms of the application of just *one* of the categories (quality) to pure intuition. In this way Kant's transcendental philosophy makes the question of *reality* secondary to that of *objectivity*; but this downplaying of the epistemological significance of matter is misleading to the extent that without matter objects would lose all empirical reality just as much as if they were deprived of their objectivity.

Maimon takes the opposite path, making the question of reality primary and objectivity secondary. It is of great importance therefore that the difference that the differentials identify is real. To secure this he asserts the reality of difference:

Difference pertains to all things; or all things must be – or must be thought – different from one another, for it is just because of this that they are all things.

('Short Overview', s.179–80)

INTRODUCTION TO THE TRANSLATION

And he argues that difference in the appearance must reflect a difference in the objects themselves:

> I agree with Kant that for us the transcendental object of all appearances considered in itself is *x*. *But I maintain that if we assume there are different appearances, we are also forced to assume there are different objects corresponding to them* and that these can be determined *per analogium* with their corresponding appearances even though they cannot be determined in themselves. In the same way, those born blind cannot think each colour in itself, although they can nevertheless think the refraction peculiar to each colour by means of lines constructed from haptic intuition [*Anschauung des Gefühls*] and so make each colour into a determinate object.
> ('Short Overview', s.201, emphasis added)

Thus difference is so to speak the magical quality that can pass through the absolute barrier that Kant sets up between the knower and the thing in itself. This way of thinking the reality of difference probably has its roots in Leibniz's notion of perception as a confused understanding, so that as more differences are made out, understanding increases, but there is no thought that more differences might be being seen than are actually there. This view also accords with the modern information theory idea of entropy only increasing, or the idea that in the transmission of a signal the ratio of noise to information (difference) never decreases. It is important to note that when Maimon calls the differentials 'elements' of intuitions he does not mean that they are very small intuitions that are too small to cross the threshold of consciousness – they are not extended at all.[40] Hence he does not regard them as so to speak small pieces of matter but as themselves relational:

> But I differ in that the transcendental idealist [i.e. Kant] understands by matter what belongs to sensation in abstraction from the relations in which it is ordered, whereas I hold that what belongs to sensation must also be ordered in relations if it is to be perceived (even if I cannot directly perceive these relations). I also hold that

---

[40] In a letter to Kant dated 21 September 1791, Maimon attacks Leibniz's theory of 'petit perceptions', obscure representations that fall below the threshold of consciousness (I. Kant, *Philosophical Correspondence 1759–99*, p. 177).

xliii

INTRODUCTION TO THE TRANSLATION

> time and space are the forms of this relation in so far as I can perceive it, and I understand by matter not an object, but merely the ideas that perceptions must ultimately be resolved into.
>
> ('Short Overview', s.205)

Indeed one of the most striking aspects of Maimon's philosophy is the way it presents a thoroughgoing philosophy of difference in which relations and differences are prior to their objects:

> It is an error to believe that things (real objects) must be prior to their relations. The concepts of the numbers are merely relations and do not presuppose real objects because these relations are the objects themselves.
>
> ('Short Overview', s.190)

> When a perception, for example **red**, is given to me, I do not yet have any consciousness of it; when another, for example **green**, is given to me, I do not yet have any consciousness of it in itself either. But if I relate them to one another (by means of the unity of difference), then I notice that red is different from green, and so I attain consciousness of each of the perceptions in itself. If I constantly had the representation red, for example, without having any other representation, then I could never attain consciousness of it.
>
> (Chapter 8, s.131–2)

There is an important difference between Maimon and Leibniz on this issue. For Leibniz it could be said that the reason space and time are not real is precisely because they are relations. Relations are not real, only that is real that exists as substance, independently, and hence without relation to everything else: hence the theory of monads. Now I have already remarked that when Maimon introduces his theory of differentials of sensation he remarks in a footnote his belief that Leibniz discovered the differential calculus through his system of the *Monadology*. But it would be completely wrong to infer from this association that Maimon's differentials are monads; and perhaps in order to prevent this identification Maimon in the text immediately after the note specifies that they are 'not mathematical but *physical points*', for Leibniz described the monads as not physical but *metaphysical points*. The differentials are inherently relational

INTRODUCTION TO THE TRANSLATION

and as such are completely at odds with Leibniz's definition of substance. What is more, Maimon is true to the spirit of Kant's critical philosophy in treating substance as a category. Maimon's solution to the question '*quid juris?*' of the applicability of the categories is to say that they apply directly to the differentials: the differential of sensation is only thought as substance in applying that particular category to it. The way Maimon thinks this is well summarized in the following passage:

> The metaphysically infinitely small is real because quality can certainly be considered in itself abstracted from all quantity. This way of considering it is also useful for resolving the question, *quid juris*? because the pure concepts of the understanding or categories are never directly related to intuitions, but only to their elements, and these are ideas of reason concerning the way these intuitions arise; it is through the mediation of these ideas that the categories are related to the intuitions themselves. Just as in higher mathematics we produce the relations of different magnitudes themselves from their differentials, so the understanding (admittedly in an obscure way) produces the real relations [356] of qualities themselves from the real relations of their differentials. So, if we judge that fire melts wax, then this judgement does not relate to fire and wax as objects of intuition, but to their elements, which the understanding thinks in the relation of cause and effect to one another.
>
> ('Notes & Clarifications', #15, s.355–6)

In Chapter 3 Maimon claims that what his theory of cognition presents is the objective order of how the mind works in contradistinction to its subjective order of operation. The subjective order goes from (1) receiving sensations to (2) ordering them into intuitions in space and time (which he says gives consciousness but not thought) to (3) thinking intuitions under concepts to (4) thinking the totality of concepts in ideas of reason. He doesn't state that this is a description of Kant's account but it fits it reasonably well, although without mentioning the transcendental machinery at work producing objects. However, it may be that by calling it subjective he means rather that this is how we might naturally assume things work, or how things seem to our consciousness. On the other hand, the objective order goes from (1) the differentials of sensation to (2) the grasping of these by concepts of the understanding to (3) thinking the

xlv

totality of concepts in ideas of reason. Thus objectively intuition plays absolutely no role in cognition, we only imagine it does. And on the most radical interpretation of what Maimon is saying, consciousness plays no role either: consciousness requires some extension in time but thought, differentials, concepts, are all differential, relational, intensive.

Maimon's conception of how categories apply to the differentials is further clarified in Chapter 8 where after some chapters defining concepts he returns to the discussion and criticism of Kant's theory of knowledge undertaken in the first three chapters. In Chapter 8 he deals with issues dealt with by Kant in the 'Analogies of Experience', that is to say persistence and alteration. He argues that the only criterion of something altering rather than being replaced is that the alteration be minimal, and this means that there is an *a priori* principle of continuity in all experience. He says that in order to preserve self-identity the successive determinations of an altering substance must be minimally different:

> to make experience possible, they [the determinations] must therefore be united in the object so that they make the least break ... This leads us to search for the cause of this appearance, i.e. the continuity in it, and to fill in the gaps in our perceptions in order to make then into experiences. For what else is understood by the word 'cause' in the doctrine of nature than the development of an appearance and its resolution, so that between it and the preceding appearance the desired continuity is found. Everyone can explain this for themselves by means of countless examples, so I do not need to dwell on it.
>
> (Chapter 8, s.139–40)

It is interesting to note how this identification of alteration and cause, and the reduction of both to a differential, is exactly what happened to the concept of cause in the history of science. Bertrand Russell wrote several attacks on the anachronism of the way philosophers still spoke about cause at the beginning of the twentieth century, chiding them for their ignorance of actual scientific theory. In discussing this issue in *The Analysis of Mind* he points out that the usual concept of cause lacks rigour because there is generally a gap in time between the cause and the effect (e.g. when we say 'taking the poison caused the person's death' although some event might have intervened to stop the cause having its effect, such as the person being shot dead before the poison took effect). He continues:

> Thus, if we are to take the cause as one event and the effect as another, both must be shortened indefinitely. The result is that we merely have, as the embodiment of our causal law, a certain direction of change at each moment. Hence we are brought to differential equations as embodying causal laws. A physical law does not say 'A will be followed by B,' but tells us what acceleration a particle will have under given circumstances, i.e. it tells us how the particle's motion is changing at each moment, not where the particle will be at some future moment.[41]

Similarly in Maimon's theory cause, alteration and substance coalesce in the single reality of continuity of change, expressed by the non-extended differentials at each point.

I have compared Kant's and Maimon's accounts of space and time, but I have not yet compared their accounts of difference. Difference takes centre stage in Maimon's transcendental philosophy; the concept is not absent from the *Critique* but the role it plays is less visible. Kant does not discuss the concept of difference explicitly until after the 'Transcendental Analytic' in the 'Amphiboly of the Concepts of Reflection', a chapter that stands as if it does not quite know where it belongs, between the 'Analytic' and the 'Dialectic', being described as an appendix to the former. Much of this chapter is taken up with criticism of Leibniz's philosophy and of his misuse of concepts, in particular his misuse of the concept of difference. In this respect the chapter has an affinity with the 'Dialectic' that is to follow, since it shows how the misuse of concepts can lead to false metaphysical claims. Difference and identity are one of the four pairs of 'concepts of reflection' that are discussed (the others are agreement/opposition, inner/outer, matter/form). Kant calls them 'concepts of reflection' because reflection on the domain of their use is required if they are to be used correctly. With respect to difference, Leibniz's error is to assert that the principle of the 'identity of indiscernibles' is universally valid. Kant argues that on the contrary it is only valid of concepts, not of intuitions. It is quite possible for several

---

[41] Bertrand Russell, *Analysis of Mind* London: George Allen & Unwin, 1921), p. 68.

conceptually identical things to exist as different objects of sensible intuition, whereas identical concepts are just one and the same concept. In this sense it could be said that difference is equivocal for Kant: difference used of concepts does not mean the same thing as difference used of sensible objects. Because Maimon grounds spatial or temporal difference in real differences, he is on the contrary committed to the univocity of difference: mere difference of place is only real to the extent that it represents an underlying real difference.

But beyond the criticism of Leibniz there is another important aspect to the 'Amphiboly of the Concepts of Reflection'. This is the fact that the concepts discussed therein have already been used in the *Critique* prior to this reflection on their correct use.[42] In particular, identity and difference have been used in the descriptions of synthesis in the 'Transcendental Deduction' and 'Schematism'. In the 'Schematism', as we have seen, the synthesis of extensive magnitude is a synthesis of the homogeneous; equally in the first edition version of the 'Deduction', in the synthesis of apprehension that precedes the further syntheses that bring an intuition under a concept, a synthesis of the homogeneous is necessary:

> for the unity of intuition to come from this manifold (as, say, in the representation of space), it is necessary first to run through and then to take together this manifoldness, which action I call the synthesis of apprehension.
>
> (A99)

In the first edition deduction, this synthesis of apprehension as a pure synthesis that unites perceptions into a pure intuition underlies all use of *a priori* concepts; if it is incoherent then Kant's solution to the question '*quid juris?*' fails. The difficulty is how can what is completely homogeneous nevertheless be grasped hold of and synthesized into a whole. I think this difficulty lies at the heart of Maimon's rewriting of the *Critique*; in criticizing the possibility of synthesis of the homogeneous, Maimon is arguing that one can only think it if one illegitimately models the pure synthesis on an empirical synthesis. We only think that there is no problem in putting together different pieces of time or space because

---

[42] For example, the concepts of matter and form structure sensibility according to the 'Transcendental Aesthetic', equally the concepts of inner and outer distinguish the two kinds of sense, and so on.

INTRODUCTION TO THE TRANSLATION

we are imagining these pieces as identifiable pieces of matter, but in fact they are not identifiable at all. So Maimon feels entitled to apply the term 'transcendent' which Kant introduces in the 'Dialectic' to describe principles that encourage us to go beyond the bounds of experience, to Kant's own invention of the imaginary domain of pure intuition.[43] To sum up: within the Kantian framework, although the question of the legitimacy of the application of the concept of difference to experience is dealt with in the 'Amphiboly' this treatment is not adequate according to Maimon. Its inadequacy can be summarized by saying that in that chapter Kant considers the *empirical* and *conceptual* application of the concept but not its *transcendental* application. This allows his error of using it *transcendentally* in the 'Analytic' in accordance with the principles of its *empirical* use.

In Chapter 2 Maimon poses a startling question: what is the legitimacy of the judgement that red is different from green:[44]

> if I say that **red** is different from **green**, then the pure concept of the understanding of the difference is not treated as a relation between the sensible qualities (for then the Kantian question *quid juris?* remains unanswered), but rather either (according to the Kantian theory) as the relation of their spaces as *a priori* forms, or (according to my theory) as the relation of their differentials, which are *a priori* ideas of reason.

This seems an odd question from the Kantian viewpoint, since Kant only seeks to answer the question *'quid juris?'* with respect to the categories (not the concepts of reflection), and with the categories it is always in terms of a determination of time (a schema) not of space. However, it should now be clear why Maimon thinks the problem of the legitimacy of the concept of difference is fundamental to the *Critique*. According to Maimon, we are entitled to use *a priori* concepts to the extent that we grasp the ultimate differences of things, hence the concept of difference is

---

[43] See A296/B352 ff., and 'Short Overview', s.179.

[44] The topic no doubt has its source in Leibniz's argument against Locke that even an apparently purely empirical judgement like 'red is different from green' involves innate ideas (in this case the idea of difference). See Leibniz, *New Essays on Human Understanding*, trans. and ed. P. Remnant and J. Bennett (Cambridge: Cambridge University Press, 1982), Book 1.

the most fundamental of the *a priori* concepts, the others, cause, substance, alteration, are specifications of difference. We cannot apply *a priori* concepts directly to intuitions because intuitions contain what we do not understand.

Ideas of the understanding: from the 'differential' to 'material completion'

Maimon calls the differentials 'ideas of the understanding'. In so doing he takes ideas from the purely regulatory role they are allowed in the *Critique* as 'ideas of reason'[45] and by attaching them to the understanding gives them as 'differentials' a constitutive role in knowledge. I want to look now at another 'idea of the understanding' that Maimon puts forward, an idea also associated with a concept from the calculus, but this time with integration. Before explaining this idea I need to discuss some of the other concepts Maimon deploys in his frequent discussions of mathematical examples in the *Essay*.

There are two concepts of mathematical objects whose definition Maimon discusses again and again: the straight line and the circle. The underlying reason for the importance of these two examples for Maimon lies, I think, in their special status in Euclid's axiomatic system of the *Elements*: they are the only geometrical objects whose possibility is postulated rather than demonstrated by construction. They are first defined and then postulated: everything else is constructed *from* straight lines and circles, but it is simply postulated that a straight line of any length and a circle of any size can be drawn. There is no problem with this of course, but if one could reduce the number of postulates the system would be more elegant – for example, if one could construct a straight line from a point or a circle from a straight line. According to Heath, Saccheri in 1697 introduced the terminology of 'real' and 'nominal' definitions into his account of Euclid to make the point that for Euclid the definition of a geometrical figure does not establish that its construction is possible.[46] Saccheri terms Euclid's definitions 'nominal', and states that in order to become 'real' they must be supplemented either by the postulate that the figure is possible or by the proof of this through construction. Maimon uses the same terms but also draws on a distinction Spinoza

---

[45] See A671/B699 ff.
[46] See the discussion of definitions in the introduction to Euclid *The Elements*, Vol. 1, trans. and intro. Sir T. L. Heath (New York: Dover Books, 1956), pp. 143–51.

makes between 'incomplete' and 'complete' definition in the *Treatise on the Emendation of the Intellect*.[47] Spinoza writes:

> If a circle is defined as a figure in which the lines drawn from the centre to the circumference are equal, it is obvious that such a definition by no means explains the essence of a circle, but only one of its properties.[48]

To rectify this fault, a complete definition (of a created thing) must satisfy the following requirements:

1 It ... must include its proximate cause, for example, according to this rule a circle would have to be defined as follows: a figure described by any line of which one end is fixed and the other movable ...
2 The conception or definition of the thing must be such that all the properties of the thing, when regarded by itself and not in conjunction with other things, can be deduced from it, as can be seen in the case of this definition of a circle. For from it we clearly deduce that all the lines drawn from the centre to the circumference are equal.[49]

Maimon, contra Sacceri and in agreement with Spinoza does not allow the mere *postulation* of existence to provide a real definition but requires the *production* of the figure. A nominal definition, he says (Chapter 2, s.50), identifies the condition that the concept must satisfy, for example, 'a figure in which the lines drawn from the centre to the circumference are equal'. Maimon agrees with Sacceri that the problem with this kind of definition is that it fails to establish the possibility of what is defined. A real definition, on the other hand demonstrates that an object is possible by 'explaining how it arises' [*die Erklärung der*

---

[47] We know from his autobiography that Maimon had read Spinoza, but the only evidence I am basing the claim that he read this particular text upon is the similarity in their discussions of the definition of the circle.

[48] Spinoza, *Treatise on the Emendation of the Intellect*, in Spinoza, *Ethics & Treatise on the Emendation of the Intellect*, trans. S. Shirley (Indianapolis, IN: Hackett, 1992), pp. 257–8 (§95).

[49] Spinoza, ibid. p. 258 (§96).

li

INTRODUCTION TO THE TRANSLATION

Entstehungsart], that is to say, how it comes into being. But what Maimon adds to this from Spinoza is the notion that *a real definition would give the essence of a circle from which all its properties could be derived*. Or in other words that we do not fully comprehend the circle unless we have a real definition for it. So the real definition is required not just to show that the circle is possible but *in order to understand what a circle is*. And it is understood through its method of generation: the figure produced by rotating a line around one of its endpoints.

This requirement of being able to provide what Maimon calls the 'way of arising' or 'mode of genesis', is one of the fundamental concepts of the *Essay*. It is supplemented by another notion that adds a further requirement for the 'completion' of a concept, beyond what Spinoza demanded in a complete definition, viz. *material completeness*:

> The material completeness of a concept, in so far as this completeness cannot be given in intuition, is an idea of the understanding. For example, the understanding prescribes for itself a rule or condition: that from a given point an infinite number of lines that are equal to one another are to be drawn, from which (through the connection of their endpoints) the concept of the circle is to be produced. The possibility of this rule, and consequently also of this concept itself, can be shown in intuition (through the movement of a line around the given point), and consequently also its formal completeness (unity in the manifold). But its material completeness (of the manifold) cannot be given in intuition, because one can only ever draw a finite number of lines that are equal to one another. It is thus not a concept of the understanding to which an object corresponds, but only an idea of the understanding, which one can ever approach to infinity in intuition through the successive addition of such lines, and consequently a limit concept [*Gränzbegrif*].

(Chapter 3, s.75–6)

This then is the second 'idea of the understanding': it and the differential are in a sense opposite extremes. Let us examine this idea of 'material completeness'. Maimon states that the 'formal completeness' of the concept of the circle is shown in intuition, by which he means that the circle is a unity in intuition – a complete circle. But nevertheless the intuition cannot present the infinity of the positions of the rotating line that produced it and so the manifold united into a formal unity is not itself complete in intuition. Kant discusses this in his letter on the *Essay* and firmly rejects Maimon's claim that the nominal or formal definition of the circle ('from a given point an infinite number of lines that are equal to one another are to be drawn') is inadequate – Kant insists that its possibility is already grasped in the definition because in so defining it we imagine it in pure intuition, so the definition does not lack anything in order to be complete. But Kant does not mention Maimon's explanation of *why* he thinks material completion matters. Maimon's claim is in effect that Spinoza's second definition of the circle (the figure generated by a rotating line) which he claims is complete, is not, because it fails to satisfy Spinoza's own second requirement for a complete definition, viz. that all the object's properties can be derived from it alone. Maimon states: 'if we want to derive the measure of the area of the circle, or its relation to a square, then we must necessarily assume the circle as already complete, because otherwise this relation cannot be exact' (Chapter 3, s.78). It is in this way that Maimon introduces the integral calculus into transcendental philosophy in terms of 'material completeness' as an 'idea of the understanding'. Kant does not recognize that underlying the disagreement about the adequacy of definitions is the fact that Maimon is appealing to a very different conception of geometry from that presented in Euclid's *Elements* which always seems to be Kant's reference; and that this new approach gives geometry a material and productive character that it lacks in Euclid. This genetic approach is not in actual fact new, since it was inaugurated by Archimedes in *On the Sphere and the Cylinder* where he introduced the 'method of exhaustion' in order to attempt to solve the problem of 'squaring the circle' by identifying the circle with a regular polygon with an infinite number of sides and approximating this figure by imagining polygons with an ever greater number of sides inscribed inside and outside the circle, the circle being larger than one and smaller than the other. Each side of a polygon determines a triangle whose other sides are radii and whose apex is the centre, and the sum of these triangles is the area of the polygon, and the more sides the polygons have the closer this area is to the area of the circle. In the seventeenth century this method had been rethought and universalized into a method for finding the area under a curve in general by the invention of the integral calculus by Newton and Leibniz. This method breaks down the barriers between what for the Greeks were different classes of objects: points, lines, areas and volumes, and allows points to generate lines, lines areas and so on. As Newton describes his new method in *On the Quadrature of Curves*:

> I consider mathematical quantities ... as generated by a continual motion. Lines are described, and by describing are generated, not by any apposition of parts, but by a continual motion of points. Surfaces are generated by the motion of lines, solids by the motion of surfaces, angles by the rotation of their legs, time by a continual flux, and so on in the rest. These geneses are founded upon nature, and are every day seen in the motion of bodies.[50]

So to return to Maimon's argument about the circle, he is thinking the area as the limit of an infinite synthesis of lines, and pointing out that if the synthesis is merely finite (not materially complete) then the result will be inaccurate – for example, it will give the area of a many-sided polygon not a circle. If we don't understand the circle in this way then we cannot know, for example, that its area is πr^2 and so our understanding of it is incomplete.

Maimon takes the calculus to show that understanding does not lie in intuition but in getting behind intuition to grasp its production. Sensible intuition, whether it is of the objects of pure geometry or of the empirical world, always contains the arbitrary, that we do not understand. The arbitrary extension of the objects of geometry and the associations of concepts in an empirical concept such as gold (yellow colour, distinctive weight, etc.) into which we have no insight. It is in leaving behind the domains of pure and empirical intuition that we move towards understanding the real.

Maimon provides a striking account of how the two ideas of the understanding, the differential and the completed synthesis, exceed our consciousness in an endnote to Chapter 2:

> We should note that both the primitive consciousness of a constituent part of a synthesis (without relating this part to the synthesis) as well as the consciousness of the complete synthesis are mere ideas, i.e. they are the two limit concepts of a synthesis, in that without synthesis no consciousness is possible, but the

[50] See Appendix.

consciousness of the completed synthesis grasps the infinite in itself, and is consequently impossible for a limited cognitive faculty ... So we start in the middle with our cognition of things and finish in the middle again.

('Notes & Clarifications', #15, s.349–50)

The world of consciousness in which we live, in which we begin and in which we end, is the finite world. We can be conscious neither of the differentials from which we synthesize the finite nor of the result of this synthesis, the integral, because to understand it is to understand it as infinite. Reality and understanding escape intuition and conscious representation at both ends.

Conclusion: The Productive Fleeting Activity of Thought

In the Preface to the second edition of the *Critique of Pure Reason*, Kant speaks of the poor state of metaphysics in comparison with the sciences. Mathematics became scientific in ancient times and in the last 150 years the study of nature has also become a science, yet metaphysics has not progressed and remains stuck in an interminable debate between opposing schools. Kant suggests that philosophy would do well to learn a methodological lesson from the sciences. He maintains that the breakthrough to science that happened in geometry in ancient Greece and in natural science as recently as the seventeenth century occurred in both cases when scientists replaced a method of passive observation with one of active intervention. The geometers found that the properties of figures could be demonstrated through constructing them in accordance with prior concepts; and the natural scientists learnt to conduct experiments, for *'they comprehended that reason has insight only into what it itself produces according to its own design'*.[51]

Kant invents transcendental philosophy in accordance with this methodological insight: *the understanding can attain necessary* a priori *knowledge of the world precisely to the extent that the world is its own construction*. Maimon transforms transcendental philosophy by making it more thoroughly consistent with this principle. He sees an insurmountable gap between intuition and understanding: whatever Kant's claims for pure intuition, Maimon believes intuition as such always involves

[51] Bxi–iii.

something given that is not produced by the understanding, and as such it cannot contribute to knowledge. The understanding cannot think the objects of intuition, only their production:

> The understanding can only think objects as flowing (with the exception of the forms of judgement, which are not objects). The reason for this is that the business of the understanding is nothing but **thinking**, i.e. producing unity in the manifold, which means that it can only think an object by specifying the way it arises or the rule by which it arises: this is the only way that the manifold of an object be brought under the unity of the rule, and consequently the understanding cannot think an object as having already arisen but only as arising, i.e. as flowing.
>
> (Chapter 2, s.33)

But rather than simply applying Kant's principle of successful scientific method more rigorously to transcendental philosophy, Maimon finds in the calculus a specific scientific model for transcendental philosophy. It too conforms to the principle of understanding something through understanding how it is produced, and it is the method that underlies the success of the Newtonian scientific revolution. In so doing Maimon reveals the strange fleeting character of a thought that is a stranger to consciousness.

Note on the Translation

General Issues

Manfred Frank, one of the originators of the current revival of interest in Maimon, describes Maimon's German prose as 'tricky [*vertrackt*]' (and his punctuation as 'highly arbitrary'). In some ways however the problems presented by Maimon's German are more challenging for the modern German editor than for the translator since German was not Maimon's first language and his knowledge of it – although impressive – never achieved native-speaker fluency. As a result, the text is in some ways already a translation; and its (further) translation into English less likely to introduce distortion than in the case of highly polished German prose writers like Schopenhauer or Nietzsche (not that Maimon's prose – never without an austere beauty – fails to achieve a certain characteristically eighteenth-century rhetorical flourish, in the Dedication and final remarks, for instance).

But perhaps the root of its trickiness is not linguistic at all, but rather a reflection of Maimon's own intellectual energy: he is almost always arguing (very often using a *reductio*) and practically every clause of the work is positioned in a logical relation with the rest. It would not unusual for him to begin a clause 'but since although ..'. Maimon naturally exploits the more structured syntax and richer inflections of the German language for his argumentative purposes, but there have been relatively few occasions on which we have needed to substantially modify the syntax of the text for English readability.

We have tried to produce an English translation that is as readable as

NOTE ON THE TRANSLATION

Maimon's German without any sacrifice of accuracy. Reproduction of characteristically German syntax however is not accurate translation, but a failure of translation and we have avoided this.

There are some (rare) instances where Maimon's own knowledge of German may be lacking (see below under *sich vorstellen* and *sich auf etwas beziehen*) but we have never translated on the basis of this assumption without interpolating the original in the text. Almost always we translate Maimon's words without interpretation, but sometimes with a comment.

Maimon uses the now rapidly obsolescing forms of noun declension in German (e.g. additional –e on dative masc./neut. singular nouns). Indeed, he declines Latin nouns when using them inside a German sentence. Where we give individual German terms we have normalized the spelling, and we have put Latin nouns into the nominative case.

Frank describes Maimon's punctuation as 'highly arbitrary' and so we have tried to preserve as much of it as is compatible with readable English. In particular, there seemed to be little reason to break up Maimon's semicolon separated clauses into separate English sentences (although this would be the norm in contemporary English prose). We have therefore left the reader a flavour of the density of Maimon's German without hindering readability. Maimon sometimes makes a claim in one clause and then gives the reason for it in a new clause separated from the first by a semicolon. Occasionally we have simply bound these two clauses together using ' ... because ..' in English.

Specific Issues

There are relatively few lexical difficulties with Maimon's German, and in general, given his extremely close relation to Kant, we have selected our English terms from the now standard Guyer and Wood translation of Kant's *Critique of Pure Reason*. (One exception is '*Zugleichsein*', which we have usually translated as 'coexistence', following the older Norman Kemp-Smith translation because Maimon uses the term to describe the relations of things both in time and in space. We have however occasionally translated it as 'simultaneity' when it is specified as a determination of time alone.)

The following translations warrant some comment however:

1 Mass versus count nouns: *Erkenntnis, Realität*
'*Erkenntnis*' and '*Realität*' ('cognition' and 'reality') are only mass nouns in English, that is, they refer to a notional non-decomposable mass of

cognition/reality that cannot be denumerated. This is why their plurals are unusual in English. In German however these terms can act both as mass and as count nouns. In other words, it is appropriate to say *'eine Erkenntnis'* in German where it is not appropriate to say 'a cognition' (or 'a knowledge') in English. Similarly, the plural *'Erkenntnisse'* implies a set of denumerable individual items of cognition. Used as a mass noun, *'Erkenntnis'* denotes cognition in general; used as a count noun it denotes an individual cognitive particular (e.g. a judgement). When Maimon uses these nouns we have translated them literally ('a cognition', 'a reality') rather than introduce non-textual material ('a cognitive particular' or 'an item of cognition' that might be misleading. The reader should bear in mind this difference between German and English usage.

2 *Ansehung*

Maimon uses the phrase *'in Ansehung ..'* a lot. It means 'with respect to ..', and this is how we have usually translated it, avoiding near-synonymous phrases in English ('in relation to ..' and 'with reference to ..' to avoid confusion with Maimon's technical vocabulary). When used of a person (e.g. *'in Ansehung Kants'*) we have sometimes however shortened it to e.g. 'for Kant'.

3 *Auseinander*

Maimon uses two locutions with slightly different meanings to characterize space: (1) *'das Auseinandersein'* which means 'being separate' or 'being apart', which has been translated by 'being-apart', (2) *'außer einander'* meaning 'outside one another' or 'external to one another'. Maimon seems to regard these as more or less synonymous, so the reader should not take 'separateness' to mean 'being kept apart by something else' or 'having a space between them', but just 'being in different places'. For Maimon space and time are continua (see Chapter 8 where he introduces the *principle of continuity*).

4 *bedeuten/bezeichnen* (and cognates)

In the chapter on 'Symbolic Cognition' Maimon introduces a technical distinction between *'bedeuten'* and *'bezeichnen'*. The latter is always translated as 'to designate' in this context; but the former is given as either 'to mean' or 'to signify' because Maimon often uses *'bedeuten'* with non-propositional direct objects and 'to mean' does not allow this so easily in English whereas 'signify' does.

NOTE ON THE TRANSLATION

5 *Bestimmen/(un)bestimmt/Bestimmung*

We have almost always translated '*bestimmen*' as 'determine' and '*Bestimmung*' as 'determination' (exceptions are where the context is obviously non-technical). The pair '*unbestimmt*'/'*bestimmt*' poses some more problems however: 'indeterminate'/'determinate' is the natural translation, but this is often gives a misleading impression because 'determinate' and 'indeterminate' have the inappropriate connotation of 'a particular object' and 'not any particular object' whereas for Maimon determination does not have to do with picking out an object from other objects, but rather with determining more closely what has already been picked out. In Maimon's language, the determinable (subject) is determined by the determination (predicate) and prior to this determination the determinable is undetermined but not indeterminate. Because determination is an action of the understanding (or of judgement), 'determined' gives the past participle sense of the result of the action whereas 'determinate' has the adjectival sense of 'particular', which can be misleading. In contexts where this contrast is evident, we have therefore chosen the pair 'undetermined' and 'determined', but the reader should keep in mind the same German terms are being used where the translation has 'indeterminate' and 'determinate'.

6 *Denkbarkeit*

We have chosen to translate this using the neologism 'thinkability' because its meaning is clear, it brings the German word to mind, it is more concise than 'possibility of thinking', and it does not prejudge the identity of thinking with the use of concepts as would 'conceivability'. (In addition, 'conceivable' and 'comprehensible' have been used to translate '*begreiflich*'.)

7 *Einerlei, Einerleiheit, Identität*

Maimon usually expresses identity using '*einerlei*' (literally, 'one and the same') and '*Einerleiheit*' (literally 'one-and-the-same-ness'). Where possible we have translated the adjective form literally as 'one and the same', but where this has not been possible we have used 'identical'. For the abstract noun we have used 'identity'. Occasionally we have used other translations, and in these cases we have given the German original in the text.

Maimon also uses the Latinate term '*Identität*', but almost exclusively in the phrase '*Satz der Identität*' (the principle of identity). We have marked the German for the one exception to this on s. 253. He uses the

NOTE ON THE TRANSLATION

Latinate term *'identisch'* a little more frequently, and the German is also given in these cases. Maimon seems still to be reserving these Latinate forms to express propositional identity. In all other (unmarked) cases the words being translated are *'einerlei'* or its cognates.

Maimon uses the phrase *'ein und derselbe'* quite often. We have translated this 'the very same ..' to distinguish it from *'einerlei'*.

8 *Einartig/ungleichartig* versus *gleichartig/verschiedenartig*

We have translated both of the former pair of words as 'homogeneous' and both of the latter pair as 'heterogeneous', but marked the originals in the text. There is a slight difference of meaning between the pairs: the former pair literally signifies 'of one kind'/'not of one kind'; whereas the latter pair literally signifies 'of the same kind'/'of different kinds'. But Maimon does not appear to be exploiting this difference in his use of the terms. Of these terms, Kant only uses *'gleichartig';* he uses it (1) negatively in the context of the lack of homogeneity of concept and intuition (hence the need for schemata) and (2) positively in the context of the pure syntheses of time and space – of extensive quantity. It is this latter use that is relevant to Maimon's use of these terms.

9 *Entstehung, entstehen, Entstehungsart, Entstehungsregel*

These mean literally 'arising', 'to arise', 'way of arising' and 'rule of arising'. We have preferred to keep as close as possible to these literal meanings, often by choosing periphrasis in the case of compounds: 'way that ____ arises', 'rule by which ____ arises', 'rule for ____ to arise. These terms are central to Maimon's thought, and we have preferred to bring out the semantic continuity of these terms in the text in English. The reader should bear in mind where Maimon uses strong compound noun formations.

10 *Erfindung/Entdeckung*

Strictly *'Erfindung'* is 'invention' and *'Entdeckung'* 'discovery'. However, Maimon often talks about *'Erfindungen in den Wissenschaften'* in a way that suggests he means 'discoveries'. We have opted for the English term most consistent with the context and put the German term in brackets if our translation is unorthodox.

11 *Evidenz*

This term means 'evidence', but in some contexts it seems to be used to

NOTE ON THE TRANSLATION

refer to the especially high degree of evidence characteristic of, for example, mathematical claims. In these cases we have translated it as 'self-evidence' or as 'evident nature' and given the German.

12 *Folge*

This word has been translated as 'succession' or 'sequence' in chronological contexts and as 'consequence' both in logical contexts (where it is contrasted with '*Grund*') and in causal contexts (where it is contrasted with '*Ursache*'). Maimon uses the term '*Konsequenz*' to describe the consequent of a conditional (hypothetical) statement, and this is always translated 'consequent'.

13 *Leiden/Handeln, handeln, Handlung*

We have used either 'passivity' and 'activity' to translate these terms or the adjectives 'passive' and 'active' (in particular in the related phrases '*durchs Leiden*' and '*durchs Handeln*' s. 168). Maimon uses this pair to describe the difference between the non-spontaneous and spontaneous aspects of our cognitive faculties. The distinction is Kantian, although Kant himself doesn't use exactly these terms.

Elsewhere (Chapter 1) Maimon characterizes the difference between understanding and imagination in terms of the '*tätig*' character of the former in comparison to the (partly) '*leidend*' character of the latter. These terms have also been translated as 'active' and 'passive'.

As a verb, '*handeln*' is translated as 'act' and the much more frequently occurring '*Handlung*' is translated either as 'act' or 'action' depending on context.

Occasionally Maimon contrasts '*Leiden*' with '*Wirken*', and in these cases we have resorted to periphrasis: 'what it does, and what it undergoes' (s. 102).

14 *Idee*

This has always been translated by 'idea'. Maimon always uses this word in the special sense that Kant gives to it in the *Critique of Pure Reason* when he speaks of 'ideas of reason', although Maimon extends this use to include a new kind of ideas he calls 'ideas of the understanding'. 'Idea' used in this Kantian sense is often given a capital letter in English in order to mark it out from the everyday sense of the term or from the sense in which is used by other philosophers, but we have thought this unnecessary given that Maimon never uses it in these other ways.

NOTE ON THE TRANSLATION

15 *Mensch*

'Mensch' means 'human being' or 'person', and these have been our usual translations, but occasionally it has been necessary to use the gendered English term 'man'. The reader should bear in mind that the German term carries no gendered connotation.

16 (*Immer*) *nähern*

Maimon uses this term to describe the idea of approaching a limit (an idea that he takes from mathematics but applies considerably more widely). *'Nähern'* means 'to approach', and also, in a mathematical context, 'to approximate'. We have chosen not to translate *'immer'* as always because this runs the risk of obscuring the continuous nature of the approach or approximation. Rather we have used various methods modelled on the use of *'immer'* in phrases like *'immer mehr'* to mean 'more and more' or 'ever more'.

17 *Objekt/Gegenstand*

Maimon does not appear to make any distinction between these terms, and we have accordingly translated them both as 'object'. Very occasionally we have interpolated the German terms to distinguish them, for example when the two different terms are used in the same sentence.

18 *Materielle, Stoff, Materie*

All these words mean approximately 'matter', and this is how we have translated them. Where the German is *'Materie'* we have not generally provided the German, but have always done so where it is *'Stoff'* or *'Materielle'*.

19 *Verschieden* and cognates

This term means 'difference'. Because the concept of difference is so central to Maimon's thought, we have endeavoured always to translate it by the same word, 'difference' (if another word is used we interpolate the German). Often, however, we have chosen a verbal formation 'to differ' instead of the noun 'difference'.

20 *Verhältnis/Beziehung, sich beziehen auf, Größenverhältnis*

Maimon does not appear to make any systematic distinction between *'Verhältnis'* and *'Beziehung'*, and we have accordingly translated them both as 'relation'. However, Maimon does sometimes use the special verb

NOTE ON THE TRANSLATION

phrase *'sich beziehen auf . .'*, which means ' refer to . .' rather than 'relate to . .'. It is not always obvious that Maimon means 'refer' as distinct from 'relate', but we have usually translated this as 'refer', and we note the German when we depart from this translation. The special mathematical term *'Größenverhältnis'* is the equivalent of the English 'proportion' or 'ratio' and has been translated accordingly. The German term has however been included in order to show that it is literally a 'relation of magnitudes'.

21 *Verknüpfung/Verbindung*
Maimon does not seem to make a distinction between these terms and both have been translated as 'connection'.

22 *(sich) vorstellen*
'Vorstellen' means 'to represent', but *'sich vorstellen'* means 'to imagine'; sometimes, however, Maimon appears to mean something more like 'represent to oneself' and in these cases we have interpolated the German.

23 *Wissen/Erkennen (Erkenntnis, kennen)*
We have observed the standard distinction between *'Wissen'* and *'Erkennen'* (and their many cognates, especially *'Erkenntnis'*) by translating *'Wissen'* as 'knowledge' and *'Erkennen'* as 'cognition' (and their corresponding cognates in English). Maimon does not appear to make a technical distinction here: rather his topic is *'Erkennen'*, and he uses *'Wissen'* only in informal contexts. We have used the full range of English cognates, especially 'recognize' for the verb form of *'erkennen'*, but have generally avoided 'cognize' and used periphrases like 'have cognition of' instead. Any departures from this standard are accompanied by the German in the text.

On a few occasions, Maimon also uses the term *'kennen'*, almost always in the context of claiming that we do not *'kennen'* the inner nature of things. We have translated *'kennen'* here as 'be acquainted with' or 'be familiar with'.

Note on Page Numbering, Notes, References and Typography

Marking of footnotes and endnotes in the text

There are three kinds of notes to the text: (1) the translators' footnotes, (2) the original footnotes, (3) the original endnotes.

Maimon's footnotes were marked by an asterisk in the original German text, but his endnotes (the extensive 'Notes & Clarifications') were not marked. The endnotes were not numbered and were linked to the text by being preceded by the number of the page to which they referred and a quotation of the first words of the part of the text to which they referred.

We have modified this system in order to mark all the notes in the text whilst still allowing the different kinds of note to be distinguished. Translators' footnotes and Maimon's footnotes are numbered in a single series through each chapter, with translators' footnotes distinguished by the customary prefix 'T.N.'; their numbers are inserted at the place in the text to which they refer. The endnotes have been numbered in one continuous series and are linked to the text by the appropriate number appearing in the page margin opposite the first line of the passage to which they refer.

Page references to the *Essay on Transcendental Philosophy*

The page numbers of the corresponding pages of the original edition are marked at the top of each page of the translation, and the page breaks are marked in the text with a vertical stroke. References to passages from the

NOTE ON PAGE NUMBERING, NOTES, REFERENCES AND TYPOGRAPHY

Essay in the 'Introduction to the Translation' and in translators' footnotes are to these page numbers of the original edition, not to the page numbers of this translation. To remind the reader of this fact, the letter 's' (abbreviating 'Seite' the German word for 'page') has been prefixed to such page number references. The page numbers in the index also refer to the original edition.

Page references to the *Critique of Pure Reason*

References to page xx in the first and second editions of Kant's *Critique of Pure Reason* are given in the now customary abbreviated form Axx and Bxx respectively.

Scope of the index

The scope of the index is restricted to the translations of the texts of the original edition (and employs its page numbers); it does not cover the 'Introduction to the Translation' or the appendices.

Typography

Maimon's original text was set mainly in *Fraktur* (i.e. Gothic type) with foreign language words in roman type; emphasis was indicated by *Sperrdruck* (spaced letter type). To preserve the distinction between emphasis and the indication of foreign language terms we have used boldface for emphasis and reserved italics for indicating foreign language terms.

Acknowledgements

The translators would like to express their thanks to Frank Beetham for providing translation of the Latin portions of the text and Adrian Haldane for his excellent work on an earlier draft of this translation.

Essay

on

Transcendental Philosophy

with an

Appendix

on

Symbolic Cognition

and

Notes

by

Salomon Maimon

From Lithuania in Poland

Dextrum Scylla latus, laevum implacata Charybdis Obsidet ...

Virgil, *Aeneid* Bk 3, v 420.[1]

Berlin
Christian Friedrich Vos and son
1790

---

[1] TN. 'On your right waits Scylla in ambush and on your left the insatiable Charybdis', as translated by David West (Penguin Books, 2003).

DEDICATION

To His Majesty the King of Poland, Grand Duke of Lithuania, etc., etc.[2]

Sire,

From time immemorial people have recognized reason's mastery over them, and have willingly placed themselves under its sceptre. They have however recognized it as merely a judicial and not as a legislative power. The will has always been the highest legislator; and reason is supposed to determine connections between things only in relation to the will. In recent times people have acquired the insight that free will can be nothing other than reason itself, and therefore that reason must not only determine the connection of means to end, but must also determine the end itself. The fundamental principles of morality, politics, and even of taste, must bear the stamp of reason if they are to be of any use at all. It is therefore an important task, before we apply the laws of reason to these objects, first to determine and firmly establish these laws themselves by means of an inquiry into the nature of reason and into the conditions of its use as well as its limits. This is not some particular speculation that has merely the satisfaction of a thirst for knowledge as its end, and that should therefore be postponed and undertaken only after other important tasks; it must rather precede all other tasks, because, before this has been done, nothing rational can be undertaken in human life. This is the investigation that I have taken up in this work, and that I now venture to place at the feet of **Your Royal Majesty's** throne.

If it is true that the inner worth of a man of high rank can be more reliably recognized from the way that he spends his free time than from his official occupations (which seem to further his sublime position, and for which he has a whole nation, or even half the world, as witness), then how highly must we value the service of a regent who seeks respite in the arms of the Muses and in the bosom of the sciences from the most honourable as well as the most difficult of occupations, that of making people happy; and who therefore remains great even in his recreation and free time! With that quiet consciousness of his worth which this continual striving after perfection must guarantee him, he moreover combines the lovable quality of being popular, which tempers the glory of his throne, and gives this modest seeker after truth the courage to place his investigations at His Majesty's feet. How ardently then must each heart fly to Him, how must His

---

[2] TN. In his autobiography Maimon expresses his regret that the copy he entrusted to the king's representative in Berlin, to his knowledge, never reached the king.

example summon all of His subjects to become like Him, at least to the extent that this is possible, and to direct all their powers to science, to which their sublime monarch is able to devote only a small part of his precious time; and especially since they may expect from Him not only protection and forbearance, but also guidance and instruction.

It is my pride to have been born in the land of a regent who possesses these sublime merits in such full measure, who protects and encourages the sciences because He recognizes their influence on the state and because He knows it ennobles human nature and lends our spirit both liberty and breadth. Fearful despots are suspicious of these qualities, but the good father of the people has nothing to fear from them, and therefore rather than begrudging them will grant them to His children as their inalienable birthright. It is my pride to have been born under **Your Royal Majesty**'s sceptre. And although my fate has lead me to the Prussian States, even at a distance, the happy efforts of **Your Majesty** on behalf of science have remained ever holy and unforgettable to me, and have moved me to dedicate, in deepest humility, these enquiries into some objects of transcendental philosophy to **Your Majesty**.

I would account myself fortunate if these first fruits of my modest talent were not found to be completely unworthy of being honoured with the high approval of **Your Royal Majesty**; and if I could thereby contribute something to giving the noble Poles an advantageous opinion of my nation (that is, of the Jews who live under their protection), and contribute something to convincing them that the Jews, if they have not been useful to the state that is so patient with them, have lacked neither in capacity nor good will, but only in a purposeful direction for their powers. I would be doubly fortunate if I should succeed at the same time in making my nation alert to their true advantages, and in encouraging their boldness and enthusiasm in the task of making them, through enlightenment and honesty, ever more worthy of the respect of the nation under which they live, and of the favours that they enjoy under the wise government of **Your Royal Majesty**.

With warmest wishes for **Your Royal Majesty's** long and happy life, I remain ever

Your Majesty's most humble servant,
Salomon Maimon.
Berlin, in December, 1789.

DEDICATION

Ad Kantium

*E tenebris tantis tam clarum extollere lumen
qui primus potuisti inlustrans commoda vitae,
te sequor, o G...ae gentis decus, inque tuis nunc
ficta pedum pono pressis vestigia signis,
non ita certandi cupidus quam propter amorem
quod te imitari aveo; quid enim contendat hirundo
cycnis, aut quidnam tremulis facere artubus haedi
consimile in cursu possint et fortis equi vis?
Tu, pater, es rerum inventor, tu patria nobis
suppeditas praecepta, tuisque ex, inclute, chartis,
floriferis ut apes in saltibus omnia libant,
omnia nos itidem depascimur aurea dicta,
aurea, perpetua semper dignissima vita.*[3]

Lucretius, *De Natura Rerum*, Bk 3, v. 113.

---

[3] TN. Below is William Ellery Leonard's translation. In this passage Lucretius is paying tribute to his master Epicurus, whose principal work, *On Nature*, was the basis of his own. Maimon directs the tribute instead to Kant and accordingly replaces 'Graecae' in the third verse with 'G...ae', allowing it to be read as 'Germaniae'.

> O thou who first uplifted in such dark
> So clear a torch aloft, who first shed light
> Upon the profitable ends of man,
> O thee I follow, glory of the Greeks,
> And set my footsteps squarely planted now
> Even in the impress and the marks of thine-
> Less like one eager to dispute the palm,
> More as one craving out of very love
> That I may copy thee! – for how should swallow
> Contend with swans or what compare could be
> In a race between young kids with tumbling legs
> And the strong might of the horse? Our father thou,
> And finder-out of truth, and thou to us
> Suppliest a father's precepts; and from out
> Those scriven leaves of thine, renowned soul
> (Like bees that sip of all in flowery wolds),
> We feed upon thy golden sayings all-
> Golden, and ever worthiest endless life.

Introduction

If it is true that every being strives as much as it can to persist in its **existence**,[1] and if it is true that the existence of a thinking being[2] consists in **thinking** (in accordance with the Cartesian identity claim [*identischer Satz*]: *cogito, ergo sum*): then it quite naturally follows from this that every thinking being must strive as much as it can to think. It is not difficult to prove that all human drives (in so far as they are human drives) can be resolved into the single drive to think; but I shall save this for another opportunity. Even those who despise thinking must admit this truth, if they would only pay careful attention to themselves. All human activities are, as such, simply more or less thinking.

However, since our thinking being is limited, this drive is restricted, at least subjectively, although not objectively. Thus, there is here a *maximum* that we cannot overstep (allowing for all external obstacles), although we can fall short of it through negligence; as a result, a thinking being strives not just to think in general [*überhaupt*], but rather to reach this *maximum* in thinking. So it cannot be denied that the **sciences**, in employing this faculty of thought [*Denkungsvermögen*], have a direct use, beyond their indirect use in human life.

However, there are only two sciences properly so called, in so far as

---

[1] TN. '... *daß jedes Wesen sich bestrebt, so viel an ihm ist, sein Daseyn zu verlängern*' which may be presumed to be Maimon's translation of Spinoza's famous Proposition 6 of Book 3 of *The Ethics*: '*Unaquæque res quantum in se est, in suo esse perseverare conatur*'.

[2] TN. Here and in the rest of the Introduction, 'being' and 'thinking being' translate '*Wesen*' and '*denkende Wesen*' respectively.

they are based on *principia a priori*,[3] namely, **mathematics** and **philosophy**. Science is to be met with in all the remaining objects of human cognition only in as much as they contain these two within them.[4] Mathematics determines its objects completely *a priori* through construction; as a result, the faculty of thought produces both the **form** and the **matter** of its thinking out of itself. But this is not how it is done with philosophy: in philosophy the understanding produces only the **form** of thinking | out of itself; but the **objects** it is **applied** to must be given to it from elsewhere.

So the question is: how is **philosophy** as a **pure** *a priori* cognition possible? The great **Kant** posed this question in his *Critique of Pure Reason*, and answered it as well, by showing that philosophy must be **transcendental** if it is to be of any use; that is, it must be able to relate *a priori* to objects in general, and is then called transcendental philosophy. This is therefore a science that relates to objects determined through *a priori* conditions, and not *a posteriori* through particular conditions of experience: this distinguishes transcendental philosophy as much from **logic** (which relates to an undetermined object in general) as from the **doctrine of nature**, which refers to objects determined through experience. I want to clarify this with examples. The proposition '*A* is *A*' or, a thing is one and the same as itself, belongs to logic, because here '*A*' means a thing in general that is indeed determinable, but is not in fact determined by any condition, whether *a priori* or *a posteriori*: | it is therefore valid of every thing, without distinction. However, the proposition: 'snow is white' belongs to the doctrine of nature because both the subject (snow) and the predicate (white) are objects of experience. On the other hand, this proposition: 'everything changing (accident) is necessarily connected with something that persists in time (substance)' does not belong to logic because neither the subject nor the predicate are undetermined objects, that is to say objects in general; rather the subject is determined as something that persists in time, and the predicate as something that changes. But the proposition does not belong to physics either because, although the objects are indeed

---

[3] TN. *A priori* principles.
[4] TN. Compare Kant's statement in *Metaphysical Foundations of Natural Science*: 'in every special doctrine of nature only so much science proper can be found as there is mathematics in it'. In I. Kant, *Philosophy of Material Nature*, trans. J. W. Ellington (Indianapolis, IN: Hackett, 1985), p. 6.

determined, they are so only through *a priori* determinations (of time, which is an *a priori* form). It therefore belongs to transcendental philosophy. The propositions of logic are **analytic** (their principle [*Prinzip*] is the principle [*Satz*] of contradiction); those of physics are **synthetic** *a posteriori* (the subject is connected with the predicate in a proposition because they are perceived as connected in time and space) and their principle is the association of ideas (as mere perceptions, before they are made into experiential propositions by means of a concept of the understanding). The propositions | of transcendental philosophy are indeed also synthetic, but their principle is not experience (perception), it is rather the reverse: they are the **principles** or the **necessary conditions of experience** by means of which what in perception merely **is, must be**.

We succeed in doing this in the following way: first of all, we presuppose as indubitable the fact that we possess a set of experiential propositions, that is to say, propositions that contain not merely a contingent but a necessary connection between the subjects and predicates given in perception. For example, 'the fire warms the body', 'the magnet attracts the iron' and so on. Out of these particular propositions however, we construct a **universal proposition**: that, if the one (*A*) is posited, then the other (*B*) must necessarily also be posited. Now, one might think that we have produced this universal proposition through **induction** since we presuppose that the proposition will be confirmed through a completed induction. But since our induction can never be complete, so a proposition produced in this manner can only be used as far as the induction | reaches. More detailed investigation however reveals that a universal transcendental proposition behaves quite differently: such a proposition is already in itself *a priori* universal, before particular experiences, and this is true because we could not have any experiences (subjective perceptions related to objects) without it, as is to be shown in the treatise itself; as a result, far from deriving such a proposition from experience, we rather derive experience from it, since it is a condition of experience.

Again, one could say: it is true that in the **particular** cases we observe of this proposition, it is not a mere perception, that is to say a subjective connection between subject and predicate, but an experience, that is an objective connection; but still it can only be a **particular proposition**, that is to say it can only be valid for already constituted [*gemacht*] experiences, and cannot be valid *a priori* for experiences yet to be constituted. So, for example, although the proposition 'a straight line is the shortest line between two points', is objective, it is nonetheless valid only for the straight line, and not universally valid for all objects that could be constructed; and this is because the proposition is not based on the conditions of construction in | general, but only on this particular construction. Could this proposition 'if something is given in experience, then something else must necessarily be given' also then only be valid for this particular experience and not for experience in general? The following serves as an answer to this question: the presupposition is impossible, because it means that the proposition would have to be expressed like this: '**a few** [*einige*] objects of experience are so constituted that if the one is posited, the other must necessarily also be posited'. But then the conditions through which these few objects are determined and through which they are distinguished from all the other objects to which the proposition does not refer, would also have to be given in perception. And the particular experiences (the fire warms the body, etc.) would have to arise by means of the comparison of these experiences with the determinations expressed in the proposition, and through the judgement that they are one and the same. (For if these few objects were left undetermined in the proposition itself, then we would have no criterion by which we could recognize that these particular cases belonged to the few the proposition refers to; and so we could not make any use at all of the proposition.) But the understanding (as the faculty of rules) is not | at the same time the faculty of intuitions; as a result, the proposition or rule cannot relate to particular perceptual determinations but [must] relate to perceptions in general: so we must look for something *a priori* universal in perception (because if this universality were itself an *a posteriori* determination, then the difficulty could not be overcome), and in fact we find it in **time**, which is a universal form or condition of all perception, and which as a result must accompany all perceptions. So the proposition in question is now expressed in this way: 'the preceding [*das Vorgehende*] determines the succeeding [*das Folgende*] in time'. It therefore refers to something *a priori* universal, namely time. From this we see that the propositions of transcendental philosophy refer first to determined objects (not, like the propositions of logic, to an object in general), and so to intuitions; and second, they refer to objects determined *a priori* (unlike the propositions of physics). The propositions of transcendental philosophy must either be universal, or not be propositions at all.

The great Kant supplies a **complete idea** of transcendental philosophy (although not the whole science itself) in his immortal work *The Critique of Pure Reason*. | My aim in this enquiry is to bring out **the most important truths** of this science. And I am following in the footsteps of the aforementioned sharp-witted philosopher; but (as the unbiased reader will remark) I am not copying him. I try, as much as it is in my power, to explain him, although from time to time I also make some comments [*Anmerkungen*] on him. In particular, I present the following remarks to the thoughtful reader for examination. First, the distinction between mere *a priori* cognition and pure *a priori* cognition, and the difficulty that still remains with respect to the latter. Second, my derivation of the origin of synthetic propositions from the incompleteness of our cognition. Third, doubts with respect to the question *quid facti?*, to which **Hume's** objection appears to be irrefutable. Fourth, the clue I give to the answer to the question *quid juris?* and the explanation of the possibility of a metaphysics in general, through the reduction of intuitions to their elements, elements that I call ideas of the understanding [*Verstandsideen*]. The reader will find the remaining remarks in their appropriate places. To what extent I am a Kantian, an anti-Kantian, both at the same time, or neither | of the two, I leave to the judgement of the thoughtful reader. I have endeavoured, as much as I could, to avoid the difficulties of these opposed systems (something that I also wanted to show in my motto).[5] How far I have succeeded in this, others may decide.

As far as my style and literary performance are concerned, I frankly admit that they are very lacking (since I am not a German by birth nor have I practice in written essays). I would not even have wanted to publish this work had not some learned men, to whom I had given it to read through, assured me that I am still comprehensible despite the faults in my expression; in any case, I do not write for readers who look more to the style than to the matter itself. Moreover, this work is only supposed to be an attempt [*Versuch*][6] that I intend in the future to rework completely. Should a reviewer still have something to object to (besides the style and organization) against the substance itself, I will always be ready either to

---

[5] TN. Maimon is referring to the quotation from Virgil on the title page.

[6] TN. The work is entitled *Versuch über die Transzendental Philosophie*, which we have translated as '*Essay on Transcendental Philosophy*' since '*Versuch*' is generally used in German book titles where English has 'Essay' (for example Locke's *Essay* is *Versuch* in German). However the German word retains the sense of 'attempt', which the English word indeed also possesses but has almost lost.

defend myself, or to admit my error. My primary motivation is simply progress in the knowledge [*Erkenntnis*] of truth; | and anyone who is familiar with my situation will themselves see that I cannot have pretensions to anything else on earth. To censure my style would therefore not only be unjust, because I have myself admitted my weaknesses in this respect, but also completely futile, because my defences against such accusations would presumably be couched in just the same style, which would then have to produce a *progressum in infinitum*.[7]

---

[7] TN. Progress to infinity.

Chapter 1
Matter, Form of Cognition, Form of Sensibility, Form of Understanding, Time and Space

A limited cognitive faculty requires two parts: 1. **matter**, that is to say something given, or **what** [*das was*] is to be cognized in the object of cognition; 2. **form**, or that **for which** [*das wofür*] the object is to be cognized. Matter is the particular in the object, through which it is cognized and distinguished from all other objects. Form, on the other hand, (in so far as it is grounded in the cognitive faculty in relation to this kind [*Art*] of object) is the universal that can belong to a class of objects. The **form of sensibility** is therefore the mode [*Art*] of the cognitive faculty in relation to sensible objects; the form **of the understanding** is its mode of operation [*Wirkungsart*] in relation to | objects in general, or (what amounts to the same thing) in relation to objects of the understanding.

For instance, the colour red is given to the cognitive faculty (we say '**given**' because the cognitive faculty cannot produce the colour out of itself in a way that it itself prescribes, but behaves merely passively in relation to the colour). This colour is therefore the matter of the perceived object. But the way we perceive the red colour as well as other sensible objects is this: we order the manifold [that is] in them in **time and space**. These are the forms. For these ways of ordering the manifold do not have their ground in the red colour, as in a particular object, but in our cognitive faculty in relation to all sensible objects without distinction. And this is why we are convinced *a priori* not only that all sensible objects that we have already perceived in these forms must have these forms, but also that all objects that are yet to be perceived must have them as well.

CHAPTER 1

As a result, we can see that these forms **do not first arise in us** with the perception of objects (if they did then they would have their ground in particular objects, and hence could not be universal forms), but rather were already in us beforehand as universal conditions of this perception. Perception itself is therefore a cognition of these universal forms in particular objects; and it is the same with the forms of the understanding, as will be shown below.

Here we want to deal with the forms of sensibility in themselves; in the next chapter, however, we will consider the forms of sensibility in connection with the forms of the understanding, in relation to the matter of sensibility itself that is their ground.[1] So, first let us deal with the forms of sensibility, or time and space.

Space and Time

Space and time are not concepts abstracted from experiences because they are not constituent parts [*Bestandteile*] of experiential concepts: that is, they are not the manifold, but rather the unities through which the manifold of experiential concepts is gathered together [*zusammen genommen*]. For example, gold is an experiential concept [comprised] of extension, impenetrability, yellow colour, etc., which make up the manifold within gold; but this manifold is only gathered together into a concept because it is together in time and space; consequently time and space are not the constituent parts themselves, but rather merely their ligaments [*Bande*]. Considered in themselves, independently of their connection with each other, impenetrability, yellow colour etc. are concepts abstracted from experience; but time and space, through which this connection is possible, are not. But neither are they themselves experiential concepts ([that is,] unity in the manifold of experience) because in themselves they do not contain any manifold consisting of heterogeneous [*ungleichartigen*] parts. The parts of time and space are not possible **prior** to them, but only **in** them; they can be viewed as a plurality [*Vielheit*] only quantitatively not qualitatively.

So what are space and time? **Kant** asserts that they are the forms of

---

[1] TN. '*die ihnen zum Grunde liegende Materie der Sinnlichkeit selbst*'. Grammatically '*ihnen*', 'their', could refer either to the forms of sensibility or to the forms of the understanding, but that it should be taken to refer to the former will become clear when Maimon explains the grounding of space and time on material differentials.

our sensibility, and here I am of completely the same opinion as him. I add only that these particular forms of our sensibility have their ground in the universal forms of our thought in general, because the condition of our thought (consciousness) in general is unity in the manifold. So if *A* and *B* are completely identical, there is in this case no manifold. There is therefore no comparison, and consequently no consciousness (and also no consciousness of identity). But if they are completely different, then there is no unity and, once again, no comparison, and consequently also no consciousness, not even consciousness of this difference, since, considered objectively, difference is just a lack of identity (even though, considered subjectively, it is a unity, or relation of objects to one another). As a result, it cannot have objective validity. So space and time are these special forms by means of which unity in the manifold of sensible objects is possible, and hence by means of which these objects themselves are possible as objects of our consciousness.

I also note that each of these forms on its own is insufficient, and that both of them are necessary for this purpose, but not in the sense that positing one necessitates positing the other; but rather the reverse, namely, that positing one necessitates cancelling out the other in the very same objects. So positing one necessitates positing the other in general, because otherwise it would not be possible to represent (as a mere negation) the cancelling out of the other. I will explain this point more precisely. Space is the being-apart [*das Auseinandersein*][2] of objects (being in one and the same place is not a determination of space, but rather its cancellation). Time is the preceding [*Vorhergehen*] and succeeding [*Folgen*] of objects with respect to one another (simultaneity is not a determination of time, but its cancellation). So if we are to imagine things in space, that is, outside one other [*außer einander*], we must imagine them simultaneously, that is, in one and the same point in time (because the relation of separateness is an indivisible unity). If we want to imagine things in a temporal succession, one after the other, then we must

---

[2] TN. Maimon uses two locutions with slightly different meanings to characterize space: (1) '*das Auseinandersein*' which means 'being separate' or 'being apart' (2) '*außereinander*' meaning 'outside one another'. Maimon seems to regard these as more or less synonymous, so the reader should not take 'separateness' to mean 'being kept apart by something else' or 'having a space between them', but just 'being in different places'. This issue should also be considered in relation to the *principle of continuity* introduced in Chapter 8.

imagine them in one and the same place (because otherwise we would have to imagine them at one and the same point in time). Now, since movement is change of place in a temporal succession, you might certainly think that movement must unite space and time in the same objects. On closer inspection, however, we find that it does not actually do so, i.e., in this case too space and time are not united in the same objects. Take | two things (a and b) that are outside one another, and further, a third thing (c) that is moving from a to b. Here a and b are represented as simultaneous (without temporal succession) in space (outside one another). But c, i.e. its different relations ca and cb, are represented only in a temporal succession and not in space; this is because relations (as concepts) can be thought only in a temporal succession, but not as outside one another.

Space and time are as much concepts as intuitions, and the latter presuppose the former. The sensible representation of the difference between determined things is the being-apart of those things; the representation of the difference between things in general is being-apart in general, or space. As unity in the manifold, this space is therefore a concept. The representation of the relation of a sensible object to different sensible objects at the same time is space as intuition. If there were only a uniform intuition, then we would not have any concept of space, and hence no intuition of space either, since the latter presupposes the former. On the other hand, if there were nothing but different types of intuition, then we would have merely a concept, but not an intuition, of space. And it is the same for time. | As intuition, space (and it is the same for time) is therefore an *ens imaginarium*: it arises because the imagination [*Einbildungskraft*] imagines as absolute what exists only in relation to something else: absolute place, absolute movement, and the like are of this kind. Indeed the imagination even goes as far as determining these, its fictions [*Erdichtungen*], in manifold ways; the objects of mathematics arise in this way (the difference between the absolute and relative way of looking at things [*Betrachtungsart*] is merely subjective, and changes nothing in the object itself). The validity of the principles [*Grundsätze*] of these fictions is based only on the possibility of their production. For example, 'a triangle arises from three lines, of which two together are longer than the third', or 'a figure cannot arise from two lines', and the like. In this case even the imagination (as the faculty of fictions, for determining objects *a priori*) serves the understanding. As soon as the understanding prescribes the rule for drawing a line between two points (that is, that it should be the

14

shortest), the imagination draws a straight line to satisfy this demand. This faculty of fictions [*Erdichtungsvermögen*] is, as it were, something intermediate between the imagination properly so-called and the understanding, since the latter | is completely active [*tätig*]. The understanding does not merely take objects up (from whatever ground they may be given), but also orders them and connects them with one another; and in this its procedure is also not merely arbitrary, rather it looks[3] first to an objective ground, and then also to increasing its activity [*Tätigkeit*]. That is to say, the understanding counts as an object only a synthesis that has an objective ground (of the determinable and of the determination) and that must thus have consequences, and no others.[4] On the other hand, the synthesis of the imagination is only active in so far as it does not merely take objects all at once but orders them under one another and connects them; but it is also passive [*leidend*] here in that it brings this about in a determined way, that is, according to the law of association. On the other hand, the synthesis of the faculty of fictions is completely spontaneous [*freiwillig*], and can therefore at least conform to a rule [*regelmäßig*], even if it cannot comprehend one [*regelverständig*].

I want to explain this point more precisely.

A synthesis in general is unity in the manifold. But the unity and the manifold can be either necessary (given to the understanding, but not produced by it), or arbitrarily [*willkürlich*] | produced by the understanding itself, but not according to an objective law, or again spontaneous [*freiwillig*], that is to say produced by the understanding itself according to an objective ground. The given (*reale* in sensation) is a unity of the first type. Time and space, as intuitions, and in so far as they are quanta, belong to the second type. A determined (limited) space can be arbitrarily taken as a unit[5]

---

[3] TN. Following Ehrensperger in reading '*sieht*' in place of '*steht*'.

[4] TN. How this sentence explicates the preceding sentence becomes clearer in Chapter 4 where Maimon presents a new criterion for the Kantian distinction between analytic and synthetic *a priori* propositions. The reference to the understanding 'increasing its activity' concerns what Kant calls the 'amplificatory' character of synthetic judgements (analytic judgements being merely 'clarificatory'); Maimon understands this in terms of the synthesis generating new consequences.

[5] TN. '*Einheit*' means both 'unity' and 'unit' (in the arithmetical sense) and the choice of translation has been determined by the context. The reader should bear this in mind with all subsequent occurrences of 'unit' and 'unity', which always translate '*Einheit*'; the double meaning is particularly important with respect to the differentials which, although they are the ultimate real units, are nevertheless not simple but are rather unities of difference (syntheses of difference).

15

[*Einheit*] so that an arbitrary plurality [*Vielheit*] emerges out of it through the successive synthesis of such units with each other (this plurality is arbitrary as much in relation to the unit that is adopted, as with respect to the ever possible continuation of this synthesis). For example, a triangle is a unity produced by the understanding (according to the law of the determinable and the determination). A right-, obtuse-, or acute-angled, triangle[6] is a plurality produced[7] by the understanding (according to the law of determination). Time and space as concepts (of being-apart and of succession) contain, as differentials of the plurality, a necessary unity in the manifold.[8] This is because the synthesis of the relation of preceding and succeeding one another, can never be thought separated [into parts] by the understanding, for otherwise the essence of time would be completely destroyed. By contrast, if I assume a determinate time (duration) as a unit, and produce a greater time through successive synthesis of the | same units with one another, then this synthesis is merely arbitrary. And it is the same for space. This makes clear the difference between treating time and space as concepts and treating them as intuitions. In the first case, they exclude one another, as I have already remarked; in the second case it is just the reverse, that is to say, they presuppose one another. They do so because they are extensive magnitudes (i.e. magnitudes of such a kind that the representation of the whole is only possible through the representation of the parts), so that to be able to imagine a determinate space, it is necessary to assume another determinate space as a unit in order to produce the required space through successive synthesis of the unit. But this successive synthesis presupposes the representation of time. On the other hand, the thought of a determinate time can only take place when a determined space arises, i.e. through the movement of the hand on a clock or the like. The object of pure arithmetic is number, whose form is pure time as a concept; on the other hand, the object of pure geometry is pure space, not as concept, but as intuition. In the differential calculus, space is

---

[6] TN. This example occurs again in Chapter 7 where Maimon explains that while a triangle in general is a unity that is only potentially right-angled or obtuse, because these properties are mutually exclusive they must produce a plurality when actual; in other words, through being determined, the general triangle (unity) becomes several triangles (plurality).

[7] TN. Ehrensperger has '*gedachte*' ('thought') where the original has '*hervorgebrachte*' ('produced').

[8] TN. See Chapter 2 for the theory of differentials.

considered as a concept abstracted from all | quantity, but nevertheless considered [as] determined through different kinds of quality in its intuition.[9]

I believe I can maintain that representations of space and time have just the same degree of reality as the pure concepts of the understanding or **categories**; and that therefore what can rightly be maintained of one can also be maintained of the other. Take for example the category of **cause**. Here I find first of all the form of the hypothetical judgement: if something, a, is posited, then something else, b, must necessarily be posited. a and b are thereby determined only through this relation to one another, but we do not yet know what a and b may be in themselves. On the other hand, if I determine a through something other than its connection to b, then b is determined as well. Applied to determined objects, this logical form is called a category. Time is a form, that is to say, a way of relating objects to one other. In it, two points must be assumed that are distinct from each other (the preceding and the succeeding). These points must however be determined by the objects that occupy them. Pure time (the preceding and the succeeding without determining either of these positions) can | therefore be compared to a thought form, i.e. a logical form [*mit gedachter logischer Form verglichen*] (both are relations of objects to each other). Points in time that are determined by objects can be compared to the categories themselves (cause and effect). And so, just as categories can are meaningless, and hence useless, without time-determination;[10] so time-determinations are meaningless without the categories of substance and accident, and these categories are meaningless without determined objects. And it is the same for space.

Apart from this conception [*Ausser diesem Begriffe*], I do not know why time and space should be intuitions. An intuition is treated as a unity only because its distinct parts in time and space are identical in relation to a concept. So, to determine time and space themselves as intuitions, another time and another space would have to be assumed. If I posit two points, a and b, that are separate, then neither of these points is yet a space, only their relation to one another is. So in this case there is no unity of the manifold of space, but rather an absolute unity of space, that

---

[9] TN. '*In der Differentialrechnung wird der Raum als Begriff abstrahiert von aller Quantität, aber doch durch verschiedne Arten der Qualität, seiner Anschauung bestimmt betrachtet.*'

[10] TN. '*Zeitbestimmung*' is the word Kant introduces in the 'Schematism'(A139/B178) to describe the nature of a schema.

is to say, it is not yet an intuition. Perhaps someone will say that, although it cannot be an intuition, it can be the element of an | intuition if one assumes another point, c, besides b, so that the intuition of space will arise from the being-apart of a and b, and then of b and c? But this is to forget that when we describe relations and connections as separate, this only amounts to saying that they are different from one another (because a concept cannot be something outside another concept in time and space). But in themselves and abstracted from objects, these two relations are not different from one another. Consequently no intuition of space can arise from adding them together [*Zusammenrechnung*]. And it is the same for time. Time is thought through the preceding and the succeeding (simultaneity is not a time-determination but only the cancelling out of time). Preceding and succeeding time points are nothing with respect to time; only their relation to one another represents time. Different relations of this kind cannot be thought at all. Consequently, time is not an intuition either (gathering together in one representation what is given as identical according to concept, but different according to time). This would require, in addition to the perception [*Perception*][11] of each given in itself in time, | a reproduction of the preceding given with the perception [*bei Wahrnehmung*] of the present[ly] given (by virtue of their identity according to the law of association). So, in order to be able to gather together different temporal unities into one intuition, the preceding unity would have to be reproduced with the present temporal unity, which is impossible. Space and time can therefore only be called empirical intuitions (as predicates of intuitions) and not pure intuitions.

---

[11] TN. This is the only occasion where Maimon uses the Latinate term '*Perception*'; wherever else 'perception' occurs in this translation, the German is '*Wahrnehmung*'. Kant also does not in general use this term in the *Critique*, it only occurs when he is defining his concept of 'idea' in the 'Dialectic', where he defines 'perception' as 'representation with consciousness' (A320/B376).

Chapter 2
Sensibility, Imagination, Understanding, Pure *A Priori* Concepts of the Understanding or Categories, Schemata, Answer to the Question *Quid Juris?*, Answer to the Question *Quid Facti?*, Doubts about the Latter

Considered in itself as a quality, every sensible representation must be abstracted from all quantity whether extensive or intensive.[1] For example, the representation of the colour red must be | thought without any finite extension, although not as a mathematical but rather as a physical point, or as the differential of an extension. It must further be thought without any finite degree of quality, but still as the differential of

---

[1] I am not ignorant of what can be said against the introduction of mathematical concepts of infinity into philosophy. In particular, since these concepts are still subject to many difficulties in mathematics itself, it might appear as if I wanted to explain something obscure through something yet more obscure. However, I venture to claim that these concepts in fact belong to philosophy and were taken from there over into mathematics; as well as that the great **Leibniz** came upon the discovery of the differential calculus through his system of the Monadology. A magnitude (*quantum*) is not treated as a large quantity [*Auch ist etwas Großes (quantum), doch nicht als eine größe Quantität betrachtet*], but rather as a quality abstracted from quantity. However, in mathematics as much as in philosophy they are mere ideas that do not represent objects but only the way objects arise, i.e. they are mere limit concepts [*Gränzbegriffe*], which we can approach nearer and nearer to, but never reach. They arise through a continuous regress or through the diminution to infinity of the consciousness of an intuition. TN. Ehrensberger changes the passage cited in German above to: '*Auch ist etwas Großes (Quantum) doch nicht als eine Größe (Quantität) betrachtet*'; he notes that he has made an alteration but does not justify it. Maimon had already corrected the wording in the Errata to the original text.

19

CHAPTER 2

a finite degree. This finite extension or finite degree is necessary for consciousness of the representation, | and is different for different representations according to the difference of their differentials; consequently sensible representations in themselves, considered as mere differentials, do not yet result in consciousness.[2] Consciousness arises through an activity of the faculty of thought. But in the reception of individual sensible representations this faculty is merely passive. If I say: I am conscious of something, I do not understand by this something that is outside consciousness, which is self-contradictory; | but merely the determinate mode of consciousness, i.e. of the act [*Handlung*] itself. The word '**representation**', used of the primitive consciousness, here leads us astray; for in fact this is not representation, i.e. a mere making present of what is not [now] present, but rather presentation, i.e. the representation of what was previously not as [now] existing. Consciousness first arises when the imagination takes together **several** homogeneous[3] sensible representations, orders them according to its[4] forms (succession in time and space), and forms an individual intuition out of them. Homogeneity is necessary because otherwise there could be no connection within a single consciousness.[5] They are however (although not with respect to our consciousness) each in themselves several [*mehreres*] representations; for although we **perceive** no temporal succession in them, we must nevertheless **think** it in them because time in itself is infinitely divisible.

Just as, for example, with an accelerated movement, the preceding

---

[2] It follows that as their differentials, they are neither absolute, nor merely arbitrary, but determinate units such that when they are added to themselves successively, an arbitrary finite magnitude [*Größe*] then arises. But we must assume that these units are different in different objects: for otherwise all things would be one and the same thing, and their difference would consist only in their magnitude, which no one would accept. The possibility of different units (which are not arbitrarily assumed) is shown by mathematics, in which both incommensurable magnitudes and likewise differentials, necessarily presuppose different units. TN. As remarked in a translators' note to the previous chapter, 'unit' and 'unity' are the same word, '*Einheit*', in German.

[3] TN. 'Homogeneous' translates [*einartige*], literally 'of one kind'.

[4] TN. '*ihren Formen*' – this is ambiguous. We have translated '*ihren*' by 'its' rather than 'their' on the assumption that time and space are being described as forms of the imagination rather than forms of the sensible representations.

[5] TN. By 'in a single consciousness [*in einem einzigen Bewußtsein*]' Maimon evidently means 'in a single conscious representation' (made up of several representations each alone too small to cross the threshold of consciousness), not in one person's consciousness as opposed to in several different persons' consciousnesses.

velocity does not disappear, but ever joins itself onto the following ones, so that an ever increasing velocity arises, so equally the first sensible representation does not disappear, but ever joins itself onto the following ones, until the degree necessary for consciousness is reached. This does not take place by means of the comparison of these sensible representations (because the imagination does not compare) nor by insight into their identity (as occurs later by means of the understanding when it has already achieved consciousness of different objects), but takes place merely in accordance with the universal Newtonian law of nature, namely that no action [*Wirkung*] can be eliminated [*vernichtet*] of itself without an action being opposed to it (that is, we are not conscious of any comparison in us, although it must proceed in us obscurely because comparison is a condition of unity in the manifold, or of a synthesis in general, by means of which an intuition first becomes possible).

Finally the understanding joins in: its job is to bring the different sensible objects that have already been given (intuitions) into relation with one another by means of pure concepts *a priori*, or to make them into real objects of the understanding by means of pure concepts of the understanding, as will be shown below. Aristotle, their discoverer, called these pure concepts of the understanding **categories**. Sensibility thus provides the differentials to a determined consciousness; out of them, the imagination produces a finite (determined) object of intuition; out of the relations of these different differentials, which are its objects, the understanding produces the relation of the sensible objects arising from them.

These differentials of objects are the so-called *noumena;* but the objects themselves arising from them are the *phenomena*. With respect to intuition = 0, the differential of any such object in itself is[6] $dx = 0$, $dy = 0$ etc.; however, their relations are not $= 0$, but can rather be given determinately [*bestimmt angegeben werden können*] in the intuitions arising from them.

These *noumena* are ideas of reason[7] serving as principles to explain

---

[6] TN. '*Das Differential eines jeden Objekts an sich ist in Ansehung der Anschauung = 0*'. The concision of '= 0' makes this a little difficult to read, but if read as 'equal to zero' the meaning becomes clear: for intuition the differential is equal to nothing (we cannot imagine or be conscious of differentials).

[7] TN. In Chapter 3 Maimon defines these *noumena* as ideas of the understanding [*Verstandsideen*] and as such differentiates them from Kant's ideas of Reason [*Vernunftideen*]. It seems that at times, as here, he uses 'ideas of reason' in a loose sense to cover both these kinds of idea (which have in common that they cannot be objects of experience), and at other times opposes them.

how objects arise according to certain rules of the understanding. For example, if I say that **red** is different from **green**, then the pure concept of the understanding of the difference is not treated as a relation between the sensible qualities (for then the Kantian question *quid juris?* remains unanswered), but rather either (according to the Kantian theory) as the relation of their spaces as *a priori* forms, or (according to my theory) as the relation of their differentials, which are *a priori* ideas of reason. The understanding I can only think objects as flowing [*fliessend*][8] (with the exception of the forms of judgement, which are not objects). The reason for this is that the business of the understanding is nothing but **thinking**, i.e. producing unity in the manifold, which means that it can only think an object by specifying [*angiebt*] the way it arises or the rule by which it arises [*die Regel oder die Art seiner Entstehung*]: this is the only way that the manifold of an object be brought under the unity of the rule, and consequently the understanding cannot think an object as having already arisen [*entstanden*] but only as arising [*entstehend*], i.e. as flowing [*fliessend*]. The particular rule by which an object arises, or its type of differential, makes it into a particular object; and the relations of different objects arise from the relations of the rules by which they arise or of their differentials. I will explain myself more precisely on this point. An object requires two parts [*Stücke*]. First, an intuition given either *a priori* or *a posteriori*; second, a rule thought by the understanding, by means of which the relation of the manifold in the intuition is determined. This rule is thought by the understanding not as flowing but all at once.[9] On

---

[8] TN. In the *Critique of Pure Reason* Kant introduces this term in the 'Anticipations of Perception' but restricts its use to characterizing intensive magnitude: 'magnitudes of this sort can also be called flowing, since the synthesis (of the productive imagination) in their generation is a progress in time, the continuity of which is customarily designated by the expression 'flowing' ('elapsing'). (A170/B211). Kant may be using '*fliessend*' to translate Newton's term 'fluent'; in the *Tractatus Quadratura Curvarum* of 1704 Newton introduced the concepts of 'fluent' and 'fluxion' in expounding his infinitesimal calculus and part of the introduction to this work has been included as an Appendix. He states there that he will be dealing 'with mathematical magnitudes not as made up of small parts but as generated by a particular movement' and goes on to say that 'I have looked for a way of determining magnitudes from the speed of movements or from the increments with which they are generated; calling these speeds of growth fluxions, and the quantities generated, fluents'. Mapping this terminology onto Maimon would make the differentials fluxions and the objects generated from them (as thought by the understanding), fluents.

[9] TN. '*Diese Regel wird vom Verstande nicht fliessend, sondern auf einmal gedacht*'. This could also be translated as: 'This rule is thought by the understanding not in a flow but all at once'.

the other hand, the intuition itself (if it is *a posteriori*), or the particular determination of the rule | in the intuition (if it is *a priori*), is such that the object can only be thought of as flowing. For example, the understanding thinks a determined (although not individual) triangle by means of a relation of magnitudes [*Grössen-Verhältnis*, i.e. proportion or ratio] between two of its sides (their position being given and thus unalterable), through which the position and magnitude of the third side is also determined. The understanding thinks this rule all at once; but because the rule contains merely the universal relation of the sides (according to any arbitrarily adopted unit), the magnitude of the sides (according to a determinate unit) still remains undetermined. But in the construction of this triangle the magnitude of the sides can only be presented as determined; so, in this case, there is a determination that was not contained in the rule and that is necessarily attached to intuition; this determination can be different in different constructions even when the rule or relation is kept the same. Consequently, in view of all the possible constructions, this triangle must never be thought by the understanding as having arisen, but rather as arising, i.e. flowing. On the other hand, the faculty of intuition | (that certainly **conforms to rules** but does not **comprehend rules** [*das zwar* **regelmässig** aber nicht **regelverständig** ist]) can only represent the manifold itself, and not any rule or unity in the manifold; so it must think its objects as already having arisen not as [being in the process of] arising. Indeed even if the relation is not a determinate numerical relation, but a universal relation or function, the relation [*Verhältnis*] of the objects and the consequences to be drawn from it is never exactly correct except in relation [*Beziehung*] to their differentials. For example, to claim of every curved line that the [ratio of the] *subtangent*: $y = dx:dy$ and consequently *subtangent* $= \dfrac{y\,dx}{dy}$ is not

exactly correct in any construction, because it is in fact another line and not the subtangent that must be expressed through this relation, and the subtangent cannot be expressed unless $\Delta x : \Delta y$ is made into $dx:dy$, i.e. unless this relation [*Verhältnis*] that can only be thought in intuition is related [*beziehet*] to its elements.[10] For the understanding to think a line, it must draw it in thought, but to present a line in intuition, it must be

---

[10] TN. See the Appendix: Newton's *Introduction to the Quadrature of Curves*, for a fuller account and a diagram that illustrates Maimon's argument.

CHAPTER 2   35 | 37

imagined as already drawn. For the intuition of a line, only consciousness of the apprehension[11] | (of the taking together of mutually external parts) is required, whereas in order to comprehend [*begreifen*] a line, a real definition [*Sacherklärung*] is required, i.e. the explanation of the way it arises [*die Erklärung der Entstehungsart*]:[12] in intuition the line precedes the movement of a point within it; on the other hand, in the concept it is exactly the reverse, i.e. for the concept of a line, or for the explanation of the way it arises, the movement of a point precedes the concept of the line.

So sensibility has no connection at all; the imagination has connection through the determination of coexistence and succession in time and space, although without determining objects in relation to time and space, i.e. the form of the imagination is such as to relate things in general to one another, so that one is represented as preceding and the other as succeeding in time and space, although without determining which is the preceding and which the succeeding; so if we find in experience (perception) that things are determined with respect to the preceding and the succeeding, this is merely contingent. According to my definition, pure concepts (concepts that do not contain any, even *a priori*, intuition) | can only be relational concepts, for a concept is nothing but the unity of the manifold; but the manifold can only be thought as a unity if its constituent parts have to be thought at the same time, either reciprocally or at least one-sidedly.[13] The first case [reciprocal dependence of parts]

---

[11] TN. In the first edition of the *Critique*, the synthesis of apprehension [*Apprehension*] is the first of the three syntheses that progressively transform the manifold of intuition into the unity of experience; in this synthesis the *manifold* of intuition is merely taken up into *one* representation, further syntheses are required to bring it under a concept (see A99).

[12] TN. '*Sacherklärung*' or 'real definition' is here being used as a technical term (elsewhere Maimon calls it '*definitio realis*') in opposition to mere '*Namenerklärung*', '*definitio nominalis*', or 'nominal definition'. '*Erklärung*' means both 'definition' and 'explanation', and the choice of translation has been determined by the context. An alternative translation of '*Erklärung der Entstehungsart*' would take '*der Entstehungsart*' to be merely qualifying '*Erklärung*' ('definition') giving something like: 'definition in terms of the way it arises'.

[13] TN. '*Entweder wechselseitig oder zum wenigsten einigseitig zugleich gedacht werden müssen*'. This distinction of two kinds of synthesis is discussed further in Chapters 4 and 8. The meaning is that the components of a synthesis must be either mutually dependent (e.g. cause and effect – neither can be without the other) or one must depend on the other but not the reverse (e.g. accident and substance). Hence cause cannot be thought without effect, nor accident without substance, or in Maimon's words they 'have to be thought at the same time'; it is the necessity involved in this dependency which distinguishes synthesis from mere contingent association.

gives rise to a relational concept, i.e. a concept that is thought by the understanding not only with respect to its form but also its matter; or where matter and form are one and the same, and consequently are produced through a single *actus* of the understanding; for example, the concept of cause and its relation to the effect by means of which it is determined are one and the same, hence the proposition 'a cause must have an effect', is not merely identical [*identisch*], i.e. already **contained** in the definition, but is the **definition itself**.[14] A cause is something of this type: when it is posited something else must be posited. On the other hand, an absolute concept is thought only one-sidedly in a unity because it is a relation that is thought in the intuition; so the intuition can also be thought without this relation, but not the reverse. See Chapter 4.[15]

| On the other hand the understanding has a connection through *a priori* forms – inherence, dependence, etc. But because these are not intuitions, and consequently cannot be perceived (indeed even the possibility of the latter is inconceivable) they acquire their meaning only through a universal rule in the form of intuitions (time), to which they are related. Thus if I say, for example that *a* is cause and *b* effect, this means that I relate objects to one another through a determined form of judgement (dependence); but I still note that they are not objects in general, but determined objects *a* and *b*; and their reciprocal relations to one another in the shared concept of dependence (i.e. that *a* is the cause and *b* the effect) are determined by means of a universal rule in the form of intuitions, namely that *a* must necessarily precede and *b* must necessarily follow. This is the case with any arbitrarily assumed concept where the determination of its *essentia nominalis* leaves its *essentia realis*[16] still doubtful until it has been presented in intuition. For example, the understanding thinks the arbitrarily assumed concept of a circle according to the rule that it | is a figure delimited by a line of such a kind that all the

---

[14] TN. Maimon's point seems to be that the notion of having an effect is not merely contained in the notion of cause (so that the proposition is identical in the sense of merely stating explicitly what is already included in the notion of cause), but that cause and effect are reciprocally defining, and that the proposition expresses this reciprocal definition.

[15] TN. The original refers to Chapter 3 but the topic is not discussed there. The meaning of the previous sentence is not entirely clear even in the light of what is said in Chapter 4; but it may be understood as saying that an object of intuition as substance can be considered both in relation to its accidents and independently of them, but that this relation (of substance and accident) has no meaning ('cannot be thought') outside the domain of objects of intuition.

[16] TN. Nominal essence and real essence.

lines that can be drawn from a given point inside the figure are equal to one another; this is the *essentia nominalis* of a circle. However, it is still doubtful whether these conditions are also possible until it is presented in intuition by means of the movement of a line around one of its endpoints; thereupon the circle becomes an *essentia realis*. It is the same in the following case: a **something** is thought (by means of the form of hypothetical judgement) such that when it is posited, something else must be posited. But this procedure is arbitrary and there is no insight into its possibility from concepts alone; now if the understanding finds a given intuition, *a*, (namely one that it has itself introduced for the sake of experiential propositions) such that when it is posited, another intuition, *b*, must be posited, then as a result this concept acquires its reality. I will explain myself more clearly. The form of the hypothetical judgement is merely the concept of the dependence of the predicate on the subject; the subject is as undetermined in itself as it is with respect to the predicate, | whereas, in relation to the subject, the predicate is determined by the subject (although it is certainly undetermined in itself). In itself the concept of cause is undetermined and so it can be arbitrarily posited; by contrast, the concept of effect is determined in relation to and by means of the assumed cause, although it is certainly undetermined in itself. Or, in other words, every possible object can without distinction be the cause of something, and this not merely in itself, but also in relation to a determined effect, if the effect is determined arbitrarily. But if the cause has already been arbitrarily chosen, then the effect can no longer be anything at all, but only one determined thing.[17] Dependency can thus be conceived without relation to determined objects (as the form of hypothetical | judgements in logic); but cause and effect cannot be conceived unless related to determined objects; i.e. the rule of under-

---

[17] In order to explain this through an analogy, imagine the following: a curve, where the same y gives several values of x (i.e., where its directrix intersects the curve at several points). The form of the hypothetical judgement in general can be compared with the expression of this curve, where y is a function of x and [some] determinate magnitudes [*wo y eine Funktion von x und bestimmten Grössen ist*]. Here y represents the *cause*, and x the *effect* , | both x and y are in themselves undetermined or variable. But if x is determined then so is y, but not the reverse; consequently, x is undetermined, both in itself (as an undetermined part of the directrix) and by y (if the latter is determined); on the other hand although y is indeed in itself (as an undetermined ordinate) undetermined, it is determined by x (if the latter is determined). TN. For example, the function $y = x^2$ where x is undetermined by the value of y because $x = +\sqrt{y}$ or $-\sqrt{y}$.

standing concerning hypothetical judgements relates only to determinable and not to determined objects; but its objective reality can only be demonstrated by its application to determined objects of intuition. But this determination of the effect by the cause cannot be assumed *materialiter* (as when I say: a red thing is the cause of a green one, and the like) because then the question arises: *quid juris?* i.e. how is it conceivable that *a priori* concepts of the understanding like those of cause and effect can provide determinations of something *a posteriori*; these determinations must rather be assumed | *formaliter*, i.e. with respect to the common form of these objects (time) and their particular determinations in this form (the one as preceding and the other as following) because then these concepts of cause and effect are determinations of something *a priori*, and hence determinations of the objects themselves (since objects cannot be thought without these concepts).

So experiences and these concepts (cause and effect) are in a reciprocal relation that is asymmetrical:[18] on the one hand, experience does not first make these concepts possible, but only shows that they are in themselves possible; on the other hand these concepts not only show that experience in itself is possible, but they make it possible. It is the same with the construction of mathematical concepts.[19] For example, the construction of a circle through the movement of a line around one of its | endpoints does not make the concept of the circle possible in the first place, but merely shows that it is possible. Experience (intuition) shows that a straight line is the shortest line between two points, but it does not make it the case that the straight line is the shortest. The possibility of a circle (a figure of the following kind: all lines that can be drawn from a given point within it to its limit are equal) is proven analytically; namely an intuition is given (a line that is moved around one of its endpoints), and then this intuition is compared to the arbitrarily chosen concept, and they are found to be identical because a line moved about one of its endpoints is identical to itself in every possible position, consequently this line in all its possible positions is identical to the concept of the circle (to its conditions).

---

[18] TN. '*haben eine wechselseitige Beziehung von ganz verschiedener Art auf einander*'. Literally: 'have a reciprocal relation of a completely different kind to one another'.

[19] By this I understand the empirical construction performed in accordance with the definition by means of the postulate or practical corollary for describing a circle. On the other hand, pure construction in the imagination shows not merely that the figure is possible, but makes it possible in the first place.

This identity is not given by experience; experience only gives something that is represented absolutely and this allows what cannot be comprehended in itself[20] (the forms and categories) to be comprehended. The matter [*das Materielle*] of intuition, what is directly related to an object, makes the form [*das Formelle*] of intuition comprehensible; that is to say, it makes comprehensible both the forms of intuition with all their possible connections and relations [*Beziehungen und Verhältnissen*], and also the pure concepts of the understanding or forms of thought, which do not relate directly to an object but only indirectly, by means of the categories.[21] As a result we are entitled to assert that all concepts of the understanding are innate, even though they only come to light (to consciousness) at the instigation [*Veranlassung*] of experience. It is just the same with judgements; indeed, the very nature and possibility of judgements is incomprehensible from experience; so they must be possible in themselves before all experience. Intuition shows us that a triangle can be constructed from three lines, two of which are together longer than the third; but it is not intuition that makes this possible in the first place, rather it is already possible in itself, etc. For example, if I judge: red is different from green, then I imagine first red in intuition and then green; afterwards I compare the two with each other, and from this the judgement arises. But how are we to make this comparison comprehensible? It cannot happen of its own accord [*vor sich*] during the representation of **red** and the representation of **green**; it does not help if someone says the imagination reproduces the first representation along with the second because they cannot flow together into one representation; and even if this were possible there would still be no comparison and for the very same reason. It is even more striking with disjunctive judgements: for example, a triangle is either right-angled or oblique-angled; if we suppose that this judgement becomes possible in the first place by means of intuition, then we must first bring a right-angled and then an oblique-angled triangle into intuition.

---

[20] TN. i.e. a relational concept [*Verhältnis-Begriff*].

[21] TN. Kant speaks of 'pure concepts of the understanding or categories' (e.g. A76/B102), treating 'pure concepts of the understanding' and 'categories' as synonymous terms, whereas Maimon here speaks of 'pure concepts of the understanding or forms of thought' and seems to be using 'categories' in Kant's sense but using 'pure concepts of the understanding' to include, for example, the concept of identity (classified as a concept of reflection by Kant – see A261/B317), whose application to intuition he has just demonstrated in the case of the circle.

But how can this judgement be comprehended, for these predicates are mutually exclusive and yet it is supposed to be possible to think both at the same time in the same subject? Experience cannot therefore make the possibility of such concepts and judgements conceivable, on the contrary they must be already to be found in the understanding *a priori* where they are not subject to experience and its laws: from this we can see the mysterious nature of our thought, namely that the understanding must have every possible concept and judgement in itself before coming to consciousness of them. Besides those [concepts and judgements] already discussed, this is also shown not only by the forms of thought and their determining concepts (categories) and *a priori* principles but also by all concepts and judgements in general (these principles | are not mere dispositions, as some may believe;[22] they are not perceived first obscurely and then clearly, as is the case with sensible representations; for dispositions, capacities, etc., are the objects themselves coming to actuality, only to a weaker degree, whereas these concepts and judgements are indivisible unities); as has already been mentioned, this is because intuition yields merely the data to which they are applied, and by this means helps to bring them to consciousness (without this we could make no use of them), but does not contribute anything to their reality. It is the same in the following case. The concepts of cause and effect contain the condition that if something determined, A, is arbitrarily posited, something else that is necessarily determined (by means of the former), B, must be posited. The concepts are thus far merely problematic. But now we come to experiential judgements, for example that heat expands our air, and the like (this does not just mean that heat comes first and the expansion of the air follows, i.e. a mere perception, but that if heat comes first, then the expansion of the air must necessarily follow on from it). In this we find something that is identical to | the arbitrarily assumed concept, that is to say, the heat is given assertorically (arbitrarily) as something determined, from which the expansion of the air must follow as something necessarily determined by the heat. Only in this way do we see [*einsehen*] for the first time that the arbitrarily adopted concepts are possible. So experience does not make these concepts

---

[22] TN. Maimon is no doubt referring to Leibniz's defence of innate ideas against Locke's attack in *New Essays on Human Understanding*. There Leibniz's spokesman Theophilus states: 'truths, in so far as they are within us when we do not think of them, are tendencies or dispositions' (p.86, §26).

possible in the first place, rather, we merely recognize their possibility through it: on the contrary it is these concepts that make experiential judgements possible in the first place because judgements of experience cannot be thought without these concepts. There is the same reciprocal relation between every universal concept and the particular contained under it. A figure (a delimited space) is in itself possible; in order to have insight into [*einsehen*] this, I must construct a particular figure, for example a circle, a triangle, and the like. These particular figures are however only possible by means of the universal concept of a figure in general because they cannot be thought without the universal concept, but the reverse is not true because a figure lacking this particular determination is also possible. Such important concepts as the categories and their legitimate use can never be explained at sufficient length. I have endeavoured to explain these things as far as I was able; | I want now to do so in even greater detail.

An object [*Objekt*] of thought is a concept of an object [*Gegenstand*] produced by the understanding according to universal rules or conditions that therefore requires two parts: 1) **Matter** [*Materie*] of thought, or something given (intuition) whereby these universal rules or conditions are applied to a determined object of thought (for they cannot [themselves] determine an object just because they are universal). 2) **Form of thought**, i.e., these universal rules or conditions themselves without which the given can still be an object (of intuition) but not an object of thought: for **thought** is judging, i.e. finding the universal in the particular, or subsuming the particular under the universal. Now the concepts can arise at the same time as the intuition, or the concepts can precede the intuition, in which case they are merely symbolic, and their objective reality is merely problematic. So the question *quid juris?* is relevant to these concepts, i.e. [the question] whether or not these symbolic concepts can also be made intuitive [*anschauend*] and thereby obtain objective reality. I will explain this by means of examples. | The concept of a straight line requires two parts: first, matter or intuition (line, direction); second, form, a rule of the understanding in accordance with which this intuition is thought (sameness [*Einerleiheit*] of direction, being straight); here the concept arises at the same time as the intuition, for the drawing of this line is from the beginning subject to this rule. The reality of the synthesis of the expression (straight with line) or the symbolic reality is based on the reality of the synthesis of the concept itself (the closest possible connection [*die möglichste Verbindung*] between matter and form). This, however, applies only where intuition is *a priori* like the rule itself, as is the case with mathematical concepts, which can be constructed *a priori*, i.e. presented in a pure intuition; in this case I allow an *a priori* intuition to arise in conformity with an *a priori* rule: but if the intuition is *a posteriori* and I want to give the matter a form and thus make it into an object of thought, then my procedure is manifestly illegitimate [*unrechtmässig*][23] because the intuition has arisen *a posteriori* from something outside me, not *a priori* from myself, and so I can no longer prescribe it a rule for it to arise. Now there are also cases where the synthesis of the symbolic object precedes the synthesis of the intuitive one. For example, the understanding forms [*bildet*] the concept of a circle by prescribing the following rule or condition for it: that it be a figure for which all lines that can be drawn from a determinate point in it (centre) to its limit (circumference) are equal to one another: here we have a merely nominal definition [*Namenerklärung*], i.e. we know the meaning of the rule or condition of the circle, but we still lack a real definition [*Sacherklärung*], i.e. we do not know whether this rule or condition can be fulfilled or not. Should it be incapable of fulfilment, then the concept here expressed in words would have no objective reality: its synthesis would be found only in words but not in the thing itself [*der Sache selbst*]. So we leave this open and assume its objective reality merely problematically in order to see whether we can make it assertoric by means of an intuition. Fortunately **Euclid**[24] has actually discovered a method for bringing this concept into an intuition *a priori* (through movement of a line around one of its endpoints);[25] in this way the concept of a circle obtains an objective reality. Now we also find concepts or rules that are the forms of judgements in general; as for example, the concept of cause, which is the

---

[23] TN. I.e literally not in accordance with a rule or law, and because of this illegitimate, or begging the question *quid juris?*

[24] If space and time are *a priori* forms of sensibility, then I do not understand why movement is not as well (i.e. alteration of relations in space)? Indeed I even believe that the representation of space is only possible through that of movement, or rather at the same time as it. A line cannot be thought except through the movement of a point.

[25] TN. This claim about Euclid is false. In *The Elements* Euclid first *defines* the circle (the nominal definition given by Maimon is similar to Euclid's) and then *postulates* that a circle of any size can be drawn, but he does not provide a method for accomplishing this (see *The Elements*, Bk I, Definition 15 and Postulate 3). Because Euclid was used as a school textbook for centuries there were many different versions and abridgements in circulation and Maimon may be basing his claim on a variant version of the third postulate.

31

CHAPTER 2

form of the hypothetical judgement in relation to a determined object. Its meaning is this: if something determined, *a*, is posited assertorically, then something else, *b*, must be posited apodictically. The question then is: *quid juris?*, i.e. is the objective use of this concept legitimate or not? – and if it is, what kind of law does it belong under:[26] for the concept is related to objects of intuition given *a posteriori* and hence is certainly illegitimate with respect to the matter of intuition, which is given *a posteriori*. How then can we make it legitimate? The answer to this, or the deduction, is as follows: we do not apply this concept directly to the matter of intuition, but merely to its *a priori* form (time) and by this means to the intuition itself. So, if I say *a* is the cause of *b*, or if *a* is posited, *b* must also necessarily be posited, then *a* and *b* are not determined with respect to their matter or content, but only with respect to particular determinations of their form (the preceding and the succeeding in time): i.e. the reason that *a* is *a* and not *b* is not that *a* has a material determination that *b* lacks (for this cannot be subsumed under the *a priori* rule in so far as it is something *a posteriori*), but rather because *a* has a formal determination (the preceding), that *b* does not have. And it is the same with *b*: it does not become a determined object different from *a* through a material determination but rather through a formal determination (the succeeding) of their common form (time). So in this case the preceding stands to the succeeding [*folgende*] as the antecedent stands to the consequent [*Konsequenz*] in a hypothetical judgement. This procedure enables the understanding not only to think objects in general, but also to **have cognition of determined** objects. If there were no *a priori* concepts determining objects, determined objects could still be intuited in themselves, but there would be no way to **think** them, i.e. they would be mere objects of intuition, and not of the understanding: if on the other hand there were no intuitions, then objects could indeed be thought in general, but we would have no concepts of **determined** objects: in other words, the one would be thought as something of the kind that if it is posited, then something else must be posited at the same time; and the other as something of the kind that, if the first is posited then it must also be posited. But then we could not have cognition of objects; i.e. we would be unable say whether anything particular contains this universal concept. So, in the first case we would have no understanding; but in

---

[26] TN. '*ist der objektive Gebrauch dieses Begriffs rechtmäßig oder nicht? – und ist er es, was für eine Art Rechtens ist es, worunter er gehört.*'

the second no faculty of judgement [*Beurtheilungsvermögen*].²⁷ And even if we had both, but had no *a priori* form of intuition, then we would indeed have the constituent parts of judgement (universal concepts that are to be found in particular objects *in concreto* and particular objects to which universal | concepts can be applied), but we would have no available means of carrying this judgement out in a legitimate way; this is because universal concepts or rules *a priori* and particular objects of intuition *a posteriori* are completely heterogeneous. But this deduction now removes all difficulties at a stroke. However, the following question can still be raised: what determines the faculty of judgement to think the rule-governed succession as corresponding to the rule of the understanding itself (so that, if *a* comes first and *b* follows, but not the reverse, then the faculty of judgement thinks the relation of cause and effect between them), and to think each particular member of this sequence as corresponding²⁸ to each particular member of the rule of understanding (the preceding corresponding to cause and the succeeding to effect)? The following serves as an answer to this question: we do not in fact have any insight into the ground of this correspondence, but we are not for all that any the less convinced of the *factum* itself. We have several examples of this type: for example, in the judgement that the straight line is the shortest line between two points we have an apodictic cognition of a correspondence between two rules that the understanding prescribes to itself for the construction [*Bildung*] of a certain line: (**being straight** | and **being the shortest**). We do not comprehend why these two must be combined in one subject, but it is enough that we have insight into the possibility of this correspondence (in so far as they are both *a priori*). It is the same here [i.e. with the concept of cause] – we did not want to explain this correspondence analytically by answering the question *quid juris?* by means of a deduction, but merely to demonstrate its possibility since the fact is synthetically certain through intuition; in other words we merely wanted to make this cognition into an *a priori* cognition and not

---

²⁷ TN. Maimon uses both '*Beurtheilungsvermögen*' and '*Beurtheilungskraft*' and these have been translated as 'faculty of judgement' and 'power of judgement' respectively; he does not use Kant's word '*Urteilskraft*'. Like Kant he almost always uses '*Urtheil*' and '*urtheilen*' for the noun 'judgement' and verb 'to judge' and these both occur very frequently, however there are also a handful of occurrences of '*Beurtheilung*' and '*beurtheilen*'.

²⁸ TN. Here and below, 'correspondence' and 'corresponding' translate '*Übereinstimmung*' and '*übereinstimmend*'.

into a pure cognition. See the 'Short Overview of the Whole Work' below.

I want to explain the difference between these two kinds of cognition more precisely. An *a priori* cognition is a universal cognition, which is the form or condition of all particular cognitions and hence it must precede the latter, but this condition of all particular cognitions is not [itself] a particular cognition. An intuition is *a priori* if it is the form or condition of all particular intuitions, not itself a particular intuition but again a condition of all particular intuitions. For example, time and space. Consciousness of all intuitions in general presupposes consciousness of time and space; but consciousness of time and space does not presuppose any particular intuition, but I rather intuition in general. A concept is *a priori* if it is the condition for thinking any object at all, but no particular object is a condition for it. Examples of such concepts are identity, difference and opposition [*Gegensetzung*]: *a* is identical to *a*, *a* is opposed to *not a*; here no **determined** object is thought under *a* but merely a **determinable** object, i.e. for consciousness of identity or opposition no particular object is needed but only an object in general, or at least if the concept does condition a particular object, then it is treated as abstracted from this. Something is **pure** when it is a product of the understanding alone (and not of sensibility). Everything that is pure is at the same time *a priori*, but not the reverse. All mathematical concepts are *a priori*, but nevertheless not pure: I have cognition of the possibility of a circle from out of my self [*aus mir selbst*] without having to wait for it to be given in experience (which I could never be certain of if it were to be given). So a circle is an *a priori* concept, but it is nevertheless not on that account pure, because it must be grounded in an intuition (that I have not produced from out of myself according to a rule, but that has been given to me from somewhere else, though it is still *a priori*). All relational concepts [*Verhältnisbegriffe*], I for example, identity, difference, substance, cause, and the like, are *a priori* and at the same time pure because they are not given representations themselves but merely thought relations between given representations. It is the same with propositions. *A priori* propositions are propositions that necessarily follow from concepts by means of the principle of contradiction (without regard to whether or not the concepts are pure). Only propositions that follow from pure concepts are pure: mathematical propositions are all *a priori* but they are not pure. On the other hand, the proposition that every effect has its cause is *a priori* and at the same time pure because it follows necessarily from a pure *a priori* concept (cause; since neither a cause without an effect, nor the reverse, can be thought). This is why the representations of time and space are still not pure (since they themselves arise from sensible representations) although they are *a priori* (prior to every particular sensible representation). They are not unities connecting the manifold of intuitions, but are themselves a **manifold** that is connected through **unity**, and at the same time they are the forms of all other intuitions.

To conclude this chapter, I want to add something about the possibility of synthetic | *a priori* propositions. The explanation [*Erklärung*][29] of the possibility of an object or of a synthesis in general can mean two different things. First, [it can be] the explanation of the meaning of a rule or condition, i.e. the demand that a merely symbolic concept be made intuitive. Second, [it can be] the genetic [*genetische*] explanation of a concept whose meaning is already familiar. According to the first type of explanation of possibility, the concept of colour is something impossible for someone born blind: this is not only because the way these intuitions arise cannot be explained to him, but also because the meaning of this symbol cannot be explained to him. But for a sighted person this concept certainly does have a meaning, it can be made intuitive *materialiter*[30] to him, but its possibility is merely problematic, for we cannot explain the way it arises to him. See Chapter 5. A root of 2 has a meaning (a number that gives the number 2 when multiplied by itself) and is thus possible *formaliter*. But it is not possible *materialiter* because in this case no object (determinate number) can be given. Here the rule or condition of the production of an object is conceivable and yet the object in itself is | not possible (as a result of material lack [*Mangel an Materie*]). $\sqrt{-a}$ is also impossible *formaliter* because the rule itself cannot be made conceivable (since it contains a contradiction). The possibility of the principles of mathematics is only of the first kind, i.e. they can be given a meaning in intuition, but not of the second kind, because, even if I already see the meaning of the proposition that a straight line is the shortest between two points (by constructing a straight line), I still do not know how I arrived at this proposition. The reason is that this relation does not specify merely a

---

[29] TN. As was remarked in an earlier footnote, '*Erklärung*' means both 'explanation' and 'definition' and although translated as 'explanation' throughout this paragraph, '*genetische Erklärung*' could, for example, be rendered as 'genetic definition'.

[30] TN. Throughout this paragraph *materialiter* and *formaliter* are the Latin terms for 'materially' and 'formally'.

universal form that must be in me *a priori*, but rather specifies the form or rule of a particular object (the necessary connection between being straight and being the shortest), so that here the question *quid juris?* of the explanation of possibility understood in this sense, is totally unanswerable; for how is it conceivable that the understanding can establish with apodictic certainty that a relational concept (the necessary being together of the two predicates) that it thinks must be found in a given object? All that the understanding can assume with certainty in the object is what it itself has put into it | (in so far as it has itself produced the object itself in accordance with a self-prescribed rule), and not anything that has come into the object from elsewhere. So, assuming that time and space are *a priori* intuitions, they are still only **intuitions** and not *a priori* **concepts**; they make only the terms of the relation intuitive for us, and by this means the relation itself, but not the truth and legitimacy of its use. So the question remains: how are synthetic propositions possible in mathematics? or: how do we arrive at their evident nature [*Evidenz*]?

For a cognition to be true, it must be both given and thought at the same time: **given** with respect to its matter (that must be given in an intuition); **thought** with respect to the form that cannot be given in itself, although it receives its meaning in an intuition (because a relation can only be thought, not intuited). That is to say, the form must be of such a kind that it also belongs to the symbol considered as object, as in the principles of identity and contradiction: *a* is identical to *a*, *a* is opposed to *not a*. In this case the question *quid juris?* falls completely aside because the | principles are rules of the thinkability[31] of things in general, without regard to their matter. On the other hand, with synthetic propositions (whether mathematical or physical propositions), the question *quid juris?* always returns, i.e. although the fact is indubitable, its possibility remains inexplicable. This can be extended generally to the relation between every essence [*Wesen*] and its properties because the properties do not follow [*folgen*] analytically from the essence according to the principle of identity (as is the case with the essential parts) but merely synthetically, and so the possibility of the properties' following is incomprehensible. By virtue of the *factum* we can at best ascribe the highest degree of probability to

---

[31] TN. '*Denkbarkeit*', we have chosen to use this neologism because its meaning is clear, it brings the German word to mind, it is more concise than 'possibility of thinking', and it does not prejudge the identity of thinking with the use of concepts as would 'conceivability' ('conceivable' and 'comprehensible' been used to translate '*begreiflich*').

propositions of this kind, but there is no way that we can ascribe apodictic certainty to them. To be able to do so we must assume that the (for us) synthetic connection between the subject and the predicate must have an inner ground so that if we, for example, had insight into [*einsehen*] the true essence [*Wesen*] of a straight line, and accordingly could define it, then this synthetic proposition would follow analytically. On this supposition the evident nature [*Evidenz*] of mathematics would indeed be saved but we would then have no synthetic propositions. | So I can only think that **Kant** assumed the reality of synthetic propositions merely with respect to our limited understanding; and in this I am readily in agreement with him.

If we want to consider the matter more carefully, we will find that the question *quid juris?* is one and the same as the important question that has occupied all previous philosophy, namely the explanation of the community [*Gemeinschaft*] between soul and body, or again, as the explanation of the world's arising (with respect to its matter) from an intelligence. For we ourselves as well as the things outside of us (in so far as we are conscious of them) can be nothing other than our representations themselves, representations that are rightly divided into two principal classes. 1) The forms, i.e. the representation of the universal modes of our operations [*Arten unserer Operationem*], which must be in us *a priori*. 2) The matter, or the representation of particular objects that is given to us *a posteriori* and that, in connection with the first, yields consciousness of particular objects. As a result, we call the former soul, but the latter body (namely modifications of them, through which we have cognition of them).[32] So the question of the explanation | of the soul's union with the body reduces to the following question: how is it conceivable that *a priori* forms should agree with things given *a posteriori*? and the second question reduces to the following: how can we conceive of matter arising, as something merely given but not thought, by assuming an intelligence, since they are indeed so heterogeneous? This question would not come up if our understanding could produce objects out of itself according to its self-prescribed rules or conditions without needing to be given something from elsewhere. But this is not the case, and because the objects that are subject to [its] rules and conditions must be given to it from elsewhere, so the difficulty arises of its own accord. That is to say, how can the understanding

---

[32] TN. '*nämlich Modifikationen derselben, wodurch sie erkannt werden.*' '*Derselben*' ('of them') probably refers back to the 'particular objects' mentioned in the previous sentence.

subject something (the given object) to its power (to its rules) that is not in its power? In the Kantian system, namely where sensibility and understanding are two totally different sources of our cognition, this question is insoluble as I have shown; on the other hand in the Leibnizian-Wolffian system, both flow from one and the same cognitive source [*Erkenntnisquelle*] (the | difference lies only in the degree of completeness of this cognition) and so the question is easily resolved. I will take as an example the concept of cause, i.e. the necessity of *b* following from *a*. According to the Kantian system it is inconceivable by what right we connect a concept of the understanding (of necessity) to determinations of an intuition (of temporal sequence). **Kant** certainly tries to get around this difficulty by assuming that space and time and their possible determinations are *a priori* representations in us, and therefore that we can legitimately ascribe the concept of necessity, which is *a priori*, to determined succession in time, which is also *a priori*. But we have already shown that even if they are *a priori*, intuitions are still heterogeneous with concepts of the understanding, and so this assumption does not get us much further: on the other hand, for the Leibnizian-Wolffian system, time and space are, though not distinct [*undeutliche*], still concepts of the understanding of the connections and relations [*Beziehungen und Verhältnissen*] of things in general, and so we are completely justified in subjecting them to the rules of the understanding. We assume an infinite understanding (at least as idea), for which the forms are at the same time objects of thought, | or that produces out of itself all possible kinds of connections and relations of things (the ideas). Our understanding is just the same, only in a limited way. This idea is sublime and will, I believe (if it is carried through), overcome the greatest difficulties of this kind.

I will now explain by means of the following example what I have claimed above about synthetic propositions, namely that they derive their existence from the incompleteness of our concepts. **Kant** advances the following as an example of a synthetic *a priori* proposition: a straight line is the shortest between two points.[33] But let us see. **Wolff** defines a straight line like this: a line whose parts are similar to the whole (presumably its parts share one and the same direction because we can only have cognition of a line and differentiate it from other lines by means of direction); and since lines abstracted from any magnitude can

[33] TN. B16 (this example does not appear in the first edition of the *Critique*).

differ only in their position, so a straight line means the same as **one** line (by position), and a non-straight (curved) line means the same as several lines (thought as a single line by means of their common law).[34] So I want | to try to prove this proposition analytically: namely that **one** line (between two points) must be shorter than several lines (between the same points). So I suppose two lines that I will compare with **one** line between the same points. From this a triangle arises in intuition. Concerning triangles, **Euclid** has proved (Bk 1, Prop. 20) that two lines taken together (sides of the triangle) must be greater than the third,[35] and this merely by means of some axioms and postulates that follow analytically from the concept (e.g., extending [*verlängern*] a straight line, the position of figures does not alter their size, etc.[36]). The same can also easily be proved for the relation of this one line to several lines that lie with the first line between the same points; the reason is that a rectilinear figure will always arise that can be resolved into triangles. | Let us

---

[34] My intention here is merely to show that according to this definition of a straight line, the proposition: 'a straight line etc.', is not an axiom but a proposition derived analytically from other propositions. And supposing that in the end we arrive at synthetic propositions lying in turn at the ground of all these propositions (something I leave open for now), nevertheless, I maintain that by means of my definition I can make these propositions too analytic, just as I have made the former allegedly synthetic propositions analytic. What is more, I will explain below that I am not content with this definition borrowed from **Wolff**, I only wanted to show the possibility of my claim, even assuming that I could not apply it in this case.

[35] TN. It is worth noting that Euclid's proof of this proposition is a *locus classicus* of the debate as to the virtue of proving what common sense takes as self-evident. The Epicureans ridiculed Euclid's elaborate proof on the grounds that even an ass knows its truth – for if it is standing at one corner of a triangle and its food is placed at another corner, it will reach it by walking along one side not two. See Heath's discussion in *Euclid's Elements* with Intro and Commentary by Thomas Heath, 2nd edn (New York: Dover, 1956), Vol. I, p. 287.

[36] TN. Proposition 20 states: 'In any triangle two sides taken together in any manner are greater than the remaining one'. The proof makes use of Postulate 2, 'to produce a finite straight line continuously in a straight line', Common Notion 5, 'the whole is greater than the part' and of two previously proven propositions about triangles. However Maimon's second example of an axiom or postulate used in the proof, 'the position of figures does not alter their size' is not present in Euclid; if it states that translations in space preserve size (i.e. that space is isotropic), it is irrelevant since Proposition 20 does not involve translations of triangles in space; the more likely alternative is therefore that it states that lines in different positions (and orientations) can be equal. This is presupposed by Euclid's definitions of a circle, and of an equilateral triangle and an isosceles triangle (Definitions 15 and 20), and an isosceles triangle is indeed constructed in the proof of Proposition 20.

suppose, for example, the line *ac* which, along with the three lines *ad*, *de*, *ec*, lies between the two points *a* and *c*. Then I say: the line *ac* must be shorter than the three lines *ad*, *de*, *ec*, taken together, for it clearly follows from the preceding proposition that *ac* < *ab* + *bc* and *bc* = *be* + *ec*, consequently, *ac* < *ab* + *be* + *ec*: but *be* < *bd* + *de*, consequently *ac* < *ab* + *bd* + *de* + *ec*, Q.E.D.

Admittedly the unity or plurality of the lines (according to their position) must be constructed, i.e. presented in an intuition, without this it would be completely meaningless: but that means only that the terms of the comparison (the objects) are presented in an intuition and not the relation itself. Just as if I say the **red** in *a* is identical to the **red** in *b*, then the proposition is analytic even though the objects of the comparison are given intuitions.[37] The present case is just the same: a straight line is given in an intuition in just the same way as a non-straight line (many lines brought under a unity); but nevertheless the relation itself (that the former is shorter than the latter) is proven analytically (through the principle of identity and contradiction, *per substitutionem*).

If **Kant** does not want to adopt the Wolffian definition of a straight line[38] (for there is, to my knowledge, no other), but maintains that a straight line is a concept determined only through intuition, then we will here have an example of how the understanding can make a concept of reflection into the rule for the production of an object (although a concept of reflection should really be thought between already given objects rather than as producing the objects in thinking them). The reason is that in order to produce a straight line as object, the understanding thinks the rule that it should be the shortest between two points (it cannot make 'it should be straight' into a rule because being straight is an intuition and consequently outside its domain); this rule is in fact a concept of reflection (a relation of difference with respect to magnitude), concerning pure magnitudes prior to their application to

---

[37] TN. The proposition is ambiguous, but Maimon evidently does not intend the proposition to express the thought that the shade of red is the same in both *a* and *b*, which would be an empirical judgement, and contingently true or false; he appears rather to be asserting that it is analytic that the property of being red is the same of whatever it is asserted.

[38] TN. In the letter commenting on the *Essay* that is included in this volume, Kant objects to this definition: 'as for defining a straight line, it cannot be done by referring to the identity of direction of all the line's parts, for the concept of direction ... already presupposes the concept [of straight line]'.

intuition, and cannot be supposed otherwise, because it is only by means of such relations that the magnitudes become objects in the first place. Here the inner (the thing in itself) does not precede the outer (the relation to other things) as is the case with other objects, but rather the reverse; i.e. without the thought of a relation [*ein gedachtes Verhältnis*] there is indeed no object of magnitude (in pure arithmetic; geometry does provide us with objects prior to their subsumption under the category of magnitude, namely figures that are already determined through their position). Being straight is, as it were, an image [*Bild*] or the distinguishing mark [*Merkmal*] of this relational concept: as a result it cannot be used as a concept of the understanding in order to infer any consequences from it. If we go through all the propositions concerning the straight line, we will find that they follow not in so far as it is straight but only in so far as it is the shortest; similarly, nothing can follow from any other sensible intuition than that it is what it is. It is the same with all propositions that hold of everything without distinction (as well as of nothing), because they too are correct symbolically, i.e. not of determined objects, but of objects in general. The expression **straight line** is used merely because it is short.[39] | But the fact that we already have cognition of this proposition by means of intuition alone prior to its proof rests only on the following: we perceive its distinguishing mark or image in intuition (although it can only be made clear, not distinct), and so we already have a presentiment of the truth in advance (a presentiment that, I believe, must play no insignificant role in the power of invention [*Erfindungskraft*]). It appears to be a paradox because in this case it is customary to believe that being straight is an inner determination (a relation of the parts to one another) and being the shortest is an outer determination. But on closer inspection we find just the opposite, namely, that being straight or the identity of direction of the parts already presupposes that they have arisen. So this definition of the straight line is useless as well. The Wolffian definition cannot avoid this difficulty because the similarity of the parts to the whole can only be in direction and consequently it already presupposes lines. However, the property of being the shortest begins precisely when it arises and is at the same time an internal relation.

---

[39] TN. Maimon is playing on the shortness of the straight line and the shortness of the expression 'straight line'.

I come now to the question *quid facti?* **Kant** mentions this merely in passing, but I hold it to be of great importance with respect to the deduction of the categories. Its meaning is this: how do we know from our perception that *b* succeeds *a* that this succession is necessary, whereas the succession of the very same *b* upon *c* (which is equally possible) is accidental? **Kant** indeed notes (and rightly) that the answer to this question depends only on the power of judgement [*Beurteilungskraft*] and further that no rules can be given for this. But if we let it depend on this, we would have nothing solid to lean on in determining the reality of the categories and their complete enumeration. Let us look into this.

Kant derives the concept of cause from the form of the hypothetical judgement in logic. But we could raise the question: how does logic itself come by this peculiar form, that if one thing *a* is posited, another thing *b* must necessarily also be posited? It is not a form of possible things (like the form of the categorical judgement, or the *principium exclusi tertii*,[40] that is based on the principle of contradiction that every subject *A* has either *a* or *not a* as a predicate). The reason is that we do not come across it at all in this context where predicates are stated categorically of the subject and properties of the essence; even if a categorical proposition can also be expressed hypothetically, this only makes the expression not the form of the judgement itself hypothetical. So we have presumably abstracted it from its use with real objects, and transferred it into logic; as a result we must put the reality of its use beyond doubt before ascribing reality to it as a form of thought in logic; but the question is not whether we can use it legitimately, which is the question: *quid juris?*, but whether the fact is true, namely that we do use it with actual objects. Yes, it will be said, the fact is indubitable. We say, for example: the fire warms (makes warm) the stone and this signifies not merely perception of the succession of the two appearances in time, but the necessity of this succession. But to this **David Hume** would reply: it is not true in this case that I perceive a necessary succession; I certainly use the same expression that others use on this occasion, but I understand by it only the often perceived succession of the warming of the stone upon the presence of the fire and not the necessity of this succession. It is merely an association of perceptions, not a judgement of the understanding. It is just what in animals we call the expectation of similar cases; and even if **Kant** has

---

[40] TN. Principle of the excluded middle.

proved that we cannot have abstracted these forms from experience because experience only becomes possible in the first place by means of them, **David Hume** (or his representative) can gladly admit this. He will say: the concept of cause is not in the nature of our thought in general such that it would also occur [*stattfinden*] in symbolic cognition, and it is also not grounded in experience in the sense in which **Kant** uses this word; consequently there are no experiential propositions properly so called [*eigen*] (expressing necessity) and if I say this concept is taken from experience, I understand by this mere perception containing a merely subjective necessity (arising from habit) that is wrongly passed off as an objective necessity. So, in order to prove the fact itself against **David Hume**, we would have to be able to show that when they first have this perception, | children too instantly make the judgement that the fire is the cause of the warming of the stone. But this will be difficult to do. From this we see that logic is unable to yield a trustworthy distinguishing mark of the reality of these forms (in so far as the fact, or the use of its forms, is itself doubtful); and that concepts like these that determine particular objects, must be completely excluded from logic, which abstracts from all matter.

Chapter 3
Ideas of the Understanding, Ideas of Reason, etc.

§1 An idea of the understanding is the material completeness[1] of a concept, in so far as this completeness cannot be given in intuition. For example, the understanding prescribes for itself this rule or condition: that an infinite number of equal lines are to be drawn from a given point, so that by joining their endpoints together the concept of a circle is produced. The possibility of this rule, and hence of the concept itself, can be shown in intuition (by rotating a line around the given point); and this also shows the formal completeness of the concept (completeness of unity in the manifold). But its material completeness (completeness of the manifold) cannot be given in intuition, because only a finite number of

---

[1] TN. In this chapter 'completeness' and its cognates 'to complete' and 'completed' respectively are always used to translate '*Vollständigkeit*' and its cognates '*vollenden*' and '*vollendet*'. In some contexts 'fulfill(ed)' might seem the obvious translation of the latter, and an explanation of why it has been avoided may shed some light on this chapter. This issue goes to the heart of Maimon's criticism of Kant's way of answering the question, *quid juris?* For Kant the problem is how can *a priori* concepts apply to objects of intuition, and his solution is *pure intuition* determined as schemata that bridge the gap between the two. For Maimon (and his thought here stands in relation to both Leibnizian infinite analysis of concepts and Spinozan mind/body parallelism), the answer is *not* to bridge the gap between concepts and intuitions, but rather to carry both to the point of completion where they cease to differ. We have, for example, neither a complete concept nor a complete intuition of a circle – but only an idea in which they are one. Thus the issue is not of objects more or less completely fulfilling concepts but of concepts or objects being completable in themselves and hence converging at infinity (or for an infinite intelligence).

equal lines can be drawn. So this concept is not a concept of the understanding to which an object corresponds, but only an idea of the understanding, something that we can come infinitely close to in intuition by means of the successive addition of such lines, and consequently a limit concept [*Gränzbegrif*]. I think that there is an obvious difference between the totality of conditions by means of which an object of intuition is thought, and the totality of the intuitions themselves that are subsumed under these conditions. The equality of the lines in this example is a condition (a determination of their relation to one another): I can subsume any number of lines whatever under this condition and yet the condition itself always remains one and the same. So, when I think that all the lines drawn from a given point on a plane are to be equal, this totality does not concern the condition as the form of the concept, but rather its matter [*Stoff*]:[2] the former is already complete with any two lines (the lines A and B do not become more equal because C is also thought as equal to them). But if the totality [*Allheit*] of lines is also thought as [being part of] the condition, then there is again no plurality of conditions; the reason is that I may think as many equal lines as I want to, but as long as I suppose their number to be finite, I still do not thereby think a circle; on the other hand I cannot, for example, think the concept of an individual without the concept of the species, nor the species without the concept of the genus, etc. In this case the thinkability of the individual is conditioned by the thinkability of all the general concepts: we do not find the complete condition in any two of these concepts, but in all of them taken together; but if this totality [*All*] is infinite, then it is an idea of reason. In a geometric series, the condition is completed [*vollendet*] by the relation of two successive terms, but if the series is required to be equal to a given sum, then this belongs to the condition as well, and as long as the number of the terms is not complete [*vollendet*] the series is not the one that satisfies the condition. On this view, the series expressing an irrational root must never come to an end, because if it could, the condition would not be satisfied [*erfüllt*] (that its value should be equal to the required root). Concerning the definition of a circle, it could indeed be said: it is not necessary to suppose that all the lines drawn from the centre are equal, but merely that each line I draw be equal to those already drawn; and on this definition the concept will not

---

[2] TN. Both '*Materie*' and '*Stofff*' have been translated by 'matter', but where the original is '*Stoff(f)*' this has been marked.

be an idea.[3] But we should take into account the fact that mathematical concepts are not copies of anything, so that we would have to compare them with their originals to determine their completeness; rather they are themselves the originals produced by the understanding out of itself *a priori*. From this it follows that the completeness of mathematical concepts can be judged only relatively, with respect to the consequences to be drawn from them. Suppose, for example, that we want to derive the following proposition from the concept of a circle as a consequence: every line drawn from any point on the circumference to intersect the diameter at right angles is the mean proportional line between the sections of the diameter it cuts.[4] To derive this proposition, we do not need to suppose in the definition of the circle that all the lines drawn from the centre are equal, but only that three of them are. But if we want to derive the area of the circle, or its relation to a square, then we must necessarily regard the circle as already completed, because otherwise this relation cannot be exact.

These ideas are indispensable for extending [*Erweiterung*] the use of the understanding. The extent [*Umfang*] of this use is always proportional to the degree of completeness attained. For example, take the following rule for drawing three lines *ca, cb, cd*: two of them, *ca, cb*, run in opposite directions from a given point *c* on a line *ab*, but the third *cd* makes an acute angle, *acd*, with one of them, *ca*. If I have drawn three lines in accordance with this rule, then I can deduce with certainty that the perpendicular line, *de*, drawn from the endpoint *d* of *cd*, to *ca*, is the mean proportional line through the parts it separates (*ae* and *ec*) and that it is perpendicular to the other line, *cb*, etc. It is the same with the concept of a straight line, that is to say of a line all of whose parts have the same direction: the line itself, the direction of some of its parts, and the identity of this direction, can all be given in an intuition, but not the identity of direction of all of its parts. In a similar way, the asymptotes of a curved line are complete according to their rule, but in their presentation they are always incomplete. We grasp how their construction must be completed without being able to construct them completely. In spite of

---

[3] TN. Maimon here presents the rebuttal of the need for ideas of the understanding to account for the circle that Kant presented in his letter responding to the manuscript of the *Essay* (see Appendix). This discussion was therefore evidently added in a revision of the manuscript.

[4] TN. See Euclid, *Elements*, Book VI, Prop. 13 and the corollary to Prop. 8.

their material incompleteness, these concepts, or rather ideas of the understanding, are nevertheless correct because their rules can be made comprehensible by means of what is always given in intuition. For their material completeness they require only a continual repetition of this very rule. But since this repetition, in accordance with the concepts' conditions, must be infinite, they remain mere ideas, and their application has the same degree of correctness as the degree of their material completeness. For example, the principle that a straight line is the shortest between two points is all the more correctly applied to a given line, the more straight parts can be identified in it. It is just the same with the concepts or intuitions employed in the synthesis of the imagination such as the concept of succession in time and space. By means of these forms the imagination relates different sensible representations to one another and lends unity to its manifold. Here once again the understanding insists on material totality; in other words, by means of this *a priori* form it considers an intuition to be in a succession in time and space (without which we could not have any intuition) even when the imagination does not notice any succession.

On the other hand, the formal completeness of a concept is called an **idea of reason**. For example, we know about the concept of cause (or the judgement that follows from it), i.e. of something that exists presupposing something else from which it must follow in accordance with a rule. Let us then suppose the following: one thing, g, presupposes a cause, f, that in turn presupposes its own cause, e, and so on to infinity. Here f contains, so to speak, the first dignity [*Dignität*] of the concept of cause with respect to g, the effect and e the second, since it is the cause of the cause, and so on. So an infinite dignity of cause is presupposed with respect to g, and this is an idea of reason. It is the same with all pure concepts of the understanding. I want to explain myself still more clearly on this point. The subjective order (with respect to our consciousness) of all the operations of the mind is the following:

1 Sensibility (which certainly does not provide consciousness itself, but rather the matter [*Stoff*] for consciousness).
2 Intuition. The ordering of homogeneous [*einartigen*] sensible representations under their *a priori* forms (time and space); from this consciousness arises, although certainly no thought.
3 Concepts of the understanding (categories); from this a thought arises, i.e. the representation of a unity in the manifold.

CHAPTER 3

4   Ideas of reason. Totality of the concepts of the understanding.[5]

| The objective order considered in itself is, on the other hand, the following:

1   Ideas of the understanding, that is to say the infinitely small of every sensible intuition and of its forms, which provides the matter [*Stoff*] to explain the way that objects arise.
2   Concepts of the understanding, and
3   Ideas of reason, whose use has already been explained.

So for the understanding and for reason there is neither sensibility nor intuition (these belong to sense and imagination) but only ideas and concepts that always accompany the former[6] and that appear (or come to consciousness) at their instigation [*Veranlassung*]. As a result, the understanding does not subject something given *a posteriori* to its *a priori* rules; rather it lets it arise [*läßt entstehen*] in accordance with these rules (which I believe is the only way to answer the question *quid juris?* in a wholly satisfactory way). These three operations are the conditions of intuitions themselves. For example, intuition of the colour red requires: 1) Ideas of the understanding, i.e. the representation of any one of the red points in itself (abstracted from any quantity). 2) Concepts of the understanding (their **homogeneity** [*Einartigkeit*]: what allows them | to be brought into a single intuition; **cause**: if a red point comes first, then only a red point can follow within the same intuition, otherwise we could not have any intuitions, i.e. any connection of several intuitions in one representation, in which case we would live in a perpetual dream; **substance**: something must always remain self-identical in the succession of these points in time and space otherwise they could not be taken together in one intuition, and it is the same with all the other concepts of the understanding). 3) Ideas of reason: the totality of concepts of the understanding.

---

[5] TN. *Totalität der Verstandsbegriffe*. This phrase does not mean all the concepts of the understanding taken together, but rather the totality or 'formal completeness' of each such concept, which is an idea of reason.

[6] TN. 'the former' probably refers to sensibility and intuition.

Chapter 4
Subject and Predicate. The Determinable and the Determination

If one of the constituent parts of a synthesis can be thought without 35
reference to the other, i.e. either in itself or in another synthesis, but the
other cannot be thought without reference to the first, then the first is
termed the subject of the synthesis and the latter the predicate. For
example, a triangle or a space enclosed by three lines can be thought just as
well in itself, without reference to its **being right-** or **oblique-angled**, as
it can be thought disjunctively in these different kinds of synthesis. On the
other hand, being right- or oblique-angled cannot be thought without
triangle in general. So in this case triangle is the subject, but being right- or
oblique-angled is the predicate, and the concept this synthesis gives rise to
is an absolute concept. In general [*allgemein*] logic, the forms of thought are
viewed in relation to an object in general (*a priori* or *a posteriori*); but in
transcendental logic, they are viewed in relation to objects determined *a
priori*. As a result, subject is not distinguished from predicate through any
condition in general logic; whereas in transcendental logic they are
distinguished by means of an *a priori* condition: I will therefore now try to
establish this condition. It is nothing other than the objective possibility of
a synthesis in general. It should also be noted that in this case we are
talking about an objective synthesis (where the ground of the synthesis lies
in the objects), so that negative predicates or determinations are excluded
(ones that do indeed determine a concept, but not an object). Only positive
ones are taken into consideration, in so far as they exclude one another
through difference (not opposition) and cannot be thought in an object at
the same time in relation to one and the same thinking subject.

49

If, on the other hand, neither of the two [constituent parts] can be thought without reference to the other, then each is at the same time subject and predicate in relation to the other, and the concept arising from this [synthesis] is a relational concept, as for example cause and effect.[1] I think everyone will admit that in the absolute concept the same subject can be thought disjunctively with different predicates. But people will not so readily accept that the same predicate can only belong to one subject and the same subject can only have one predicate. They will object that although it is true that a predicate cannot be thought without any subject at all (since it is a predicate and not a subject), it can perfectly well be thought without any particular subject. As a result, I want to explain this more fully: it is natural for one abstract concept to make another abstract concept necessary: if in the synthesis AB I treat A as separate from B, then I must also treat B as separate from A; but this is only possible in symbolic cognition: in intuition I must treat AB together since otherwise the synthesis would have no ground. Yet there is indeed a difference between these two abstractions since A is still a real concept (that has consequences) even though it cannot be presented in intuition as such (abstracted from AB); on the other hand, B is not a real concept,

---

[1] For a finite understanding this kind of synthesis [i.e. a reciprocal synthesis such as cause and effect] is a mere form that (viewed in itself and apart from its application to a determined object of intuition) does not determine any object. It can be compared to an algebraic expression where x is a function of y and vice-versa: these determine one of the quantities by means of its relation to the other and hence only by means of the determination of the other. Consequently, for a finite understanding only the first kind of synthesis [i.e. an absolute or one-sided synthesis] takes place, **as object**; whereas for an infinite understanding the second kind takes place, since an infinite understanding thinks all possible things by this means. For an infinite understanding everything is in itself fully determined because it thinks all possible real relations [*Real-Verhältnisse*] between the ideas as their principles [*Principien*]. For example, let us suppose that x is a function of y, y a function of z, etc. A necessary relation of x to z etc arises out of these merely possible relations. Through this new function, x is more determined than before, and through being related to all possible relations, it is completely determined. For the infinite understanding the subject is what is thought merely as possible, and the predicate is what follows necessarily from this. The former (as in itself possible) can be thought without the latter, but the latter (as necessary consequence of the former) cannot be thought without the former. However, for a finite understanding, the subject is not what is **thought** in itself but only what is **given** in itself; and the predicate is what is thought only in relation to it, as object. For the infinite understanding, concepts are judgements of the possibility of things, and judgements are conclusions as to the necessity of things, deduced from the former; for a finite understanding, concepts are also judgements of the possibility of things, but they are in a one-sided synthesis.

although a new real concept (which has new consequences) arises when it is added to *A*. So in this case *A* is the subject and *B* the predicate of the synthesis; as a result the subject contains more reality than the predicate, because, besides the share of reality it has with the predicate in the new consequences, it has in addition, firstly its own consequences (that the predicate has no share in), and secondly the possibility of new consequences.

So let us take two subjects *A* and *B* with a common predicate *C*, so that two different syntheses arise from them: *AC* and *BC*. If these two syntheses are both to be real (not merely symbolic), then, considered in itself, *C* cannot be | a real concept, i.e. it cannot have any consequences as a real concept. On the other hand, the syntheses *AC* and *BC*, must have consequences that in themselves *A* and *B* did not have. As a result, these new consequences must be grounded in the synthesis alone; further, the consequences of the first synthesis *AC* must be different from the consequences of the second synthesis *BC* because the first synthesis is different from the second synthesis. But then I ask: where does the ground of this difference lie? It cannot lie in the predicate *C*, because *C* is necessarily self-identical in both syntheses. It also cannot lie in *A* and *B* in themselves. The reason for this is that if the ground of the difference (as determination) of the consequences were to be found in *A* and *B* in themselves, then the consequences themselves must also already be found in *A* and *B* in themselves (because being different is not a new determination that synthetically extends the concept of the object, but merely a concept of reflection enabling us to think a particular kind of relation), and so the synthesis would not be real (because *AC* and *BC* can yield no new consequences, i.e. ones not already arising out of *A* and *B* in themselves). The ground [of the difference] also cannot lie in the connection of subject and predicate; for what does it mean to have a ground in the | connection, if not that both have a share in it?

In short: I hope everyone will agree that different grounds cannot have the same [*einerlei*] consequences. The reason is this: if the grounds are completely different, i.e. if to posit one is to eliminate [*heben*] the other, then the following is certain: if *A* is a ground (condition) of something, then *non A*,[2] or the elimination [*Hebung*] of the ground, cannot at the same time be the ground of the same something. On the

---

[2] TN. Latin for 'not *A*'.

CHAPTER 4

other hand, suppose they are only partially but not completely different, and so in part the same [*einerlei*]: in this case, if A is the ground of something, then B can be the ground of the same something at the same time only to the extent that it is identical with A. Then the ground of this something is neither A nor B, but instead merely what they have in common [*was bei ihnen einerlei ist*]. If it is objected that being different is not (either wholly or in part) opposition, but rather a special form, then it must still be admitted that, although it is not opposition itself, it still presupposes the latter, because [things] that are different necessarily exclude one another; in other words, to think something different from A, one must first eliminate [*heben*] A and then put this something in its place.

Or to put it yet another way: we recognize that a synthesis is not merely symbolic but real because one part of it can be thought without the other (thought in itself), but not the reverse; but none of these parts can be presented in itself, as an abstract concept in intuition, so we cannot know whether one of them can be thought in itself unless we actually present it in intuition by means of different syntheses; only by doing this can we recognize that none of these syntheses is necessary for it to be thinkable and that as a result we must also be able to think it in itself, i.e. without them. The necessity of such a synthesis thus rests on the other part, the one that cannot be thought without the first (thought in itself). So if we assume that there is a determination common to two determinables, then this determination becomes a determinable (because it can be thought in different syntheses) and also the reverse, contrary to the assumption. If people still doubt whether what is presented in different syntheses can also be thought in itself, let them simply consider universal concepts with respect to their consequences; they will find that nothing that is connected with such concepts in any synthesis has the least share in their consequences; and from this their independence from all synthesis in general (with respect to their consequences, although not with respect to their presentation in an intuition) is evident enough.

In addition, I do not believe that this claim of mine will be overturned by any induction. For example, take the objection that the predicate 'figure' belongs to every body as subject, or that a determined colour, for example red, can belong to different bodies, etc. We only have to consider these examples more closely to discover that in the first example figure is not predicated directly of body, but of its form, namely of space; and that in the second colour is as little a predicate (determination) of body in general as it is of any particular body: for what could it be a determination of? – extension, impenetrability, weight, hardness, etc.? Only those who have no insight into the nature of a determination and treat things of the imagination as things of the understanding could believe this. The gathering together of these qualities is merely a synthesis of the imagination, based on their simultaneous coexistence [*Zugleichseyn*] in time and space (the assumption of an inner ground is and remains merely an assumption – that is, for us,[3] although it must be admitted that for the infinite understanding the assertoric-synthetic propositions must be apodictic and the apodictic-synthetic propositions analytic); but not a synthesis of the understanding: we can think a red body as little as we can a **sweet** line.

The understanding's procedure in forming [*Bildung*] concepts is opposed to its procedure in judging. In the former case it acts synthetically, but in the latter analytically. In forming concepts it starts from the universal and achieves the particular by means of determinations; on the other hand, in judgements it is the reverse: it thinks the particular first, and then subsumes it under the universal by omitting determinations; as a result, the terms subject and predicate must be exchanged in the two cases. With concepts, the subject is the universal and the predicate the particular. With judgements it is the reverse, but only in name, for in fact concept and judgement are identical. For example, if I say a triangle can be right-angled, then this is no different from thinking a right-angled triangle by means of this procedure; and if I say that a human being is an animal, this is tantamount to saying that the concept of a human being arises by means of a closer determination of the concept of animal. A re-membrance [*Wiedererinerung*] of the concept takes place with these and other similar judgements. So if I say *A* is the cause of *B*, then the concept of cause arises at the same time as the judgement because, as has already been shown, the mere form of the hypothetical judgement does not contain the concept of cause until it is applied to determined objects. The reason is that a cause is something by means of which something else is determined, and determined means not

---

[3] TN. '*In Ansehung unsrer*'. Maimon has omitted the feminine noun which '*unsrer*' ('our') would be expected to qualify. To keep this open we have translated the phrase by 'for us'. One possibility would be 'our reason' since he uses this phrase when speaking of our need to hypothesize or assume something which the infinite understanding can know *a priori* in endnote 22. See also the next footnote.

merely **posited**, but **determinately posited**. As a result, the mere form (if something in general is posited, then something else in general must be posited) does not yet contain the concept of cause.

I have thus established that a determination cannot be thought without the determinable, and so it follows of itself that a determination with respect to our consciousness[4] can only be a relation,[5] and as such either an inner or an outer one. For example, in the concept of a straight line the predicate 'straight' is an inner relation, i.e. the identity of the direction of the parts; but in the concept of a perpendicular line, being perpendicular is an outer relation, namely in relation to another line, etc. In a synthesis of intuition and concept, either the intuition or the concept can be subject or predicate, etc. Applied to objects of experience, the concepts of subject and predicate provide us with the concepts of **substance** and **accident**. That is, if an object of experience (intuition) can be thought in different syntheses, then it is termed substance (and because it is an object of experience, we can only be convinced that it can be thought in different syntheses if we actually think it as given in different syntheses); but the different determinations with which it is thought in synthesis are known as its accidents. But because time is the form of intuition, different representations cannot be thought at the same time. As a result, these different syntheses can only be thought as following one another in time, while the subject must be self-identical in all of them, i.e. substance must be something that persists in time while the accidents are something changing. From this we see that the concepts of substance and accident can on no account be applied to things that do not exist in time (things in themselves rather than intuitions) since they would then be completely meaningless: I do not know how it is possible that a thing is supposed be thought either in itself or through another thing. It must not be objected that this can be explained using examples from mathematics (whose objects are *a priori*). For example, in the concept of a straight line, the line is the subject and being straight the

---

[4] TN. '*In Ansehung unseres Bewusstseins*'. Maimon generally uses this phrase to mean 'for *our* consciousness' as opposed to that of an infinite understanding, rather than in the sense of 'for *consciousness*' as opposed to in itself.

[5] This is valid for an absolute concept; for the determination of a relative concept is only the particular object to which it is applied, i.e. an intuition. For example, if I say that the fire warms the stone, then in this case the universal relational concept of cause is determined through a particular object, namely, fire.

predicate because the former can be thought without the latter but not the reverse. We need only bear in mind that space and all its possible determinations are forms of sensibility, and at the same time themselves intuitions, i.e. something given (although *a priori*), | but not something thought; it follows that I am entitled to think a line as something given without the relation-determination [*Verhältnissbestimmung*] of being straight. But this is not the case with *a priori* objects (*noumena*); with respect to such objects the pure concepts of the understanding are completely meaningless because, apart from the fact that we have no insight into [*einsehen*] the possibility of the mere form of synthetic judgement without intuitions, we can in any case only think an object by means of this form, but we cannot have cognition of it. Cognition takes place only by means of the distinguishing marks of persisting and changing existence in time.

Chapter 5
Thing, Possible, Necessary, Ground, Consequence, etc.

A possible thing is opposed (1) **to the impossible, of which we have** *formal*-positive cognition, and in this case signifies the absence of contradiction; (2) **to the formally nothing or to the** *formally*-problematically possible and impossible,[1] and in this case 'possible thing' signifies a synthesis of which we have positive cognition and in which the predicate can belong to the subject as the determination to the determinable. This synthesis is one-sided [*einseitig*]. The determinable is the part of this synthesis that can be thought in itself as well as *disjunctively*[2] with other determinations (besides the one actually thought). On the other hand, the determination cannot be thought in itself without at least something determinable in general (see Chapter 4[3]). For example, in the synthesis of a straight line, 'line' is the determinable and can be thought both in itself as well as with other determinations (**crooked**), whereas 'being straight' is the determination and cannot be thought in itself in the absence of something it can determine. This synthesis thus differs from a synthesis of relational concepts [*Verhältnißbegriffe*], which is reciprocal [*wechselseitig*] so that neither of the parts of the synthesis can be thought without the other, as for example with cause and effect where each of the parts is both

---
[1] TN. The italicized 'formal' and 'formally' are both the Latin *'formaliter'* in the original.
[2] TN. The italicized 'disjunctively' is the Latin, *'disjunctive'* in the original.
[3] TN. The original mistakenly refers to Chapter 3.

determinable (by the other) and determination (of the other) at the same time. But if several things that can each be thought in itself are taken together arbitrarily, then this synthesis is formally[4] problematic and opposed to the possible.

(3) **To the materially nothing:** in this case 'possible thing' signifies the given intuition that comprises the *substratum* of a synthesis, without which the synthesis would be a merely subjective form, without objective reality.

(4) **To the actual:** in this case, by contrast, 'possible thing' signifies the absence of either contingent (pure concept) or essential matter (idea). For example, the concept of a triangle, abstracted from the body that the imagination connects it with in space and time (through coexistence), is of the first kind; whereas the asymptotes of a curved line are of the second kind. In this second kind, the synthesis of a finite and the synthesis of an infinite understanding are formally identical and only materially different in that a finite understanding can make only part of the synthesis intuitive while the rest remains merely symbolic, whereas an infinite understanding represents everything to itself intuitively.[5]

(5) **To the necessary:** either *formally*, i.e. if the synthesis is not necessary according to the laws of identity or relation; or *materially*, if the synthesis is not necessary in intuition, as it is for example in the judgement that a straight line is the shortest between two points.

A thing is thus either merely **negatively** or also **positively** possible; it is negatively possible if the concept of the thing does not contain a contradiction, i.e. if a predicate is not at the same time both attributed and not attributed to one and the same subject (without regard to the content of subject and predicate). Its positive possibility indeed presupposes the negative possibility but it also requires something in addition: (1) an intuition that grounds the concept along with the relation thought in that intuition, for example, a straight line; (2) an objective ground of possibility, so that the synthesis is not merely arbitrary but is grounded in the object itself (as I have already shown, this objective ground of possibility amounts to being able to think the subject without the

---

[4] TN. In this and the next four paragraphs, 'formally' and 'materially' are translating the Latin terms *formaliter* and *materialiter*.

[5] TN. '*der letztere hingegen stellet sich das Ganze intuitive vor*'. '*Sich vorstellen*' means 'imagine', whereas '*vorstellen*' means represent. But here 'represents to itself' is a better translation, since it would be wrong to suggest that the infinite understanding employs images.

predicate but not the reverse). The straight line can serve as an example of this as well; (3) a *definitio realis*[6] or the explanation of the way it arises. This demonstrates that the positively possible contains more reality than the merely negatively possible.

The actual is not, as some philosophers claim, an *ens omni modo determinatum*[7] because even if I should admit that everything actual is an *ens omni modo determinatum*, it would not follow from this that the reverse is true, that every *ens omni modo determinatum* must be actual. A right-angled triangle of a determinate size is certainly an *ens omni modo determinatum* but is still not actual, etc. Indeed it is doubtful whether even the first proposition is correct, namely that everything actual must be an *ens omni modo determinatum*. We have cognition of the actual only by means of | its causal connection with other things, i.e. by means of what it does or what it undergoes.[8] But what I would really like to know is what can convince me that an actual thing, gold for example, is *omni modo determinatum*? After all, its determinations are just its particular kinds of capability, its causal connection with other things, e.g., that fire can melt it, that *aqua regis* but not *aqua forti* can dissolve it,[9] etc. But all of these determinations can only be known *a posteriori* from experience, not *a priori*, so that I can only be convinced that it is *omni modo determinatum* by means of an experience continuing to infinity (but that is impossible), and so an *ens omni modo determinatum* is merely an idea. As a result, actuality needs another definition, namely this: actuality is certainly that within which I perceive a synthesis; however, this synthesis does not proceed in accordance with the laws of the understanding (the determinable and the determination), but merely in accordance with the laws of the imagination. For example, gold is a perceived synthesis of yellow colour, distinctive weight, hardness, etc. It is not a synthesis of the understanding because these characteristics can be thought without one another and hence are not in the relation of subject and predicate (the determinable and its determination); | instead they are combined only because they accompany each other in time and space. I freely admit that the synthesis of imagination must have an inner ground, i.e., an

---

[6] TN. Real definition.
[7] TN. A being determined in every way, or a completely determinate being.
[8] TN. *Wirken oder Leiden.*
[9] TN. Literally 'strong water' and 'royal water', the former referred to nitric acid and the latter to a concentrated mixture of nitric and hydrochloric acids.

understanding that is acquainted with the inner essence of gold has to construct its concept of gold so that these properties must necessarily follow from the essence; nevertheless, for us this synthesis will always remain a mere synthesis of the imagination.

The merely possible, as opposed to the actual, is the fictional [*erdichtete*], i.e. a completely arbitrary synthesis rather than one that has been perceived, for example, green colour, distinctive weight, etc. Such a synthesis does not differ in kind from actuality but merely in degree, i.e. they differ in terms of the fact that their representations are not found together in time and space so often, or in terms of the reduced forcefulness [*Stärke*] of the representations themselves.[10]

Thing in itself. Concept of a thing. The concept of a thing can be distinguished from the thing itself only with respect to completeness, either material or formal. A right-angled triangle of a determinate size brought into a construction [*in einer Construktion gebracht*] is both the thing and its concept | at the same time; on the other hand, a triangle in general is merely the concept of a triangle and not the thing itself because it still lacks determinations required for its presentation in intuition; only its material incompleteness distinguishes it from the thing itself. The thing gold is an unknown [*unbekannt*] essence with the properties of yellow colour, distinctive weight, etc. Our concept of gold is constituted by the synthesis of the properties and this concept is distinguished from the thing itself only because of its formal incompleteness (our lack of insight into the objective connection of these properties), etc.

The claim that everything actual is possible, signifies three things: (1) the actual must not be positively impossible, in other words, the actual must not contain a contradiction; (2) the actual must not be positively possible for us [*in Ansehung unserer*],[11] i.e. we must not be able to comprehend the synthesis made by the imagination; (3) the actual must be positively possible in itself, i.e. it must in itself be grounded in a synthesis of the understanding.

---

[10] TN. Maimon seems to be hinting at a comparison between his distinction between the actual and the fictional and Hume's distinction between impressions and ideas: the former only differing from the latter through possessing a greater degree of vivacity or forcefulness.

[11] TN. '*In Ansehung unserer*'. As in a similar usage of this phrase in the previous chapter Maimon has omitted the feminine noun which '*unserer*' ('our') would be expected to qualify; one possibility would be 'for our reason' but we have preferred to simply leave this open by translating the phrase as 'for us'.

The claim that the impossible cannot be actual does not signify that the constituent parts of an actual synthesis must not contradict one another (in fact they cannot contradict one another because each of them can be represented in itself, | whereas contradictory things are only contradictory in relation to one another). Instead the meaning is this: each of the parts must not be self-contradictory, as for example when one says: a golden square sphere.[12]

The actual is opposed (1) **to the impossible**, of which we have *formally*[13] **positive cognition**; in this case the claim that everything actual is possible is correct. (2) **To the problematic** in so far as the synthesis of the actual is not wholly arbitrary, but a real synthesis of the imagination in time and space (although it is not a synthesis of the understanding). (3) **To the material nothing**. (4) **To the necessary**. The necessary is opposed to all of these, and is explained by what has already been said.

The ground of an object is a rule or condition according to which an object can be represented. The object itself is what is grounded in the rule. For example, the understanding prescribes itself a rule or condition to draw an infinite number of equal lines from a given point; a circle | can be presented in accordance with this rule by means of the connection of the endpoints. In this case, the equality of the lines is the ground and the circle what is grounded. But this ground remains insufficient for the grounded (the object) to arise until the understanding has in turn managed to discover [*ausfündig gemacht hat*] its ground (the rule or condition for the equality of the lines, i.e. through the movement of a line around one of its endpoints). So the ground is a concept of the

---

[12] TN. This claim can be understood in the light of the theory of determination expounded in Chapter 4. According to Maimon all *actual* syntheses are 'one-sided', i.e. are of subject and predicate (determinable and determination); because of this the two components of the synthesis cannot contradict one another, a contradiction can only be present if one of these components is self-contradictory. Turning to the example of a golden square sphere, here 'golden' is the predicate and 'square sphere' the self-contradictory subject. Implicit here is Maimon's rejection of the classical example of a contradiction, 'a square sphere' where 'sphere' is the subject and 'square' the predicate, subject and predicate thus appearing to contradict one another; according to Maimon's doctrine of determination this synthesis is not impossible because it is contradictory but because it is badly formed – 'square' and 'spherical' are both determinations of 'delimited space' and hence cannot determine one another.

[13] TN. formaliter

understanding; but the sufficient ground[14] is merely an idea of reason, which we can approach ever more closely (and in so doing extend the use of reason), but can never reach.

The ground of a cognition (of a judgement) in the strictest sense is a universal judgement regarded as the major premise [of a syllogism] with the given judgement as the conclusion so that the latter becomes an analytic proposition.[15] 'Ground' in a broader sense is just the subject regarded as the condition of a judgement that is thus merely a synthetic judgement. The first kind of ground is expressed by '**because**' and the second by '**if**'. A triangle is a triangle **because** every thing is identical with itself; a straight line is the shortest between two points, that is to say, **if** a line is straight then, etc. The definitions of mathematics are conditions but not grounds (in the strictest sense) of propositions. If judgements precede concepts, or if judgements express relations that are definitions of concepts (as do all pure judgements *a priori*, according to my account), then they are subjectively analytic judgements but objectively synthetic judgements. For example, every cause has an effect; this synthesis of cause and effect is not analytic (considered objectively) because cause and effect are not identical, nevertheless they must be thought together (by the thinking subject [*in Ansehung des Subjekts des Denkens*]) because they define one another reciprocally.

Moreover, the term 'ground' is also used merely of cognition without regard to the existence of a thing, as has already been mentioned; in this usage it signifies a previously attained cognition considered as the condition of a new cognition. If this new cognition does not concern the thinkability [of the objects] in general, but rather the mode of existence of the objects, then this ground is called a **cause**. I will explain it using examples: the sum of the angles of a triangle is equal to two right angles. This is a new cognition: its ground is an already attained cognition, namely that a thing is equal to itself, and that if two parallel lines are cut by a third, the corresponding angles are equal. So in this case the

---

[14] TN. '*zureichender Grund*'. The Leibnizian concept traditionally translated as 'sufficient reason'. To avoid confusion '*Grund*' has usually been translated as 'ground' and '*Vernunft*' always by 'reason' (although in appropriate cases where there was no risk of confusion '*Grund*' has been translated as 'reason').

[15] TN. '*das als Obersatz von den gegebenen Urtheil, als Schlusssatz gedacht wird*'. The meaning of this, using the example Maimon offers in the next sentence, would be: major premise: all things are identical to themselves; minor premise: a triangle is a thing; conclusion: a triangle is a triangle (*because* all things are identical to themselves).

antecedent is the **condition** of the consequent in this new judgement, and the preceding judgement the **ground** of this new judgement. On the other hand, if I am looking for the ground of the following judgement: 'if a comes first, then b must necessarily follow', which concerns the existence of these objects, then this means that I am looking for its cause. If I do not find this ground or cause in any already attained cognition, then in this case there is no ground or cause (because to say that a thing is cause of itself is to say no more than that it has no cause) and the antecedent is instead the condition of the consequent, as in the following judgement for example: the straight line is the shortest between two points. So it is an error to say that in the hypothetical judgement, 'if a precedes then b must necessarily follow', the preceding a is the cause of the following b; instead is it merely its **condition**. There is in fact no **cause** in this case. As a result, this judgement cannot be used of things in themselves, because in this case a is not determined as condition. Instead we would have to express ourselves in this way: 'what is the ground or the cause, that if a precedes, b | must follow?' The answer to this would be: 'it is necessarily so', that is to say it has in fact no ground or cause. It is the same as asking: 'what is the reason [*Grund*] that the straight line is the shortest between two points?', the reply is: 'because it is a straight line', that is to say the ground of the predicate is in the subject itself; or to be more exact, this judgement does not in fact have any ground, that is to say, there is no universal judgement from which this can be deduced as from some prior cognition. So it is strange that we think we know the ground of a judgement in placing it in its own subject, since it is precisely in doing this that we demonstrate that do not know it.

Chapter 6
Identity, Difference, Opposition, Reality, Logical and Transcendental Negation

Identity and difference. These concepts have a more general usage than the categories. Identity and opposition refer[1] to a thing in general: *a* is identical with *a*, *a* is opposed to *non a*.[2] Although difference does not refer to a thing in general, this is not to say that it refers (by means of conditions) to determined things; rather it refers merely to determinable things; on the other hand, the categories refer to things determined by conditions. Identity, difference, etc. are relational concepts [*Verhältnißbegriffe*][3] so that one cannot be thought without the other. To say that

---

[1] TN. The verb 'to refer' throughout this paragraph translates '*sich beziehen auf*', which accurately translates the standard meaning of this verb. However, the usage here suggests that Maimon is not making any principled distinction between 'is referred to', 'relates to' and 'applies to'.

[2] TN. Not *a*.

[3] TN. See the first paragraph of Chapter 5 where Maimon asserts that relational concepts are reciprocally determining. In the next paragraph of this chapter he goes on to say that identity is defined as lack of difference and in Chapter 7 states that identity and difference, like all relational concepts, are reciprocally defining. Thus substance and accident, cause and effect, identity and difference, unity and plurality are all reciprocally defining pairs of relational concepts, and further all concepts of the understanding are, according to Maimon, of this kind. A glance at Kant's table of categories (A80/B106) will show how differently Kant arranges things (only substance/accident, cause/effect and community are called relational concepts; unity/plurality, and reality/negation are not correlates as are the pairs of relational concepts but separate categories; identity and difference are excluded from the table of categories as mere reflective concepts of comparison). Maimon's basis for treating all the categories in this same way is that they are all syntheses that unite under a relation while at the same time determining their terms as different.

63

a and *b* are identical is only true in a certain respect; in another respect they must necessarily be thought as different (in as much as they are more than one thing). Even to say that a thing is identical with itself is at least to consider it twice, i.e. at different times; and this temporal difference makes the thing in a certain respect different from itself. We can be certain that a concept is completely identical with itself, but not that an object is (i.e. a concept grounded in an intuition); besides the temporal difference in thought, an object can also differ with respect to the concept itself, i.e. we can make an error in judgement. In addition, no objects can be completely different without at the same time also being identical in a certain respect; the reason is that otherwise they would not just be different, but opposed, and this would mean that we are not comparing two objects, but one object with nothing, if we accept Baumgarten's definition[4] (if there is something in *a* that is not in *b*). It follows from this definition that either all things are identical and merely differ in magnitude, i.e. are similar, or *a* must contain an infinite number of distinguishing marks. The former follows if we take $b = \frac{a}{n}$; the latter if we suppose $a = \alpha \beta$, $b = \alpha$. For if *a* has two marks $\alpha \beta$, then α must in turn be different from β, and so on *ad infinitum*.[5]

Difference is not actually a special form in its own right, but signifies simply lack of identity, or of objective unity, despite the fact that the *actus* of the relation of objects to one another is always a subjective unity of consciousness. In fact, as with all relational concepts, it cannot be defined without circularity; relational concepts are universal forms of thought by means of which the understanding brings unity to the manifold. In themselves (abstracted from their *a priori* forms, time and space) intuitions can no more be described as identical than as different (here the Kantian question: *quid juris?* is totally unanswerable), unless it is with respect to their differentials or elements, as I have shown above. We can apply these concepts only to the forms of intuitions, or on my account, to their differentials, and by this means to the intuitions themselves. So only *a priori* concepts or ideas can be judged identical or different, and intuitions can be judged only by means of their forms, namely in terms of whether they are in one and the same time and space or not.[6]

---

[4] TN. Baumgarten, *Metaphysica*, §38.
[5] TN. The original has: '*Denn wenn a zwei Merkmale βα hat, so muss wiederum a von b verschieden sein, u.s.w. ins Unendliche*', which seems to be a mistake.
[6] TN. '*in so fern sie nämlich in einerlei Zeit und Raum sind, oder nicht.*'

Opposition [*Gegensetzung*][7] is also a relational concept and its mutually relating terms or *extrema* are reality and negation. These concepts are derived from the universal logical functions of affirmation and negation [*Verneinung*][8] and these in turn teach us nothing about the matter or the content of judgements (subject and predicate), but merely express their form, or the way they relate to one another. We also make these forms themselves into objects of thought, and think reality and negation as if they were things in themselves that are given to us. Opposition, (as what these two extremes have in common in relation to one another), reality and negation (as the *extrema* themselves), cannot be understood independently of one another; this is no more possible than to think magnitude in general without greater and smaller (the ingredients of the definition of magnitude), or these in turn without one another, and without magnitude in general. So it is inconsistent to say (as is customarily done) that reality and negation are opposed to one another, | for negation is the correlate of reality, and correlates can never be opposed to one another; i.e. one does not cancel out [*aufheben*] the other, but they are instead defined by one another. Thus to say that negation is opposed to reality is like saying that the effect is opposed to the cause. But if negation is understood not merely as the cancelling [*Hebung*] of reality but the concept of cancelling in general, then to say that reality is opposed to negation is like saying that the concept of greater or smaller is opposed to the concept of magnitude in general when in fact the latter cannot be thought without the former because magnitude in general is what is common to the two correlates (greater and smaller). So in this case too, opposition is what the two correlates reality and negation have in common: this is exactly the nature of such relational concepts and what distinguishes them from all other products of the understanding. That is to say that for those other products of the understanding, the concepts

---

[7] TN. This word does not occur in the *Critique*. Kant uses *Entgegensetzung* for the opposition of reality to negation discussed in the Schematism (A143/B182), and *Widerstreit* for opposition as opposed to agreement – the second of the four pairs of concepts of reflection discussed in the Amphiboly (A260/B316 ff), the first pair being identity and difference.

[8] TN. In the *Critique*, *Bejahende* (affirmative) and *Verneinende* (negative) are two of the three possible qualities of judgement and as such are logical categories (Kant also uses their substantive forms *Bejahung* (affirmation) and *Verneinung* (negation)), while *Realitaet* (reality) and *Negation* (negation) are their corresponding transcendental categories of quality. In this chapter 'negation' has been used to translate both '*Negation*' and '*Verneinung*', but where the German is the latter it has been included in brackets.

precede the judgement, i.e., in order to judge or to grasp the relations and connections of these things, or to determine the form by means of the copula, we must first acquire the concepts of the subject in itself and of the object in itself, i.e., the matter precedes the form; but with relational concepts it is only by means of judgements that we acquire concepts of subject and predicate in the first place, i.e., the form precedes the matter, or to speak more correctly, they both arise at the same time.

There are no other grounds besides this for saying that logical reality is opposed to logical negation. The reason is that these forms or acts of affirming and negating [*Verneinens*] are themselves not just opposed to one another, i.e. to posit the one is not merely to cancel the other, but the one is instead a different positing from the other. It is also impossible to make this claim about the objects of logical opposition because logic does not distinguish between its objects; we can make it only about transcendental objects, in so far as the one is thought with the subject of thought[9] under the form of affirmation, and the other under the form of negation [*Verneinung*]. I will explain this matter in more detail. Reality and negation are as much logical (affirmation and negation [*Verneinung*]) as transcendental (something and nothing). In the first case they are the two universal forms of judgement, or ways that objects are related to one another; they are in fact forms of the forms themselves, and this in two ways: either through being ways that forms are related to one another, as when I say that accidents belong to a substance (this is a relation of affirmation between substance and accidents, and these are themselves in turn explained by means of relations, etc.); or by virtue of constituting the universal, itself determined in different ways by the forms. For example, if I say: a is the cause of b, then this is as much as to say: I determine the universal form of affirmation by means of cause, etc.; and if I say: a is not the cause of b, then I determine the universal form of negation [*Verneinung*] by means of cause, etc.; i.e. if I say: a is not the cause of b, then in so doing I leave the relation of the objects to one another undetermined, but for me the positive thought that a is not the cause of b is a relation of these things to my faculty of thought. In the second case they are indeed logical relations but merely of something to the subject of thought and not of objects to one

---

[9] TN. '*in so fern das eine mit dem Subjekt des Denkens*'. That '*mit*' ('with') here means 'in relation to' is suggested by the use of the phrase '*in Beziehung auf der Vorstellungskraft*' ('in relation to the power of representation') with apparently the same meaning in the next paragraph.

another. So in this sense, reality is a something subsumed under logical affirmation for the subject; whereas a negative thing is a something subsumed under the relation of negation [*Verneinung*].

The concept of the act of negation [*Verneinung*] is, like that of affirmation, a transcendental reality; and if we say that reality and negation are opposed to one another, then we must understand by these terms not logical but transcendental reality and negation, i.e. we compare what in relation to the power of representation is subsumed under the form of affirmation with what is subsumed under the form of negation [*Verneinung*], and then we subsume them both under the form of logical negation [*Verneinung*] (opposition). But if we should want to claim that logical reality and negation are opposed to one another, then this would be meaningless. The reason is that logical negation [*Verneinung*] is nothing other than opposition, and so a constituent part of the matter of the judgement (opposition) would at the same time be its form, and this would mean about as much as if we were to say, for example, that the concept of identity is identical with a, which is completely senseless.

Logical reality is as much a subjective as an objective synthesis or relation of objects to one another. On the other hand, logical negation is merely a subjective relation of objects to one another because I cancel the relation of objects to one another by means of this very negation. So logical reality is fruitful [*fruchtbar*], i.e. it produces an object, whereas logical negation is sterile [*unfruchtbar*]. If I say that a is or can be b (a triangle is or can be right-angled), then a new concept ab (a right-angled triangle) arises from this. On the other hand, when I say a is not b, no object arises from this.

Transcendental reality is a something that can be brought into a relation of logical reality with the power of representation. But transcendental negation is a something that can be brought into a relation of logical negation with transcendental reality as well as with the power of representation. As I have already shown, the *minimum* of transcendental reality is an idea of the understanding; but transcendental negation is an idea of reason. The failure to distinguish between these two kinds of reality and negation has led to two important errors. 1) The error already mentioned, namely that these logical forms have been treated as opposed when they are merely different. 2) That transcendental reality is regarded as something in itself and outside the power of representation, when in fact it is merely a special relation of something in general to the subject of thought.

Chapter 7
Magnitude

Magnitude is either plurality thought as unity or unity thought as plurality. In the former case the magnitude is extensive and in the latter, intensive.

To construct [*machen*] the concept of an extensive magnitude requires the following: (1) given sensible representations that are different (in terms of the forms of intuition)[1] but homogeneous (in terms of their concept), and that are (2) gathered together in a concept and (3) gathered together in an intuition. But to construct the concept of an intensive magnitude requires: (1) a sensible intuition that (2) is compared with another intuition homogeneous to it. For example, two drops of water are different in terms of intuition[2] (in terms of their spatial relation or position [*Ort*]), | but homogeneous in terms of their concept. Taking these together in an intuition constitutes the concept of extensive magnitude. On the other hand, a determined red is an individual intuition and comparing it with another determined red produces the concept of intensive magnitude or of degree. Now time and space are the forms of intuition and these are by their nature extensive magnitudes (because in both of them we perceive a taking together of different but homogeneous representations: in time, the preceding and the succeeding; in space, the

---

[1] TN. '*der Formen Anschauung nach*'. Maimon requested the interpolation of '*Formen*' in the errata to the original publication, we are assuming he meant to interpolate '*Formen der*'.

[2] TN. For consistency it seems likely that Maimon would have wanted to have changed this too to read 'in terms of the forms (or form) of intuition'. (See first footnote to this chapter).

right and the left, etc.). As a result, intuitions themselves must be extensive magnitudes in accordance with these forms. But in addition, the material (real) [*Materiale* (*reelle*)] can also be compared to something else homogeneous with it (irrespective of form). In this case it has an intensive magnitude. In an extensive magnitude plurality is given, but unity is thought (through abstraction); in an intensive magnitude, on the other hand, it is the reverse. The extensive magnitude is, so to speak, the schema of the intensive magnitude because intensive magnitude, along with its relations, cannot be perceived directly and in itself but only by means of extensive magnitude. For example, the different degrees of | heat and cold are perceived by means of the rising and falling of a thermometer: it is given as a unity and thought as a plurality through comparison. With quanta, intensive magnitude is the differential of the extensive, and the extensive is, in turn, the integral of the intensive. For example, if I say that a right-angled, an obtuse-angled and an acute-angled triangle are all triangles, then a right-angled, an acute-angled [triangle], etc. comprise a plurality because they exclude one another so that they are incapable of being thought at the same time: unity is thought only through abstraction. On the other hand, if I say that a triangle can equally well be right-angled or obtuse-angled as acute-angled, then in this case there is a unity (triangle). The reason is that the '*can be*' must be thought at once along with right-angled, obtuse and acute; but in relation to actuality they must be thought as a plurality. The first plurality can be compared with the extensive, the second with the intensive. A right- obtuse- and acute-angled triangle is an inner plurality (without comparing it to anything else) because the thought of one excludes the thought of the others. On the other hand, a triangle in general is an inner unity; it contains plurality only potentially, and this plurality is thought externally, i.e. | by comparison with the mutually exclusive determinations that can still be added to it. A line with determinate magnitude contains an inner plurality: for example, if a line of 10 inches is to be drawn, then a line of one, two, three, etc., inches must be drawn first. But with, for example, a determinate degree of heat, no plurality is found in the object itself, its heat must be compared with another object in order to perceive this plurality.

Chapter 8
Alteration, Change, etc.[1]

If each of two representations or concepts is capable of being thought in itself, then they cannot be thought together in a synthesis. A synthesis is only possible if one of its constituent parts cannot be thought without the other. This can take place either one-sidedly – as with the synthesis of the subject and predicate (determinable and determination) of an absolute concept – or reciprocally as with the synthesis of the correlates of a relational concept. Black and a circle cannot be thought in synthesis (black circle) because each of them is capable of being thought in itself. In the realm of possibility they are both independent of one another for all time, or to speak more precisely, independent of time. By contrast, a synthesis of the understanding is to be found in a | straight line. For although 'line' can be thought in itself, being straight cannot be thought without 'line', so being straight can only be thought by means of this synthesis. This synthesis is thus at least one-sidedly necessary. Despite being different, cause and effect define one another, and so cannot be thought without one another. The synthesis (that a cause has an effect and the reverse) is thus reciprocally necessary: they must both be thought at the same time (without temporal sequence). By contrast, a triangle cannot be thought as right-angled and oblique-angled at the same time, but only in a temporal sequence.

---

[1] TN. Throughout this chapter, 'alteration' and 'change' translate respectively *'Veränderung'* and *'Wechsel'*, and similarly with their cognate verbs, 'to alter' translates *'verändern'*, 'to change' *wechseln*. Maimon is following Kant's usage in the First Analogy (A187/B230), and our choice of English words agrees with Guyer and Wood's translation according to which substances are said to *alter* when their states *change*.

The preceding and the succeeding in time itself are correlates of time, and as a result they cannot be represented without one another because they are what they are only in relation to one another. Change means: succession of determinations one after the other in time; alteration is the relation of the determinable to these successive determinations, in other words it is the synthesis of the very same determinable with different and mutually exclusive determinations in a temporal sequence; it is derived from the logical | function in disjunctive judgements, but can be perceived only as in a temporal sequence (its schema).[2] Time itself is not altered because its different determinations (the preceding and the succeeding) do not change (if they did, another time would have to be assumed in which this change was perceived), and the reason for this is that time cannot be thought without both these determinations. Time is represented neither by the preceding in itself, nor by the succeeding in itself, but only by their relation to one another; from this it follows that something determinable must be connected with different determinations in a temporal sequence in order to represent an alteration, i.e. change of determinations. If I should want to represent an alteration not only as possible (e.g. a triangle that is first right-angled, and then oblique-angled), but also as given to me, then something must be given that persists in time (substance), and this must be of such a kind that it can be represented in itself without relation to any determination; and this substance must be perceived in a synthesis with different determinations succeeding one another in time, i.e. with changing determinations. But if the order of these different | syntheses in time is arbitrary (i.e. it is arbitrary which precedes and which follows), then there will be no difference between a merely possible subjective synthesis and an actual objective synthesis; and if, for example, I perceived a triangular body become round, I would think the delimited space [*beschränkter Raum*] as in two different states in a temporal sequence (the very same determinable with two different determinations); this is the basis for the following judgement: 'in terms of its form, i.e. as a delimited space, a body can be thought as both triangular and round in a temporal

---

[2] TN. There is a notable divergence from Kant here, in that Kant in the *Critique* derives the category of *community* (simultaneous interaction of substances) from the logical form of the disjunctive judgement, whereas Maimon here describes *alteration* (succession of mutually exclusive determinations of a substance) as deriving from the schematizing of disjunctive judgement.

sequence'; but it is not the basis for the judgement that it actually is so. So in this case I would have only perceptions succeeding one another in time and these are objects of sensibility and imagination that I would connect according to the subjective laws of my mode of representation [*Vorstellungsart*]; but I would have no experience, i.e. no perception of something that would determine what is left undetermined by the subjective laws of my mode of representation. For just as I can imagine a body first as triangular and then round, I can also imagine in time, and just as I can imagine water as first fluid and then | solid (frozen), so I could also do the reverse, etc. So, if I am to have experience, then these perceptions must not be undetermined with respect to their sequence but rather determined according to a rule of the understanding, i.e. it must not be the case that any possible appearance follows every possible appearance, but rather one out of all the other possible appearances must necessarily follow. As has already been shown, the determination of appearances (as to which of them is to come first and which is to follow) must not be thought as in them *materialiter*[3] because this would raise the question *quid juris?*, i.e. how can we presuppose something given *a posteriori* (the material determination of appearances) to be *a priori* congruent [*konguierend*] with a rule of the understanding (the necessity of the sequence)? Rather, it must be thought only *formaliter*, i.e. if I perceive something preceding and something necessarily following it (without looking to their matter, but to the particular determination of succession in general), then I judge that the succession of these objects one after the other | is objective (whether the perception is itself correct amounts to the answer to the question *quid facti?* It is based only on the power of judgement [*Beurtheilungskraft*] and no further rules can be given for this).[4] And where this is not the case, the succession is merely subjective (because with respect to my subject this succession is not necessary but merely possible). This is shown in the previously cited examples where the different syntheses of the triangle, and the different states of the water considered in themselves, are merely subjective. By contrast, there is a

---

[3] TN. Throughout this paragraph *materialiter* and *formaliter* are the Latin terms for 'materially' and 'formally'.

[4] TN. Maimon's uses '*Beurtheilungskraft*' here as an apparent equivalent of Kant's '*Urteilskraft*' (see translator's note to Chapter 2). In the 'Analytic of Principles' (A132-3/B171-2) Kant defines the power of judgement [*Urteilskraft*] as the faculty of subsuming under rules, and argues that no further (second-order) rules can be provided to govern this activity.

necessity connected with the actual perception of fluidity following heat and of solidity following cold, from which I judge that heat makes the water fluid (is the cause), cold makes it solid etc.

A universal law of nature with respect to objects of experience follows from this. Everything that happens (objectively or actually)[5] must follow necessarily upon something preceding; if not, if it merely follows contingently, then it does not happen objectively or actually, but is merely a play of the imagination. So we cannot have any objects of experience, and consequently we cannot have any experience (objective connection of these objects of experience) unless we apply the concept of cause to objects of perception. I will explain this more precisely. The concepts of reflection, identity and difference,[6] are the highest (most universal) forms of thought because the use of the categories properly so called extends only to objects of experience (to the objective reality of subjective perception), while the use of these concepts of reflection extends not only to objects of experience but also to objects of perception itself. Consciousness in general rests on unity in the manifold; something manifold must be given, the understanding relates this together [*auf einander bezieht*] by means of some concept (unity of identity); or in other words, something must be given that is thought by the understanding as a manifold (through unity of difference), i.e. either the unity in the manifold is objective (as identity) or subjective (as difference). For example, two objects *a* and *b* are each given in themselves. Consciousness of them requires: 1) subjective unity of consciousness (that *a* is given to the same subject as *b* is; if this were not so, then there could not be any relation between the given objects). 2) Objective unity, i.e. something must be found in these objects that destines them for this relation. Again, this can take place in two ways: either by this means the objects are thought together merely with regard to the subject, or they are thought

---

[5] TN. '*objektive wirklich*', 'or' has been inserted on the assumption that these adverbs are being used almost as synonyms and as independently qualifying their verb ('objectively actually' might suggest on the contrary that 'objectively' was qualifying 'actually').

[6] Opposition is only a logical form and no intuition can be subsumed as matter under it; that is to say, this unity is merely subjective because only a negation is opposed to reality and no intuition can be given to a negation. The opposed directions in the movement of two bodies are only different not opposed because they do not cancel one another in different objects, i.e. as long as both preserve their movement; if they collide with one another, however, so that their movement ceases, then there is once again no opposition because there is only negation with negation.

in themselves as a unity (the ground of this particular relation must be found not in the subject alone but also in the objects since the understanding has more than one form or mode of relation of things to one another).

Difference and identity are the forms of perceptions in general (of individual sensible intuitions). When a perception, for example **red**, is given to me, I do not yet have any consciousness of it; when another, for example **green**, is given to me, I do not yet have any consciousness of it in itself either. But if I relate them to one another (by means of the unity of difference), then I notice that red is different from green, and so I attain consciousness of each of the perceptions in itself. If I constantly had the representation red, for example, without having any other representation, then I could never attain consciousness of it. This is certainly true with respect to our consciousness; however, as I have already shown above, it is also true that I cannot attain consciousness of any individual intuition without the concept of the identity of individual sensible representations by means of which they can be taken together in an intuition. Indeed I cannot do so without consciousness of this identity because the consciousness of an intuition presupposes the presence of objects, but objects can only arise through this identity.

The forms of concepts in general are identity (unity in the manifold), but also difference, by means of which the manifold is thought as a manifold. For example, suppose that two triangles are given to me (they are determined differently and hence are two triangles and not one). I relate them to one another and notice that they are both triangles, i.e. that they are identical. | The concept of triangle in general arises from this. So let us see what must necessarily follow from these forms or conditions of our consciousness. The difference in our perceptions, i.e. being outside one another in time and space, makes the forms of our sensibility necessary (I speak here as a Leibnizian, who treats time and space as universal undetermined concepts of reflection that must have an objective ground); in other words, the form of sensibility is a schema of this difference, and through it this difference is determined *a priori*; i.e. what is given *materialiter*[7] as different, can also only be thought *formaliter* as different. The reason for this is that, although form precedes matter, i.e.

---

[7] TN. Throughout this paragraph *materialiter* and *formaliter* are the Latin terms for 'materially' and 'formally'.

our mode of representation (the constitution of our mind) determines the representation itself, it is nevertheless the reverse with respect to our consciousness, in other words, in this case consciousness of the form presupposes the matter (because unless something determined is given to us, we cannot attain consciousness of the form). Being outside one another in time and space has its ground in the difference between things, i.e. the imagination, which is the ape of the understanding, represents the things *a* and *b* as external to one another in | time and space because the understanding thinks them as different. So this concept of the understanding is the imagination's guiding principle and it must not lose sight of it if its procedure is to be legitimate; but if it does lose sight of it, then it falls into fictions no longer subject to any rule of the understanding. The concept of **being different** is more universal than that of **being outside one another** because the latter applies only to intuitions whereas the former can be applied to concepts as well, i.e. everything that is different must be perceived in intuition in space and time, but not the reverse. So if we nevertheless still represent in space things like water that are identical in intuition, this takes place only in relation to something different, i.e. the representation is transcendent. It is the same with time: if I have slept for, say, a few hours, then I can only perceive the time by means of the different position of the hands of a clock for example; but time and space exist merely in perception and hence are not there where they are not perceived. So the original (the objective) necessarily determines the copy (the subjective) with respect to | existence, but not the reverse, even though at times there is no way for us to have cognition of the original other than by means of the copy, as for instance we have cognition of the category from out of a determinate temporal sequence. The latter is thus the ideal ground of the former, but the former the real ground of the latter. The imagination is used in a transcendent manner when it imagines [*die Einbildungskraft sich vorstellt*] a series of things that are identical by concept in a sequence in time and space, i.e. it transfers its form from a real matter to an imagined matter (in which the understanding does not notice any difference). Each of us can perceive in ourselves that in order to represent things that are identical in a sequence in time and space we are compelled to relate them to things that are different; if we did not, then this representation would be impossible. So although time and space are forms of our sensibility, they presuppose forms of the understanding and these in turn presuppose something objective (matter). In this case, the question *quid juris?* is not

75

applicable because these forms are conditions of perceptions, and on this ground the question of our right to subsume objects under their forms (time and space) must be inapplicable as well. |

The concept of continuity in time and space is also derived from the continuity of difference between things. The reason is that if I had only one representation and it was identical to itself (and without determinate duration), then I would not be able to attain consciousness of it. So I would not have a concept of difference, and hence I would also not have any representation of temporal sequence. Or again, suppose that I had nothing but different representations (i.e. none of them lasting for any time, but such that one could say of them that they were self-identical at different points in time), then again I would not have any consciousness. Consequently, with respect to sensibility, duration for some time [*Dauer einiger Zeit*] is necessary for consciousness, and with respect to the understanding this is identity in difference. Duration, i.e. the unalterability of something, cannot be imagined without the determination of some period of time [*einiger Zeit*], i.e. by means of its relation to something alterable (through which the representation of temporal sequence arises). Nothing can be thought as self-identical without being related to things different from one another [*auf etwas von einander verschiedenes zu beziehen*] (substance to its accidents, for example); so in the same way, to be able to represent an object as at the same time identical with and different from itself, | i.e. as altering and enduring in time, this difference must be assumed to be as small as possible, so that the time in which the object remains self-identical can be imagined only by means of this difference. In other words, every alteration must be continuous because if this is not the case, then we would no longer be able to tell whether it was the same object that is altered or a quite different [*anderer*] object and so the concept of alteration would become meaningless.

Experience is the perception of the very same persisting thing [*Beharrlichen*] connected with different determinations that are changing in time. This presupposes firstly the concept of the persisting (substance) and then of the changing [*Wechselnden*] (accident); it further presupposes the necessary succession of determinations one after the other (cause and effect). We cannot say that cold water has become sweet, but we can say that it has become warm, i.e. in order to constitute an experience, it is not enough to perceive the substance in connection with any arbitrary determinations that change in time, but only with those that are related to one another by excluding one another in the very same substance:

however, to preserve | self-identity, this exclusion must be *minimal*. The perception that the water is cold and afterwards that it is sweet indeed contains a subjective succession of determinations, but not an objective one, because both these determinations can be united in one object, i.e. they can exist at the same time, whereas the same water cannot be hot and cold at the same time. If this self-excluding synthesis [*diese sich ausschliessende Synthesis*] is indeed perceived, then it can only be represented by means of the change of these determinations over time. So the mode of change necessary for experience is determined: the preceding determination is the cause of the one that follows, or the latter presupposes the former because without succession in general, indeed without determined succession, no experience is possible.

But to be perceived in intuition a determination must be something positive (since a negative determination is merely logical) and yet the determination that follows must be opposed to the preceding one; but what is opposed to something positive cannot be anything but something negative, and these two opposed qualities are nevertheless necessary to experience: in order | to overcome this contradiction and consequently to make experience possible, they must therefore be united in the object so that they make the least break [*Abbruch*], i.e. their opposition must be a *minimum*. In this case therefore we have experience, i.e. perception of the same persisting thing connected with different determinations that change over time. These determinations are at the same time also positive because the observed opposition between them (which is necessary to experience) is the smallest possible, and this is the so-called **principle of continuity**.[8]

This principle is accordingly not, as is customarily assumed, an experiential principle,[9] i.e. merely abstracted from experience, but an *a priori* principle, through which experience is first made possible. When we notice that something happens suddenly (without continuity), if for example a small child were to instantaneously turn into a giant, then we cannot persuade ourselves that it is the same thing, and has only altered,

---

[8] TN. '*Satz der Stetigkeit*'. Note that although '*Satz*' has usually been translated by 'proposition', in this context, as with '*Satz des Widerspruchs*' (principle of contradiction) it has been rendered as 'principle'; in the next paragraph 'principle' also translates '*Satz*'.

[9] TN. '*Erfahrungssatz*'. Note that here and elsewhere that Maimon uses this term as a synonym for 'empirical proposition'. In Kant's terminology, an 'experiential' (as opposed to an 'empirical') principle would imply a principle involving the application of *a priori* concepts, rather than a principle abstracted from experience.

rather we rather think they are different things (in this case where the difference is so great, the similarity does not matter); it is just as impossible for us to believe that Peter and Paul are same person because the universal concept of person is identical in both of them, and were we to see before us first Peter and then Paul in his place, we would not judge that Peter had become Paul, but that Peter had disappeared and Paul had taken his place (without us knowing how).

This leads us to search for the cause of this appearance, i.e. the continuity in it, and to fill in the gaps in our perceptions in order to make them into experiences. For what else is understood by the word 'cause' in the doctrine of nature than the development of an appearance and its resolution [*Auflösung*], so that between it and the preceding appearance the desired continuity is found. Everyone can explain this for themselves by means of countless examples, so I do not need to dwell on it.

If I do not find this continuity in the succession of determinations of the very same determinable, then I resort to another determinable and look for this continuity between two successive determinations; as for example if I say: the father is the cause of the son (he goes along with the development of the whole process),[10] or the fire warms the stone. This gives rise to the distinction between having a cause in itself or outside itself. Representations of the soul are of the first kind when they carry on uninterrupted, following the law of association; but if they are interrupted by an outer sensation they belong to the second kind. Continuity is still always to be found in them; however it must not be sought in the connection of the present representation with the preceding, but rather in the analogy between bodily movements and sensations, and rests on the question *de commercio animi et corporis*.[11]

This latter kind gives us the representation of necessary simultaneity, just as the former gives us the representation of necessary succession. Since representations are always successive we cannot know whether the objects succeed one another in themselves as they do in our subject (if we were to find that this succession was merely arbitrary, in the sense that we could also represent it in the reverse order, then this reversed order of succession must happen in another time than the preceding one so that in each time only one kind of succession can be actual). But we can

---

[10] TN. '*versteht sich mit*'. This phrase means to 'get along with' (usually a person).
[11] TN. Of the interaction of mind and body.

recognize this by means of the following distinguishing mark: when we find an appearance whose determination cannot be made continuous with the preceding determination of the very same appearance but only with that of another appearance, then we judge that the determinations do not follow one another (in the very same determinable) but that they are simultaneous (in different determinables). From this it follows that a determinable (subject) can have two mutually exclusive determinations (predicates) in a temporal sequence where one is something real [*eine Realität*] and the other is its negation (in accordance with the principle of continuity as has already been mentioned); but, on the other hand, it cannot have two determinations in a temporal sequence that are not mutually exclusive, as has already been demonstrated. But I also maintain that it cannot have two mutually exclusive determinations at the same time, and I will demonstrate this in the following way.

A determination in general is something that cannot be thought in itself, but only as a determination in relation to the determinable. So let us assume that a determinable A has two simultaneous determinations b and c; c is either an indirect or a direct determination of A, i.e. either c is a determination of b, and this in turn of A, or c is not a determination of b, but both are direct determinations of A. In the first case A has in fact only one determination, b, and the latter also only one determination, c. But in the second case b and c can each be thought without the other (otherwise they would have to be determinations of one another, contrary to the hypothesis), so that I can think Ab in itself and Ac in itself. But then where does the necessary synthesis of all three, Abc, arise? It is true that if b is to be thought, it must be thought in a synthesis with A, and the same is true of c (from the nature of determination). But why must they be thought at the same time in this synthesis, since they are in fact not determinations of each other? Consequently this synthesis is totally arbitrary, i.e. the determinable, A, cannot have two determinations b, c at the same time. I have already shown (in Chapter 4, s. 89) that the reverse is also true, one and the same determination cannot belong to different determinables.

It follows from this that a substance is also incapable of having two different accidents at the same time (it cannot be brought into experience). The reason is that if one accident cannot be thought without the other, then the former is an accident of the latter, but it is not directly an accident of the substance; if each of them can be thought without the other, then the substance must be represented along with each of them successively and so they cannot be perceived in the same substance at the same time.

Chapter 9
Truth, Subjective, Objective, Logical, Metaphysical

First of all, truth and falsity cannot be applied to thoughts, but only to signs *qua* signs, or expression *qua* expression (in relation to thoughts). For example, 'a right-angled triangle' is a true concept because in this expression I actually think the triangle as something determinable and being right-angled as its determination, and gain insight into their unity or the real connection between subject and predicate (determinable and determination). Consequently this expression has a meaning, and is therefore **true**, because being right-angled is a relation within the triangle and accordingly cannot be thought in itself so that this synthesis is necessary. On the other hand, 'a black triangle' is not a true concept, but also not a false one, because I do not actually think anything in this expression. The reason is this: the black colour can be represented in itself and so cannot furnish a determination of the triangle; consequently in this case I lack the unity of inherence, or the real connection between subject and predicate, that is required for every concept in so far as it contains something *materialiter*[1] manifold: so, in itself, the concept is merely problematic. On the other hand, this expression is false if it is taken to refer to something (a thought unity) that it cannot refer to.

There are no true and false concepts with respect to thought considered in itself; rather something either is a concept or it is not. But if it is not, the sign related to it is false because it is both a sign and not a sign at the same

---
[1] TN. materially.

time. From this it can be seen that here too, where falsity with respect to the concept is tantamount to thinking nothing, the highest criterion of truth is the principle of contradiction because there is indeed a contradiction in the subject of thought, although not in the object itself. The difference between the two kinds of contradiction amounts to this: if I say, for example, 'a square circle', then only the form (the connection of the two as belonging to one another) is false; the parts of the matter (square, circle), can remain the same and I need only subsume them under the form of difference instead of that of determination for the thought that a square is different from a circle to be true. By contrast, 'a black triangle' cannot be subsumed under any form. In the former case both are determinations of shape which cancel one another out; in the latter case, on the other hand, only one (triangle), but not the other (black), is a determination of the subject, shape. Now I would very much like to know what philosophers want to achieve with their distinction between truth in speech [*Rede*] and truth in thought. There is certainly no truth in speech in itself, i.e. in the use of words as empty sounds. There is also no truth in thought in itself without signs, rather there either is a thought or there is not. Truth is thus the special relation of speech to thought, i.e. that a thought corresponds to the expression; falsity is the opposite, i.e. that no thought corresponds to the expression, although a thought is claimed to correspond to it, for otherwise it would be an empty sound.

Logical truth is the connection of objects of thought (concepts) according to the laws of the understanding. In so far as they have not been produced by any connection, axioms are the elements of truth, but not truth itself. The results produced by the connection are products of truth, but not truth itself because, following my definition, truth signifies merely the procedure [*Gang*] of the understanding, or its way of thinking in conformity with law, not the principle [*Prinzip*] that it started out from, nor the result that it finally attained. Any proposition (including metaphysically false ones) could be used as the principle [*Prinzipium*] of logical truth, not only because truths can accidentally be produced from false principles [*Prinzipien*], but also absolutely, that is to say, if these false propositions are supposed to be true, then such and such must follow. Neither these consequences nor their principles [*Prinzipien*] will be of any practical use; but here I am only considering their use in thought. If Euclid had assumed false axioms instead of his metaphysically true ones, then I am sure that he would not, because of this, have bequeathed a lesser or worse work to the world than the one that we now possess. For example, if I assume that the outer angle of a triangle is not the sum of the two opposite inner angles, but is equal to this sum plus a half of it, then it would necessarily follow that the angle at the centre of a circle would not be twice (as it actually is) but three times as big as the angle at the circumference, and so on. If I assume that a part is bigger than the whole, then following the laws of thought, I would derive consequences from this axiom that are different from the consequences of the opposite axiom. Doubtless a judge would not allow that I should pay my creditor a groschen rather than the thaler I owe him because it follows from this presupposition that a groschen is more than a thaler; but this is not relevant to the use of the understanding. I thus prefer to divide propositions into real and not real, instead of true and false. The difference between real and not real[2] (in relation to thought) amounts only to this: the latter requires at least one real proposition, namely the principle of contradiction (without this it would not even have a use in thought). This claim is not only required by the interest of reason but is also useful in the application of reason to morality: in the former it offers us new prospects for the use of reason (for example, it could invent a new mathematics); in the latter it is useful in cases where we should moderate our zeal for furnishing the truth and reducing error (and where doing so would have no serious consequence) because there are falsehoods that are much more useful to some people than their opposing truths.

Logical truth is merely the principle of contradiction (or equally the principle of identity derived from it) as well as everything subsumed under it. The relation of this truth to determined objects is only contingent because these principles are valid of every object in general, and are comprehended through the latter.[3] By contrast, the form of difference [*Verschiedenheit*], as well as of categorical, hypothetical and disjunctive propositions, and everything that is subsumed under them, these are all

---

[2] TN. This sentence does not make sense as it stands. It is possible that there is a mistake here and that it should read: 'The distinction between false and not real ..', so that the sentence would express the claim the not real in contrast with the false must be at least internally consistent even though nothing corresponds to it in reality (as would be the case with Maimon's example of a non-Euclidean geometry). Or the contrast could be between the non-real (which must contain only one real claim, the principle of contradiction) and the real (which must contain only real propositions).

[3] TN. '*weil sie von jedem Gegenstand überhaupt gelten, und durch dasselbe begriffen werden*'. Because its verb is plural we have translated '*sie*' by 'these principles' on the supposition that it refers back to the two principles cited in the previous sentence.

metaphysical truths | because they necessarily refer to determinable, although not determined, objects, and are grasped by this means. If I think a and b as different, then I cannot think objects of thought in general under a and b, but only determinable objects, for an *objectum logicum* cannot differ from an *objectum logicum*,[4] i.e. from itself. It is the same when I say that b as predicate belongs to a as subject, or a is condition of b.

Subjective and objective truth. A truth recognized by any particular thinking being is to this extent merely a subjective truth. But it is an objective truth if this being recognizes it in such a way that every thinking being in general (in so far as it is a thinking being) must recognize it. For example, in so far as our sensible intuitions agree with certain forms, they are merely subjective because there can always be thinking beings that have completely different forms of intuition from those we have. Consequently these forms themselves have merely subjective reality even though they are in us *a priori*. And it is the same with the forms of our thought because there can always (problematically) be thinking beings, | that connect appearances (if they have them) and make them into objects of the understanding, but use completely different forms to do so.

In fact, it seems that we do not have any criterion of objective truth. But if we look into the matter more closely, we will find that this doubt cannot do any harm to our thinking. [Suppose], for example, that I have proved a mathematical proposition to someone by reducing its opposite to a contradiction, and he says to me: this follows quite correctly from our common form of thought, but perhaps there are beings that do not have this form. I would reply that my proposition is in fact valid only for the two of us and not for such beings. But if he were to claim that the form of his thought was different from mine, I would certainly have nothing more to do with him. Nevertheless, it must be noted that in the first case, no one can carry his doubt so far on pain of self-contradiction. The reason is this: since he says there may be thinking beings with completely different forms from ours, so he must | admit that these thinking beings, in so far as they are thinking beings, must have something in common with us. As a result, what any thinking being recognizes as true in so far as it is a thinking being is objective truth. Assuming that this commonality [*Gemeinschaftliche*] comprises only the subsumption of a

---

[4] TN. Logical object.

manifold under a unity in general, then however greatly this manifold and this unity may differ from ours, this alone is already sufficient to prove the reality of objective truth. As a result, just as every particular concept must contain the universal under which it belongs, so here every subjective truth must contain something objective. I will not take on the task of determining what this commonality is; this is rather for my opponent to do, that is to say, he must determine what he understands under the expression 'thinking being', and as soon as he has defined it, he will see himself forced to acknowledge certain objective truths. With the second case there is also no danger to thought, for we have never yet met someone who claims to be able to think a contradiction (to think things that contradict one another | in a synthesis). The history of all ages and all lands, particularly the history of the arts and sciences, demonstrates rather the opposite, namely that people have always taught one another and convinced one another of certain truths, and the common form of their thought must follow from these.

Chapter 10
On the I, Materialism, Idealism, Dualism, etc.

What am I? An important inquiry, according to the famous Delphic saying 'know thyself'! What *psychologia rationalis*[1] understands by the word 'I' cannot be either an intuition (even if *a priori*) or a concept because these are what they are, something outside me; they are something intuited or thought, but not the subject of thought itself. So this can only be the universal form of thinking and intuiting in general, namely the unity of consciousness, a condition of all intuitions and concepts in general. As a result, it can be thought as an object in general, but we do not have any cognition of it as a determined object (just because it is common to all objects). So categories cannot be applied to this I because they gain their significance only by means of their relation to determined objects of experience, and are correctly used when applied to a schema. Thus I cannot say: 'I or this thinking faculty in general is a substance' because this transcendental concept is far from determining an individual (which the word 'I' nevertheless expresses); indeed it does not determine any object, and so I can certainly say that I am substance, i.e., that the concept of a thing in general is permanent in time, or there must be a thing at all times (because I cannot think time without some thing); but this amounts only to thinking a substance and there is no way for me to have cognition of it because no intuition is subsumed under it.

It is the same with unity (simplicity): the concept of a thing in general certainly must be a unity, but no intuition is thought in this as a unity.

And it is the same again with personality (identity of consciousness at

---

[1] TN. Rational psychology.

different times). | Admittedly, the **I** must be identical with itself at different times, otherwise no thought would be possible at all. For example, the thought of a triangle is only possible because I relate the representation of three lines to that of space. So a thought could never arise from these representations if I had the one and another thinking being had the other. It is the same if I think, for example, the judgement that *a* is *b*, but someone else thinks that *b* is *c*: the conclusion that *a* is *c* could never arise from this, etc. This is all correct. However, because time is not something objective, but merely a subjective form of our sensibility or a way of relating objects (intuitions) to one another, so the particular determinations of objects in time are persistence and change; but these determinations can be represented only in relation to one another so that I can only say something is persistent in relation to something changing that is connected to it and the reverse. As a result, my **I** must indeed be something permanent in relation to my changing representations in me; but it can itself be changing in relation to something else. For example, if I remain stationary in my cabin in a ship, | i.e. my state does not alter with respect to the objects in the cabin, I can still, along with the ship, nevertheless alter my state with respect to the objects viewed as being at rest on the bank. With respect to the sequence of my representations, my **I** accompanies them all and must be viewed as persistent (substance) because otherwise they would not all be my representations. But another **I**, or another thinking being, for which my I is not me [*ich*] myself, but a representation of me, i.e. for which this representation is not what every representation must be related to, as it is for me, but rather something that must be related to its I, along with all its other representations. This I can think my I as a representation in it, as changing in relation to its own I. Consequently the subjective judgement: 'my I must remain identical with itself for all time in relation to my consciousness', is not valid objectively, i.e. [as claiming that] my I must also remain identical with itself in relation to another consciousness.

We can see from this that we cannot have a *psychologia rationalis*[2] because we do not possess a | concept of its domain [*von ihrem Vorwurf*] that determines an object; but we can certainly have an empirical psychology.

---

[2] TN. Rational psychology.

CHAPTER 10

Idealism, Dualism, Materialism, etc.

If each of these sectarians were to understand what they were saying, then the materialist ought to express himself as follows: I must admit the difference between inner perceptions that I represent to myself in time, and outer perceptions that I represent in space, and that these are two completely heterogeneous kinds [*heterogene Arten*]; but I claim that the transcendental object, or the substrate that grounds the outer perceptions, and that they refer to as representations, is the very same as the ground of the inner perceptions, that is to say the real existing in itself and independently of our way of representing it is something manifold. Both our inner as well as our outer perceptions are modifications of this something, that is to say they refer to it as predicates do to their subject. Let us imagine that this something does not exist; then we I (the unity of this consciousness in all these perceptions) cannot exist either, and nor can the perceptions themselves. But if we cancel out [*aufheben*] our existence in thought, then the existence of this something is still not cancelled [*gehoben*], and I am entitled to call this something matter. Consequently nothing exists in itself except matter.

The idealist will say: the manifold as such cannot exist because it is an apprehension of unities and only unities exist outside the representation and we can only think unities by analogy with ourselves, i.e. as powers of representation [*Vorstellungskräfte*]. The representations time and space, and what is determined by them, are only confused thoughts of the connections and relations of things to one another.

The dualist says: inner and outer perceptions are too heterogeneous [*heterogen*] to be taken as merely different degrees or modifications of one and the same being [*Wesen*]. So we assume that the transcendental object of the one (outside representation) is different from the transcendental object of the other. If there were no matter, we could not have any representations of I things in space, although the faculty of representation could still exist in spite of this; and if there were no faculty of representation, matter (its transcendental object) could still exist in spite of this.

But I would like to ask what compels them all to assume the existence of a transcendental object (of which they have not the least knowledge) and to relate the modifications of their consciousness to something outside it (as the word representation already indicates)? Let us attempt to solve this riddle; perhaps we will be lucky enough to succeed.

CHAPTER 10

An object of thought is a manifold considered as a unity, for example a right-angled triangle. What cannot be thought in itself in the manifold, but only in relation to the other, i.e. the predicate of this synthesis, is a distinguishing mark or representation of this synthesis. It is the same with a mere synthesis of the imagination. For example, gold comprises extension, impenetrability, exceptional density and hardness, etc. Taking these properties together in an intuition constitutes the essence of gold, each of them | is a distinguishing mark or representation of it. From this it can be seen that taking these distinguishing marks together in a single intuition does not refer to something outside this intuition, and nor does each of them in itself; rather the whole of this synthesis represents itself and every part or distinguishing mark represents the whole in relation to the remaining ones. So, according to this account, we do not need to assume any transcendental object. Besides, we cannot deny that there are different kinds of perceptions; they provide us with the matter[3] that thinking makes into different objects: this is the Kantian transcendental idealism and empirical realism. Objects in space are real with respect to their matter, outside the power of representation, but dependent on it with respect to their form. If there were no form, then this matter would remain in itself, only it would not have this form; but if there were no matter, then the form could still exist, but it would only be able to think objects in general [*im Allgemeine*] but could not have any cognition of particular objects.

If the representation of an object as the objective substrate is rejected | (because we in fact represent nothing by this), then all these opinions can easily be reconciled, and their differences reduced to a merely verbal dispute. That is to say, what the materialist understands by matter is the merely given, what exists in itself not by the operation of the power of representation. So the materialist claims that matter exists only in itself, not as modification of the power of representation. For the materialist, the I itself, or the power of representation, is a mere idea, and existence cannot be attributed to it. But the idealist claims that everything is mere modification of the power of representation, even if it is not produced by any operation of this power (according to our consciousness), and hence the idealist claims that even what is given has no existence in itself, whereas the power of representation itself must necessarily exist as the

---

[3] TN. 'Matter' in this paragraph translates '*Stoff*' rather than '*Materie*' which Maimon uses in a similar context elsewhere. There is no apparent difference in meaning.

condition of all existence, and that the I is the thing in itself, although it is at the same time a mere representation. Admittedly, we cannot think of it as a determined object, for what is thought as a determined object is not the I but something different from it; as a result, it is the only example of something that can be thought of as an object but not as a determinate object. | The dualist can also be reconciled with these two.

As for me, with the idealist I claim that my **I** is a mere idea (in so far as it is thought as not determined by anything), but it is at the same time a real object because by its nature it cannot be thought as determined by anything outside itself. I add that even if it cannot be determined as an object in itself, it can nevertheless be determinately thought as an object in its modifications, by dint of approaching a determined object ever more closely to infinity. This continuous approach takes place by means of an ever increasing isolation and universalization of concept and judgement; by this means we continuously distance ourselves from matter, and approach form ever more closely, although the complete attainment of the latter is not merely an idea, but in fact contains a contradiction, since it is both an object and not an object at the same time. An irrational root is an example of this: we can approach ever closer to it by means of an infinite series, but its complete attainment is not just an i5dea (| in so far as this series must be continued to infinity), but contains an impossibility, since an irrational number can never become rational.

The sine of an arc behaves in a similar way. It increases as the arc increases, and if the angle of the arc becomes = 90 degrees, its sine becomes = ∞, but at the same time it ceases to be the sine of an arc, because it fails to satisfy the condition that it be cut by the secant.

We therefore have not only a method by means of which we can approach the idea **I** ever more closely in construction, but also a practical rule by which we go into ourselves [*in uns selbst gehen*], as it were, or better, by which we, as such, attain ever greater reality. The reason is, as I have already remarked, that the more universal the modifications of our **I** become, the more we become substance (subject of our representations), and the more universal these become, the more interconnected they become, and hence the simpler we become; and the longer the | series of representations thus connected becomes, the more we become identical with ourselves at different times. That is to say, we achieve a higher degree of personality by this means, and it is the same with all the properties of our **I** or **soul** dealt with in psychology.

Short Overview of the Whole Work

In truth, this overview cannot be so very short. Some matters are dealt with in more detail here than in the work itself, while others are completely neglected or only touched upon. My aim here is to set the results of the whole work in an appropriate order before the eyes of the reader so that he can review the *statum controversiae* at a glance. |

Short Overview of the Whole Work

Sensation is a modification of the cognitive faculty that is actualized within that faculty only passively[1] (without spontaneity); but this is only an idea that we can approach by means of ever diminishing consciousness, but can never reach because the complete absence of consciousness = 0 and so cannot be a modification of the cognitive faculty.

Intuition is a modification of the cognitive faculty that is actualized within that faculty in part passively and in part actively. The former is termed its matter, the latter, its form.

Appearance is an undetermined intuition, in so far as it is based on passivity.

The absolutely *a priori* [*a priori absolut betrachtet*] is, for **Kant**, a type of cognition that must be in the mind prior to any sensation. For me, on the other hand, the absolutely *a priori* is a type of cognition that precedes cognition of the object itself, i.e. [it is] the concept of an object in general along with everything that can be asserted about such an object, or [a type of cognition] in which the object is only determined by means of a | relation, as for example the objects of pure arithmetic.

So, taken in its strictest sense, absolutely *a priori* cognition [*Erkenntnis a priori im engsten Verstande und absolut betrachtet*] is the cognition of a relation between objects that is prior to the cognition of the objects themselves between which this relation is found. Its principle is the principle of contradiction (or identity). But if cognition of the object must precede representation of the relation, then, in this strict sense, it is termed *a posteriori*. From this it follows that we do not have *a priori* cognition of the axioms of mathematics, that is to say, they are not *formaliter a priori*, although they are *materialiter* (in time and space) *a priori*. Suppose I do not possess a representation of a straight line, and someone asks me, 'can a straight line be non-straight at the same time?' I will certainly not put my judgement off until I have a representation of it (assuming that I don't know what a straight line is), rather I will have my answer on hand at once: that this is impossible. By contrast if he asks me, 'is a straight line the shortest?' I will answer, 'I don't know, perhaps yes,

---

[1] TN. '*durchs Leiden*', passively as opposed to actively [*durchs Handeln*] – see next paragraph. Kant does not use this term to characterize the occurrence of sensation in the *Critique*, but he does define sensation as the effect of an object on our capacity to 'be affected' or our 'receptivity' (see A19–20/B33–34).

perhaps no', until I have acquired a representation of a straight line. The reason for this is that the principle of identity is the most universal form of our cognition, and hence it must apply to all objects in general, no matter how they are otherwise constituted. By contrast, 'a straight line is the shortest' is merely the form by means of which we think this determined object, so that as long as we do not possess any representation of the object, we cannot know if this form pertains to it or not.

For **Kant**, the **pure** is that in which nothing belonging to sensation is to be found, i.e., only a connection or a relation (as an activity [*Handlung*] of the understanding) is pure; but for me the **pure** is that in which nothing belonging to intuition is to be found (in so far as intuition is only incompletely active [*eine unvollständige Handlung ist*]).

The possibility of a concept can signify two things:

(1) Absence of contradiction. It is so used only in symbolic cognition because if I have an intuitive cognition of a concept, then I do not need to compare the determinations with one another beforehand to see whether they are not contradictory, for the fact or actuality of them is proof enough of their possibility.

(2) A real ground of possibility, and this in turn in two ways; either (a)[2] it signifies the absence of contradiction, not just in the combination of symbols, but in the object itself. Suppose someone who does not possess the concept of a point is asked, 'is an extended point possible, or not?' he will say it is possible because, by considering only the rules of combination, how could he recognize the impossibility when he does not have any representation of the object? This is not the case when he is asked 'is an unextended extended point possible'? Here it is not at all necessary for him to know what a point is to be convinced of the impossibility of this concept, as the contradiction is here already to be found in the symbolic combination.

Or (b) 'the real ground of possibility' means not only that the symbol can be realized, but also signifies the comprehensibility of the way that this real thing arises [*Entstehungsart dieses Reellen*]; or, if I may be permitted the expression, it signifies the necessity of the possibility. The concept of an equilateral triangle is indeed possible in the former sense if I construct a triangle in general and then simply

---

[2] TN. (a) and (b) are not in the original.

add the equality of the sides in thought; but this possibility is merely arbitrary. By contrast, if I construct an equilateral triangle by means of two equal circles, whose circumferences pass through each other's centres,[3] then I see the necessity of the equality of sides in thought; but this possibility of the concept; it is the same with *a priori* judgements.

Kant raises the question, how are synthetic *a priori* propositions possible?[4] The question means this: the possibility of analytic *a priori* propositions is readily comprehensible since they depend on the principle of contradiction and this refers to an object in general rather than to a determined object so that the analytic propositions must also be found in the understanding prior to the representation of determined objects. By contrast, synthetic propositions refer to a determined object, so how can they precede the representation of the object itself, i.e., be *a priori*?

In order to preclude the possible objection: 'what need is there to inquire into the possibility of synthetic propositions when there are in fact none?', Kant starts out by trying to put the fact itself beyond doubt, citing synthetic propositions from both mathematics and the natural sciences that express necessity and consequently must be *a priori*.

I note, however, that even if such propositions express necessity, this does not establish that they contain (objective) necessity. For example, my judgement that a straight line is the shortest between two points can derive from my having always perceived it thus so that for me subjectively it has become necessary. The proposition has a high degree of probability, but no objective necessity. Now suppose that the criterion I gave above[5] for *a priori* propositions with objective necessity is also valid the other way around so that where the criterion is not fulfilled, there is no objective necessity; in this case, the propositions mentioned here not only **could be** merely subjective, but definitely are merely subjective because they do not fulfil the criterion. On the other hand, suppose the

---

[3] TN. See Euclid, *Elements*, Bk 1, Prop. 1.
[4] TN. See B19–24. Kant brings this question to the fore in the *Prolegomena* and in the Introduction to the second edition, identifying it as 'the general problem of pure reason'. It is less prominent in the first edition.
[5] TN. i.e. that if a cognition is to be *a priori*, it must be a cognition of a necessary relation between objects that precedes any cognition of objects themselves.

criterion only serves to demonstrate the objective certainty of those propositions that do fulfil it, then in this case it is at least true that the fact remains | uncertain, and a fact that is uncertain is no fact at all. This doubt does not detract from pure mathematics, as its propositions can be derived hypothetically from its axioms, 'if a straight line is the shortest, then ..' and so on, but applied mathematics and the doctrine of nature will suffer a loss. Metaphysics as speculative science will also be none the worse for this doubt: I will always be able to claim, 'if the soul is simple, then it is indestructible', and so on; and just as any science can make satisfactory progress in using these propositions by making the hypothetical absolute, so metaphysics can do the same. I think that the proposition 'everything has its cause' possesses the same degree of self-evidence [*Evidenz*] as the proposition 'a straight line ...', and if Kant has also proved that space is an *a priori* form, i.e. is prior to the objects of the senses themselves, then the proposition 'the straight line ...' is only *a priori* in this sense, i.e., *materialiter*, but not [in the sense of] being prior to all objects in general, indeed not even [in the sense of] being prior to cognition of the object of the judgement itself. But objective necessity can be attributed only to propositions that refer to an | object in general, such as the principle of contradiction.

If I am asked: but must this subjective necessity not have an objective ground? I reply, yes, certainly it must, but this is precisely because the judgement is grounded in the object, and so the judgment can only be made after a representation of the object itself has been obtained.

But if we want to consider the matter more precisely, we will find that the expression, 'objective necessity' is actually meaningless, because necessity always signifies a subjective compulsion to accept something as true. With respect to evidence [*Evidenz*] in the sciences, we must pay attention to the generality [*Allgemeinheit*] of the propositions, but again, not in and for itself (since a more general proposition is not more true than a less general one), but rather [because] it depends only on the correct application of these propositions, that is, the more general a proposition is, the less we run the risk of applying it incorrectly. The reason is this: suppose we would like to apply a proposition to some particular case, then there is no problem because this particular case is contained in the general. On the other hand, if it is merely a particular proposition, and we | would like to make it general, then we would be making a big mistake because the general is not contained in the particular. Once we are completely sure about the scope [*Umfange*] of a proposition, then it is all the same to us whether it is more or less general in itself. As a result, the fewer the determinations that a subject can accept, the more general the judgement made by it must be; mathematical axioms are like this. **A straight line is the shortest between two points**. A straight line cannot accept any more determinations beyond magnitude; but in this case, the determination of the subject cannot exert any influence on the predicate because it is the predicate itself and so the judgement must be general.[6] What if someone says, 'perhaps this proposition is only valid between two points at the distance I had already introduced into the predicate by means of construction, but not at any other distance?' Then let us first assume that it is valid for the points at distance, *ab*, but not for the points at twice the distance, *ac*, i.e. that the shortest line between *a* and *c* is not the straight line *ac*, but *adc*, which is not straight.[7] Now I have assumed that the line *ab* is both a straight line and the shortest line between *a* and *b*, and because the position of a line does not alter its quality or magnitude, I can substitute *ab* for *bc*, so that if I position the point *a* at *b*, the point *b* must coincide with *c*, consequently *ac* = 2*ab* and must be both straight and the shortest line between *a* and *c*. The reverse can also be proven, namely that a straight line would still be the shortest for distances smaller [than the one introduced into the construction]. Let us suppose (through construction) that *ac* is both a straight line and the shortest line between *a* and *c*, then I say that half of this line will also be both straight and the shortest line between *a* and *b* because if *ab* were not the shortest, then twice *ab* = *ac* would not be the shortest, contrary to the assumption. And it must also be straight because, in bisecting *ac*, I have not disturbed its position and hence have not altered its nature. In fact this result is already present in the words themselves because if I say that perhaps a

---

[6] TN. '*nun aber kann hier diese Bestimmung des Subjekts aufs Prädikat keinen Einfluß haben, weil sie das Prädikat selbst ist*'. By 'the determination having no influence on the predicate' Maimon seems to mean that the second determination (shortest) does not further determine the first determination (straight), i.e. that shortest lines are not a subset of the straight lines but are the very same lines. '*Weil sie das Prädikat selbst ist*' – because what are apparently two different predicates are actually the same.

[7] TN. The original translates as: 'i.e., the shortest line between *a* and *c* would not be the straight line *ac*, but *adc*, which is not the shortest, would be straight', which we take to be a mistake.

straight line is not the shortest at twice the distance, | then I contradict myself because distance can be determined only by means of the shortest line.

The proposition, 5 + 7 = 12 (the second example of synthetic propositions in mathematics)[8] is also universal [*allgemein*], namely because it is a singular proposition (which logicians rightly count as universal).

The self-evidence [*Evidenz*] of mathematics can thus stand firm, even if we do not wish to assume with Kant that **space** is an *a priori* form of intuition.

By contrast,[9] I pose the question in the following way. Since all *a priori* cognition must be analytic, and can be derived from the principle of contradiction, how can we make those propositions that are synthetic due to a lack in our cognition into analytic ones? Or, how can we define the subject so that the predicate is identical [*identisch*] to it? For if we look closely at all such propositions, we always find that their subject is either not defined at all but merely presented in intuition (as in the Kantian example, '7 + 5 = 12'), or that it is badly defined, as in the example 'a straight line is the shortest between two points'. So how should we improve it? I do not want to take | on the task of developing all such propositions in this way in order to make them satisfy my requirement; it is enough that I hold it not to be impossible.

'**Space**', says Kant,[10] 'is not an empirical concept which has been drawn from outer experiences. For in order for certain sensations be related to something outside me, [...] or in order for me to be able to represent them as outside one another, [...] the representation of space

---

[8] TN. Maimon is apparently referring to Kant's discussion of synthetic *a priori* propositions in mathematics in the Introduction to the second edition of the *Critique* (B14–17), in which the two examples are 'the straight line between two points is the shortest' and '7 + 5 = 12'. In the first edition these examples are not cited in the Introduction; the former is never cited and the latter appears only in the 'Axioms of Intuition' (A164). The same two examples are also used in the Preamble to the *Prolegomena*.

[9] TN. At this point the discussion of Kant's way of posing the question 'how are synthetic *a priori* propositions possible' (begun seven paragraphs above) comes to an end, and Maimon presents his own approach to the question.

[10] TN. In this and the following paragraphs Maimon quotes from and discusses the five characteristics that Kant attributes to space in the 'Transcendental Aesthetic' – see A23–25/B38–41. There are some ellipses in the quoted passages that Maimon does not mark, where this is the case [...] has been inserted. The translation here and in other quoted passages follows Guyer and Wood.

must already be their ground ...' But this only proves that space is a universal concept, not that it is an *a priori* one (according to my definition). By contrast, I claim that as intuition space is a schema or image of the difference between given objects, that is, a subjective way of representing this objective difference, a difference that is a universal form or necessary condition of thinking things in general; without this objective difference it would be an empty space, i.e., a transcendent representation without any reality (as when I imagine a homogenous object in space, without relating it to something heterogeneous). So, considered in itself, space is indeed a universal concept but not an *a priori* one; only when considered in relation to what it represents (difference) is it an *a priori* concept, namely because difference pertains to all things; or all things must be – or must be thought as – different from one another: for it is just this that makes them all things.

Secondly, he says, 'space is a necessary representation ...' As I have already remarked, this necessity is merely subjective with respect to space viewed in itself (since it is certainly objective with respect to what it represents, namely difference). As I have already mentioned, the possibility of thinking space without objects is purely transcendent.

Thirdly, he says, 'the apodictic certainty of all geometrical principles [...] is grounded in this *a priori* necessity ...' For me, this apodictic certainty rests on their universality alone. Either this needs no proof, in so far as the relation can be perceived between individual objects of intuition, as in, for example, the proposition '5 + 7 = 12' where an individual proposition is included within the universal proposition; or at the very least it can be proved that if the proposition is perceived in any intuition, then it must also be perceived in every future intuition, as with propositions like 'the straight line is the shortest between two points'. This universality certainly must have an objective ground, i.e., to an infinite understanding the proposition must be analytic; but we cannot have any insight into this ground.

Fourthly, he says, 'Space is not a discursive or [...] general [*allgemein*] concept of the relations of things in general'. This is correct with respect to space as it appears to us, but not with respect to what space represents (the difference between sensible objects in general). In this case, difference in general is abstracted from particular differences because things are different in different ways. Red is different from green in a different way than sweet is different from bitter. But we should not be surprised that copy and original are not completely alike, or that there are not different spaces corresponding to the different kinds of differences, any more than we are surprised that a mathematical figure drawn on paper and its concept are not completely alike.

Fifthly, he says, 'space is represented as an infinite [...] magnitude'. The extent [*Umfang*] of space can never be greater than the extent of the things that fill it, and since the latter can only be finite in intuition, so space can only be represented as finite. The representation of the infinity of space is therefore transcendent and has no objective reality. I am therefore in agreement with Kant that space, regarded as an intuition in itself (but not as the image of a relation), has a merely a subjective reality, and that things appearing to us in space may perhaps not appear in space to other thinking beings; but I would add that this subjective appearance must have an objective ground, which, precisely because it is objective, must be thought in the same way by all thinking beings. I could say the same with respect to Kant's theory of time because for me time is an image of the difference between mental states in general.

Kant claims that sensibility and understanding are two completely different faculties. But I argue that an infinite thinking being must think them as one and the same power [*Kraft*] despite the fact that we must represent them as two different faculties in us, and that for us sensibility is incomplete understanding. This affects us in three ways: 1) we are not conscious of the concepts contained within sensibility; 2) with respect to the concepts that we can attain, we must attach them to sensibility in order to achieve consciousness of them; 3) so, for the most part, we come by both these concepts themselves as well as their relations to one another incompletely and in a temporal sequence according to the laws of sensibility. By contrast, the infinite thinking being thinks all possible concepts all at once with the greatest completeness without any admixture of sensibility.

The table of the logical functions in judgements, and hence the table of categories as well, seem to me to be suspect.[11] 1) The reality of hypothetical judgements is doubtful. In the pure *a priori* sciences, such as mathematics, we never come across them; although I can say things like, 'if a line is straight then it is the shortest between two points', this is only

---

[11] TN. Maimon now moves on from the 'Transcendental Aesthetic' to discuss the 'Transcendental Analytic', beginning with the table of judgements at A70/B95.

a peculiar manner of speaking, that in this case does not mean anything in particular (because it is tantamount to saying 'a straight line is ...', which would in fact be a categorical judgement). It follows that hypothetical judgements must have been adopted [by the pure sciences] *per analogiam* from somewhere else, where they do seem to mean something. But we come across such hypothetical judgments only in our judgements about natural events; and if this too is denied by claiming that in fact we do not have any judgements of experience (expressing objective necessity), but only subjective judgements (that have become necessary through habit), then the concept of a hypothetical judgement would be and would remain merely problematic.

Moreover, I ask, what are assertoric and what apodictic judgements, and how are these kinds of judgement distinguished from one another? If mathematical axioms are assertoric judgements (because according to my definition of *a priori*, we do not have any insight into the ground of their necessity *a priori*), then there are in fact no apodictic-categorical judgements because the axioms themselves are certainly categorical, but they are not apodictic; and what is derived by the principle of contradiction after assuming them, is | certainly apodictic with respect to its relation to the axioms, but its reality in itself cannot be any greater than the reality of the axioms themselves, i.e., it is, like them, merely assertoric. By contrast, if these axioms are apodictic (because they express necessity), then in turn I do not know what a merely assertoric judgement might be: it cannot be an experiential (or perceptual) judgement, for example, that a body is heavy, because this is not in fact a judgement, but just an expression of fact that we always perceive the subject accompanied by the predicate in time and space. So we can see that logic cannot guide us here.[12]

By contrast, I claim that the synthetic propositions of mathematics are certainly true and universal propositions, but that they are nevertheless not apodictic; rather they are merely assertoric and neither *a priori* (in my sense of the word) nor pure.

The concepts of substance and accident are just the logical concepts of subject and predicate understood in their transcendental signification.

---

[12] TN. '*die Logik hier zu keinem Leitfaden dienen kann*', a reference to Kant's claim that the logical forms of judgement provide a clue or guiding thread [*Leitfaden*] for the discovery of the categories. See A66/B91 ff.

SHORT OVERVIEW OF THE WHOLE WORK

That is to say, if two things are determined only by means of this relation, then the former can be thought without relation to the latter | but the latter cannot be thought without relation to the former. I freely admit that the distinguishing marks of these objects must be given in experience in order for them to be subsumed under these concepts. So I agree with Kant that these concepts, as well as the judgements grounded in these concepts, are valid only of objects of experience; I only claim that they are not, as K. assumes, directly valid of objects of experience as they appear to us, but rather that they are valid only of the limits of objects of experience (ideas), and that they are valid of the objects of experience themselves by means of these ideas.

The difference between Kant's deduction[13] of these concepts and mine amounts to this: Kant assumes there is no doubt that we possess experiential propositions (that express necessity), and he proves their objective validity by showing that experience would be impossible without them; but on Kant's assumption, experience is possible because it is actual, and this is why these concepts have objective reality. But I doubt the fact itself, that is to say, I doubt whether we possess experiential propositions and so I cannot prove their objective validity the way Kant does; instead I prove only the possibility that they are objectively | valid of the limits of objects of experience (which are determined as objects by reason in relation to their corresponding intuitions), not [that they are valid of] of objects of experience themselves (which are determined in intuition). As a result, the question, *quid juris?* must fall aside (in as much as pure concepts are applied to ideas). So things *can* stand in this relation to one another; but whether they do so in fact is still in question. For example, Kant[14] proves the reality of the concept of cause (or the necessity with which *b* follows *a*, but not the other way around, i.e., succession according to a rule) as follows: apprehension of the manifold of appearance is always successive [*sukzessiv*][15] (whether this [succession] is subjective or objective). So the objective can only be distinguished from the subjective by the perception that in the former case the sequence is necessary in accordance with a

---

[13] TN. Following both Scherrer and Ehrensperger in reading *Deduktion* for *Reduktion*.
[14] TN. Maimon now considers the arguments of the Second Analogy (A189ff./B232ff.) and Kant's examples of the successive perception of a static house and of a moving ship.
[15] TN. In this and the next paragraph '*Sukzession*' (and cognates) will be translated by 'succession' (and cognates), while '*Folge*' will be translated as 'sequence'.

rule, but in the latter it is merely contingent. Now I maintain that a necessary sequence in accordance with a rule is not to be found in perception, i.e., I deny the fact: if a sequence is supposed to be necessary because I am unable to perceive one sequence while perceiving another, then it could not be distinguished | from a merely contingent sequence, since the perception of one sequence during the perception of another is impossible in this case too.

Succession [*Sukzession*] in the representation of a house (for example, from bottom to top) is represented as arbitrary and so the house itself is not represented as having arisen by means of this succession of movements; by contrast, the movement of the ship is represented as actual and hence as having arisen in the course of the succession. The reason is that we do not have cognition of the house as an object only by means of this succession, but also by means of other distinguishing marks that are perceived simultaneously and without succession during the same apprehension (it does not matter if they in turn, in their apprehension, are perceived successively, as long as they are not treated as successive during the given apprehension). By contrast, the movement of the ship is perceived only by means of this single successive apprehension; prior to this apprehension as well as after it, there are no distinguishing marks that could make its existence an object of cognition. This is why we believe that the object first arises in this succession, whereas the former succession presupposes the existence of the object. Regarded in themselves, these two kinds of succession | are not in fact distinct from one another and so when someone asserts that the ship **actually** moves down the stream, he does not in fact know what he means by the word 'actually'.

Kant takes the categories or pure concepts of the understanding to be mere forms of thought that are incapable of definition and hence completely useless outside the conditions of intuition. But I maintain that the categories, as pure concepts of the understanding, can and must be defined without any condition of intuition. They concern the thinkability of things; their actuality and their conditions are merely contingent to them. For example, substance is that part of a synthesis that can be thought without the other part (even if it in turn can be thought as predicate in relation to something else), i.e., it is the subject of the synthesis. Accident is that part of a synthesis that cannot be thought without the other part, i.e., the predicate. We can explain and clarify these concepts by means of examples drawn from the pure sciences such as mathematics. A cause is something that, when it is posited, must be viewed as the ground for positing something else; it is again subject, but of a judgement rather than of a concept. An effect is | something that must necessarily follow (although not in time) when what precedes it has been posited.

Accordingly, I view the understanding as merely a capacity for thought, that is, for producing pure concepts by means of judging. No real objects are given to it as material for it to work on. Its objects are merely logical and they only become real objects in the first place by means of thought. It is an error to believe that things (real objects) must be prior to their relations. The concepts of the numbers are merely relations and do not presuppose real objects because these relations are the objects themselves. For example, the number 2 expresses a ratio [*Verhältnis*] of 2:1 at the same time as it expresses the object of this relation; and if the latter [being an object] is necessary for its consciousness, it is certainly not necessary for its reality. All mathematical truths have their reality prior to our consciousness of them.

These pure concepts of the understanding and relations (that always come in pairs) define one another reciprocally, i.e., in a circle; and this is quite natural because if a concept were not defined circularly, it could not be altogether pure, i.e., it would have to possess a constituent part | that could not be defined at all but that is merely given (to sensibility) and not thought by the understanding; or it would have to be defined by means of an infinite series of predicates. But the latter does not provide a definition because if I say the distinguishing mark of *a* is *b*, that of *b*, *c*, etc., then I can never know what *a*, *b*, *c*, etc. are. So there are only two ways that a concept or objective synthesis (unity in the manifold) can be defined. Either (1) it is grounded in an intuition that the understanding thinks according to a rule; this gives rise to a concept defined so that the subject is the grounding intuition and the predicate is the rule thought by the understanding. This approach produces an impure or mixed concept, all concepts other than relations are of this kind. In this case the constituent parts of the concept must precede the concept itself, i.e. precede its synthesis. In other words, the constituent parts of a judgement about the possibility of an objective synthesis must precede the judgement itself, as in the example of a straight line. Or (2) the understanding merely thinks a rule that determines a relation between two completely undetermined logical objects by means of which the objects themselves are determined; | this gives rise to a pure concept **with** or **through** the judgement. Take, for example, cause. Unlike identity, this concept is not merely a form that remains undetermined by any condition; instead it is a real object that is produced by thought and does not precede it. But if 'object of thought' means merely what precedes thought, then pure thought has only the concept of a thing in general (*ens logicum*) as its object. By contrast, the object of applied thought is neither an intuition (which is not an object of the understanding) nor any mere *ens logicum*, but rather the *ens reale* or what I call an idea of the understanding, the element of a particular intuition. It is a limit concept between pure thought and intuition by means of which the two are legitimately bound together.

Suppose it is true that we possess experiential propositions (in Kant's sense) and that we apply the pure concepts of the understanding to appearances for their sake; then the possibility of all this or the *quid juris?* is easily explained according to my theory because the elements of appearances, what | the pure concepts of the understanding are subsequently applied to, are not themselves appearances. If someone asks me: but how does the understanding recognize that these elements pertain to these relations? I answer: because the understanding itself makes them into real objects by means of these relations and because the appearances themselves approach these relations more and more closely (to infinity). For example, suppose I say that the **I** or my thinking being is a substance or the ultimate subject of all my representations; how do I know this? For the following reason: in thinking I approach such a substance more and more closely because the more I think or judge, the more universal the predicates of the subject of the judgement become relative to those of the subject in the object; and the more universal these are, the less they present the object and the more they present the subject of my thought. For example, I judge that I am a human being, that human beings are animals, that animals are organized bodies, that organized bodies are things. In this series of connected judgements the representation of the **I** as object becomes smaller and smaller while the representation of it as subject becomes larger and larger because the **I** is the ultimate subject. So the more universal the predicates become, the more they approach this ultimate | subject, until at last I reach the limit between subject and object (the thinkability of an object in general); and it is the same when we think synthetically or produce concepts by means of a synthesis. In this case we appear to approach the object by means of continual determination and to get further away from the subject, but actually it is the other way around. This is because abstraction is not accomplished easily, and I begin thinking with a more particular predicate, and hence one that is more easily grasped: for example, 'thinking thing in general' determined by 'human being'. But if I take a closer look at this determination, I find that it is not and cannot be an absolute determination because it is itself already composed of something determinable and a determination. So I take 'animal' as the determination of a thing in general and proceed as before, i.e., through thinking I approach more and more closely to a determination as subject until at last I come to the **I** that is itself both determinable and determination. This **last thing** [*dieses Zuletzt*] is of course never to be found because the I that I reach is still always a predicate (of inner sense). I approach the true **I** ever more closely as something that for my consciousness is only an idea, but in itself I is a true object, and precisely because we can approach it ever more closely by means of a determinate series, so it follows that an infinite understanding must actually think it.

I am equally entitled to say that I am simple, on the grounds that thinking allows my representations (as my predicates) to be ever more closely connected and so brings me ever closer to this simplicity, ultimately giving rise to complete simplicity. Now, someone might say that all of this is true only of the representation of the I, not of the object itself. I reply that what distinguishes the thing itself from its representation is only that it is less complete; when they are both taken in their greatest completeness (as is here the case), then they are necessarily one and the same.

So the result of the theory is the following. With Kant, I maintain that the objects of metaphysics are not objects of intuition and cannot be given in experience. But I depart from him in this respect: he claims that they are not objects that can be thought by the understanding as determined in any way; by contrast, I I hold them to be real objects, and although they are in themselves only ideas, they can nonetheless be thought as determined by means of the intuitions that arise from them. Further, just as we are in a position to determine new relations between magnitudes[16] themselves by reducing them to their differentials (and these in turn to their integrals), so by reducing intuitions to their elements, we are in a position to determine new relations between them, and in this way to treat metaphysics as a science.

---

[16] TN. '*neue Verhältnisse unter diesen (den Größen)*', that is *Größenverhältnisse* or ratios.

I share Kant's opinion about the impossibility of an ontological proof of the existence of God;[17] and I add the following grounds for this impossibility.

The ontological definition of God is: **a being that contains all possible realities**. But I will prove that not only such a being, but also any being in general containing several realities, is impossible as an object, and is only an idea. For example, let us assume that a being consists of two realities *a* and *b*; we must then assume that each of these consists of two parts, namely one that is common to both | (by means of which they are realities at all) and another part that is proper to each of them (by means of which they are differentiated from each other). Now, what they have in common is certainly a reality because it is what makes both of them into realities; but what is particular to each of them must also necessarily be a reality. The reason is this: if we assume it is a reality in one but a negation of this reality in the other, then the other would not be a particular reality, but the universal concept of reality in general; and this is contrary to our assumption. So we have turned the two realities assumed in the thing into four. Each of the two realities contained in each of the assumed realities must in turn consist of two parts, and so on to infinity. From this it follows that this concept can never be thought as a determinate object. It further follows from this that things in general cannot be distinguished by means of the number of realities that they contain, but only by means of what is comprehended in one and the same reality.[18]

Now it could be objected that although this proposition is correct with respect to a **thing** thought through a concept, it is not correct with respect to the **concept** | itself since the latter is necessarily a synthesis of several realities. For example, a straight line (which contains two realities); a right-angled triangle or a space enclosed by three lines that is right-angled (which contains three realities) and so on. But on reflection there is in fact no plurality of realities here because the reality of a concept lies only in its synthesis. If its constituent parts are separated, no reality (as synthesis) remains. A right-angled triangle does not contain more realities than a triangle in general, i.e., more unities; it merely

---

[17] TN. A592/B620 ff.
[18] TN. '*die Intension eben derselben Realität*', taking '*Intension*' as the opposite of '*Extension*', i.e., referring to the comprehension of a concept as opposed to its extension.

contains a greater reality or unity. And if we do not want to take our inability for objective impossibility, then this idea is correct, namely, that in the end all concepts must be reduced to one concept, and all truths to a single truth; at least as ideas these cannot be denied, since we approach ever closer to them. So if the expression 'a being that contains all possible realities' is to mean anything, it must mean a being that contains all possible degrees of one and the same reality, which is in turn a mere idea that we | can approach ever more closely by means of successive syntheses, but that can never be thought as an object.

God is either what grounds all possible concepts, i.e., the given; or he is the sum total of all possible concepts or realities and is necessarily connected to this given.[19] So the proposition 'God exists' is either analytic or synthetic. In the first case it amounts to saying that the given in all our concepts, i.e. the existence synthetically connected with concepts, is existence. In the second case it is tantamount to saying the most real being, or the sum total of all possible realities, is necessarily connected with existence. In both cases it is an axiom that requires no proof. But it yields only a new name not a new concept because in the first case it amounts to no more than saying that existence is existence, and in the second, that all realities are merely every reality [*alle Realitäten bloß jede Realität*], and this amounts to saying just that every reality (concept) must be based on something given; but it must first be proved that all realities can come together in a single synthesis because, although I claim that all concepts must be reducible to a single concept, | this is still a mere idea. So we can never treat the concept of the most real being as an object. Accordingly, I do not need to join Kant in destroying the ontological proof by showing that even if realities do not contradict themselves as such in the concept, they can cancel each other's consequences in the thing itself. This would show merely that God's most perfect[20] effect (the best world) cannot be produced from this concept, but not that he himself has no real synthesis. The first definition of God is a *definitio realis* whose corresponding *definitio nominalis* is 'God is a necessary being', this is because real (not merely logical) necessity is nothing but the given,

---

[19] TN. '*Gott ist entweder das allen möglichen Begriffen zum Grunde liegende, d. h. gegebene; oder der Inbegrif aller möglichen Begriffe oder Realitäten, das mit diesem Gegebenen nothwendig verknüpft ist.*'

[20] TN. '*allervollkommenste*', later in this paragraph 'most perfect' translates '*vollkommenste*', the sense 'most complete' should also be kept in mind.

without which nothing can be thought. On the other hand, the *definitio nominalis* corresponding to the second definition is 'God is the most perfect being'.

As far as the cosmological proof is concerned,[21] the world is contingent not with respect to its existence, but with respect to the way it exists. The law of causal connection amounts to this: as a formally determined thing, b necessarily presupposes another formally determined thing, a; | but as determined forms both b and a necessarily presupposes matter [*das Materielle*] (the given). So we must seek the unconditioned of these conditioned forms, but not an unconditioned existence that is already given as a condition of each of these forms. This is because neither what is given [*das Gegebene*] in itself (what in the thing pertains to its existence) nor what is thought [*das Gedachte*] in itself (what pertains to its essence) is either necessary or contingent; rather, only their relation to one another in a synthesis [is]. And the contingency of this relation does not lead us in any way to the unconditioned as object, but [leads us] merely to resolve it into an infinite series.[22]

I agree with Kant that for us the transcendental object of all appearances considered in itself is x. But I maintain that if we assume there are different appearances, we are also forced to assume there are different objects corresponding to them and that these can be determined *per analogium* with their corresponding appearances even though they cannot be determined in themselves. In the same way, those born blind cannot think each colour in itself, although they can nevertheless think the refraction peculiar to each colour by means of lines constructed from haptic intuition [*Anschauung des Gefühls*] and so make each colour into a determinate object. To claim | that intuition is analogous only to intuition and not to the thing itself is to completely cancel [*heben*] the concept of intuition, i.e., of the relation of a determined object to a determined subject. Indeed it is impossible to prove that intuitions are the effects of something outside ourselves, so that if we want to go by our consciousness alone, then we must accept transcendental idealism, in other words, we must accept that these intuitions are merely modifications of our I, modifications that the I

---

[21] TN. A603/B631.
[22] TN. There is no paragraph break here in the original, but it seems demanded by the change of topic.

itself produces, but produces as though they were produced by objects completely different from us.

This illusion can be thought of in the following way. The representations[23] of the objects of intuitions in space and time are like images produced in a mirror (the empirical I) by the transcendental subject of all representations (the pure I, thought by means of its pure *a priori* form); but they appear as if they came from something behind the mirror (from objects that are different from ourselves). The empirical [component] (material [*Materiale*]) of intuitions is actually (like the light rays) from something outside us, i.e. something given (different from us). | But we must not let ourselves be misled by the expression 'outside us', as if this something were in a spatial relation to us; the reason is that space itself is only a form within us, whereas this 'outside us' signifies something in whose representations we are not conscious of any spontaneity, i.e. something that (with respect to our consciousness)[24] is purely passive and not active in us.

Kant very often uses the word 'given' in connection with the matter of intuition; by this he does not mean (and nor do I) something within us that has a cause outside us, for this cannot be perceived directly, but merely inferred. But inference from a given effect to a determinate cause is always uncertain because an effect can arise [*entspringen*] from more than one cause so that in the relation of perception to its causes it always remains in doubt whether these are internal or external; hence 'given' signifies only this: a representation that arises in us in an unknown [*unbekannt*] way.

Idealists in general do not in fact deny the existence of external sensible objects outright (how could they?); instead they merely deny that we can have cognition of this existence directly, through | perception, and from this they infer that we can never be certain of the actuality of external sensible objects through any possible experience.

A transcendental idealist maintains that the matter of intuitions (the empirical) as well as their form (time and space) exist only within us and that there may indeed be things outside us (things in themselves, or intellectual things that differ from us and so are distinct from ourselves),

---

[23] TN. '*Die Vorstellung*', singular subject of the sentence, changed to plural to match the plural verb.

[24] TN. Maimon generally uses this phrase to refer to his distinction between *our* (limited) understanding of things and that of an infinite understanding.

but that we can never be certain of their existence. The transcendental realist is opposed to the transcendental idealist and affirms existence in itself outside our representation; the transcendental realist agrees with the transcendental idealist to the extent of treating both matter and its forms, time and space, as modes of our intuition, not to be found in the things themselves outside this mode of intuition. But the transcendental realist hypothesizes (it cannot be asserted with certainty) that the matter of intuition has its ground in things in themselves, and its forms have their ground in the relations of these things in themselves. If we now assume that no intuitive being exists, then for the transcendental idealist nothing will exist at all, i.e. nothing can be posited as determined; by contrast, according to the transcendental realist nothing will exist with | certainty, but nevertheless something determined may exist.

As for me, since I cannot go outside my immediate [*unmittelbar*] perception, I accept that both the matter of intuition (the empirical in intuition) and its form exist only within me; and to that extent I agree with the transcendental idealist. But I differ in that the transcendental idealist understands by matter what belongs to sensation in abstraction from the relations in which it is ordered, whereas I hold that what belongs to sensation must also be ordered in relations if it is to be perceived (even if I cannot directly [*unmittelbar*] perceive these relations). I also hold that time and space are the forms of this relation in so far as I can perceive it, and I understand by matter not an object, but merely the ideas that perceptions must ultimately be resolved into. So I agree with the transcendental realist that intuition has an objective ground with respect to both its matter and its form; but I disagree in that the transcendental realist assumes that objects are determined in themselves, whereas I take them to be mere ideas, that is, | objects that are not in themselves determined and that can only be thought as determined in and through their perception (just as the differential is thought through its integral). If my mode of intuition was destroyed, then there would be no intuitions, and no objects of thought that were determined in themselves [*an sich bestimmte Objecte des Denkens*]. But since my faculty of thought might still remain, this faculty of thought could always produce objects of thought out of itself (ideas that become determined objects by being thought). The reason is, I maintain that thought has a merely contingent relation to any faculty of intuition in general, not merely to a particular mode of intuition; and I believe that the understanding considered purely in itself (although not according to our current

109

consciousness) is a faculty for determining real objects through thinking a relation that refers to an object in general (*objectum logicum*), as I have already explained on various occasions. I could also easily show that this system agrees very precisely with the Leibnizian one (if this system is correctly understood), although I take it to be unnecessary to do so now.

We have here[25] (if I may be permitted to use the expression) a **trinity**: **God**, the **world**, and the human **soul**. That is to say, if by world, we mean simply the intellectual world, i.e. the sum total of all possible objects that can be produced from all possible relations thought by an understanding; and if by **soul**, we mean an understanding (faculty of thinking) that relates itself [*sich darauf bezieht*] to this world, so that all these possible relations can be thought by it; and if by **God**, we mean an understanding that actually thinks all these relations (I don't know what else I should think by *ens realissimum*), then these three things are the very same thing. But if by world we mean merely the world of the senses, something that can be intuited by our faculty of intuition and according to its laws, and thought according to the laws of thought (although through a progression *in infinitum*); and if by soul, we mean this faculty in so far as it is determined through an actual intuition; and if by God, we mean an infinite understanding that actually does relate to everything possible through thought, then they are certainly three different things. But since the second way of regarding the issue does not derive from our absolute faculty of cognition, but only from its limitation, so it is the first way that is true and not the second. This is therefore the point at which materialists, idealists, Leibnizians, Spinozans, and yes, even theists and atheists can be united (if only these gentlemen would understand one another, instead of maliciously rousing the rabble against one another). Certainly, it is a *focus imaginarius* – ! How far I am in agreement with Kant here, I leave to the judgement of Kant himself, as well as to the judgement of every thinking reader.

Kant maintains that, as the object of psychology, the I is a representation empty of content, and hence that all the claims deriving from it are mere paralogisms.

By contrast, I maintain that the **I** is a pure *a priori* intuition

---

[25] TN. Maimon now proceeds to a discussion of the three classes of transcendental ideas set out at A333/B390 ff. By 'here' he refers to the discussion of the previous paragraph – he will now specify the content of these ideas that are objects only for an infinite understanding.

accompanying all our representations, although we cannot assign any distinguishing marks to this intuition because it is simple. Given this, let us now look at the paralogism more closely. 'That the representation of which is the **absolute subject** of our judgement, and hence cannot be used as the determination of another thing, is **substance**. I, as a thinking being, am the **absolute subject** of all my possible judgements, and this representation of Myself cannot be used as the predicate of any other thing. Thus I, as thinking being (soul), am **substance**.'[26]

Kant makes this into a paralogism because by the word **I** in rational psychology he understands the thing in itself (*noumenon*). So, on his principles, the concept of substance is not applicable to it because there is no intuition in this case by means of which we could have cognition of it. But I maintain that the **I** is an intuition, indeed even an *a priori* intuition (because it is the condition of all thought in general). So the category of substance can be applied to it and the question, *quid juris?* does not arise. But if we inquire further: how do I recognize the fact that my I endures in time? Then I reply: because it accompanies all of my representations in a time series. How do I recognize the fact that it is **simple**?[27] Because I cannot perceive any manifoldness in it. How that it is numerically identical [*identisch*]? Because I have cognition of it at different times as one and the same as itself. Kant no doubt objects that perhaps all this is correct only of our representation of the I, but not with respect to the real thing that grounds it. But I have already explained that I hold the representation or concept of the thing to be one and the same as the thing, and that they can only be distinguished through the completeness of the latter with respect to the former. So, where there is no manifoldness, as in this case, the thing itself is one and the same as its representation, and what is valid of the latter must be valid of the former. But I must still deal with a doubt that Kant has raised with respect to personality,[28] and that does not concern the difference between the representation of a thing and the thing itself, but the truth (objectivity) of the representation itself. He says, 'the identity [*Identität*] [...] is inevitably to be encountered in my own consciousness. But if I consider myself from the standpoint of another (as an object of his outer intuition), then it is

---

[26] TN. Maimon is quoting directly from the First Paralogism, A348/B406 – quotation marks and original emphasis added.

[27] TN. This is the subject of the second paralogism, A351 ff.

[28] TN. The subject of the third paralogism, A361 ff.

this external observer who originally considers **me** as **in time**; for in apprehension, time is properly represented only in me. Thus from the **I** that accompanies [...] all representations at every time [...] he will still not infer the objective persistence of my self', for we cannot explain this as valid | from the standpoint of a stranger, etc.[29] However, I note that at least this stranger cannot perceive any absolute alteration in me [considered] as his outer intuition because the alteration of the relation is the same on both sides. So if I assume a third person observing both of us, then he will perceive my alteration with respect to the other just as well as the other's alteration with respect to me. What persists and what alters are always only relative. Suppose that my state is persistent in relation to one body, *a*, but not in relation to another, *b*; then I know only that together with the body *a* I have altered my state with respect to body *b*, and that it in turn has altered its state in relation to us. But I know nothing of an absolute alteration, because alteration in general can only be relative, and the concept of an absolute alteration contains a contradiction. So if I say, 'I persist', I can only assert it in relation to my time. |

On the Categories[30]

The forms of thought, or of judgements in general, are relations between undetermined (logical) objects thought by the understanding. These objects come to be real objects of thought – but not of cognition – by means of their reciprocal determination in these relations. So if these forms are to have objective reality, i.e., if we are to be able to ascribe them to objects and recognize them in objects, then the objects must already be thought beforehand as determined by something (since these forms serve only to connect objects but not to produce them). However, because of the question, *quid juris?*, this cannot happen by means of *a posteriori* determinations, but only by means of *a priori* determinations; and because these in turn can only be relations of objects to other objects (since the understanding cannot intuit, but only think, i.e., relate objects

---

[29] TN. A363, quotation marks added, the ellipses are not marked by Maimon, and the final clause is not a direct quotation. All emphasis is Kant's apart from where explicitly stated otherwise. Note also that Maimon substitutes apprehension [*Apprehension*] where Kant had apperception [*Apperzeption*].

[30] TN. This section largely refers to the 'Analogies of Experience' (A176 ff./B218 ff.).

to one another), this relation must be of such a kind that it can refer to all objects without distinction (and hence also to *a posteriori* objects). Since this first relation refers directly to objects, it is, so to speak, the matter of the second relation, which is its form, i.e. the second relation can only refer to objects indirectly, by means of the first relation.[31] This takes place using the concepts of reflection: identity, difference, etc. For example, the understanding thinks objects determined in relation to one another by means of the relation of *maximum* of identity or, what amounts to the same thing, *minimum* of difference. It thinks these in turn in the form of hypothetical judgements, i.e., in such a relation to one another that, if one of them, *a*, is posited, the other, *b*, must be posited. This is the source of the advantage that we not only think objects by means of a reciprocal relation to one another, but we also recognize them in perception ([i.e. in perception] of the inner relation that is thought by the understanding as a condition of the outer relation and that is expressed in the form of the hypothetical judgement). If we find that *a* stands to *b* (that directly follows *a*) in a relation of *maximum* identity (here the question, *quid juris?* falls aside, since time is the form of the objects, and this relation is valid of all objects, including those given *a posteriori*), then we recognize the fact that they are also in the relation of cause and effect to one another. But it remains to be determined which is the cause and which the effect (since this inner relation is common to both of them). This cannot take place by means of a concept of reflection because these do not determine objects, but presuppose them as already determined.[32] As a result, we must look for something else to do this. But we find nothing suitable *a priori* except time, which is directly related to objects (since it is a necessary form of objects) and at the same time is *a priori*. So we distinguish the cause from the effect by means of time-determination, that is to say the cause is always what comes first, and the effect what follows in time. And it is the same with all the other categories. The term 'categories' is applied to the forms of judgements in so far as they distinguish not only the subject from

---

[31] TN. In other words the second kind of relation cannot be applied to objects directly but needs to be supplied with objects that have first been picked out by the first kind of relation.

[32] TN. This sentence contradicts what has just been established, viz. that the concepts of reflection determine objects directly, whereas the categories only determine objects that have previously been determined by the concepts of reflection. Therefore this sentence should perhaps read: 'This cannot take place by means of any category …'

SHORT OVERVIEW OF THE WHOLE WORK

the predicate for all remaining possible things (through a real relation), but also distinguish them from each another through a time-determination. How far I depart here from **Kant's** opinion will be made clear by the following.

1) **Kant** maintains that the categories are conditions of experience, i.e., he asserts that without them we could have perceptions, | but not experience (necessity of perception). By contrast, I join Hume in doubting the reality of experience, and so I maintain that logical forms, along with the conditions of their use (given relations of objects to one another), are conditions of perception itself. As a result, I claim that the categories of substance and accident are conditions of the perception of objects in themselves, and [those of] cause and effect are conditions of the perception of alteration. The reason is this: an object of thought or of consciousness in general requires unity in the manifold, but this synthesis presupposes that not all of its constituent parts can be thought in themselves (or else the synthesis would have no ground), i.e. it presupposes that at least one constituent part of the manifold is impossible without the unity, that is to say, without its connection to the other part, whereas its other constituent part must also be thought in itself (or else we would have a mere form but not an object) – and these just are the concepts of substance and accident. Again: the perception of an alteration requires unity in the manifold, i.e., the relation of two states of a thing to one another. If these states were | completely different, then only a manifold would be possible, but no unity in the manifold (because in this case there would be no reproduction – depending as it does on the law of association – and hence no comparison). On the other hand, if they were completely identical [*völlig einerlei*], then there would be no manifold, i.e., they would then not be two [states] at all, but one and the same state. In both cases no unity in the manifold would be possible, and hence no perception of alteration, and [so] not even the representation of a temporal sequence. So these states must be in part identical and in part different so that reproduction of the past state (through the law of association) in the perception of the present state and hence their comparison with one another becomes possible. But this difference must be a *minimum*, or else it would not be the same thing that had merely altered, but something completely different from the first thing (as happens in other cases of reproduction). A green leaf is different from a white one because this difference can be | perceived (even though both

have something in common [*Einerlei*], namely, leaf, and so are suitable for association). This is why the difference must be infinitely small so that the thing acquires merely a differential to a state different from the former state, and for this reason cannot be taken as a different thing itself, and just this, as I have already remarked, is the relation that the understanding subsumes under the form of hypothetical propositions.

2) According to **Kant**, the latter [i.e hypothetical] proposition is expressed like this: if *a* comes first, then *b* must follow necessarily, according to a rule. Here the succession [*Folge*] of *a* and *b* is the antecedent, and the determination of this succession according to a rule is the consequent. By contrast, I express it like this: if *a* and *b* follow one another, then they must themselves be thought in relation to one another according to a rule. So succession in general is the antecedent, and the inner relation the consequent. Without **Kant's** rule, we could not distinguish a merely subjective succession (perception) from an objective succession (experience); without my rule we could not even perceive a subjective sequence, and the same holds with respect to all the other categories. |

3) Which follows from the above. For **Kant**, the rule determines not only the form under which the object must be subsumed, but also the objects themselves with respect to this form – (i.e., not only must the objects perceived in a rule-governed sequence be subsumed under the form of hypothetical propositions, i.e., supposing one undetermined object makes it necessary to suppose another undetermined object); but also, what comes first is what is supposed hypothetically (i.e. the cause, and what follows is what must necessarily be supposed on supposing the first, i.e. the effect). By contrast, for me the rule determines merely the relation of the objects to one another (the maximum of identity), but not the objects themselves with respect to the relation. So, for **Kant** cause and effect are distinguished in perception, and we recognize them as a result of this. But for me we have perceptual cognition only of the way these objects are related to one another and not of the terms of this relation.

That we do in fact distinguish cause from effect rests simply on the following: |

a) We assume that the objects in this relation possess other determinations in addition to those under which this relation is thought

115

(these additional determinations are only contingently connected to the essential ones under which the relation is found); as a result, the objects can of course be distinguished by means of these superfluous determinations (determinations that are merely *a posteriori* and hence are not contained in this relation's *a priori* rule): that is to say, we take the object [*Objekt*] that is found in its contingent synthesis before the immediate succession (and subsequently becomes the true object [*Gegenstand*][33] of the comparison) to be the **cause**, i.e. to be something that makes it necessary to suppose something else when it is supposed; and, on the other hand, we take the object [*Objekt*] that only acquired this object [*Gegenstand*] of comparison in the succession, to be the **effect**, i.e. something that must be supposed if the first is supposed. The cause of this error is this: we relate the concepts of cause and effect to the existence of the objects, i.e., we believe that the existence of the cause makes the existence of the effect necessary. But because these concepts refer merely to the the way they exist (since the concepts are supposed to have their origin in logic, which abstracts from the existence of objects), we should instead express ourselves this way: 'if two things, A and B, immediately follow one upon the other, then they must be in a relation of maximum identity to one another'; i.e., we ought to presuppose the existence of objects in a sequence and think only the way that they exist according to a rule, instead we express ourselves in this way: 'the existence of A makes the existence of B necessary'; and because of this, we believe the proposition to be irreversible, since A exists before B, but not the other way around. In fact the existence of A prior to this immediate succession is of no concern to us: this sequence is thought in the relation of cause and effect, i.e., this sequence of objects (determined by a rule with respect to their relation to one another) is the cause of their possible perception, but not of the objects themselves.

Now it might be thought that the existence of the effect presupposes not only that the cause exists but also the way that it exists (maximal

---

[33] In this passage Maimon is differentiating *Gegenstand* from *Objekt*, which he does not do consistently in the *Essay*. *Objekt* apparently refers to the object existing with all its contingent properties outside the causal relation, and *Gegenstand* to the object *qua* cause or *qua* effect. This distinction does not therefore map onto the one that Kant sometimes observes between *Objekt* as object in general (or of thought) and *Gegenstand* as actual sensible object.

sameness of cause and effect).[34] For example, a body *a* moves towards body *b*, collides with it, and sets it in motion as well; here the motion of *a* preceded the motion of *b*, and from this we can deduce that the motion of *a* is the **cause** (condition of the motion of *b*) and the motion of *b* the **effect**. But on reflection, while the motion of *a* did precede the motion of *b*, it did not in fact precede it as cause; the reason is this: had the motion of *a* begun only on its contact with *b*, then the motion of *b* would have had to have followed no less than it did in the present case where the motion of *a* began prior to this contact. It follows that in this case the cause (condition of the motion of *b*) never existed prior to the effect. But in the effecting [*Wirken*] itself we have no means of recognizing cause and effect and distinguishing them from one another, for because *a* and *b* move off after the contact with the same degree of motion we can view each one equally well as cause or as effect; or rather, we must view their common motion as the effect of a cause external to both of them because at contact they constitute one body. In the case of an accelerated motion we might well think that the cause precedes the effect because in this case the degree of the effect is determined by the magnitude of the preceding motion. For example, if a ball falls from a given height and makes a hole in soft clay, then the depth of this impressed hole is proportional to the given height. But my question is this: what distinguishes cause from effect in this example? Because according to one and the same law this can be understood equally well as either an attraction (working with renewed effect [*aufs neue wirkt*] at every point of the distance so as to produce a uniformly accelerated motion), or as an impulse.

All of this makes it clear that we can only recognize the relation of cause and effect within objects of experience, but that we cannot have any cognition of the terms of this relation, i.e. which the cause is and which the effect. To recognize something as cause or effect within an action, we must be acquainted with the nature of the things outside the action. So we cannot have any direct cognition of it [as cause or effect], in the action, but only indirect cognition. For example, if we see a round body in a round hole, then we cannot know whether the body was already round and the hole was made round through its pressure or the other way around (the hole was already round and the body took on its

---

[34] TN. '*nicht nur das Dasein der Ursache dem Dasein der Wirkung vorausgesetzt werden muß, sondern auch die Art des Daseins selbst (das, was in beiden die größte mögliche Einerleiheit hat).*'

shape), until we | can make out whether the body is harder than the matter containing the hole, or the other way around. But in the action itself (in the resting of the round body in the round hole), either of the bodies could be cause or effect, or equally neither of them (if both the body and the hole were already round). However, we can only have cognition of the nature of the body prior to the action by means of a comparison of its state before the action with its state after the action. If we find that its state before the action was not altered by the action, but the state of the other body was altered by the action, then we judge the current state of the former to be the **cause**, and the current state of the latter to be the **effect**. And this makes it clear that it is not in fact the cause that must precede the effect, but rather that something by means of which we have cognition of the cause must precede cognition of the effect.

If we want to consider the matter more closely, we will find that the concept of alteration cannot be thought of as an inner modification of things, but only of their relations to one another. So we cannot say, 'the alteration in the relation of a to b is the cause of the alteration in the | relation of b to a', since the latter is one and the same as the former. Besides the thought relation of a to b and the reverse, we must assume another relation, namely the relation that both have to something outside of them so that a does not alter in this relation, but b does. Now we [can] say, 'this unaltered relation of a to some third thing is the cause of the altered relation of b to a'. For example: body A is in motion, it collides with body B and sets it too in motion. In this case A and B have simultaneously altered their relations to one another because at first they were at a distance from one another (and then they touched one another) and the alteration of the one is in this case not the condition (cause) of the alteration of the other but is rather identical [*identisch*] with it. However, in relation to other bodies A has not altered its state (making allowance for its loss of motion, i.e. the reaction), whereas B has altered [its state], so we say, 'the unaltered state of A, i.e., its motion, is the cause of the alteration in the state of B (from rest to motion)', and in this way we are in a position to distinguish cause from effect. As a result, the existence of one object is not (as is commonly thought) the | cause of the existence of another object; rather the existence of an object is only the cause of the cognition of the existence of another object as effect, and the other way around. Without the motion of a – given that b acquires this motion (in whatever way) – we would certainly perceive an effect, i.e. an alteration in the relation of b to other objects; but we would not have any cognition of the object of this alteration [i.e of which object altered] because this alteration could just as well be related [i.e. attributed] to other objects as to a. But now [i.e. in the case in which a is in motion] we are in a position to determine the object of this alteration, b, by relating it to a. Since (as we have already remarked) existence does not need a cause, the motion of b (the alteration of its relations to other objects) could exist without the motion of a; but then I would have no grounds for attributing it to b rather than to the other things, i.e. to any object at all. But although the alteration of b relative to a (from motion to rest) is opposed to the alteration of b relative to other objects (from rest to motion), yet the former serves as the distinguishing mark of the latter, or rather, as the condition of its cognition. And should we instead suppose the reverse (because the choice is indeed arbitrary), namely that a is at absolute rest, and b (together with the other objects) is in motion towards a, then we would indeed rightly attribute the motion after the impact to b and not to a because b's state has altered both relative to a (from motion to rest) and relative to other objects (from rest to motion), whereas a has altered its state merely relative to b (from motion to rest) but not relative to other objects.

Antinomies. Ideas

For **Kant**, ideas are principles of reason that by their nature demand the unconditioned for every conditioned. Since there are three kinds of syllogism (namely, categorical, hypothetical and disjunctive) there are also necessarily three kinds of idea, and these are none other than the three complete categories (ultimate subject, cause, world-whole) that ground the antinomies (conflict of reason with itself), which can be resolved only by his system of sensibility and its forms.

By contrast, I extend the sphere of the ideas (as well as the sphere of the antinomies arising from these ideas) much further because I maintain that they are to be found not only in metaphysics but also in physics, and even in the most self-evident of all sciences, mathematics, and hence that the antinomies require a far more general solution. For me the solution rests on this: that the understanding can and must be considered in two opposed ways. 1) As an absolute understanding (unlimited by sensibility and its laws). 2) As our understanding, in accordance with its limitation. So the understanding can and must think its objects according to two opposed laws.

SHORT OVERVIEW OF THE WHOLE WORK

The theory of infinity in mathematics and the objects of this theory in physics necessarily lead us into such antinomies. For us, the complete series of all the natural numbers cannot be an object given in any intuition; it can only be an idea by means of which the successive progress to infinity is treated as an object. Here reason comes into conflict with itself because it treats as an object something that according to its conditions can never be given as an object. The solution to this antinomy is the following. Since our perception is tied to the form of time, we can only produce an infinite number by means of an infinite succession [*Sukzession*] in time (and so we can never think of it as complete). But an absolute understanding thinks the concept of an infinite number all at once, without temporal sequence. So, what is treated as a mere idea by the understanding considered as a limited understanding, is a real object for the understanding considered as existing absolutely. What is more, we are sometimes in a position to substitute objects for ideas, or the other way around, to resolve objects into ideas, as is the case with convergent infinite series. We can calculate their value with the greatest precision, and in turn convert determinate numbers into such series.

But there are also ideas that approach determinate objects ever more closely, but are not of the kind to ever reach them and allow us to substitute determinate objects for them. Irrational roots are like this. We can approach them ever more closely by means of infinite series (according to the binomial theorem, or with the help of a *series recurrens*), and yet we are convinced *a priori* that we will never find their exact value because they cannot be either whole numbers or fractional numbers, and hence cannot be numbers at all. In this case reason falls into an antinomy because it prescribes a rule according to which this number must definitely be found, and at the same time proves the impossibility of accomplishing this. These are examples of ideas and the antinomies arising from them in mathematics.

I also want to provide some examples of this kind from physics.

1) The movement of a body is the alteration of its relation to another body in space, so we are unable to ascribe this merely subjective representation (one that is thought between things, but is not in them) to one body rather than the other. If this subjective representation is to have objective validity (to determine an object), then we must attribute to one body, *a* for example, besides this movement (alteration of its relation to *b*), another movement that is not in *b*. That is to say, we attribute the

movement to *a* but not to *b* because *a* has not only altered its relation to *b* but has also altered its relation to another body *c*, whereas *b* has only altered its relation to *a* and not to *c*. But just as *a* has altered its relation to *c*, so *c* has altered its own relation to *a*, and therefore we have no ground for thinking this motion as actually in *a* rather than in *c*, and hence we must assume yet another body, for example *d*, and so on to infinity. In this case we have an antinomy because we can never think the motion as actually in *a*, and yet see ourselves forced to suppose for the sake of experience that this is true; in other words, reason commands us to assume an absolute motion, but we cannot do so because the concept of motion can only be thought as relative.

2) A wheel moves around its axle, and so all of its parts must move simultaneously. But the nearer a part [*Teil*] is to the centre, | the smaller its velocity becomes (since it travels through less space than a more distant part in the same time). From this it follows that there is an infinitely small movement in nature. So there is a velocity that is *omni dabili minor*,[35] i.e. infinitely small because the movement is not limited by actual division [*Teilung*]. We have another antinomy in this case because an infinitely small movement is thought as an object and at the same time not as an object of experience.

3) A wheel turns around its axle along the straight line *AB*, from *A* to *B* so that gradually every part of its circumference covers every part of the line *AB*; so, **after** a complete **rotation**, the described line *AB* is equal to the complete circumference of the circle. But at the same time, consider a smaller circle *CFG* within the larger circle *AHI*: it turns around the very same axle from | *C* to *D*, so that after a complete rotation it describes the line *CD*, parallel to *AB* and equal to it. But this gives rise to a difficulty, namely to explain how it is possible that the line *CD*, described by the smaller circle *CFG*, should be the same as the line *AB*, described by the larger circle *AHI*. And they must indeed be equal because

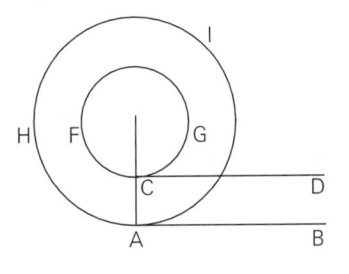

---

[35] TN. Smaller than any given.

SHORT OVERVIEW OF THE WHOLE WORK

the rotations of both circles (since they make up one body) must happen at the same time. Aristotle remarked on this difficulty in his questions on mechanics,[36] and ever since then mathematical minds have endeavoured to resolve it. in his *Analysis Endliche Größen*,[37] §601, Court Counsellor Kästner tries to resolve this difficulty in the following way (following Galileo).[38] He says:

> This case depends on the concept of rolling. If the condition of this is required, then of all concentric circles, only one can roll, and it is arbitrary which is taken to do so. Of the remaining similar arcs, all the points do indeed gradually fall on all the points of the lines parallel and equal to *AF*; but this does not prove equality because lines are not sums of points[39] and similar arcs of concentric circles I have an equal number of points, since a radius can be drawn through each point of one, and that radius provides a point on the other. To explain this, imagine regular polygons of a particular kind, hexagons for example, placed concentrically, one inside the other. Now, if the outer one rolls along a straight line so that its sides cover one part of the line after another, then these parts will join up, and if the entire polygon has rolled around, it will have covered a length of the line equal to its perimeter. But at the same time a smaller concentric polygon will roll along a line parallel to the former line in such a way that the parts of the latter line consecutively covered by its sides do not join up. If it has completely rolled around, and at the same time the large polygon has done the same, then it has gone over just the same length on its parallel that the outer polygon has gone over on its line, but it has not covered all of this length with its sides, but only parts that did

---

[36] TN. This is the 'paradox of the wheel', problem 24 of *The Mechanics*, customarily but probably erroneously attributed to Aristotle. Available in English in *The Complete Works of Aristotle*, ed. J. Barnes (Princeton: Princeton University Press, 1984) Vol. 2, pp. 1299–319.

[37] TN. A. G. Kästner, *Anfangsgründe Analysis Endliche Größen*, 2nd edn (Göttingen, 1767), pp. 302–3.

[38] TN. Galileo discusses the problem in *Dialogue Concerning the Two Chief World Systems*, trans. Stillman Drake (Berkeley, CA: University of California Press, 1967), §68–73.

[39] TN. Here Kästner inserts a reference to the fifth definition of his *Geometry*: 'The point is the limit of the line, and thus of all extension. Consequently, it itself has neither extension nor part, and an aggregate of points joined together does not constitute a line.' *Anfangsgründe Geometrie* (Göttingen, 1767), p. 159.

not join up; the sum of these parts makes up the perimeter of the small polygon. If we imagine such polygons having more and more sides, | then they will approach the circle, and through this, the difficulty is explained.

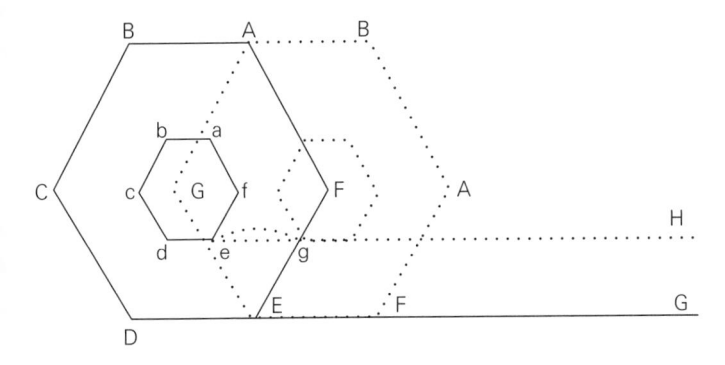

As this passage is somewhat obscure, particularly because Kästner did not include a diagram, I want to clarify it by means of the above figure. The condition of the rotation or rolling of a wheel requires that all points on its circumference must little by little touch all points on the line that it describes in this process. Another concentric circle certainly describes a line parallel and equal to the former line, but not all its points touch all the points of the [original] line; rather, some of its points describe arcs whose chords make up some parts of the [original] line. This becomes clear if we think of regular concentric polygons, for example, hexagons, instead of the circle. The parts of the outer polygon *ABC* etc. cover the line *DG* gradually and continuously. | By contrast, the parts of the inner polygon *abc* etc. do not cover the line *dH* continuously, since during the time that the side *DE* of the larger polygon ceases to cover the line *DG* and before the side *EF* begins to cover it, the point *e* of the smaller polygon moves in the arc *efg*, before the side *ef* begins to cover the line *dH*. Consequently, the line *dH* is not merely the sum of the sides *ab*, *bc*, *cd*, *de*, etc., but this sum plus the chords of the previously mentioned arcs, which is the difference between the sum of the sides of the larger and smaller polygons. But [the length of] this arc is directly proportional to the magnitude of the sides, and the magnitude of the sides is inversely proportional to their number. So, if the number of the sides is infinitely great (as when the polygon becomes a circle) and as a result the sides themselves are infinitely small, then this arc is also infinitely small. But I claim that as long as we replace the circle by a polygon with a finite number of sides, we do not need an explanation like this (at least as long as it cannot be proved that the circumference of the smaller circle plus the difference between its and the larger circle's beginning and endpoints must be smaller than the circumference of the larger). This is because the line *dH*, which the smaller polygon | *abcd* gradually covers by means of its rolling, is in fact shorter than the line *DG* that the larger polygon *ABCD* covers, since we have no reason [*Grund*] to begin this covering from the middle of the side, and in turn to end it there, because the covering of the side must take place all at once. By contrast, if we suppose the number of sides to be infinitely large, and hence the sides themselves to be infinitely small, then the one way of explaining things is of no more use to us than the other: in this case each instant of the rolling only covers a single point of the line being described; consequently both lines begin and end at the same time and so my explanation cannot be used. But Kästner's approach resolves this difficulty no better: if the sides are infinitely small, then the previously mentioned arcs must also be infinitely small, and so their chords must be infinitely small as well; and yet, taken infinitely many times [*unendlichemal*], these chords are supposed be equal to a finite line (the difference between the circumferences of the larger and smaller circles). We must therefore admit an actual infinity as the element of the finite (and not merely a mathematical one, i.e., the possibility of infinite division). So | this case also gives rise to a true antinomy because (through the idea of the infinite divisibility of space) reason commands us never to reach the end of the division of a determinate line so that we finally arrive at an infinitely small part; and yet at the same time reason proves to us that we must actually arrive at such an infinitely small part. I could cite many more such examples from mathematics as well as from physics, but for now these should suffice.

All of this makes it clear that for us the infinite (the ability to produce it) is indeed a mere idea; but that it nonetheless can be and is in a determinate way actual so that the antinomies this gives rise to can only be resolved in my way. Further, these antinomies are just as real and pose just as much of a challenge to reason to resolve them as the Kantian antinomies do. So let us grant that the mathematical antinomies can also be resolved according to Kant's system of sensibility and its forms (in which space can only exist | in our representation so that the infinite in space cannot be thought as an already completed object, but merely as an idea);[40] nevertheless, the physical antinomies I have discussed are found within what is actual outside of our mode of representation and so cannot be resolved in his way, but only in mine.

---

[40] TN. In terms of the examples Maimon has just provided, only the three physical antinomies involved the infinity of space, whereas the mathematical antinomy involved infinite time. So in referring to mathematical antinomies that may be resolved by Kant's theory of the ideality of space he must have other examples from pure geometry in mind.

My Ontology

After what has already been said, it is easy to think that I associate a quite different concept with the word ontology than the concept usually associated with it. That is to say, for me ontology is not a science that is applicable to the thing in itself, but only to appearances. It cannot have a wider domain [*Umfang*]. Here I will deal specifically with those points where I differ from the Wolffians, and hence also from Kant; for to say what others have already said would be superfluous. My exposition follows Baumgarten's paragraph ordering, so that the reader may more easily grasp the difference between our approaches.[1]

---

[1] TN. Maimon's paragraph numbering in fact follows not the original Latin text of Baumgarten's *Metaphysica*, but that of Georg Friedrich Meier's abridged German translation (Alexander Gottlieb Baumgarten, *Metaphysica* trans. G. F. Meier, (Halle: 1783)).

My Ontology

§1 Ontology is the science of the most general properties of things; that is to say, not the properties of a thing in general (of a thing determined through no condition), but the properties of every *a priori* determined thing. As a part of metaphysics, it differs from logic as much as from the doctrine of nature as follows: logic relates merely to the form of thinking, without relation to any determined object (whether determined *a priori* or *a posteriori*), while the doctrine of nature relates itself [*beziehet sich auf*] only to an object determined *a posteriori*. For example, the form of hypothetical propositions in logic is expressed like this: if one thing is supposed, then another thing must necessarily be supposed. Here the subject (thing) is determined only by the predicate (relation of antecedent to consequent). In physics the form is expressed like this: 'heat expands air'; here the subject of the relation ([between] heat and air) is determined by means of *a posteriori* conditions. In metaphysics, on the other hand, it is expressed like this: if *A* comes first, and *B* follows it according to a rule, then the supposition of *A* makes it necessary to suppose *B*. In this case the subject of the relation (of cause and effect) is determined by means of a time-determination (succession [*Folge*] according to a rule) that is *a priori*. So the concept or principle of cause belongs to metaphysics. The objects of logic can be compared to transcendental magnitudes (which are not determined in relation to one another by any algebraic equation), while the objects of metaphysics can be compared to variable magnitudes (which are determined only by means of their relation to one another), and the objects of physics to continuous magnitudes.

§7 The principle of contradiction is the formal principle of all negative judgements, and can also indirectly become a principle of positive judgements.

§8 This is the formal **nothing**; the material **nothing** is however the not-thinking [*Nichtdenken*] of something determinate.

§14 A cognition, that is to say, a judgement, has a ground. By contrast, a real object has merely a condition, not a ground. A cognition is the ground of another cognition if it contains it. So ground and consequence [*Folge*] cannot be interchanged. A determinate object, *A*, is identical with itself. Why? Because every object is identical with itself. In this case, the latter judgement is the ground of the former, which is its consequence. But if the one judgement is not a ground, but merely a condition of the other, then the condition can be interchanged with the conditioned. As, for example, in this judgement: a straight line is the shortest between two points. The judgement that a line is straight can be viewed as the condition of the judgement that it is the shortest, and the reverse.

§18 According to my definition of ground, the principle that nothing is without a ground[2] must be expressed like this: only what is self-evident [*an sich evident*] is without a ground (no judgement can be accepted unless it is derived from a self-evident judgement).

§25 The principle that nothing is without a consequence must be expressed like this: no universal judgement is without a consequence (i.e. without the particular judgement it contains) because an individual judgement does not in fact have any consequences (what follows from an individual judgement is not grounded in it, but in the universal judgement that contains it). With respect to ground in the second sense, namely, *qua* condition, great care must be taken about what this ground really is; i.e. whether it comprises the whole subject (the synthesis of determinable and determination) or is merely a predicate of it. For example, a right-angled triangle is as such the ground or condition of its properties, namely that the square of its hypotenuse is equal to the sum of the squares of the other sides; in this case the condition of this property is neither the triangle in itself, nor being right-angled in itself, but their synthesis. By contrast, in the proposition, 'the straight line is the shortest between two points', only the determination '**straight**' is the condition of the property ('line' cannot be this condition because it is also the condition of the opposite property). Disregarding this distinction leads to error: namely, we believe that one effect can be the consequence of different causes because we have not noticed that in this case the ground of this consequence (i.e. the cause of the given effect) does not lie in the different objects, but rather in something common to both of them. In what follows I will explain this in more detail.

§22 The determinable is the universal, and the determination is what makes something particular out of the universal. Now in some cases it is hard to recognize which is which, as for example in the concept of an equilateral triangle: in this case I can treat the triangle as the universal (in that it can be either equilateral or non-equilateral) and the equality of the sides as what makes it into a particular concept. But conversely, I can also

---

[2] TN. '*nichts ist ohne Grund*', or, 'nothing is without a reason'.

treat the equality of the sides as the universal (in so far as there can be many equal-sided figures), and the number of sides (triangle) as what makes it into a particular concept. So the question is: are determinable and determination interchangeable in this case? Or, in other words, is there any distinguishing mark that would allow me to recognize them and distinguish them from one another? To which I answer: there is in this case no direct distinguishing mark, but there is an indirect one, i.e. I can determine them only in relation to the consequences derived from this concept. If I want to use the concept of an equilateral triangle for the judgement that it has equal angles, then I treat the equality of its sides as the determinable, and their number as its determination; because in fact equality of angles can be predicated not only of an equilateral **triangle**, but also of every equal-sided figure in general, at least with respect to sides which have the same direction.[3] So in this case determining the number of sides as three turns what otherwise merely **can be**, into what actually **is**. But if I want to judge that each of its angles is $\frac{2}{3}$ of a right angle, then this can be predicated only of a triangle, not of any other equilateral figure. The reason is that if the angles are unequal, then they cannot each be $\frac{2}{3}$ of a right angle, i.e. equal; but if they are equal, then it is a regular polygon: it has been shows that for a regular polygon (assuming that the number of sides is equal to n) the sum of its angles = $2n - 4$ right angles so that each angle = $\frac{2n-4}{n} = 2 - \frac{4}{n}$ right angles. As a result, each n gives a different value, and only $n=3$ can give the value $= \frac{2}{3}$. So, with respect to this consequence, equality of sides is not the determinable, and their number is not the determination, but the reverse; this is because this consequence (that each of its angles is equal to $\frac{2}{3} R$)[4] can belong to a triangle in general, and if it is equilateral, must belong to it; and it is the same in all other cases.

But there is a point of view that allows us to judge what the determinable is and what the determination is in any object (synthesis of intuition and concept). It is this: if the intuition is *a priori*, then it is the determinable and the concept is the determination; this is because the

---

[3] TN. It is not very clear what Maimon means by the final clause of this sentence. But he is likely taking note of the fact that not all equilateral polygons are equiangular, the simplest example being the rhombus. It consists of two pairs of sides of the same direction, so Maimon could be associating one angle with one pair of sides and the other angle with the other pair and on this ground asserting that sides that have the same direction have the same angle.

[4] TN. Maimon here uses R to stand for the right angle.

MY ONTOLOGY

spontaneous production of an intuition according to a rule presupposes the possibility of the intuition in itself (since what is possible in connection must also be possible in itself). For example, in the concept of a straight line, line in general is possible, even without the [determination of] 'being straight', so in this case it is the determinable; whereas 'being straight' is only possible through 'line', and so on. But if the intuition is *a posteriori*, then it is the other way around: the concept is the determinable because it can also be thought in itself prior to its connection with the *a posteriori* intuition (by means of its connection with an *a priori* intuition), whereas the intuition is its determination because it cannot be thought without the concept; for example, the *a posteriori* intuition of fire is subsumed under the concept of cause because we say 'the fire warms the stone'. Here the concept ('if something is posited, then must something else must be posited') is the determinable because it can also be thought without the fire by means of an *a priori* intuition, namely time (if something comes first and something follows according to a rule); but the reverse is not possible because without the concept fire can only be intuited not thought (in a necessary relation).

The possibility of a thing either concerns the form of its thinkability, in which case it signifies the absence of contradiction, or it concerns the combination of matter and form, in which case it signifies an objective reality.

The judgement of the objective possibility of a thing actually comprises four judgements. 1) Absence of impossibility (of contradiction); 2) absence of necessity; 3) a positive ground of possibility; 4) absence of actuality; for example a triangle, i.e. a space enclosed by three lines, is possible: 1) because the 'enclosure by three lines', i.e. the predicate, does not contradict the subject, the concept of space; 2) the subject is not necessarily connected to the predicate, since it can also be thought in itself or with another predicate; 3) as a result there is in this case a positive ground of this possibility, namely that the predicate cannot be thought without the subject; 4) the whole concept can in turn be considered as subject in relation to a possible predicate because we can think a right- or oblique-angled triangle, and the like. From this we see that the possibility of each and every thing presupposes the possibility of both a more general and a more particular thing; as a result, in the series of subordinated things to which the given belongs, both a progress and a regress to infinity pertain to the complete possibility of a thing: this makes the idea of an infinite understanding a necessary one.

According to the Leibnizian-Wolffian school, actuality is the complete possibility of a thing. But on my theory, the actuality of a thing is its representation in time and space. From this it follows: 1) that possibility and actuality are wholly independent of one another: i.e. not everything possible is actual, and also, not everything actual is possible in a positive sense. | In so far as they are represented in time and space, all intuitions are actual; but they are not possible, in so far as we do not have any insight into the way they arise. All concepts (yes even if they are *omni modo determinata*)[5] are possible, i.e. we have insight into the ground of unity in their manifold; but they are not actual because this unity is not thought in time and space. A synthesis of concepts and intuitions is possible and actual at the same time. On the other hand, according to the Leibnizian-Wolffian definition of actuality, actuality presupposes possibility, but not the reverse, i.e. everything actual is possible, but not everything possible is actual. But from this it follows that an infinite understanding must either think of everything as actual or not think anything at all: the reason is that an infinite understanding must think everything possible all at once, for example, it must think a triangle either only as *omni modo determinatum* (right or oblique-angled, of determinate size, and the like) i.e. actual, and never as merely possible (a triangle in general) or both at the same time, which would amount to a contradiction, i.e. to not thinking at all. And because the latter is impossible, only the former remains true; from this it follows that for an infinite understanding, i.e. objectively, everything possible must at the same time be actual. But if we consider | the matter more closely we find that even this does not resolve the difficulty, because the triangle in general is just as much a real object with respect to its consequences as a triangle *omni modo determinatum* is with respect to its. Now it is a part of the completeness of an understanding not merely to think a being as possible, but also to judge synthetically, i.e. to relate its properties to its essence, and to consider them as *communia* or *propria*;[6] so an infinite understanding must think not only a triangle *omni modo determinatum*, but also a triangle in general (with respect to the *communia*, for example, that the sum of its angles is equal to two right angles) because that property,

---

[5] TN. Determined in every way, or completely determined, i.e. concepts that the Leibnizian-Wolffian school would regard as not merely possible but actual.

[6] TN. *Communia*: common properties; *propria*: properties belonging to one essence alone.

common to all triangles, is not a determination of any particular one, but rather of a triangle in general.

But on my definition, the possibility of a thing is what is thought [*das Gedachte*] (the concept), whereas its actuality is what is given in it [*das Gegebene in demselben*].[7] So, with respect to an infinite understanding this difficulty can be resolved in the same way as with a finite understanding. Namely: just as, for example, I can think both a triangle in general (in relation to its consequences) and a right-angled triangle (in relation to its consequences) by thinking them at different times, and hence as grounded on different intuitions; so an infinite understanding can think them in relation to different intuitions (according to any form) even though it certainly cannot think them at different times (because time is merely a form of our intuition).

The given intuited by an infinite understanding is either an *objectum reale*, signifying something present in the infinite understanding [*in demselben*], but not thought by it (this does not contradict its infinity because this consists only in the ability to think everything that is thinkable and the given is by its nature not thinkable); or the given is a mere idea of the relation of the concept to something outside it, which in itself is merely a modification of the understanding. In the latter case the actuality would not consist in something outside the understanding, but merely in this relation.[8]

§55 Like all relational concepts [*Relationsbegriffe*],[9] unity and plurality cannot be thought without one another; they are not opposed to one another because plurality does not cancel out unity, and this is because unity must necessarily be contained in the definition of plurality as an element (the matter [*Materiale*] in it); and so the reverse also holds.

Unity and plurality have both inner and outer forms: for example, the concept of a line is an inner unity (the line is viewed in itself); its different relations to different determinations (straight and crooked lines)

---

[7] TN. The reference of 'it [*demselben*]' is not obvious, it could refer to the thing but perhaps makes more sense if taken to refer to the understanding, as it does in a similar usage in the first sentence of the following paragraph.

[8] TN. This latter interpretation of 'the given' as idea rather than object is probably implicitly referring to the theory of differentials as ideas of the understanding presented in Chapter 2.

[9] TN. Maimon is here using *Relationsbegriffe* in precisely the sense in which he used *Verhältnißbegriffe* in earlier chapters. For a discussion of this sense see the first translators' note to Chapter 6.

constitute an outer plurality. By contrast, every synthesis is an inner plurality, while its relation to its common subject or predicate constitutes an outer unity.

§68 Truth is the relation of correspondence between a sign and the designated thing; falsity is the opposite of this. A concept or a judgement is, considered in itself, neither true nor false; instead it either exists, or it does not.

§80 Necessity and contingency are modifications of judgements (determining the value of the copula) but not of things themselves. If existence is a determination that must be added to the concept of a thing (but is not in itself a concept, because otherwise only a concept could in turn arise from it), then we cannot say that a thing exists necessarily because this does not express a perceived connection between different concepts (this presupposes the cognition of each in itself); but instead merely expresses the relation between a concept and something that is not a concept and whose necessity can never be apodictic, but merely problematic. But if existence is merely the positing [*Position*] of all the determinations of a thing, then in turn the positing [*Setzung*] of these determinations cannot be compared with these determinations in themselves, and they cannot be related to one another through an apodictic judgement, whose modification is **necessary**.

Necessity has two forms, inner and outer: inner necessity occurs in analytic judgements and outer necessity in synthetic judgements. A human being is an animal. In this case the necessity is inner because 'human being' cannot be thought without 'animal' as the concept of 'animal' is contained within that of 'human being'. But the judgement that a straight line is the shortest between two points expresses the relation of correspondence [*Übereinstimmung*] between straight and shortest; this relation of correspondence [is] not in itself, i.e. a relation of identity [*Identität*], but [is] rather [one of] coincidence in one and the same subject. The relation of the affirmation of the properties of an essence is thus a necessity of this type.

If it is true that the concept of cause contains not just a subjective but an objective necessity (although this remains to be proved), then there is a real necessity in addition to this logical necessity, a necessity that concerns the relation of things to one another in existence rather than the existence of things in general. 'If A comes first, then B must necessarily follow it' is tantamount to saying that if both A and B exist, then this existence must be of the following kind: A always comes first

133

and *B* follows. As such, the alterable can be thought only in relation to the unalterable, and the reverse. But this relation can in turn only be thought in relation to a third, and so on to infinity. Suppose there are two bodies, *A* and *B*: first they are in contact with one another and then they cease being in contact; accordingly an alteration has occurred in their relation to one another, but not in *A* in itself or in *B* in itself. For this to be possible [i.e for it to be possible to assign the alteration either to *A* or to *B*], a third body, *C*, must be assumed so that at first all three are in contact, but then only body *A* remains in contact with *C* while *B* is no longer in contact with it, and as a result *B* also ceases to be in contact with *A*. | Once again, this alteration exists only in the relations of *A* to *B* and of *C* to *B*; but if we treat the alteration in *B* as absolute, then we treat its alteration merely in relation to *C*, and so *A* must necessarily be viewed as unaltering [*unveränderlich*] in this relation. But just as *B* has altered with respect to *A* and *C*, so *A* and *C* have altered with respect to *B*, and so we must again assume a fourth body *D* in relation to which this in turn is possible (i.e. in order to be able to treat *B* as altering, but *A* and *C* as unaltering), and so to infinity. From this it is clear that only the relations of things to each other alter but not the things in themselves.

Logical reality and negation (affirmation and negation)[10] are forms or kinds of relations of things to one another. Considered as objects these forms are not opposed to one another in themselves, they are only opposed to one another in the object. Logical reality is an objective unity, but negation is a merely subjective one. Opposition cannot be thought logically, but only transcendentally; in this regard, it is an objective unity. '*A* is *B*' (identical, or determination).[11] Here the copula '*is*' | is a logical reality: it is a unity by means of which an object arises (relation of unity to the manifold). '*A* is – not *B*' (or different from *B*). Here the copula '*is not*' is a logical negation, it is certainly a unity, but one that connects *A* and *B* only in the understanding, not outside it in the object. '*A* is – not *B*'. Here there is an opposition and the unity is objective but merely

---

[10] TN. '*Die logische Realität und Negation (Bejahung und Verneinung)*.' In the *Critique*, the latter pair of concepts are two of the qualities of judgement whereas the former pair are the two corresponding *categories* of quality; see the tables of judgements and of the categories, A70/B95 and A80/B106. The word '*Verneinung*' does not occur again in the paragraph, hence wherever 'negation' occurs, the German is '*Negation*'.

[11] TN. '*A ist* B (*einerlei oder Bestimmung*)'. In other words '*A* is *B*' means either that *A* is identical with *B* or that it is determined by *B*.

transcendental. The objects *A* and *B* are not in fact determined in themselves, but are rather determined by means of their relation to one another, so that if the one is determined, then the other must also be determined; so this judgement indicates a transcendental object [*gibt uns ... zu erkennen*]. It is worth noting that opposition separates things from one another less than difference (the opposite of what is commonly believed): the reason is that things opposed to one another are defined by means of this opposition; but this is not the case with things that are different from one another. Both logical negation and reality must be conceived in themselves and the reason is this: they are opposed to one another, i.e. cancel one another, so that to claim that negation cancels reality, would fail to define anything because negation already presupposes the | concept of cancellation (logical negation). Material reality is what can be affirmed directly by the faculty of thought, whereas material negation is what cannot be thought directly, but only by means of a relation to the former so that we can maintain that it is opposed to reality.

Are there objective general [*allgemeines*] things or objective individual things, or not?

General [*allgemein*] things arise through abstraction and the more we abstract, the more general the things become. Particular things arise through determination and there can also be infinitely many degrees of determination, so we lack the capacity to go to the limit of either the generality or the individuality of things in themselves. The common understanding finds nothing general, nothing common both to a circle and a parabola, much less a general concept or expression for all curved lines, indeed even for both curved and straight lines, i.e. for all lines in general; but the mathematician has a clear insight into this; and it is the same with the concrete [*mit der Konkretion*]. So the concepts of the most general and individual things are mere ideas that reason | commands us to keep on searching for, but never in fact to find.

The author[12] maintains: 'a whole is something that is completely identical to many [things] gathered together', and so on. I am completely satisfied with this definition; I add merely that there must be a ground for this gathering together of the many in the one. This ground is [provided by] 1) [the relation of] determinability, i.e. the parts must be the kind of

---

[12] TN. i.e. Baumgarten.

things that can be thought as opposed to one another in the relation of determinables and determinations so that if we want to think the determination, then we are compelled to think the determinable at the same time (because the former cannot be thought without the latter); and 2) with respect to a consequence that can only be derived from this gathering together. So only the essential elements [*Stücke*] can be viewed as parts of the whole, not the properties accompanying the essence [*Wesen*]; they are not parts, but merely the reason [*Grund*] for treating the essence as a whole.[13]

In relation to the thing, the plurality of its determinations comprises an indivisible magnitude rather than a continuous one. In and for themselves these determinations are absolute units (in so far as they do not in turn contain a plurality | of determinations). Logic abstracts from all content so that in logic subject and predicate are not determined by any condition, either in themselves or in relation to one another. Everything can be either a subject or a predicate; indeed this is true even of **nothing**, as in the judgements that nothing is identical with nothing, that nothing is opposed to something, and the like. By contrast, transcendental philosophy considers the forms of subject and predicate in relation to real objects, i.e. objects determined with respect to their relation to one another and by means of conditions. Here the subject is the part of a synthesis that can also be thought in itself irrespective of its connection with another part; and the predicate is the other part, the part that cannot be though in itself but only as a determination of the subject; what logic terms subject and predicate are termed substance and accident in transcendental philosophy.

Subject and predicate are conditions for thinking an object in general; the reason is that thought requires unity in the manifold and this presupposes the connection of something determinable to its determination, i.e. subject and predicate. Substance and accident are conditions for perceiving an object | in general because 'perception' means 'relation of inherence of a representation in an object'. For example, I perceive that the leaf is green, and the like, i.e. relation of the accident to the substance.

When the antecedent and consequent of a hypothetical statement are

---

[13] TN. i.e. if the essence is a whole consisting of parts, and its properties follow from the essence, then they are not themselves parts. However if, for example, *AB* has different consequences (properties) than *A* or *B* alone, this is a ground for considering *AB* to be different from *A* or *B*, and thus to be a (new) whole.

applied to objects of experience, they become cause and effect. Antecedent and consequent are conditions of judgement in general because in a judgement the predicate is posited hypothetically on the presupposition of the subject. Cause and effect are conditions of the perception of an alteration. For the relation of succession of B upon A is impossible to think as a subjective unity without an objective unity at its ground. So in this case, as in the case of the relation of substance and accident (the law of the determinable and the determination), there is a rule relating the objects to one another and by means of which they are posited in a relation of cause and effect. This rule is: if the objects A and B are to stand in the relation of cause and effect, then they must have the greatest possible identity to one another and the least possible difference. All the objections that are customarily made against this claim on the basis of an experienced difference between cause and effect | are groundless and must fall immediately away if we only bear in mind that in these cases the whole [*Totum*] of A does not cause the whole [*Totum*] of B, but rather a mere modification of A is the cause of one and the same modification of B; so this modification must necessarily be identical in both (discounting the small alteration it underwent because of the different objects). Without this rule for succession, we could not perceive the succession itself because the temporal sequence is a subjective form or way of relating things to one another and so it cannot be directly related to things, but only indirectly, by means of a perceived relation.

I doubt the reality of experience itself so that for me the categories are not, as they are for Kant, conditions of experience (objective perception); rather they are conditions of perception in general, which no one can doubt. If someone objects that we do in fact have perceptions of the succession of objects upon one another even in the absence of the relation expressed in the rule; then I reply: this only occurs in relation to some perception | in which it is actually to be found, i.e. what is simultaneous with the succession is viewed as the succession. So the difference between Kant's way of presenting the law of causality and my way is as follows: for Kant this law is expressed like this: if A and B are to be recognized in perception as the antecedent and consequent of a hypothetical proposition, then they must follow one another immediately, and this succession must occur according to a rule (that the cause, or what is subsumed under the antecedent, must always come first, and the effect, or what is subsumed under the consequent, must follow). For me, by contrast, it must expressed like this: if A and B are to be recognized

MY ONTOLOGY

in perception in the relation of antecedent and consequent of a hypothetical judgement, then they must follow one another immediately, and this outer relation (of the succession) must have its ground in an inner relation (in the greatest possible identity). According to Kant, the cause determines the effect, but not the reverse. According to me, on the other hand, they determine one another reciprocally. |

On Symbolic Cognition and Philosophical Language

| Symbolic cognition is of great importance. It is by means of symbolic cognition that we attain abstract concepts and compose concepts in different ways out of these so that we are in a position to discover **new** truths from those we **already know**; i.e. to use our reason at all. On its own, intuitive cognition would certainly already give us an advantage over the irrational animals, because within their sphere they merely perceive **what is** – whereas we have cognition of what necessarily **must be**: but on its own, this advantage would be slight; like them, we could only ever perceive what is present, what we have before our eyes; whereas by means of symbolic cognition we attain cognition of what is absent and even of what is the furthest away of all, to infinity. But if it is to be of any use, symbolic cognition must be grounded in intuitive cognition; without this it would be a mere form without objective reality.
I I venture to claim that the insoluble difficulties and important disputes in the sciences have arisen from a lack of insight into the nature of symbolic cognition, and hence that these difficulties can be overcome and these disputes resolved merely by setting down the limits of the use of symbolic cognition, by specifying its different types, and by adjusting the symbolism itself (the sign system) accordingly. I shall therefore lay my thoughts on this point before the world; but for the time being I want to indicate only the idea, in order to keep the complete development of my thoughts for another occasion.

On Symbolic Cognition and Philosophical Language

What is symbolic cognition? Wolff says this: if our cognition is characterized by the fact that we express what is contained in ideas by means of words or represent it by other signs, but we do not intuit the ideas themselves that are so designated[1] – then this is termed **symbolic** cognition.[2] This definition needs explaining. For what does this sentence mean: 'We have no ideas or representations of an object – and yet we still designate them'? How is this possible, given that signs are signs only because they lead to the representations of things! Baumgarten's definition (namely that [cognition is symbolic] if the representation of the sign is greater than that of the designated thing) could indeed hold as a *definitio nominalis*. But the *definitio realis* is missing, i.e. an explanation of how it is possible that the representation of the sign should be greater than that of the designated thing. So I will try to make this clear.

It is established that the use of signs rests on the law of the association of ideas, i.e. if someone has often had [the same set of] different representations at the same time (or more exactly in an immediate temporal sequence), then they will be connected to one another in the imagination so that subsequently, if the one representation is again produced by the object, it will occasion the reproduction of the other. But this '**often**' that conditions the law ('if someone has often ..') is an indeterminate quantity and its determination must be different for different subjects and different relations of objects to these subjects; it can happen that the (contingent or arbitrary) connection of signs with the things they designate has not occurred **often enough** to be sufficient for the reproduction of the things upon the representation of the signs, so that an exertion of mind is required to accomplish this reproduction, and sometimes even every exertion is no help. In the first case, the representation of the sign is stronger than that of the designated thing;

---

[1] TN. In this chapter Maimon uses two principal verbs when speaking of the relation of signs to what they signify: '*bedeuten*' and '*bezeichnen*'. To help the reader to identify which is being used, the former has been translated by 'mean' or 'signify' and the latter by 'designate'. Likewise '*Bedeutung*' has been translated by 'meaning' or 'signification' and '*Bezeichnung*' by 'designation'. Any exceptions have been marked. The two occurrences of the verb '*andeuten*' have been translated by 'indicate'.

[2] TN. Wolff, *Psychologia empirica*, § 289, in G.W. II Abt., Bd 5, G. Olms (Hildesheim, 1986), p. 204. This is a translation of Maimon's German version of Wolff's Latin.

but in the second, only the representation of the sign is present, without the representation of the thing, and yet we represent the sign to ourselves[3] [*sich vorstellen*] as a sign (as something that refers to something else), i.e. we represent the sign to ourselves as a sign of something determinable in general, but not of a determinate thing; through the connections of signs we can even imagine the connections that the things designated by the signs maintain to each other.[4] According to these famous men, this comprises symbolic cognition, except that I Wolff limits his definition to just one case (where the representation of the thing is not present at all), whereas Baumgarten also includes in his definition the case where the representation of the thing is merely weaker than that of the sign. I note, however, that (according to linguistic usage) symbolic cognition means a particular mode of cognition that is determined by the object it refers to. But on this definition symbolic cognition would be determined merely by means of a subjective ground. The very same sentence can be both intuitive and symbolic, i.e. in relation to different subjects, or even in relation to one and the same subject at different I times. Consequently, this definition does not determine an object. As a result, I want to venture another definition: An object of cognition is a unity that is thought by the understanding in the manifold; the manifold is the given, or the matter; but the unity is the form that connects the matter of the manifold. For example, a triangle, i.e. a space enclosed by three lines, is an object of intuition; the space and the three lines comprise the matter, the manifold that becomes an object

---

[3] TN. *sich vorstellen*. This means 'to imagine', but since Maimon is claiming that we do in fact have a representation of the sign (and therefore do not need to imagine it) we have translated the phrase in this sentence according to its underlying literal meaning 'to represent to oneself'.

[4] When we read a book or hear speech, the representations or concepts of the objects are often quite obscure although their relations are clear; this is because we more often perceive the former expressed in words than in themselves so that their images become weaker and weaker until they become completely obscured; by contrast, their relations are not intuitive images but *a priori* concepts that emerge at the instigation of intuitions, i.e. indivisible unities; so they are not subject to any fading away, and because they were at one time connected with words they always remain connected in their full strength thanks to this association. Intuitive images can gradually fade away until they have been totally obliterated, i.e. they can be forgotten; by contrast, *a priori* concepts are continually present to the understanding, needing only intuitions to provoke them to emerge.

by means of unity (connection of inherence,[5] since space can be thought without the determination of three lines, but not the other way round). In this way we are in a position to have intuitive cognition not only of the object, but also, in and through this object, to have intuitive cognition of its matter in itself and of its form in itself.

This is the only way we can ever have intuitive cognition of the form, and we can have intuitive cognition of the matter only on condition that it is itself an object comprising matter and form (as is the case in the cited example), and in no other way: and nonetheless each of them must also be in itself real, outside the connection, because otherwise the connection itself would be impossible; the reason is that the connection merely makes their reality intuitive and does not bestow this reality on them, but rather presupposes it (since no synthesis can be thought without the unity of the form). In this case therefore we find ourselves forced to think of something of which we have no intuitive cognition as a real object, so that we can represent it only by means of signs, and hence it comprises an object of symbolic cognition (if it is to be an object of cognition at all).

As a result, an object of symbolic cognition is: a form, or way, of thinking an object of intuition, that is itself treated as an object (but not of intuition).

There is, however, still another sort of object of symbolic cognition that is even more abstract than the above, namely a form that we not only cannot have intuitive cognition of outside the object of intuition, but which we also cannot have intuitive cognition of in itself. The number 1000, and all large numbers in general, or the concept of a thousand-sided polygon are all examples of this sort; I cannot bring them into an intuition and in these cases, I possess only a concept of the form, or the way that the concept is possible, but not an intuitive cognition of it itself as object, that is to say: because I have an intuitive cognition of the number 10 through an empirical construction (for example through intuition of my ten fingers, and the like), I also have an intuitive

---

[5] TN. i.e. by being brought under the category of inherence (the determination of substance by accidents) – see Kant's table of categories, A80/B106. Note that Kant restricts the categories to the discursive use of reason in providing the conditions of a possible object of experience, and does not give them a role in the intuitive use of reason in constructing mathematical concepts, as Maimon appears to do here with the category of substance (although this claim as to the exclusively discursive use of the categories is complicated by Kant's saying that 'only the concept of magnitudes can be constructed'). See 'The discipline of pure reason in its dogmatic use', A712/B740ff.

cognition of 100, i.e. one that takes 10 as unit repeated ten times, and also of 1000, i.e. one that this time takes 100 as a unit repeated ten times, and so on. But in the last two cases, as in the first, I have an intuitive cognition only of 10 (albeit in relation to another unity); but I have a merely symbolic cognition of 100 and 1000 in relation to absolute unity. We comprehend the way they arise without intuiting them as having already arisen.[6] So we cannot make such concepts cognizable [*kennbar*] by means of the objects in which they are found, but only by means of signs. Let us assume that there are 1000 soldiers here and I want to teach someone the concept of the number 1000 by saying to him that it is the number of these soldiers: then he will begin to count them; but this will be no help to him because when he is finished, he will certainly be able to form a concept of the way the number 1000 arises, but not of the number itself as an object of intuition. So symbolic cognition extends to infinity (*qua materia*), as with, for example, a circle viewed as a polygon with infinitely many sides, the asymptotes of a curved line, and the like. Although we cannot think the infinite as an object this is besides the point here, since we do not make use of infinity to think the object, but merely to think the way it arises; and the possibility of the object itself makes no contribution at all to this because, even if the object were possible, we must still have cognition of its form in itself and not through the object.

This is why I also hold that geometrical propositions can be demonstrated far more powerfully through the *methodus indivisibilium*, or the differential calculus, than in the usual way. Euclid proves after his manner that triangles lying on the same base and between two parallel lines must be equal, although they may still differ from one another in shape.[7] But this equality must first be inferred (through certain tricks in drawing neighbouring lines) and cannot be seen in the triangles themselves; by contrast, if we follow the *methodus indivisibilium*, then this equality is proven directly from the triangles themselves; namely, from the fact that they arise in the same way. The lines drawn for this purpose should not be viewed as objects (because an area is not composed of lines), but instead merely as the schema of the form or way in which the triangles arise.

As a result, I cannot share the opinion of **Ben David** when he asserts

---

[6] TN. '*Wir begreifen ihre Entstehungsart, ohne sie doch als schon entstanden, anschauen.*'

[7] TN. Euclid, *Elements*, Bk 1, Prop. 37: 'Triangles which are on the same base and in the same parallels are equal to one another'. NB 'Equal' here means 'of equal area', *not* 'congruent'.

(*Versuch über das mathematische Unendliche* [*Essay on the Mathematical Infinite*]): 'That the advantage elementary geometry possesses over other sciences in regard to [its self-] evidence [*Evidenz*], it must also possess over higher geometry and algebra, namely that the reality of the former can be shown through construction, but that of the latter cannot'.[8]

But I ask: why does this matter? If we sometimes obtain an equation in algebra containing something impossible, then this impossibility must manifest itself in the solution, because this is how we obtain imaginary numbers, as, for example, if we are asked to find two numbers whose sum is 12 and whose product is 48. There are of course no such numbers, but this manifests itself in the solution because we derive $x = 12 - y$ (this is obvious), but y, which determines $x, = \sqrt{-12} + 6$,[9] making it clear that the two numbers are impossible. Higher geometry has its own constructions just as much as elementary geometry; an ellipse, a parabola, a hyperbola, etc., can all be constructed just as well as a circle.[10] Perhaps **Ben David** understands the term 'differential magnitudes' to mean something that cannot be presented in intuition; but if these cannot be represented in themselves, they can nevertheless be represented through a schema, since, if we consider the matter more exactly, the objects of ordinary geometry can also be represented only through a schema. We never find geometric figures that fully correspond to the conditions expressed in the definition. The theory of transcendental magnitudes is no less evident than the former theory; and how can we doubt the evidence of higher geometry, when its results precisely accord with those produced from ordinary geometry? Is this merely a coincidence? No mathematician would accept that. But I mention this only in passing.

---

[8] TN. L. Ben David, *Versuch einer logischen Auseinandersetzung des mathematischen Unendlichen* (Berlin, 1789).

[9] TN. Ehrensperger introduces a mistake not present in the original by writing this as $\sqrt{(-12+6)}$. The problem is expressed by two simultaneous equations which yield the quadratic equation $-y^2 + 12y - 48 = 0$, this has two roots, $y = 6 + \sqrt{-12}$ and $y = 6 - \sqrt{-12}$ of which Maimon just supplies the former.

[10] TN. 'Construction' [*Konstruktion*] is ambiguous in more than one way. First Maimon follows Kant in distinguishing pure construction in the imagination from empirical construction on paper. Second he acknowledges a distinction between mechanical construction (just as the circle can be drawn by rotating a line around one of its endpoints, so the other curves mentioned can be drawn using strings, fixed points, and straight edges) and geometrical construction (by using the equation of the curve to determine any number of points that lie on it). The first distinction is discussed in a footnote to Chapter 2, s.42, the second in the article from the *Berlinisches Journal Für Aufklärung* in the Appendices.

According to this definition, all experiential concepts and propositions will be excluded from symbolic | cognition; indeed so will all the axioms of mathematics, and even all *a priori* concepts, in so far as they are not just forms, but themselves objects of intuition; so symbolic cognition comprises only forms, or rules guiding the way that objects arise. The categories are of this kind, and so are algebraic formulae, indeed in every (moderately long) chain of inferences [*Schlusskette*] only pairs of propositions that immediately follow one another are connected by an intuitive cognition, the others are connected merely by a symbolic cognition. At the same time we can see from this that not everything signs are used for belongs to symbolic cognition, because we also use arbitrary symbols even when there are already existing natural signs, as for example all the words we use to express intuitions and concepts that can be presented in intuitions. Here the object itself is a natural sign of its representation, and also the reverse; but we make use of the arbitrary sign not so as to have cognition of the object, but rather just to renew our cognition of the object in ourselves or in others (if the object itself is absent). By contrast, with symbolic cognition of forms and their relation to one another, there is no object there that could provide a sign of this cognition except for the arbitrary symbol itself; this is because | if the object is already presented in intuition, then the concept will for this very reason not be presented in intuition, it must rather already be in itself an object of cognition, as has already been shown above. All other linguistic words are learnt through an association arising from a repeated arbitrary connection of the word with the object it designates. The words comprising symbolic cognition are not learnt through the association of words with objects, but of words with the concept that we think at the instigation of the object.

I believe that there is an obvious difference between connecting an intuition as object to another intuition so that the reproduction of one brings about the reproduction of the other and connecting a rule of the understanding (that is not itself an object) to an intuition. The first procedure is also commonly counted as symbolic cognition, in so far as the one intuition provides a sign of the other; but on a proper understanding, only the second belongs to symbolic cognition because in that case the sign is an instrument for representing something as an object of intuition that is not [in fact] an object of intuition. |

Symbolic cognition even has an advantage over intuitive cognition, since it extends further than the latter. How difficult it is to demonstrate the properties of curves using the method of the ancients, and how simple with the new analysis! The ancients certainly showed more genius in their discoveries than the moderns; but their method did not allow them take their discoveries as far as the moderns. In comparison with the moderns, the ancients are like those who can lift a certain weight without the help of a machine compared to those who need this assistance; the former show greater strength than the latter, but the latter are in a position to lift greater weights than the former. Whether modern mathematicians make too much of this (I do not mean with respect to the usefulness of their discoveries, but rather with respect to their intrinsic value) is easy to determine from the foregoing. I cannot but place here an extract of Court Counsellor **Kästner's** essay (*Unde plures insint radices aequationibus sectiones angulorum definitionibus*), which confirms what I have said with as much brilliance as wit:

> There is this in common between every calculation and machines, that they save us the trouble of constantly having under our eyes one by one all the things that we are doing, and they do this so well that in handling a calculation or a machine according to fixed laws, even people ignorant of what is happening during the operation obtain the desired result. Diderot, refusing to accept that in order to charm the ears by plucking some strings with skill it is necessary to have practised with the fingers since early childhood, invented a machine thanks to which even someone ignorant of music could achieve the same result by turning a handle. But he who uses this machine without knowing its construction would not merit the title of musician at all. And I think that musicians, like poets, painters and almost all artists who produce pleasure by their natural ability, being rather offended, would scarcely accept a person who plays on this machine even when it is thoroughly understood. If one notices the resemblance between such a machine and algebraic calculation, one will be less astonished that the English find it more elegant to employ synthetic and analytic geometry than algebraic calculus. One will also find that algebraists who take themselves seriously resemble those buffoons who run through the more densely populated states of Germany, and invite the population by yelling to admire the miracle of a magic lantern and the jumps of the Alpine mouse, a machine that Diderot admits was the model for his own. Above all, such people end up

becoming those who, having learned in passing the elements of geometry from a little summary by some recent author and having neglected to read the ancients, progress towards what they call algebra, that is to say, learn in some fashion to manipulate calculations with letters, I but do not arrive at analysis itself, which is the guide of calculations, because they have not shaped their intellect for it by a certain amount of training and do not possess the geometrical learning which it makes use of, but charm the eyes of the crowd with the frightful signs a + b − x, while often provoking laughter among those in better possession of their mathematical abc, and sometimes anger.[11]

So says a man who understands his art well, and so knows how to distinguish the real artist from the fake. I merely add that this remark about the mathematical calculus can also be applied to the philosophical calculus; I even maintain that it is far more important for the philosophical than it is for the mathematical. With the mathematical calculus it serves merely to make us aware of the distinction between those who understand the grounds of the calculus and those who do not understand them but merely act mechanically, so that we observe the

---

[11] TN. The original Latin is as follows: Est autem calculis omnibus cum machinis I id commune, ut labore singula quae agimus perpetuo ante oculos habendi, nos levent, ut calculum vel machinam certis legibus tractantes, vel eorum inscii quae durante operatione fiunt, id tamen quod desideratur obtineant. Diderotus, aegre ferens quod ad aures chordis artificiose pulsatis demulcendas, digitos fere ab infantia exercitatos habere necesse sit, machinam excogitavit, qua idem praestare possit vel ignarus musices, manubrio axis cujusdam versato. Qui hac machina nescius constructionis ejus uteretur, musici elogio omnino non esset ornandus; credo musicos ut sunt poetae, et pictores, et omnes fere ingeniosi voluptatum artifices, paulo cerebrosiores, vix eum recepturos qui machine probe intellecta luderet. Ejusmodi machinae cum calculo algebraico similitudinem qui animadvertit, is minus mirabitur cur Angli elegantius reputent synthesi aut analysi geometrica uti quam illo; idem etiam algebraicos qui sibi non contemnendi videntur, agnoscet persimiles Allobrogibus illis qui per Germaniae civitates ubi major hominum confluxus est cursitant, et ad laterna magicae miracula aut muris alpini saltus, spectators machinae talis unde Diderotus suae ideam sumsisse fatetur, ululatu inuitant. Qvales imprimis illi evadunt qui elementis Geometriae obiter ex recentioris cujusdam scriptoris compendiolo perceptis, neglecta antiquorum lectione, ad algebram quam vocant, grassantur, hoc est calculos litterales utcunque tractare discunt, ad analysin autem ipsam, que directrix est calculorum, non pertingunt, quoniam nec ingenium exercitio quodam ad illam formarunt, nec copias eruditionis geometricae quibus utitur collegerunt, vulgi tamen oculos horrendis illis signis a + b − x fascinant, prudentioribus abecedarii mathematici, saepe jocum, interdum et bilem movent.

suum cuique.[12] In this case, disregard of the distinction does not have any deleterious consequences, other than that we will take a mere calculator for an analyst. But what harm does this do? In practice, the former (someone in possession only of the rules of the calculus not the grounds) is as useful as the | latter. By contrast, with the philosophical calculus it is altogether different. Here, the calculus can be completely correct, and yet what is produced from it be of no use at all, or be quite false, because in this case the usefulness of the calculus depends on the correctness of the principles it starts out from. And anyone who has seen a little of the world will readily admit that such philosophical calculators are very common. People like this calculate according to certain systems *pro forma*, without understanding these systems themselves. They make judgements about the truth or falsity, correctness and incorrectness of particular cases without having the slightest conception of these principles. But I believe that there are certain criteria that can be used to distinguish a true philosopher from a mere philosophical calculator, or better, a philosophical machine. Namely, if (1) he does not merely rattle off formulae, but can also specify their principles and their lawful connections to one another, in so far as these are necessary to explain the way these formulae arise. 2) He presents a system discovered by someone else in such a way as not to be anxiously | holding (as commonly happens) to the particular expressions of its creator, his particular turns of phrase, his particular ordering in the presentation, and the like; but instead presents it as if he had reached this same system by his own path, so that the first inventor becomes merely the occasion for his second invention of the system. 3) He knows how to illustrate his presentation with examples. But these must be as pure as possible: in this respect I know none better to recommend than those taken from mathematics because they contain nothing superfluous and unsuitable for the explanation of the object (as do physical examples) that might confuse the object rather than clarifying it. I will clarify this point itself through examples. If someone asked me: what is a synthesis, or what is a unity in the manifold that is thought by the understanding? and I replied, I will make it clear to you using an example: a golden sphere is a synthesis, its components (the manifold) are the individual representations contained in it, the yellow colour, exceptional weight, round shape, etc. The unity is their being gathered

---

[12] TN. 'To each his own' or to render to every person their due.

together in one concept. But by doing this I would be teaching a | concept of a synthesis that is quite incorrect and at the same time I would be showing that I do not have the right concept myself because 'synthesis' signifies not merely a symbolic, but a real, and not merely a real, but a necessary, unity in the manifold. In so far as we perceive them as constantly connected in space and time, the yellow colour and exceptional weight are indeed in a real synthesis, but not in a necessary synthesis. They do not even stand in a real synthesis with the round shape (because their connection to it is not natural but merely arbitrary or contingent). But if I clarify it [the concept of synthesis] using the example of a triangle, i.e. space enclosed in three lines, only then do I teach him the true concept of a necessary synthesis because I show him that space can be thought in itself, without the determination of the three lines, whereas the latter cannot be thought without the former (because space can be thought in itself as the subject of certain predicates, e.g. infinite divisibility, but the lines cannot be thought without space).

Philosophical symbolism differs from mathematical in that everyone using mathematical symbolism understands both the signs of irresolvable concepts and | the signs of their different relations to one another in one and the same way; whereas with philosophical symbolism, there is such unanimity only with respect to the latter kind of sign, but not the former, and misunderstandings and eternal verbal disputes must necessarily arise from this. Either the atheist is a mere block-head, or the one who gives him this title is a block-head and a bad fellow as well.

Closely examined, the much-vaunted mathematical method does not actually possess any of the special benefits expected of it, for it clears the way for progress from error to error just as much as from truth to truth. So these benefits can be provided not by the mathematical method, but by the development of the principles of human cognition from the procedure of the understanding and reason in the formation of mathematical concepts and in their relation to one another.

Now that I have established the definition of symbolic cognition in general, and made it clear using examples, I will now specify its different types. Among these types are the following: 1) an | undetermined *objectum logicum*, or the concept of a **thing** in general (something thinkable), that is not determined by any conditions either *a posteriori* or *a priori*. 2) A determined *objectum logicum* that certainly cannot be determined by any *a posteriori* conditions, but can be determined by *a priori* conditions, namely by means of its relation [*Verhältnis*] to another *objectum logicum* in relation [*Beziehung*] to the faculty of thought; for example essence, predicate, and the like. 3) An *objectum reale* that is not thought in itself but by means of its connection to a real object (of intuition); the universal forms conditioning experience are of this type, for example, **substance**, **cause**, and the like. These are not merely *objecta logica*, but comprise a constituent part of an *objectum reale*, and by this means can be thought as something real. All determinations that cannot be thought in themselves separated from the determinable (see Chapter 4), but that can be thought by means of the determinable as [its] determinations, are of this type; for example, the **straightness** of a line, the **rightness** of an angle and the like. 4) A **nothing** that mathematicians nevertheless make into an object of their cognition because of the universality of their calculus | and that they express by means of signs, for example, the angle between two parallel lines, the tangent and cosine of a right angle and the like. They do not say (as is in fact the case) 'the angle between two parallel lines etc. are [*sic*] nothing', but 'the angle is infinitely small, the tangent infinitely large, the cosine again infinitely small'. They do this for the sake of the universality of their calculus, that is, when they have proved a property of a tangent, cosine or angle in general they then want to apply it to these particular cases of tangent, cosine or angle, and can legitimately do so only if they substitute the infinitely small and the infinitely large into the general formula expressing this property. But I myself fail to see the special benefits of this operation; their $\frac{a}{0} = \infty$ and other similar formulae also belong to the same type.

I do not think it is necessary to read all of the books on the topic to clarify these mysterious formulae. It is only necessary to read a **Kästner**, who says in fewer | words more than is contained in all these books.

I only remark that although all such formulae signify '**nothing**', they are still divided into particular types and these must be precisely distinguished from one another. a) A nothing containing a contradiction so that its essence is completely destroyed by the property of the infinity of the quantum, for example, an infinitely small line contains a contradiction; this is because a line is essentially infinitely divisible. So an infinitely small line (*omni dabili minor*) is a line that is not divisible (because otherwise it will not be *omni dabili minor*, since the parts must be smaller than the whole), and hence it ceases to be a line at all. The cosine of a right angle contains a contradiction because a right angle cannot have a complementary angle in order to complete a right-angled

triangle,[13] and so the cosine of a right angle, i.e. the sine of this complementary angle, is a sine that is not a sine. The sum of all natural numbers contains a contradiction because 'sum' signifies a number that is equal to several other numbers; consequently the sum of all possible numbers is itself a number, and the given | sum is not the sum required.
b) A nothing that is nothing not because it contains a contradiction but because no object can be given for it in intuition; for example, an infinitely long line. Finitude is not contained in the concept of line and so infinity cannot contradict it. But the concept cannot be constructed, i.e. presented in intuition as an object. The angle between parallel lines also contains no contradiction when it arises by moving the meeting-point of the lines enclosing a given angle to infinity; this angle is simply not an object of intuition; and it is the same with the tangent of a right angle (as the secant intersects it at an infinite distance, which is not impossible although it is inconceivable).

In addition, there is yet another type of object of symbolic cognition, c), objects that not only contain no contradiction, but are also real objects of intuition (as quanta); they can nevertheless be represented only symbolically because a contingent determination inheres in them in intuition that must therefore be excluded | from their essence. So intuition does not contribute to their possibility: we do not **think** them by means of intuition, but merely have **cognition** of them; differential magnitudes are of this type. Consider two lines (of determinate position) in a general functional relationship that gives rise to a continually varying numerical relationship. Because lines arise through movement (of a point), the two lines must have a different velocity at each instant of their movement. So the velocities of these lines at each instant are represented by the differentials, and the relations of these differentials are the relations of these velocities to one another. Now, the velocity at each instant is a real object (a determinate intensive magnitude), a quantum of determinate quantity. But we cannot have any cognition of this determinate quantity through the velocity in itself, but only through its effect, namely through the space that a body with this velocity would traverse (if the velocity remained constant); but neither the duration of the movement nor the space traversed in this time are part of the essence

---

[13] TN. 'weil ein rechter Winkel keine Ergänzung zu einem rechten Winkel haben kann'. The word 'triangle' has been added to better convey Maimon's meaning which seems clear.

of the velocity. | So we must think the latter abstracted from the former, i.e. we must reduce them to an infinitely small space and an infinitely small time; but this does not make them any the less real.

As a result I am more than a little surprised at **Ben David**. This is why: after he has announced his principal proposition, namely that the infinitely small = the infinitely large = 0, and sought to clarify it through examples (*Versuch über das mathematische Unendliche*),[14] not only does he fail to distinguish precisely these different types of **nothing** from one another (a precision we have the right to expect in a book of this kind, particularly as he himself had already noted the distinction between *nihil negativum* and *privativum*) and hence places the sum of all numbers in the same class as the tangent of a right angle (when in fact, as I remarked above, the first is something impossible, but the second, merely something incomprehensible), but he also (p. 100ff.) subjects differential magnitudes to the fate of all the types of nothing asserting that they signify simply the quality of a quantum abstracted from all quantity. I truly did not expect to find this claim here. Is a determinate velocity the mere quality of velocity | in general? And if it is, how does it acquire this quantity?[15] Through intuition, i.e. by traversing a determinate space in a determinate time? On the contrary! The magnitude of movement is not determined in the magnitude of the velocity, as I have already remarked.

Ben David goes on to say that $dx + a = a$, because a mere property cannot be added to a magnitude; but I have shown that dx is not a mere property of a quantum, but a quantum itself, and so this reason is inapplicable. The real reason is not, as **Ben David** claims, **because a property cannot be added to a magnitude**, but **because magnitudes of different types cannot be added together**. We can add dx to a about as much as we can add a pound to a cubit and the like.

As I have now defined the concept of symbolic cognition in general, as well as its different types, I will now take the different signs that can be used in such cognition and compare them to one another with respect to their final ends [*Endzwecke*]. |

In the first place, there can be natural as well as arbitrary signs; the fine arts provide an example of the former, language of the latter. The

---

[14] TN. L Ben David, *Versuch einer logischen Auseinandersetzung des mathematischen Unendlichen* (Berlin, 1789), pp. 24, 28, 34 ff.

[15] TN. By 'this quantity', Maimon is referring to the determinate quantity of the instantaneous velocity.

natural signs have an advantage over arbitrary ones, since no one apart from their inventor can understand the latter without study, whereas the former are equally understood by everyone. However: **what is easy to learn is usually of little value.** For natural signs contain either too much or too little regarding the thing they designate. They cannot represent the universal abstracted from all individual circumstances; the person in a portrait does not represent the universal concept of 'person', but is instead a person of determinate build and size. Consequently they are unsuitable for scientific use, which is grounded only in universal concepts; i.e. they contain too much, and so cannot provide signs of adequate concepts. – But looked at from the other side, they also contain too little because it is possible to designate some things, or at least certain determinations of these things, that are not sensible intuitions. For example, how would we give a sensible representation of the soul and its manifold operations? I We would have to resort to the most remote analogies! – But how would we then prevent the misunderstandings that necessarily arise from the fact that most people stop at mere sensible signs, and will not reflect upon any analogy? And those who do have this ability will reach different analogies, according to the differences in their genius. The vulgar errors of heathen mythology, and yes, the misinterpretations of Holy Scripture, where else do they come from than from this impure source? This is too well known for me to need to dwell on it.

On the other hand, while it is true that arbitrary signs must be learnt, it is also true that they can be learnt **correctly**; language is of this type, it is a collection of words arising from the manifold combinations of a small number of possible sounds. I will not here consider languages in terms of their origin, but only how they are for us today. I freely admit that nothing happens without sufficient reason [*Grund*], and that primitive words were also natural signs (of what could be heard) I of objects,[16] and that those words derived from and composed out of them were also natural signs of the concepts of objects derived from and composed out of the former objects. For us words are and remain mere arbitrary signs: so they must of necessity be learnt, and this in two regards. First, we must learn a foreign language, even with respect to its primitive words, either

---

[16] TN. '*natürliche Zeichen (des Hörbaren) der Gegenstände waren*'. This phrase is too concise for its meaning to be obvious, but Maimon may be saying that the first words imitated the sounds made by the objects to which they referred.

by being shown the object or through translation into our mother tongue. Second, we even have to learn the mother tongue itself with respect to the meaning of those words that signify objects derived from and composed out of primitive objects but that are themselves (with respect to our consciousness) not derived and composed [i.e. simple]; this we do by substituting those that are [composite], i.e. these words must be defined. For example, even in my mother tongue I must translate **person** [*Mensch*] by **rational animal** because the obscure representations that words otherwise carry with them cannot give us any precise cognition of objects. But as Locke correctly remarks, such words have occasioned only ignorance and idleness in language. People did not want | or were not able to notice that an object is derived from and composed out of other objects: they contented themselves with an obscure or at best clear representation of it,[17] and therefore instead of calling a person a **rational, living thing**, they just say **person** and the like. This makes it clear that, properly understood, philosophy is nothing other than a universal grammar [*allgemeine Sprachlehre*]. This is because 1) it gives as a universal rule for every language that the signs or words of the language must agree most precisely with the things they designate; primitive, or irresolvable things must be expressed through primitive or irresolvable signs, derived or composite things through derived and composite signs; 2) it conducts a special investigation into which things are primitive and which are derived from and composed out of the primitive, as well as into the degree of this derivation and composition by dividing things *in genera et species*, so that each is attributed the sign most precisely agreeing with it. So philosophy does not possess a dictionary of its own, but makes use of the dictionary of any language as matter so as to apply its grammar as | universal form to it. It is of no concern to philosophy whether one thing is called *animal* and another *ratio*, or the first *Thier* and the other *Vernünft*;[18] it merely prescribes that what is composed out of these two should also be designated by means of a composition of the two expressions (along with the sign of the composition itself, which is the form of the adjective). Thus

---

[17] TN. 'at best clear', i.e. clear but nevertheless not distinct, as will be explained below.

[18] TN. '*Animal/ratio*' and '*Vernunft/Thier*' are respectively the Latin and German words for 'animal/reason' In this paragraph Maimon compares the German '*vernunftige Thier*' with the Latin equivalent '*animal rationale*'. The German words have not been translated into English because of the risk of confusion arising from the lack of difference between the English 'rational animal' and the Latin.

in the first case, it will be called *animal rationale*, but in the second, *vernünftiges Thier*. (The particular way of connecting these two, namely that in the first case *ratio* is inflected by *nale*; but in the second, *Vernunft* is inflected by *tiges*, does not belong to philosophical grammar but to each particular grammar.)

However, if we look at the structure [*Einrichtung*] of actual languages, we find that although in themselves they possess this form to a greater or lesser degree, they are nonetheless far from [completely] achieving it (because these languages were not invented by philosophers according to distinct concepts, but by the common man according to confused, or at best clear, representations); and because the perfection of any thing must be judged according to its final end, so the perfection of any language must be judged according to the final end | of language in general. So if we are to compare languages with one another in this respect, then we must compare them all with an ideal language most adequate to the final end of language in general; in this way we will determine the level of perfection of each according to its degree of proximity to this ideal language.

So, first I want to specify some of the principal conditions for this ideal language, and in doing this, to determine the degree of perfection or imperfection of actual languages in general, so that the thinking reader who is also a linguist, will also be in a position to compare different languages with one another in this regard; however I consider the perfection of language here only as the perfection of signs in relation to the thoughts they designate, not its perfection in and for itself (with respect to the melodiousness of its sounds).

1) In an ideal language the signs (words) must agree most precisely with the things (concepts) they designate. To this end, the number and quality of the *partes orationis*[19] | must not be abstracted from actual languages, but determined according to *a priori* principles and arranged in a system; this postulate is possible because logic and transcendental philosophy can provide its ground since their objects can be determined and made numerically complete *a priori* (the object of the former is a thing in general, while the objects of the latter are things determined by *a priori* conditions).

So there would have to be no more and no less *partes orationis* than there are forms or types of things that are to be related to one another;

---

[19] TN. Parts of speech.

these types in turn would have to be divided into subtypes, which must again be divided into the types of which they are composed; the principal types would have to be expressed through primitive signs and the species contained under them or composed out of them would have to be expressed through signs derived from or composed out of the primitive signs. For example, if we want to take Aristotle's categories as the most general forms of thought, then we will first have two *partes orationis* designating the two principal types of concepts, namely substance and accident (since the nine categories, besides substance, are only accidents). But because these two concepts are related to one another | and reciprocally define one another, I will first express both using a common sign, and then subsequently divide [*bestimmen*] this common sign into two different types to express each of these two principal species in a particular way. For example, if I call substance, *ba*, then I will call accident, *ab*, i.e. with the same letters, only in reversed order; the identity of the letters will then indicate the identity of the relation of these concepts to one another, but the reversed order their opposed position in this relation. I will further divide substance (what can be thought only as subject and not as predicate of anything) into its subtype.

a) *Subjectum logicum*. This in turn into its subtypes:
   α) The undetermined universal thing.
   β) The determined. For example, **essence**, **property**, and the like.
b) *Subjectum reale*, this in turn into,
   α) *Subjectum reale a priori*.
   β) *a posteriori*. – And since I have termed the undetermined *subjectum logicum ba*, so | I will call the determined *bac*, the *subjectum reale a priori bai*, the *a posteriori bau*. And so I will continue with my division as long as the need to speak requires. The *adjectivum* and *adverbium* must not be described [*bezeichnet*] as property and contingency respectively. One and the same proposition should not signify different relations at the same time. In this ideal language everything would thus have its ground and all signs (except the irresolvable ones), as well as the concepts they designate, will be resolvable into irresolvable signs. We will be able to specify with certainty the way that concepts have arisen on the basis of the way that signs have arisen (and relations among concepts on the basis of relations among signs), something that will greatly facilitate our insight into truth.

How do things stand in this regard with actual languages? – We must admit that we are far from achieving this ideal, even though some progress has been made. Unlike the language of the Hurons,[20] our languages certainly have a lot of derived and composite words; but have we taken these as far as we can and should? Are the *partes orationis* precisely determined; are all concepts, along with their signs, arranged in a system (according to nature)? I think the answer to this question has to be no.

In particular, actual languages do not possess a criterion enabling us to recognize proper [*eigentlich*] expressions, and distinguish them from improper expressions: there must be improper expressions as soon as proper expressions are lacking, and there must be a criterion if the sign is supposed to agree in every detail with the object it designates. All of which has misled one famous writer (along with several others) into claiming that the greater part of every language consists of improper expressions. This claim is not only incorrect (as I will shortly show), but it is also contrary to the interests of reason and true morality (which is opposed to sentimentality [*Empfindelei*]) because it encourages materialism and makes Satan triumph over the good spirit, Ahriman over Ormuzd;[21] I mean it makes the imagination, which is constantly seeking to expand its empire and to drive out reason, triumph over reason. But in what follows I will also prove that this claim is in itself incorrect.

What are tropes?[22] It is commonly said[23] that tropes are expressions that have been diverted[24] from their original meaning into other meanings. Here, however, I am not inquiring about the nominal definition of tropes, but about the real definition, i.e. about the distinguishing marks that enable us to recognize improperly derived expressions, so that we can

---

[20] TN. Maimon is probably drawing on Monboddo's discussion of missionaries' accounts of the language of this Native American people, in Vol. 1, Ch. 5 of *Of the Origin and Progress of Language*, 6 Vols (Edinburgh, 1774); Maimon discusses Monboddo's conception of an ideal language in this work below.

[21] TN. Ahriman and Ormuzd: names of the evil and good spirits in Zoroastrianism.

[22] TN. The following pages (ss. 303–9) are taken from an article '*Was sind die Tropen?*' published by Maimon in the *Journal für Aufklärung*, Bd 5, St 2, pp. 162–79. J. H. Tieftrunk responded to Maimon in the same journal and he in turn replied with a further article. See Maimon's *Gesammelte Werke*, Bd II, pp. 443ff., 469ff.

[23] TN. Sulzer, *Allgemeine Theorie der schönen Kunste: Tropen*.

[24] TN. The word translated by 'diverted' is '*abgeleitet*'. This can mean either 'diverted' or 'derived', it was used many times with the latter meaning above ('derived' versus 'primitive' signs), and is so used again in the following sentence (in the phrase 'improperly derived expressions'). Wherever one these two terms or their corresponding nouns 'diversion' and derivation' appears below, the other meaning should also be kept in mind.

distinguish them from proper and original expressions? As long as these remain undiscovered, the nominal definition is of no help at all to us. Disregard of these distinguishing marks of determination has misled this famous writer (and others) to claim that the greater part of each and every language consists in tropes or improper expressions; and to prove this, expressions are cited that are common to heterogeneous things, such as **comprehend** [*begreifen*], **grasp** [*fassen*], and the like. But this claim allows poetry to wander too far into the domain of prose and hence to crowd prose out too much, so that in this | regard we can never make out with certainty what is poetry and what is prose. I will make an effort to solve the question I have raised, to set poetry and prose in their correct places, and to establish their distinguishing marks [*Unterschiedungsmerkmale*] according to *a priori* principles; this will at the same time make it clear that only the lesser part of language and not the greater part can consist of tropes.

In order to accomplish this, I must set out a few truths in advance: 1) The use of an improper expression must have an objective ground as well as a subjective ground. It is true that even the writers already mentioned presuppose this, since the objective ground is the ground of the possibility of an association in general, while the subjective ground is the ground for the particular determination of the series of this association. I hope everyone will allow me these truths, even without proof. 2) The similarity of objects cannot provide this ground. Suppose there is an object ab (a determined by b) whose proper expression is x. Let us also assume another object, ai, that (because of its similarity to the former, in so far as a is identical in both) is designated using the same expression, but that this expression is improper for this second object; then we must | necessarily accept that the expression cannot signify the whole object, ab; rather, it can signify only the a common to both (the determinable that is differently determined in each of them); if this were not so, then its use for ai would be groundless. So it is proper both for ai as well as for ab because it signifies one and the same a in both expressions. So, if an improper expression is still to be possible, we must look for another reason for using it. Now, however, besides the objective relation of things to one another (through unity, opposition, and the like) there are also subjective relations; I do not mean [*meinen*] contingent ones having a particular ground in the particular thinking individual, but essential relations, proper to the whole class,[25] i.e.

---

[25] TN. '*der ganzen Art eigne Beziehungen*'. 'Class' could refer back either to things or individuals.

relations that refer to objects in general by means of the forms of our cognitive faculty, for example, substance and accident, cause and effect, and the like. So this is where we must make inquiries about the ground of these derivations: these relations are none other than the forms of cognition in relation to things in general, determined from logic, and as a result we can determine the tropes that arise from them according to the same | *principia a priori* and fix the limits between poetry and prose with the greatest precision.

I want to explain myself on this point in more detail:

In every language there are transcendental expressions, i.e. expressions that are common to both material and immaterial things, as for example, the **movement** of the body and of the mind,[26] **grasping** [*fassen*] a body and **grasping** a thought and the like. Further, we know from the history of human development that sensible representations and concepts (with respect to our consciousness) precede intellectual ones. From this we infer that these transcendental expressions are originally and properly intended [*bestimmt*] for the designation of sensible objects, but subsequently diverted[27] from this application to designate the super-sensible; this notion is the source of the opinion about the tropes that I mentioned above. By contrast, I claim that, even assuming this were correct with respect to the history of our cognition and of its designation (language), it still does not follow from this assumption that these transcendental expressions should not be just as properly used for immaterial things as for material things, or more precisely, that they should not be properly used for the transcendental concept common to heterogeneous things (however I will never accept this assumption, since the cognition of particular matters [*Materiellen*] presupposes the cognition of universal forms [*Formellen*], under which they are subsumed, | and through which their[28] cognition is effected). For example, we cannot say that if in paradise Adam first saw a red cherry and called it red, and then a red apple and called that red as well, it follows that he first used a prosaic expression, and then a poetic [expression], and that the expression **red** is proper with respect to cherry, but improper (and hence a trope) with respect to apple; in fact the expression **red** does not mean

---

[26] TN. '*Bewegung des Körpers und des Gemüts*'. These same terms have been translated by 'physical movement and mental movement' below.

[27] TN. '*abgeleitet*' – see note above.

[28] TN. The pronouns 'they' and 'their' are singular in German ('*es*' and '*seine*') and have been changed to plural to match the plural noun 'matters'.

ON SYMBOLIC COGNITION AND PHILOSOPHICAL LANGUAGE

cherry any more than it means apple; instead it signifies what is common to both. It is just the same in the following case. Movement means change of determinations in time, but with the difference that in physical movement both the determination itself and its change are outer spatial determinations; whereas in mental movements they are inner relations (of identity or difference). For example, in transcendental terms, to **break off** (a flower or a speech) means: to take something that is connected to something else by means of any unity at all, and separate it. Now, in breaking off a flower, this unity is determined in a particular way so that it is a unity of actuality (coexistence in time and space); but in breaking off a speech, it is a unity of possibility or of the concept. The transcendental meaning of **movement** (of body or mind) is alteration, i.e. change in the modifications of the very same subject. Physical movement receives a further particular determination, namely that these are outer modifications (the relation of the body to different spaces). Mental movement, on the other hand, is determined by means of inner modifications. **Flowing** means a continuous sequence, one after another, of parts of a whole, with the difference that in a flowing body this continuous sequence can be thought with respect to both space and time, whereas in a flowing speech it can be thought only with respect to time. Something is **volatile**[29] if its parts can (by some means or other) be easily separated so that they cannot be recognized any more. With quicksilver, for example, this happens through the use of fire. A thought is volatile when no connection between its parts can be detected [*keinen Zusammenhang bemerkt*]. **Outside**[30] means different; however this difference is determined in a particular way according to type: with sensible objects [this is done] by means of spatial determinations but with concepts, by means of inner determinations. I will introduce one more example, from the Hebrew language, out of numerous others. The verb, אכל [*hochel*], to consume,[31] means both to eat and to burn; the transcendental concept is just the same in both; namely: maintenance of the existence of one thing through the destruction of another thing. So this expression is original and proper both for fire that

---

[29] TN. '*Flüchtig*' means 'fleeting' or 'short-lived', in scientific contexts English now prefers the Latinate term 'volatile'.

[30] TN. '*Ausser*' a preposition meaning 'outside' (spatially), that is also used more metaphorically to mean 'besides' or 'except for'.

[31] TN. '*Verzehren*'. This example in fact works as well in English with the verb 'to consume' as it does in Hebrew.

burns and for animals that consume: the flame is maintained by means of the destruction of flammable matter, just as the animal is by means of the destruction of food; so in this language, the expression: 'the fire consumes the wood', is not remotely figurative.

The invention of language reveals an extraordinary amount of both wit and acumen[32] because transcendental expressions signify transcendental concepts. But transcendental concepts are produced by comparing things and by having insight into their identity, which is an affair of wit that, at the same time, presupposes a high degree of abstraction, without which this identity could not be thought in itself. But it should be noted that in this case the effects of wit extend much further than the effects of the understanding. Hence one finds in every language expressions for transcendental concepts (those that are identical in different types of things). But expressions for concrete concepts (transcendental concepts determined in particular ways) are often lacking; for example, there may be an expression for movement in general, but not for physical or mental movement, and it is the same with all the examples mentioned above. But this does not at all serve to prove Locke's claim that understanding and wit are opposed to one another in their effects;[33] instead the cause lies merely in this, namely that the attainment of any one cognition [*Kenntnis*] presupposes another one that has already been attained, and hence cognition of what is one and the same in different things is prior to cognition of what differentiates them from one another (because it involves no comparison). But what differentiates things (the particular determinations of each) is in turn something that in each of them is one and the same as some third thing; and it is likewise recognized by this means. From this we can see that wit and understanding march in step, and that neither can in fact be thought without the other. I want to use an example to clarify this. The first person to observe a quadrilateral [*Viereck*], i.e. a figure of four sides, termed it 'quadrilateral'. But then he

---

[32] TN. '*Witz und Scharfsinn*'. In this paragraph Maimon adopts a distinction from Locke's *An Essay Concerning Human Understanding* between two faculties of the mind. The first, which Locke calls discernment or judgement and Maimon here calls *Scharfsinn* (acumen), and later *Verstand* (understanding), is the ability to carefully distinguish even similar things; the second, which Locke calls wit and Maimon *Witz*, is the ability to use similarity and metaphor to compare and combine what has been distinguished. Locke contrasts the serious labour of the former with the quick and agreeable frivolity of the latter. See John Locke, *An Essay Concerning Human Understanding*, Bk II, Ch. X1.

[33] TN. Reference provided in previous footnote.

notices another quadrilateral, although one with different angles from the first (for example, it is right-angled while the other is oblique-angled); in so far as the second is identical to the first, he also terms it 'quadrilateral.' But he still cannot determine it with respect to angle, because as yet he does not have the concept of a right or oblique angle. As a result, he is only able to recognize this determination as a determination (by comparing it with its concept), and hence achieve a distinct concept of the determined thing itself, if he has previously encountered the concept of the particular determination outside of the thing it determines. At the same time, this also makes it clear that the names of abstract things must have been invented before those of concrete things, that is, because the former presuppose only a single comparison, whereas the latter presuppose several comparisons. | I am now in a position to state both the origin of synonyms and what should be inferred about a given language from its possession of a greater or lesser number of synonyms. The course [*Gang*] language follows is like this: 1) transcendental concepts are noted and denominated by transcendental expressions; 2) their particular determinations are noted, but only by a minority of the original inventors of the language (because these require more cognition[34] [*Kenntnis*]) who consequently use different expressions from the ones originally used to designate them; by contrast, the majority still use the transcendental expressions even for particular concepts while at the same time also using the newly invented names, which therefore constitute, for this group, synonyms. The majority approaches the minority ever more closely (by achieving more and more cognitions), and in this way learns to determine the usage of words more closely; as a result, these synonyms must gradually disappear. But because the minority likewise always presses ahead and makes out new distinctions between things that in turn demand new expressions, both groups in fact always remain at almost the same distance from one another. |

Transcendental expressions that are transcendental on account of the similarity of their objects should not therefore be counted among the tropes. Tropes proper are transcendental expressions formally shared by heterogeneous things; they are diverted from one term of a relation (that they originally and properly signify) to its correlate; for things that do not

---

[34] TN. '*Mehr Kenntnis*'. This refers back to the 'several comparisons' stated as being required for cognition of particular determinations at the end of the previous paragraph.

have any relation at all to each other (either objective or subjective) cannot have a common expression (since this would then have no ground). On this basis, similar things, i.e. those having an objective relation of identity to one another, can certainly share a common expression; but it is not proper to both, rather it is proper to what is one and the same in both. By contrast, confusion [*Verwechselung*] of the correlates of a relative form has 1) a subjective ground (the subjective unification of the two by means of this form so that they can be substituted for one another); 2) this expression does not signify something common to both because, as correlates, they must exclude one another although they are at the same time certainly related to one another. These, therefore, are true tropes, and because the number of these relative forms can be determined, the number of different types of trope can also be determined. | I will cite a few examples of this type of trope that will make the difference between them and the former type (falsely so called) plain to see.

Abend[35] in the German language is a transcendental expression, common to heterogeneous things, because it signifies both the **time** and the **direction** [*Gegend*] in which the sun is to be found before it sets; but it does not at all signify something common to both (for these two refer to one another and reciprocally provide distinguishing marks for one another, but just because of this also exclude one another); so we must necessarily assume that this expression belongs originally and properly to one of them, and is diverted from there to the other. We can indeed even work out which of the two it signifies properly, and which it signifies merely as a trope: the time before the setting of the sun (when it ceases to shine above our horizon) can be conceived in itself without reference to the direction, but not the reverse, so that it is natural that this expression was originally attributed to the time, and from there diverted to the direction (on account of their subjective synthesis); | it is consequently a trope with respect to the latter. Similarly the preposition **'before'**[36] is properly used of time but improperly of space because the time determination can also be grasped in itself, whereas the space determination (i.e. before me, before the town, etc.) can only be conceived in relation to the former. Another similar expression is this: **the whole**

---

[35] TN. Meaning both 'evening' and 'the west'.
[36] TN. '*Vor*', which means 'before' in either a temporal or spatial sense, an ambiguity shared by the English word.

town is astounded. Here the word 'town' is turned[37] from its proper meaning to something related but not similar to it (the inhabitants); but another (and proper) expression for the inhabitants is already to be found in the language so that it is clear that this expression is improper.

The result of this discussion is therefore the following. 1) Poetry and prose are (leaving aside the mechanics of language) recognized with respect to their expressions as signs in relation to the things they designate and they are distinguished from one another in that the expressions of the former are proper but those of the latter improper, or derived. 2) Things whose expressions are derived from one another cannot be completely unrelated to one another because otherwise the derivation would have no ground. 3) This relation cannot be identity because otherwise the meaning would be transcendental and not derived. 4) So the relation these things have to one another must be subjective; and because the different types of subjective relation[38] of things to one another can be determined and exhaustively enumerated by logic, so it follows that all the possible types of tropes can be specified as determined *a priori* according to this principle. 5) That prose has very few expressions that are tropes: the reason for this is, as has been shown, that transcendental expressions, being far removed from tropes, i.e. from the poetic, are rather the most abstract expressions. The other tropes (more properly figures), such as personification, apostrophe, hyperbole, etc. do not concern individual expressions, but rather concern whole ways of speaking and turns of phrase that are proper to a certain state of mind and consequently do not come into consideration here; only the confusion of correlates remains to be mentioned, something that must happen only rarely in any language. By means of this discussion I think I have saved the honour of prose in a satisfactory manner, and can declare with Jourdain:

Par ma foi, il-y-a plus de quarante ans que je dis de la prose sans que j'en susse rien.[39]

---

[37] TN. *angewandt – anwenden* means 'apply', but 'wenden' means 'to turn' and Maimon seems to be using it in the more literal sense of 'turn to'; 'trope' of course itself derives from the Greek *'trepo'*, to turn.

[38] TN. Reading *'subjektiver Beziehung'* for *'subjektiver Bedeutung'*.

[39] TN. Moliere, *Le bourgeois gentilhomme*, Act II, Scene IV: 'By my faith, I have been speaking prose for more than forty years without knowing anything about it'.

The same considerations prompted a famous scholar of the last century in England, Bishop J. Wilkins,[40] to contemplate the invention of a philosophical language, that is to say one that is fully in accord with this form.

I will here cite his thoughts as presented by Lord Monboddo,[41] taking the opportunity to add a few comments; from these it will be easy to grasp both the author's plan as well as my opinion of it. First, he says: 'All things in nature are reducible to certain classes, which are termed by logicians *genus* or *species*'.[42] I add that with objects of the understanding (i.e. objects that the understanding produces out of itself, or the so called arbitrary concepts)[43] this classification and ordering into *genus* and *species* can be determined in general according to the way they arise from one another. On the other hand, it is quite different with | *a posteriori* objects; these can certainly also be classified into *genus* and *species*, and ordered under one another; but because we are not acquainted with their inner nature, this does not take place in accordance with an objective ground, but merely in accordance with a subjective one that can differ for different thinkers; as a result, a language constructed like this will be a natural [*natürliche*] philosophical language, but in no way a universal language.

Secondly: 'It is in this way only (the classification and ordering into *genus* and *species*) that we have any knowledge or comprehension [*Erkenntis oder Begriff*] of any thing: for we know nothing **absolutely**, but only **relatively**, by knowing to what genus or species it belongs, that is to say, what it has in common with other things, and what different'.[44] – To **cognize** means to subsume a particular thing under a universal concept, i.e. to subordinate it to a thing of a higher order.

---

[40] TN. John Wilkins, Bishop of Chester, *An Essay Towards a Real Character and Philosophical Language*, 2 parts (London, 1668).

[41] TN. J B Monboddo, *Of the Origin and Progress of Language*, 6 vols (Edinburgh, 1774); German translation: *Des Lord Monboddo Werk von dem Ursprunge und Fortgange der Sprache*, übersetzt v. C Schmid, Riga, 1784–85. Monboddo devotes a chapter to Wilkins' theory (Vol. II, Bk III, Ch. XIII, pp. 440–82, from which Maimon quotes). Rather than re-translating these back into English, we quote from the original English text, but have occasionally inserted the German terms used in Schmid's translation where we think this may be helpful with regard to Maimon's commentary.

[42] TN. Monboddo, op. cit., p. 444.

[43] TN. See above, Ch. 1, s.20–21, where Maimon differentiates products of the understanding as either arbitrary or spontaneous.

[44] TN. Idem, p. 444.

Thirdly, he says, 'It is these notions [*Begriffe*] [...], thus formed, by comparing things with one another, which, expressed by certain signs, audible or visible, make what we call language, [spoke or written,] and if those signs are such as to bear a reference to the class in which the thing is to be found, so that if we understand the sign, we have in effect the definition of the thing, then is the language truly a philosophical language, and such as must be universal among philosophers, who have arranged and distributed things into proper classes. It may also be said to be natural language'.[45] – Grammarians [*Sprachlehrern*] will unanimously confirm from [their knowledge of] its history that language comprises merely the signs of universal concepts because this history shows that *nomina propria* were originally *appellativa*;[46] but it also follows necessarily from the previous claim because we only achieve cognition of the unknown by comparing it with the known. Proper names always signify a universal property, although this has been forgotten over time, as can be seen in all Hebrew *nomina propria*. But as to the universality of languages formed in this way, I have already remarked that this can be attained only in the case of *a priori* things, not with *a posteriori* things. For example, the different systems of natural history require different hierarchies of things so that what, according to one system, is a *genus*, is, according to another, a *species*, and the reverse. Consequently, a language organised according to any one of these systems cannot be universal.

Fourthly, 'The difference betwixt such a language, and the common languages, is obvious. For the primitive words of those languages have no connection at all with the nature of things, or the classes to which they belong'.[47] For example, the word '**man**' has nothing in common with '**animal**', although what it designates belongs to the class designated by 'animal': by contrast, in the philosophical language the word that signifies the concept **man** would have to be the very one that signifies **animal**, only with a particular determination to indicate the difference. 'And as to the derivatives, though they have a connection with the primitive word, it is not such a connection as philosophy requires, etc.'[48]

---

[45] TN. Idem, pp. 444–45.
[46] TN. TN '*Nomina propria*' and '*appellativa*', the Latin terms for 'proper nouns' and 'common nouns' respectively.
[47] TN. Monboddo, op. cit, p. 445.
[48] TN. Idem, p. 445.

I will add some further deficiencies of common language in comparison to philosophical language. Namely, in a philosophical language the coordination of things would have to be designated as well as the different relations of subordination of things. For example, **something** and **nothing**, **light** and **darkness**, and the like, would not be designated by different words but by the very same word because they stand in one and the same relation to each other, only with different determinations that indicate the different position of the terms within the very same relation. Just as I remarked above with respect to **substance** and **accident, cause** and **effect**. Further, I also find, as was remarked earlier, that the *partes orationis* and their subdivisions are not determined or ordered in relation to one another according to any *a priori* principle. In this regard I want only to cite the example of the **article** in living languages: what is it used for? Germany's philosophical philologist [*Sprachforscher*][49] says: 'The article is used to give back to a *substantivus* the independence that is has lost as a generic name [*Gattungsnamen*], if it is necessary'. | I must admit that I cannot understand this ground. If he is talking about is the genus [*Gattung*], then, for example in the sentence, '*der Mensch ist sterblich*' [man is mortal], the article is certainly superfluous; for in this case the meaning is: **the concept 'mortal' as predicate belongs to the concept 'man' as subject**. But if he is talking about is a particular man, then 'man' is determined through a *pronomen relativum* or *demonstrativum*.[50] For example, '**the man who was there yesterday, has returned**'; or, '**this man**', etc. Indeed, sometimes even this is unnecessary, when there is no concern that the listener will confuse him with another, as for example when, Davus, Horace's slave, says to his master: *aut insanit homo*, (by which he meant Horace) *aut versus facit*, and we see clearly from his answer that the latter understood him well.[51]

Further, let us see how things stand with the subdivisions. For example, *nomen substantivum*,[52] as a particular part of speech certainly has a particular | form, but how many different kinds of *nomina substantiva*

---

[49] TN. J. C. Adelung, *Deutsche Sprachlehre* (Berlin, 1781, reprint Hildesheim, 1977), p. 248.
[50] TN. Relative or demonstrative pronoun.
[51] TN. Horace, *Satires*, Bk II, Sat. 7, final verses: '(The) man is either mad or composing verses', to which Horace replies: 'If you don't push off right away, you'll end up labourer number nine on my Sabine farm!'
[52] TN. A substantive or noun. Latin grammar distinguishes *nomina substantiva* (nouns) from *nomina adjectiva* (adjectives).

must a philosophical language distinguish, as I have already remarked? These different kinds of *nomina* would have to be designated by different forms so that they can be recognized and distinguished from one another; but common language does not possess these [forms]. It is the same with prepositions. How many different relations does the very same preposition designate in common language? For example, **to come from a place**; **to make from something** (from a material); **to infer from something**,[53] and the like. Philosophical language will of course also express all these relations with the same word because it must necessarily possess the concept common to them all: if it did not, then the identity of the designation would have no ground. But at the same time it will determine this common word in a different way in each of these relations, and it is the same with all the remaining divisions.

I believe this is enough to give an idea [*Begriff*] of the bishop's invented language. A similar idea occurred to Leibniz, | as Wolff puts it: '*pro eo quod ipsi erat ingenii acuminis*',[54] and Leibniz's names for it are: *ars characteristica combinatoria and speciosa generalis*. This is not just the invention of a philosophical language, but of a type of sign in general [*einer Art Zeichen überhaupt*] that can be used for scientific discovery[55] [*Erfinden in Wissenschaften*]. Namely, the following are required for the invention of a new proposition or the solution of a problem: first, a known or given (hypothetical) proposition expressed in signs, for example, an algebraic equation: second, signs of equal value are substituted for these signs, until you arrive at the proposition you were looking for. I want to clarify this with a simple example from arithmetic. Take the problem of finding the sum of the two numbers 752 and 183; these numbers are the given, and their sum what I am looking for; first I add 3 and 2, and so arrive at 5 (the proposition $3 + 2 = 5$ is given to me in intuition). Further, $8 + 5 = 13$, (i.e. according to our number system 3 in this column, and 1 in the next column) so I place 3 in this column and add 1 to the next column; as a result, I write 9 in it; and what I am looking for arises | from this: $752 + 183 = 935$. As a result, the thought occurred to **Leibniz** that this method of finding the unknown from the known could be established universally and not used merely to discover relations of quantities, but also of

---

[53] TN. The preposition 'from' in these examples translates the German '*aus*'.
[54] TN. By means of his ingenious mind.
[55] TN. '*Erfinden in Wissenschaften*'. Here, and for the rest of this chapter, Maimon uses *Erfinden* to designate 'discovery' rather than 'invention'.

qualities. However, he did not pursue this idea any further. He did not even show that it was possible and it remained what it was, a mere idea. We can see from this that although Leibniz's and the bishop's ideas have some similarity (with respect to their universal use), they are I think nevertheless very different from one another. Leibniz's plan is far more important than the bishop's, and its execution is correspondingly far more difficult. The bishop's plan is merely to facilitate and make universal the use of something we already possess, or at least can possess. Even without the philosophical language we can still be in possession of the correct definitions of concepts, axioms, as well as of the propositions that follow necessarily from them, and by this means we transform common language into the philosophical language. But it is hard to find | an equivalent in the philosophical language for each word we use in common language, i.e. to translate it, and this necessarily gives rise to confusion and verbal disputes, so the invention of the bishop (subject to certain constraints) would certainly be very useful.

This invention is therefore merely a means for easily learning truths, and teaching them to others, but not a means for discovering new truths; quite different expedients are required for that. How does it help me, for example, to have the correct definition of a hypotenuse, namely that it is the side of a right-angled triangle that is opposite the right angle; I will still never extract the claim that the square of the hypotenuse is equal to the sum of the squares of the other sides from this definition without construction and certain tricks in drawing some adjacent lines (called *artificia heuristica*);[56] and it is the same in other cases too.

But this plan is possible, as far as it reaches, and its possibility is even comprehensible. | By contrast, **Leibniz's** plan extends not just to the facilitation of learning; rather, it extends to scientific discovery. But how he intended to accomplish it is incomprehensible; because to do so we would have to resolve both qualities and quantities into their absolute unities (irresoluble unities); allow them to arise from these unities (and hence also from one another), and in this way determine their relation to one another. But because something is difficult to comprehend, it does not follow that it is impossible. So I was astonished to find **Ploucquet** stating in his calculus that: 'A *characteristica universalis* belongs to the dreams of excellent minds'. I must beg the astute author of this work's

---

[56] TN. Heuristic devices.

pardon; an idea is in no way a dream; it would be better to call it a divine inspiration, and my opinion is that no two things are as much opposed as an idea (if it merits this name) and a dream. Dreams have no order, no plan, and are complete chance; but ideas are nothing but order and an all-encompassing plan. An idea of something [*von einer Sache*] is, as **Kant** says: the | totality of its conditions;[57] and hence it is the highest of these conditions: its domain is the infinite and this is why it cannot be presented in an intuition while nevertheless being real, being, indeed, the ground of the reality of all our cognition.

All pure *a priori* concepts are properly ideas because we can present them in intuition only through a schema, as I have already shown on various occasions.

A categorical syllogism rests solely on an idea, and although the plan for the invention of a philosophical language, or *characteristica universalis*, can never be put into practice, we can still think of it as an ideal and approach ever closer to it. Newton's principle in his *philosophia universalis*: a body remains in itself in the state of rest or motion, until another body brings it out of this state,[58] can never be confirmed in experience because we never come across a body that always maintains its state, and yet this principle is | real as an idea; it can be presented in intuition by means of infinite approximation [*Näherung*]. The asymptote of a curved line is the same, and so are many other of the excellent ideas of pure mathematics.

All the developed languages of today were originally just as barbaric as any barbaric language that still exists today, and people have unwittingly brought them to their present degree of perfection by perpetually approaching [*Näherung*] the idea of a perfect language; and how much further might we progress, if we did this wittingly? How much a Lessing, a Mendelssohn, Wieland, and other excellent writers have contributed to it! And how much has a Kant, with his own, so unfairly condemned, language! Admittedly we will reach the highest perfection as little here as elsewhere; yet we can, if we only want to, approximate it more and more closely to infinity.

The Kantian system of categories (that he derives from the logical

---

[57] TN. See A327/B383–84.
[58] TN. An abbreviated statement of Newton's first law of motion. See Newton, *The Principia*, trans. Andrew Motte (Amherst: Prometheus Books, 1995), p. 19.

forms, and presents as complete in number) I could be especially useful for this purpose.

Now I have cited both Leibniz and the philosophers from beyond the sea – *penitus toto divisos orbe Britannos*[59] – and shown that the bishop's plan is indeed comprehensible and its execution possible even though the most important and advantageous aspect that we are entitled to expect from so difficult an undertaking cannot be realized, namely the bishop's plan cannot comprise an instrument for scientific discovery; while in its other aspect, it extends too far in that the bishop intends his universal language to be used even to designate *a posteriori* things, but these cannot be subject to any necessary universal classification, as I have already remarked; by contrast, I have shown that **Leibniz's** plan is more important because its ultimate purpose is **scientific discovery**, although he has not shown us how to execute it; – having done all this, I now want to risk offering my own opinion on this matter: It is this: I endorse the bishop's plan, but restrict it for now 1) merely to the universalization and facilitation of learning, and not to scientific discovery; 2) I restrict it further merely to the pure *a priori* sciences (pure mathematics, pure philosophy), and to this extent I believe it will be easy to execute in the following way: A dictionary could be constructed including only the conceptual appellations [*Benennungen von Begriffen*] found in *philosophia rationalis* (logic, transcendental philosophy), for example, **subject, predicate, necessity, possibility, ground, consequence, cause, effect**, etc. These appellations must be as simple as possible, i.e. monosyllabic. From these composite names could be constructed corresponding to composite concepts; for example, **force** would not receive a particular name, but instead one composed from the appellations of substance and cause; and the like.

A dictionary arranged in this way could become universal for philosophers, and it can easily be seen that this language would be far easier to learn than Greek or Latin, which a scholar must still learn, because in these latter languages, only the forms or types for thinking objects occur, but not the objects themselves. This dictionary will properly be a collection of definitions; the connection of several words from the definitions will make propositions, and this will show the different logical forms of judgement. But since I am willing to present to

---

[59] TN. Virgil, *Eclogues*, I, verse 66: 'The Britons wholly cut off from the world'.

the public a dictionary produced by me in this way, I do not want to linger any further over its arrangement.[60]

---

[60] TN. Maimon published a philosophical dictionary in 1791 (*Philosophisches Wörterbuch, Gesammelte Werke*, Vol. III), using it as a form in which to present his own philosophy, but it is not at all a dictionary based on the radical principles here described. On the other hand he does realize something of this proposal in his logic of 1794 (*Versuch einer neuen Logik oder Theorie des Denkens, Gesammelte Werke*, Vol. V), where he introduces a new logical formalism, stating: 'I have also introduced my own mode of designation, that seems to me much more natural and suitable to what it designates, than that used before'. (p. xxvii).

Notes and Clarifications on Some Passages of this Work whose Expression was Concise

Propter egestatem linguae, et rerum novitatem[1]

Looking through this work after I had finished it, I found some places where I had expressed myself at too great a length, and on the other hand places where I had expressed myself too concisely. As to the first fault, I think it can be no great disadvantage to treat these matters at length and show them from different points of view and in different connections; moreover, this evil could only be removed by a complete rewriting, and this cannot be done (at least for now). But as to the second fault, I have prepared the following remarks in order to correct it, and by this means I believe I have explained the passages in question and have made them fully comprehensible. And since I am my own commentator, I may flatter myself to have guessed my own meaning, which, if I do not betray myself otherwise, *pro statu rerum*,[2] is to be respected as no small merit in an author.

---

[1] TN. Because of the poverty of language and the novelty of things.
[2] TN. As to the state of things.

Notes & Clarifications

Introduction

1 *Mathematics determines its objects completely* a priori ... The objects of mathematics are time and space determined *a priori* according to rules or conditions. Time and space in themselves, abstracted from particular determinations, are indeed *a priori* forms of *a posteriori* objects of intuition (as will be shown), but they also comprise the matter of objects of mathematics (in so far as they are themselves intuitions). Consequently the matter of these objects is *a priori*. The forms, i.e. the rules or conditions themselves are certainly *a priori* because rules or conditions cannot be **given** but only **thought**.

2 *So the question is: How is philosophy as a pure* a priori *cognition possible?* Or for Kant: *How is metaphysics possible?* | We can comprehend that philosophy is possible as applied cognition because we possess universal experiential propositions (referring to objects of experience) that we have produced by means of induction; we subsume the particular cases of experience under these universal propositions and as a result we are in a position to state *rationem eorem quae sunt vel fiunt*,[3] i.e. to philosophize. But how is philosophy possible as pure *a priori* cognition (where the understanding produces the matter as well as the form of cognition out of itself) given that the understanding can think only rules or conditions and cannot create anything out of itself that accords with them? If philosophy were not supposed to relate to real objects but only to logical ones, it would turn into a logic, and would then have no application at all, i.e. it would not be applicable to particular objects of experience, since there would be no reason [*Grund*] to apply a particular form to one kind of object rather than to another kind: its possibility refers to all objects without distinction. Even the reality of the form in itself would be doubtful: for example, that thinking things in the relation of | cause and effect to one another involves no contradiction is not yet sufficient to prove the reality of this relation. So we will be forced to doubt not only the concept of cause and effect, i.e. particular objects of experience subsumed under the form of hypothetical judgement, but also this form

---

[3] TN. Reasons for what is or happens.

itself.[4] Consequently, philosophy does not refer to merely logical objects, nor to *a priori* objects (like those of mathematics), nor to *a posteriori* objects (like those of the doctrine of nature), and this seems already to exhaust all the possibilities. But on closer examination we find a way out, namely that philosophy refers to a transcendental object, i.e. to something required for the thought of any real object in general, namely to time and space, which constitute the matter of *a priori* objects and the form of *a posteriori* objects. The objective reality of time and space themselves, however, is based on the fact that no real object at all can be thought without them. For example, we find the form of hypothetical judgements in objects of experience, i.e. we think them through this form, and in doing so not only does this form in itself achieve objective reality, but its use is itself also justified through its relation to the time determinations of the objects of experience, as will be shown in what follows.

3 *From time to time I also make some comments* ... In order to avoid all misunderstandings, I will make my opinion on this matter known to the world. I maintain that Kant's *Critique of Pure Reason* is, in its own way, as classical a work as Euclid's, and as incapable of refutation. In order to defend this claim I will take on all of his opponents. But looked at from the other side I hold this system to be insufficient. Our thinking essence (whatever it may be) feels itself to be a citizen in an intelligible world, and although this intelligible world is not an object of its cognition (nor indeed is this thinking essence itself), nevertheless sensible objects indicate [*hinweisen*] intelligible objects to it. The existence of ideas in the mind necessarily indicates [*anzeigt*] some kind of use for them, and since this is not to be found in the sensible world, we must look for it in an intelligible world where the understanding, by means of the forms themselves, determines the objects that these ideas refer to. As a result, our thinking essence can never be satisfied with sensible objects and its way of thinking them, as the Ecclesiast says **the soul is never full (satisfied)**.[5] So it recognizes itself as, on the one side, restricted to the sensible world, but on the other side, it feels in itself an irresistible drive to

---

[4] TN. Maimon is referring to Kant's distinction between logical forms of judgement (e.g. hypothetical) and pure concepts or categories of the understanding (e.g. cause and effect). See A66/B91ff.

[5] TN. *Ecclesiastes*, Ch. 6, verse 7.

NOTES AND CLARIFICATIONS

extend these limits ever further and to discover a passage from the sensible to the intelligible world (which, whatever the politicians may say, is certainly more important than the discovery [*Erfindung*] of a route to the East Indies). Let us assume it will never be found, our thinking essence may nevertheless find out other truths by continuously looking for it (these truths may be less important, but are important enough and worthy of being sought). A little like the alchemist who was looking for gold and found Berlin blue.[6] My intention in the present writing should be judged from this point of view, rather than demanding of me what I have not promised. Taking sides, declaiming, stirring up the rabble against a system that cannot be refuted: these are not my concern. I seek truth, whether and how far I have found it, I leave to others to judge. I indeed depart from Kant in individual claims, | but concerning the principal matter, I have already made my opinion known.

Chapter 1

4 *Form of sensibility* ... The forms of sensibility and of the understanding are in a sense opposed to one another. The form of sensibility takes what would, without that form, be **outside** the cognitive faculty (the real in sensation) and makes it present **within** that faculty; whereas the understanding does the reverse: it takes what would, without it, exist merely **within** the cognitive faculty as a modification of it and makes it an object **outside** that faculty.

5 *The colour red is given to the cognitive faculty* ... [Determining] what comprises the matter and what comprises the form of cognition is a very important investigation. The nominal definition of these constituent parts of cognition could read: what is to be found in the object considered in itself, is matter; but what has its ground in the constitution of a particular cognitive faculty and not in the object itself, is the form of this object. But the question is: how can we recognize what is grounded in the object in itself and what is grounded in the cognitive faculty in relation | to the object? If we were acquainted with the object in itself, outside the cognitive faculty, and with this faculty in itself, then we could know what is proper to the object in itself, and what it has merely acquired from the

---

[6] TN. Or Prussian blue, first discovered (synthesized) by Heinrich Diesbach while working in the laboratory of the alchemist Johann Konrad Dippel in Berlin in 1704.

cognitive faculty. But since this is impossible, this question remains insoluble. For example, we know that wine in a round vessel is round only because the vessel is; if it were essentially round, then it would also have to be round outside the vessel, which is certainly not the case. On the other hand, the bottle is round even without the wine. So we are right to call the wine in itself, as it exists even outside the vessel, the matter, and the round shape that it has acquired only from the bottle, the form. But let us assume that we have never seen the wine without [*außer*] the vessel nor the vessel without [*außer*] the wine; then how would we recognize whether the wine is round in itself or merely on account of the vessel? Our case is just the same. So we can tell matter from form only by means of the distinguishing marks of particularity and universality. For example, I see a red object in space, I notice that space is to be found not only in the red object, but also in every other sensible object that I have perceived; | by contrast, the red colour is to be found only in this object, and from this I conclude that the red colour must be grounded in the object itself but that space is grounded merely in the cognitive faculty in relation to every object in general. But why to every object in general? Perhaps one day there will be an object that I perceive but not in space (or in time). So we have no ground upon which to elevate the generality of this representation, produced *a posteriori* through induction, to an *a priori* necessity. This cannot be compared to a contradiction, where we are convinced that it can never be thought because we already recognize a contradiction in the signs alone, without having to determine what they designate. Here we recognize merely that up to now we **have had** no intuition without time and space, but not that we *cannot have* any intuition without them. In the former case, we recognize the **impossibility**. In our case we merely **do not** recognize the possibility. And it is just the same with the forms of the understanding. Kant merely **presupposes** the fact, but he does not *prove* it. So these principles remain merely **probable**, but not **necessary**. |

6 *Because in themselves they do not contain any manifold* ... The different determinations of space and time (the preceding and the succeeding, the right and the left, and the like) do not constitute a manifold because they comprise merely different terms of a relational concept [*Beziehungsbegriff*], and so they cannot be thought without one another.

7 *But if they are completely different* ... I understand by this the

177

consciousness of difference that arises at the same time as the consciousness of the objects, i.e. at the same time as the consciousness of each individual intuition in itself. For if there has already been consciousness of the things in themselves on a previous occasion, then we can still attain consciousness of their difference even when they are completely different. For example, we perceive the density and weight of a body, and at the same time notice that these are completely different; but this presupposes that, in advance, we have already **attained** a concept of density in itself and of weight in itself (through comparison of different dense and heavy bodies with one another). But before this has happened, we cannot attain any concept of the complete difference, ! because complete difference is a lack of objective unity, as has already been shown.

8 *Being in one and the same place is not a determination of space ... Simultaneity [is not a determination of time]* ... That is to say, things that are in the same place are not in space in relation to one another; rather, they are both in space in relation to a third thing that is outside both of them. Equally, things that are simultaneous are not in time in relation to one another; rather they are in time in relation to a third thing that is not simultaneous with either of them.

9 *The sensible representation of the difference* ... According to Baumgarten (*Metaphysics* §33), things are different if there are determinations in one of them that are not in the other. According to this definition, difference is not a special form, but a partial opposition at the very least. This definition of the difference between things can be allowed to be valid at best when we have distinct concepts of them; it cannot be used for concepts that are merely clear, since we cannot resolve these ! into their determinations in order to see if there are determinations in one that are not in the other. Suppose some thing A has two determinations a and b, while B has only one of them, a; then A is different from B through the determination b which A has and B does not. But the question is: what makes these determinations themselves, a, b, different from one another (for if they are not different, then the A and B they determine will also not be different from one another)? Here the preceding definition does not help us because we have assumed that these determinations are simple. So we must necessarily assume that in this case the difference is a special form (rather than opposition). The form of identity refers to an

objectum logicum, i.e. to an undetermined object, because every object in general is identical with itself. By contrast, the form of difference refers only to a real object, because it presupposes determinable objects (in that an *objectum logicum* cannot be different from an *objectum logicum*, i.e. from itself). So the form of identity is the form of all thought in general (as well as the form of the merely logical); whereas the form of difference is the form of all real [*reellen*] thought, and consequently an object of transcendental philosophy. Now I maintain that the sensible representation or intuition of space in relation to particular sensible objects comprises the sensible schema or image of the difference of these things; but that the intuition of space in relation to all different sensible objects in general (which is properly empty space) comprises the schema of the difference of things in general. But this form is represented sensibly only when it cannot be represented purely, i.e. when the intuition it refers to is homogeneous [*einartig*]; by contrast, when it refers to heterogeneous [*verschiedenartig*] intuitions, it can be represented purely. For example, I take water as a homogeneous body and imagine it in space; in the water in itself I do not observe any difference between the parts (because it is homogeneous), I must first produce these by means of an inference (through the relation of the parts to different objects on the bank, for example, by reasoning in the following way: what is related to different objects must itself be heterogeneous, *atqui*,[7] etc.). The sensible representation of difference is therefore a schema of the concept of difference, i.e. space as intuition. By contrast, if I imagine nothing but heterogeneous things (none of which consist in themselves of homogeneous parts),[8] then in that case I have only the pure concept of difference and not its schema, i.e. space as concept but not as intuition. From this we can see that although space as intuition is a mere form of sensibility, as concept it is a form of all transcendental cognition in general; and the same is true of time, except that time also refers to determinations of our *I*.

---

[7] TN. The use of '*atqui*' is a reference is to one form of the hypothetical syllogism: 'if the first, then the second, but [*atqui*] the first, therefore the second'. See for example Boethius's treatise *On Hypothetical Syllogisms*. In this case, Maimon is abbreviating the following argument: (1) if something is related to different objects it must itself be heterogeneous (2) water is related to different objects (on the bank), so (3) water is heterogeneous.

[8] TN. '*wovon nicht jedes an sich aus einartigen Teilen bestehet*'. This means 'not all of which in themselves consist of homogeneous parts', which makes little sense, so we are assuming that the German should have read '*wovon nicht eines jedes ...* '.

NOTES AND CLARIFICATIONS

10 *And the latter presuppose the former ... [the intuition of space presupposes the concept of space]* ... That is to say in general, but not in the very same objects, as will be shown in the following note.

11 *The difference between the absolute and relative way of looking at things ...* Namely space, place, movement, and the like, are essentially merely relative; but if we regard them as absolute, this does not change their nature, it is only an idea of the completeness of the conditions or of the unconditioned | of this representation, and so it is merely a subjective principle.

12 *In this case even the imagination ...* The [self] evidence [*Evidenz*] of mathematics can only be explained on the following presupposition: namely, that the operations of sensibility, imagination, etc. are the very operation of understanding and reason, although with less completeness; it cannot be explained in any other way, as I will demonstrate below.

13 *Time and space ... ([this plurality is arbitrary] as much in relation to the unit that is adopted, as with respect to the ever possible continuation of this synthesis)* ... The assumed unit can be viewed as a plurality with respect to one of its parts (which is viewed as a unit). In turn, the assumed plurality can be viewed as a unit that gives rise to another plurality by means of successive self-addition.

14 *So time-determinations are meaningless without the categories of substance and accident ...* | Time presupposes alteration, this presupposes the persisting and the changing (substance and accident), and these in turn presuppose determined objects.

Chapter 2

15 *The word '**representation**' ...* Properly understood, a representation is the reproduction of a part of a synthesis in relation to this synthesis. Prior to the consciousness of this synthesis, the consciousness of each one of its parts is not a representation, but a presentation, since it does not refer to anything outside of itself. As a result, neither this, nor the complete consciousness of all parts of the synthesis, nor consequently the synthesis itself is a representation; they are rather a presentation of the thing (of the understanding) itself [*des (Verstandes) Dings selbst*]. But we should note

that both the primitive consciousness of a constituent part of a synthesis (without relating this part to the synthesis) as well as the consciousness of the complete synthesis are mere ideas, i.e. they are the two limit concepts of a synthesis, in that without synthesis no consciousness is possible, but the consciousness of the completed synthesis grasps the infinite in itself, and is consequently impossible for a limited cognitive faculty. But here I am considering only the | first kind of ideas, i.e. the ones that consciousness starts out from, because we must presuppose their existence in us for any determined consciousness. By contrast, we can never reach the other kind of ideas. So we start in the middle with our cognition of things and finish in the middle again. It is the same as, for example, in calculating with our number system, where we proceed according to the very same rules both forwards and backwards in relation to an extended magnitude (through decimal fractions), i.e. we can always think a larger or a smaller unit: after we have counted to 10, we think the 10 as a unit and in turn count 10 such units up to 100 etc., i.e. we always think a larger unit; and we also go backwards and think 0.1, 0.01, etc. as a unit, i.e. we always think a smaller unit. The absolute unit (as it is considered in pure arithmetic) is an idea that can never be presented in intuition (whose forms are time and space which are infinitely divisible). It is just the same in the case under discussion. The absolutely first in the consciousness of a thing | is a mere idea that we reach by infinitely decreasing it, i.e. that we never reach in intuition.

I further remark that there are two kinds of infinitely small, namely a symbolic and an intuitive infinitely small. The first signifies a state that a quantum approaches ever closer to, but that it could never reach without ceasing to be what it is, so we can view it as in this state merely symbolically. On the other hand, the second kind signifies every state **in general** that a quantum can reach; here the infinitely small does not so much fail to be a quantum at all as it fails to be a determined quantum. I want to explain this with examples. The angle that two parallel lines make with one another, the cosine of a right angle, and so on, are of the first kind: if I say the angle two parallel lines make with one another is infinitely small, the meaning is this: the further from their points of origin two lines meet, the smaller the angle that they make with one another, and this goes on until they are so far from their points of origin that they can no longer meet, | and in this state the angle becomes infinitely small, but it altogether ceases to be an angle. Equally if I say the cosine of a right angle is infinitely small, this means: the larger an angle, the larger its sine and the smaller its cosine, up to the point where it becomes a right angle and in this case its cosine is infinitely small, i.e. it altogether ceases to be a cosine, and so on. The only reason we are nevertheless able to designate these states (that quanta can never reach) is because they are limit concepts, i.e. a merely symbolic infinitely small. On the other hand the differential of a magnitude does not signify the state where the magnitude ceases to be what it is, but each state that it can reach, without distinction, i.e. a determinable but undetermined state. If I say: $dx:dy = a:b$, the meaning is not: x abstracted from any magnitude behaves [*verhält sich*] in relation to y abstracted from any magnitude as etc., because nothing cannot be proportional [*Größenverhältnis haben*] to nothing. The meaning is rather this: we can take x to be as small or as large as we want (as long as it has some magnitude), it always follows from the equation between these magnitudes that $x:y$, etc. So here I assume that x is *omni dabili minus*,[9] from which it will follow that $dx:dy$ etc. (for me a magnitude is something such that something else larger than it or something else smaller than it can be thought; consequently what is *omni dabili majus*[10] as well as what is *omni dabili minus*,[11] i.e. the infinitely large and the infinitely small, is a magnitude). The symbolic infinite is merely an invention of mathematicians that lends generality to their claims. For example, if they have proved certain claims of an angle or cosine in general (whatever magnitude it might have), then they also apply these claims to the case where these objects have no magnitude (I will not consider at present whether this procedure has any use in the discovery [*Erfindung*] of new truths). On the other hand, the real infinitely small can itself be thought as an object (and not merely as the predicate of an intuition) despite the fact that it is itself a mere form that cannot be constructed as an object, i.e. presented in intuition. The absolute unit in pure arithmetic is an example of this kind. This cannot provide the form of any intuition that would give rise to an absolutely determined object (because every intuition is infinitely divisible by virtue of its forms time and space, and consequently it can have no absolute unit). An absolute unit is nevertheless treated as an object of pure arithmetic itself because it can be augmented even if it cannot be diminished.

It is the same in the case under discussion. Think of two magnitudes

---

[9] TN. Less than any given magnitude.
[10] TN. Greater than any given magnitude.
[11] TN. Less than any given magnitude.

(quanta) that stand only in a relation to each another, without either standing in any relation to a third [magnitude].[12] But this relation is not an invariable numerical relation to one another, like the relation of irrational magnitudes; rather it is simply a universal functional relation [*Funktionsverhältnis*] that varies with respect to the former. They are termed infinitely small magnitudes, meaning that they are not determinate magnitudes (that they are magnitudes at all is therefore certain since they do in fact entertain a universal functional relation to one another). This way of considering these magnitudes is not only legitimate, i.e. has objective reality, but is also very useful for the discovery of new relations between these magnitudes. This is because these magnitudes stand in a universal functional relation to one another so that if one is determined, then the other is also determined, i.e. they acquire a numerical relation to one another, and hence their respective states acquire a numerical relation to one another. Now, if it appears in intuition that one of these magnitudes must stand in the same relation to a third [magnitude] that these respective states stand in to each another, then this third [magnitude] can also be determined because one of the [original] magnitudes is already determined, and so on.

The metaphysically infinitely small is real because quality can certainly be considered in itself abstracted from all quantity. This way of considering it is also useful for resolving the question, *quid juris?* because the pure concepts of the understanding or categories are never directly related to intuitions, but only to their elements, and these are ideas of reason concerning the way these intuitions arise; it is through the mediation of these ideas that the categories are related to the intuitions themselves. Just as in higher mathematics we produce the relations of different magnitudes themselves from their differentials, so the understanding (admittedly in an obscure way) produces the real relations of qualities themselves from the real relations of their differentials. So, if we judge that fire melts wax, then this judgement does not relate to fire and wax as objects of intuition, but to their elements, which the under-

---

[12] TN. '*die nur in Beziehung auf einander, nicht aber in Beziehung beider auf ein drittes, in Verhältnis stehen*'. Throughout the translation both *Beziehung* and *Verhältnis* have been translated by 'relation', on the grounds that Maimon generally uses them as synonyms. But in this mathematical context there is a divergence of use since only *Verhältnis* is used to refer to a relation of proportionality or a ratio between two numbers. In the next sentence the word which 'relation' translates is *Verhältnis*, and has this particular mathematical sense of ratio.

NOTES AND CLARIFICATIONS

standing thinks in the relation of cause and effect to one another. Namely, I hold that the understanding not only has a capacity [*Vermögen*] to **think** universal relations between determined objects of intuition, but also to **determine** objects by means of relations. As a result, it can legitimately relate different relations to one another *a priori*. This happens in the same way that, in arithmetic for example, the understanding produces determined numerical relations from the universal relations of identity and plurality and then goes on to relate these to other relations. I cannot explain myself any further on this matter.

16 *Consequently, in view of all the possible constructions, this triangle must never be thought by the understanding as having arisen, but rather as arising* ... That is to say the understanding thinks the triangle as undetermined with respect to its size; whereas the imagination can only represent it as determined. So the imagination takes the determined intuition itself as its object; but the understanding takes as its object the rule or way that the intuition arises.

17 *For the understanding to think a line, it must draw it in thought, but to present a line in intuition, it must be imagined as already drawn* ... In the understanding the concept of a line does not contain any determined magnitude so that if the understanding is to think a line with a determined magnitude, then it must first draw the line to that magnitude with the help of the imagination. By contrast, the intuition of a line already contains a determined magnitude in itself, and so there is nothing more for it to do in this respect.

18 *Pure concepts* ... Up to the end of s.37 it is a matter of developing the concept of form, whose use is to be explained (s.38). Actually this is a note to s.56 that has been inserted here in error.

19 *Indeed even the possibility of the latter is inconceivable* ... The possibility of a synthetic proposition can only be demonstrated through its actuality (its actual use). For example, before I construct a straight line, i.e. present it in an intuition, I can certainly think of it as the shortest between two points because 'being a straight line', and 'being the shortest between two points', do not contradict one another. But I have no ground for actually thinking of it as the shortest rather than not the shortest because it is also true that 'being a straight line' and 'not being the shortest' does not

184

contain a contradiction. It is even doubtful whether a more exact definition of a straight line would show whether the proposition 'a straight line is the shortest...' in fact contains a contradiction. But because this proposition is brought into an actual construction, it becomes clear both that it is not contradictory and also that it has an objective ground.

20 *Namely one that it has itself introduced for the sake of experiential propositions ...* | In relation to determinable but not determined objects, the forms of judgement have merely a subjective rather than an objective ground (they are merely different ways of thinking real objects in general, but not of thinking this or that determined object). So it is only by adding objective forms to them that the understanding is in a position to think objects and their relations with one another, i.e. to construct experiential propositions.

21 *Every possible object can without distinction be the cause of something ...* See the *Critique of Pure Reason*, p. 189.[13] For my own opinion on this matter see the *Short Overview*.

22 *Something is **pure** when ...* If someone said: on this definition we have no pure cognition, since the principle of contradiction is only a negative criterion of cognition (*conditio sine qua non*), then I reply: it is in fact true that we have no completely pure cognition, but we also do not need it. The hypothetical positing of principles is sufficient for the use of our reason. And mixed principles are also sufficient for practical use | because what follows from them and is determined by them is of the very same kind. So we do indeed have a reason for inferring the necessity of these propositions from their universality: namely the assumption that these propositions that are merely synthetic for us, must be analytic for a higher understanding.

23 *They are not unities connecting the **manifold** of intuitions, but are themselves a manifold that is connected through **unity** ...* This is precisely the unity of apprehension of the imagination, by means of which the homogeneous manifold becomes a single intuition.

---

[13] TN. The reference is to the Second Analogy, A189ff.

24 *But its possibility is merely problematic* ... This will seem a strange enough claim to many, namely that (contrary to the well-known metaphysical proposition 'everything actual is possible') I claim that even if the colour is actual, its possibility is still only problematic. But we should bear in mind that the mere lack of a contradiction does not yet yield the thought of a real object, | and that although in the present case the object is real, it is only real in relation to the faculty of intuition, not in relation to the faculty of thought. As a result, the possibility of the colour as an object of the understanding remains merely problematic.

25 *A root of 2* ... I think everyone will grant me that it is not contradictory to suppose that two has a root; and if someone says there is no number such that the number 2 arises from its product with itself, then this just means: among all possible numbers we do not find one that satisfies this condition. From this we recognize that the number 2 does not arise in this way. On the other hand, $\sqrt{-a}$ contains a contradiction because it means: a number such that $-a$ arises from its product with itself. Here I do not first need to test (as with irrational roots) whether this or that number satisfies this condition or not, rather I am already convinced *a priori* that there cannot be a number of this kind, for a negative [number] cannot arise from any product of a number with itself.

26 *If we want to consider the matter more carefully* ... | Many a scholastic [*schulgerechte*] professor who has heard something of the question *quid juris?* (if only I should have the honour to be read by these gentlemen, which I have no right to expect) will here shake his head and cry out: a strange notion to reduce the question *quid juris?* to the question *de commercio animi et corporis!* But what seems strange to many a professor, need not, on this account, be strange in fact. The professor needs only to bear in mind that he about as much of a conception of the soul as noumena as he has of the body as noumena, and these terms distinguish only between different kinds of consciousness, namely consciousness of *a priori* forms is termed 'soul', while consciousness of something merely given is termed 'matter', and the connection of the two produces what we term this or that object. Now I would like to know if a distinction of even a hair's breadth's can be discovered between the two questions that I have compared? Besides, I freely admit that neither Aristotle, nor Descartes, nor Leibniz, nor their respective disciples, have taken this question in this sense. For them it had its ground in mere philosophical

curiosity; for them, it was an object of applied rather than transcendental philosophy; for them its meaning was this: from experience we recognize two *tota* of appearances that are most precisely linked together so that each determined accident in one is always accompanied by a corresponding accident in the other (the two *tota* must be supposed to be two types of accidents in two types of substances). How can we explain this according to universal natural laws (which are likewise *a posteriori*)? For **Kant**, by contrast, the meaning of the question *quid juris?* is this: we know from experience that we connect forms of thought determined *a priori* with objects determined *a posteriori* in a necessary way, but so long as we cannot discover anything *a priori* in the objects, this is impossible, and so this necessary connection a mere illusion. So what is this *a priori* that justifies us in treating it as real? As for me, I also take a fact as ground, but not a fact relating to *a posteriori* objects (because I doubt the latter) but a fact relating to *a priori* objects (of pure mathematics) where we connect forms (relations) with intuitions; and because this undoubted fact refers to *a priori* objects, it is certainly possible, and at the same time actual. But my question is: how is it comprehensible? (*Quid juris?* for me means the same as *quid rationis?* because what is justified [*rechtmäßig*] is what is legitimate [*gesetzmäßig*], and with respect to thought, something is justified if it conforms to the laws of thought or reason.) **Kant** shows merely the **possibility** of his fact, which he merely **presupposes**. By contrast, my fact is **certain** and also **possible**. I merely ask: what sort of hypothesis must I adopt for it to be **comprehensible**? So my question has its ground, like the other question with which I have compared it, merely in a philosophical curiosity and hence does not belong to transcendental philosophy. But because my solution is universal, and can accordingly be used in relation to the objects of transcendental philosophy, and because, in addition, my question was occasioned by the Kantian question (that concerns only transcendental philosophy) I therefore think I am justified in introducing it here.

27 *We assume* [*an infinite understanding (at least as idea)*] ... Many readers will imagine they are catching a glimpse of Spinozism here. So in order to prevent all misunderstandings of this kind, I now want to explain myself once and for all: I maintain that the representation or concept of a thing is not so heterogeneous with the thing itself (or with what belongs to its existence) as is commonly believed. For me, the thing itself outside its representation, or the existence of the thing in itself, is *complementum*

possibilitatis,[14] i.e. what belongs to its possibility without us having insight into it. The reality of the former stems merely from the negation or limitation of the latter. For an infinite understanding, the thing and its representation are one and the same. An idea is a method for finding a passage from the representation or concept of a thing to the thing itself; it does not determines any object of intuition but still determines a real object whose schema is the object of intuition: for example, our understanding is the schema for the idea of an infinite understanding. In this case, the schema indicates[15] the idea, and the idea indicates the thing itself or its existence, without which this idea and its schema would themselves be impossible. | So I differ from **Kant's** opinion on these two main issues: 1) I hold a single idea (of an infinite understanding) to be sufficient, rather than the three he assumes. 2) **Kant** maintains that these ideas are not objects of our cognition; I claim instead that they are objects of the understanding (although not of intuition): we have cognition of them as determined objects of thought, even if not in themselves (directly), but rather through the mediation of their schemas (what is given of them in intuition).

So I differ from **Kant** merely in this: instead of the three ideas that he assumes, I assume a single idea (of an infinite understanding), and I ascribe objective reality to this idea (not, it is true, viewed in itself – for this is contrary to the nature of an idea – but only in so far as it acquires objective reality for us in so many ways by means of objects of intuition). And also the other way around, that is, intuitions acquire objective reality only because they must eventually resolve into this idea: as *Kant* has himself proved, intuitions possess objective | reality only when they are connected by pure *a priori* concepts. Now the understanding (or, according to **Kant**, reason) insists on absolute totality in these concepts so that this totality belongs as much to the essence of the understanding as to these concepts in general even if we cannot attain it.

---

[14] TN. The 'complement of possibility', or that which completes possibility. This is Wolff's definition of existence, see Christian Wolff, *Philosophia prima sive Ontologia* [*First philosophy, or Ontology*], 1730, §174. For Wolff philosophy is restricted to the domain of the possible.

[15] TN. *andeuten*. This word can mean either a (quite determinate) pointing, but is more usually understood as a suggestive hint and this meaning should be born in mind. Earlier in this section (s.338) Maimon describes the same relation between sensible things and the supersensible using the much more determinate verbs *hinweisen* and *anzeigen*, and this has influenced our translation here.

So it is the outline of the system I have sketched here, not its name, that must be tested and then either approved, or condemned to whatever punishment is desired. *An flamma, an mari adriatico?*[16] And yet my genie whispers to me what Horace's Sibyl divined: *Hunc neque dira venena, nec hosticus auferet enfis ... Garrulus hunc quando consumet cumque etc.*[17] Against this there is admittedly no defence, so for now may this suffice.

28 *From this a triangle arises in intuition* ... Here someone could object that a triangle can arise from this only on the presupposition that two of these lines taken together are longer than the third, and consequently that I cannot make this presupposition itself the ground of its own proof. | Note however that I have not made the following synthetic principle into the ground of my proof: 'A triangle can arise from three lines of which two taken together are greater than the third' but rather merely this one: 'A triangle can arise from three lines in general (without determining their condition)'; only now do I prove from this what the condition of these three lines [is], namely that two of them taken together must be longer than the third, and from this my claim follows at the same time, namely that two lines are longer than one line between the same two points. Although the proposition I used as the ground can itself only be presented synthetically through a pure intuition, I have nevertheless advanced a step by means of my proof, since on my account the condition of the three lines is determined analytically, whereas for Kant it is determined merely synthetically in intuition.

29 *A presentiment that, I believe, must [play no insignificant role in the power of invention [Erfindungskraft]]* ... It is well known that no general | method has yet been discovered to prove a geometrical theorem or to solve a problem; instead it comes down to certain tricks in drawing the so-called preparatory lines. But we can draw God knows how many of these and connect them both to each other as well as to those already drawn in a variety of ways, and yet still either fail to reach the goal or reach it only after much fruitless wandering. So it is a feature of genius, that is of a kind of presentiment or instinct, to see in advance that certain lines are the ones that lead straight to the desired goal. Newton says in his *Universal Arithmetic*, S.IV, Ch. I, #17:

---

[16] TN. 'Into the flames! Into the Adriatic sea!'.
[17] TN. 'No sword nor poison will ever take him off ... a babbling tongue will kill him.'

But that these Theorems may be accommodated to the Solution of Problems, the Schemes are oft times to be farther constructed, by producing out some of the Lines till they cut others, or become of an assigned Length; or by drawing Lines parallel or perpendicular from some remarkable Point, or by conjoining some remarkable Points; as also sometimes by constructing after other Methods, according as the State of the Problem and the Theorems which are made Use of to solve it, shall require. As for Example If two Lines that do nor meet each other, make given Angles with a certain third Line, perhaps we produce them so that when they concur, or meet, they shall form a Triangle whose Angles, and consequently the Reasons of their Sides, shall be given; or, if any Angle is given, or be equal to any one, we often complete it into a Triangle given in Specie, or similar to some other, | and that by producing some of the Lines in the Scheme, or by drawing a Line subtending at Angle. If the Triangle be an oblique angled one, we often resolve it into two right angled ones, by letting fall a Perpendicular. If the business concerns multilateral (or many sided) figures, we resolve them into Triangles, by drawing Diagonal Lines; and so in others; always aiming at this end, viz. that the Scheme may be resolv'd either into given, or similar, or right angled Triangles.[18]

All of this is correct, but I think you have to be a Newton to be able to use this prescription. Newton's prescription for mathematical invention seems to me like Klopstock's prescription for the higher art of poetry. Lucretius is not entirely wrong to compare the discoverer with the bloodhound: '*Ut canes* ...[19]

30 *How do we know from our perception that* b *succeeds* a [*that this succession is necessary*] ... This question means two things: 1) Given that we recognize the succession [*Folge*] of *b* upon *a* to be objective, and are therefore justified in subsuming it under the category of causality, i.e. attributing necessity in accordance with a rule to it (since without this the sequence

---

[18] TN. Maimon quotes from the original Latin text, for which we have substituted Raphson's English translation of 1720.

[19] TN. Lucretius, *On the Nature of Things*, Book 1, The Void, verses 404–9: 'As dogs full oft with noses on the ground, find out the silent lairs, though hid in brush, of beasts ...'. (William Ellery Leonard translation).

[Folge] would not be objective), then the question is: 'how do we know that the succession of *b* upon *a* is objective, but not the succession of *c* upon *a*?'. | For example, the stove in the room has been lit and then we notice that the air in the room has become warm, and that outside snow has fallen. Then we have the same right to treat each of the two consequences [*Folgen*][20] either as objective or as subjective. So what reason do we have for considering the warming of the air in the room to be the objective consequence and the snowfall the subjective consequence? I think if we appeal to common sense, both consequences would in fact be viewed as objective: on such an occasion people do not say, 'it seems to me as if snow is falling (in succession to what went before)', but absolutely: 'snow is falling'; people also do not say, 'it seems to me as if the room is (by means of this) warm', but: 'it is warm'. If someone objects that we recognize this [i.e. that the warming of the air is the objective consequence] because we know from frequent experience that this warming follows from the lighting of the stove and never precedes it, whereas, the falling of the snow sometimes also precedes it, then the use of the principle of causation, i.e. its application to particular objects, is based merely on experience and this is precisely **David Hume's** claim. How does it help us if there is a universal *a priori* rule that *b* as much as *c* | must follow something according to a rule (if this sequence is to have objective reality), since we must first learn from experience whether it is *b* or *c* that must be subsumed under this rule in relation to *a*? 2) The original fact can itself be denied, namely that we view any sequence as objective; it can be all a dream, and then not only would the use of the concept of cause fail to have objective reality in particular cases it would also fail to have objective reality in its use in general, because we would in fact not possess any objective sequences.

According to my theory, on the other hand (see the 'Short Overview of the Whole Work'), the concept of cause is not merely a condition of experience, but of perception itself. Even if the objectivity of the [particular] sequence may be doubted, it still follows first that) no one will doubt that the concept [of cause] is in general objective in relation to actual perception. That is to say, I express the principle of causation in this way: If *a* comes first and *b* is supposed to follow it (in perception), then *a*

---

[20] TN. The German word '*Folge*' means both 'succession' or 'sequence' and 'consequence', and Maimon uses it in both senses in this note. Wherever any of these three English words occur the German is '*Folge*'.

and *b* must stand under the rule of the relation of maximum identity with one another, because if they did not, then no reproduction of *a* on the perception of *b* would be possible, and hence no | relation of succession between them would be possible. Second, this rule simultaneously determines its use; i.e., I hold *b* rather than *c* to be the effect of *a* because the former conforms to this rule, but the latter does not. And if I treat the latter as also being a consequence of *a*, this does not happen directly but only through a relation of simultaneity with the former, which is a consequence of *a*.

Chapter 3

31 *The material completeness* [*of a concept*] ... According to this explanation, mathematics contains both ideas of the understanding and ideas of reason. Differential magnitudes are ideas of the understanding since they are real objects determined by means of *a priori* conditions; but they cannot be constructed, i.e. presented in intuition, because they must be viewed in abstraction from all magnitude (because they are expressed merely by means of a function-relation that, as a numerical relation, is continuously variable). So they are ideas of the understanding. By contrast, the asymptotes of a curve are not real objects, but mere limit concepts signifying something that we can approach ever closer to, but never reach, not only with respect | to an empirical construction but also with respect to a pure one. Irrational roots are also of this type. So they are ideas of reason.

32 *The series expressing an irrational root* ... Many readers will think there is a contradiction here, since in the previous note I portrayed an irrational number as an idea of reason, whereas here I count the series that expresses an irrational number as an idea of the understanding. But there is a noticeable difference between an irrational **number** and the **series** that expresses it. The number is impossible as an object, since it can be proved that no whole or fractional number can correspond to it, so that it is merely an idea of reason of the limit of the approach to a number. But this does not show that it is **nothing**, because it is still a specifiable geometrical magnitude even if it is not a number. The series that expresses an irrational number should not be understood as the sum of all its terms according to some unit, but instead as merely the following rule [*Vorschrift*]: divide the line that represents the series into *n* parts; take part

| n and then divide the line again into o parts; then take part o and add it to n, but not in the way that numbers are added (so that the sum is another number) but rather in the way that lines are added. For example, if the first part is a third and the other a quarter, then their sum should not be added (reducing to its [lowest] unit,[21] this would yield $\frac{7}{12}$); instead, the two lines should merely be gathered into one. Since the parts are infinite, this division is impossible for a finite being but not impossible in itself. The sum of all parts is always equal to the whole, whether the number of parts is finite or infinite. If the number of parts is infinite, then their sum cannot be given as a number but it can certainly be given as a line.

33 *In a similar way, the asymptotes of a curved line [are complete according to their rule, but in their presentation they are always incomplete]* ... That is, the rule of the asymptotes is the following: every part of it must be closer to the curve than the preceding part, without ever reaching the curve. To relate this rule to every particular possible part comprises an idea of the understanding because the rule contains something **impracticable** (but nothing **impossible**) when related to every particular part. This is because it means the following: draw first part a according to the rule, then b, then c, and so on without ever stopping. By contrast, applied to all possible parts (which are assumed to be already drawn) this rule is an idea of reason because it contains something impossible in that it represents the totality of the parts as complete and not complete at the same time; consequently this totality does not signify an object (not even of an infinite understanding), but merely the approach to an object.

34 *The subjective order* ... By order I do not mean the order in **time**, but the **essential** [*der Natur*] order, i.e. in this case something is **prior** to something else not if it **precedes** the latter chronologically, but rather if it must be **presupposed** by the latter according to the **essence of its thinkability**.[22] So the subjective order is this: 1) Sensibility (this constitutes the matter of consciousness, and without it we would have no consciousness at all); 2) intuition (the connection of the matter with the

---

[21] TN. '*auf eine Einheit reduziert*', i.e. expressing the fractional sum by the lowest common denominator of its terms.
[22] TN. '*sondern was der Natur der Denkbarkeit nach demselben vorausgesetzt werden muß*'.

form of sensibility); 3) concepts of the understanding (the connection of the forms | of thought with intuitions, or the connection of intuitions by forms of thought); 4) ideas of reason (the forms of thought in itself viewed as objects).

The objective order (of an unlimited cognitive faculty) is: 1) ideas of the understanding (in this case there is no sensibility and no intuition, but only the representations of all possible things; 2) concepts of the understanding (these connect these ideas in a unity of apperception); 3) ideas of reason (the representation of this cognitive faculty itself, as absolute substance, highest cause, etc).

Chapter 4

35 *If one of the constituent parts of a synthesis* [*can be thought without reference to the other*] ... Linguistic usage already shows that each part of a synthesis cannot be treated as subject and as predicate in relation to the other part at the same time. For example, we can say 'a square table', but not 'a table square', 'a black line', but not 'a line black', etc. What is the reason for this? Will it be said (as is in fact claimed) that the **universal** is the predicate, and the **particular** the subject of a synthesis? But why is square more universal than table? Perhaps because it is not only a table but also a door, a window, etc. that can be square; however it is not | only a square, but also a circle, a triangle, etc. that can be a table; and it is the same with the second example: 'black' can be attributed to more things than lines, but 'line' can also be attributed to more things than black. So the reason [*Grund*] must be the one I give, namely this: the subject comprises that part of a synthesis that also constitutes a synthesis in itself; as a result, it can also be thought in itself as an object without relation to the other part. By contrast, the predicate comprises the other part, the one that does not constitute a synthesis in itself; as a result it can be thought only as a constituent part of a synthesis, not in itself as an object.

36 *It is natural for one abstract concept to make another abstract concept necessary* ... To explain this, consider, for example, a right angle. I would not be able to have a concept of this synthesis if I did not have a concept of each of its constituent parts, namely of 'angle' in itself and of 'being right[-angled]' in itself. So as soon as one of them is possible as an abstract concept, the other | must also be possible as an abstract concept. But intuition is just as unable to present 'angle' in itself (without any

determination) as 'being right[-angled]'. Yet there is a difference between the two, namely, that 'angle' in itself is thought by means of intuition as object (of which something determinate can be predicated) although it is not presented in intuition. By contrast, 'being right[-angled]' in itself, is neither presented in intuition, nor is it ever thought as object (since nothing determinate can be predicated of it). So the former is the subject and the latter the predicate of this synthesis.

37 *In short*: [*I hope everyone will agree that different grounds cannot have the same [einerlei] consequences*] ... In the first proof I supposed the consequences of the two syntheses to be different and demonstrated from this the impossibility of different subjects sharing a common predicate. Here I suppose the consequences to be identical, and demonstrate that this is impossible from the fact that on this presupposition, the consequences do not belong to either one or the other synthesis in itself but are shared by the two of them in common, and that (according to my definition) what they share is therefore the subject of both syntheses, contradicting the presupposition. This point is more fully explained on s. 89. The claim I am putting forward here seems paradoxical and that is why I have tried to present it in different ways; otherwise of course I could have expressed myself more succinctly.

38 *With concepts, the subject is the universal* [*and the predicate the particular*] ... In the previous example of the concept of a right angle, the subject is **angle** and this is the universal because it can just as well be right[-angled] as oblique; by contrast, **right[-angled]** is the particular because (as has already been shown) this predicate can be attributed only to a single subject. The reason is that if I have also already said that each subject can only have one predicate, then it can have several predicates disjunctively although not at the same time; on the other hand, a predicate cannot have several predicates even disjunctively.

39 *and if I say that a human being is an animal,* [*this is tantamount to saying that the concept of a human being arises by means of a closer determination of the concept of animal*] ... After I had written this, I found the very same thought in **Ploucquet's** *Methodus calculandi in logicis*, namely that a judgement contains only a concept, and although a protest has already been raised against this (*Briefe über die deutsche Literatur* 217), **Ploucquet** is quite right. I will quote the whole passage. He says (n.14) 'Affirmation

195

is the grasping (intellectio) of the *identity* of subject and predicate.'[23] And he adds this in a note:

> **Every circle is a curved line**. In logic this proposition is expressed thus: **every circle is a certain curved line**. By this means what is grasped in the subject, whether or not I know that there exist other kinds of curve than the circle, is that **a certain** curved line, taken **comprehensively**, is **every** circle, or that **every** circle is **a certain** curved line. When I reflect on the meaning of the proposition: **every circle is a certain curved line**, I grasp that I conceive by it nothing but this judgement: a certain curved line is a certain curved line. This judgement, since it identifies the extremes, reduces to one concept, that of **a certain curved line** that one calls a circle. The act of the mind through which one conceives that the circle is a certain curved line is nothing other than the grasping of **one** concept. Suppose that we were deprived of all language and knowledge of terms, and that we observe a circular line, or even an infinity of circular lines, represented either by the mind alone or with the help of the sense organs, then we would think of it just as we think of it when we read or hear this proposition: the circle is a certain curved line. An affirmative judgement conceived by the mind is not the grasping of two things but of one and the same thing, and an affirmative proposition is nothing other than the expression of one and the same thing by different signs.

The reason that difficulties arise in this altogether simple matter, must be sought in ignorance of the matter and the consequent insufficiency of language itself. The insufficiency of language lies in the fact that the copula 'is' suffers from ambiguity, and that we are accustomed to use this same copula to link terms which differ in comprehension as well as extension. As to the ignorance of the matter, in this case it only concerns the determination of the predicate. Let us return to our example: **the circle is a curved line**. Consider the circle in itself, not as the subject of the proposition but as an absolute term, and one will have the concept of circle: **a curved line returning on itself, in which there**

---

[23] TN. G. Ploucquet, *Methodus calculandi in logicis* (Frankfurt and Leipzig, 1763). The original Latin is: 'Intellectio identitatis subjecti et praedicati est affirmatio'.

exists a point equidistant to each one of the points on the circumference. Now make this concept the subject to which one adds its predicate: **curved line**, giving rise to the proposition: a line returning on itself etc. is a curved line. If one compares this with this other proposition: **a parabolic line not returning on itself etc. is a curved line**, it is clear that in the second proposition a different proposition is joined to the expression 'curved line' than in the first, for the curve of a circle differs from that of a parabola. So the sense of the first proposition | is: A line returning on itself etc. is **a certain** curved line, and the sense of the second: a curved line not returning on itself etc. is a certain curved line. But from the point of view of explaining and grasping it, we have an identical proposition, which when grasped, only presents **one** concept. In the same way, '**a certain**' (which is a different sign from 'a certain' and indicates another concept) is explained by: **not returning on itself**, so that the proposition grasped becomes **identical** and comes back to **one** concept.

I foresee that it will be objected that the concept of a curved line is the same in the two propositions, since it is generic and can correctly be applied to both the circle and the parabola as predicate. Nevertheless, it is necessary to take note that in the predicate **as such** is always grasped the relation to the subject, and the concept relevant to the subject just determined. Because of ignorance of the matter, it can happen that one does not know whether the circle is **every** curved line, or a certain curved line, in the exclusive sense. Now since it is necessary that one of the two possibilities is true, it is necessary to add to the predicate a sign of particular quantity, taken **comprehensively**, because in this way, nothing can detract from the truth, whether the circle is **every** curve or **not every** curve.

One cannot object to this theory on the grounds that the predicate of an affirmative proposition, is usually only a partial concept of the concept, and is not identifiable with the subject. If it is true that | the predicate only presents a partial concept of the subject, this partial concept is nevertheless included in the subject which has just been determined as such. When I look at a round stone, saying: **this stone is round**, only **one** concept is observed in the mind. By this proposition I actually think only **one** concept, that is to say that of the round stone, whose two terms can be expressed by **one**. One can certainly say that a judgement is a comparison of ideas, nevertheless

197

one and the same thing compared with **itself**, does not make two things present but **one**.

It clearly follows from this account that every judgement comes down to **one** concept, and that it is necessary to add in the mind to every predicate its quantitative value, even if the term itself is not expressed ... [24]

---

[24] TN. G. Ploucquet, *Methodus calculandi in logicis* (Frankfurt and Leipzig, 1763). The original Latin text is as follows: '**omnis circulus est linea curva**. Quae propositio logice expressa haec est: **omnis circulus es quaedam linea curva**. Quo pacto id quod intelligitur in subjecto, sive norim, sive non norim, praeter circulum dari quoque alias curvarum species, verum tamen est **quandam** lineum curvam, sensu **comprehensivo** sumtam, esse **omnem** circulum, seu **omnem** circulum esse **quandam** lineam curvam. Dum enim cogito quid sibi velit haec praepositio: **omnis circulus est quaedam linea curva**, intelligo me nihil aliud concipere quam hoc judicium: quaedam linea curva est quaedam linea curva. Quod judicium cum extrema identificet, reducitur ad unam notionem, scilicet notionem **cujusdam lineae curvae**, quae vocatur circulus. Ille mentis actus quo circulus concipitur esse quaedam linea curva, nihil aliud est, quam intellectio **unius** notionis. Ponamus, nos omni lingua et terminorum cognitione esse destitutos, et nobis observari lineam circularem, vel infinite multas lineas circulares, sive sola mente, sive mediante organo sensorio repraesentatos, id ipsum hoc casu cogitamus, quod cogitamus, dum legimus vel audimus hanc propositionem: circulus est quaedam linea curva. Judicium affirmativum mente conceptum non est intellectio duarum, sed unius rei; neque propositio affirmativa aliquid aliud est quam expressio unius ejusque rei per diversa signa. Ratio cur in hac re simplicissima difficultates nascantur, quaerenda est ignorantia materiae, et inde pendente insufficientia linguae. Linguae insufficientia ponitur in eo, quod copula **est** aequivocatione laboret, atque per eandem termini inter se necti soleant tam comprehensione, quam extensione inter se differentes. Ignorantia autem materiae respicit hoc in negotio solam praedicati determinationem. Resumemus exemplum modo datum: **circulus est linea curva**. Consideretur circulus in se, non ut subjectum propositionis, sed ut terminus absolutus, et habebitur notio circuli, quae haec esto: **Linea curva in se rediens, intra quam datur punctum aequidistans a singulis peripheriae punctis**. Haec notio jam constituatur subjectum, cui addatur suum praedicatum: **linea curva**, sic orietur haec propositio: linea curva in se rediens etc. est linea curva. Comparetur cum hac propositione alia: **parabola linea in se non rediens etc. est linea curva**. Manifestum est in propositione posteriori cum signo linea curva jungi aliam notionem, quam in priori; nam curvedo circuli differt a curvedine parabolae. Sic igitur sensus propositionis | prioris hic est: linea curva in se rediens etc. est **quaedam** linea curva. Posterioris autem: linea curva in se non rediens etc. est quaedam linea curva. Sed explicatione et intellectione habetur propositio identica, quae intellecta non nisi **unam** exhibet notionem. Eodem modo **quaedam** (quod signum differt a quaedam et aliam innuit notionem) explicator per: **in se non rediens**, adeoque propositio intellecta fit **identica** et reducitur ad **unam** notionem. Provideo objectum iri, notionem lineae curvae in utraque propositione, esse eandem, cum sit generica, adeoque tam de circulo quam de parabola rite praedicetur. Sed observandum est, quod in praedicato **qua tali** semper intelligatur relatio ad subjectum, adeoque notio ipsi

Thus far **Ploucquet**. Now I claim that the whole business of judging consists merely in this: either attaining a distinct concept of the subject, or determining the subject of a synthesis by means of the criterion I have given. For example, the judgement that a **human being** is an **animal** presupposes that I have (prior to the judgement) a merely clear concept of the subject, 'human being', but by means of the judgement this clear concept becomes distinct (at least) in part. However, its usefulness consists in this: | I recognize certain properties of 'animal', and I can legitimately assign them to 'human being' (in so far as a human being is an animal); in other words, I already possessed a distinct concept of 'human being' prior to the judgement, namely that it is a synthesis of **animal** and **something else**. But I did not know which of these two constituent parts of this synthesis was its subject and which its predicate, i.e. (on my definition) which already constitutes a concept of the understanding or a synthesis in itself that has real consequences, and which has real consequences only by means of this given synthesis, but not outside it. And as long as these doubts remain, I can only attribute consequences to this synthesis that I perceived in it after it had arisen (*a posteriori*) and not consequences that are already found in one of its constituent parts (*a priori*) before it has arisen. But I recognize that the concept (*notio*) **animal** has also been perceived outside the given synthesis either as actual or as possible. So now I can legitimately attribute consequences to it that it has outside the synthesis as well before I know what must follow from this new synthesis. The judgement: 'a

cont.

subjecto modo determinato competens. Ex ignorantia materiae accidere potest ut dubitetur num circulus sit **omnis** linea curva, an vero quaedam linea curva, sensu exclusivo intellecta. Cum autem necessarium sit ut alterutrum cum veritate concordet, cum praedicato jungendum est signum quantitatis particularis sensu **comprehensivo** sumtae, quia hoc modo veritati nihil derogatur, sive circulus sit **omnis** curva, **sive non omnis**. Neque obverti potest theoriae huic, quod praedicatum propositionis affirmativae plerumque sit tantum notio partialis subjecti, adeoque non identificabilis cum subjecto. Si enim | praedicatum exhibet subjecti notionem partialem, ipsa hec notio partialis modo determinato inest subjecto, et sic intelligitur subjectum qua tali modo determinatum, adeoque **una** menti observatur notio, cum intueor lapidem rotundum, pronuncians haec verba: **hic lapis est rotundus.** Per hanc propositionem actu nihil aliud cogito, quam **unam** notionem, scilicet lapidis rotundi, qui duo termini etiam **uno** possent exprimi. Licet enim judicium dicatur comparatio ideae cum idea; **idem** tamen comparatum cum **semet ipso** non sistit res **duas**, sed **unam**. E qua explicatione manifestum est, omne judicium reduci ad **unam** notionem, et in mente omni praedicato addendum esse suum valorem quantitativum, licet idem terminus non exprimatur etc.'

human being is an | animal' therefore means: in the synthesis 'human being (consisting of **animal** and **something else**) I recognize the former as the subject, which is also a real concept of the understanding outside this synthesis, and which has consequences; and because of this I am already justified *a priori* in attributing the consequences of 'animal' to 'human being' as well.

Here there is therefore a difference between a judgement aiming merely at **recognition** of the subject, and one aiming at the **attribution of consequences**. With the former, the predicate can be a merely clear distinguishing mark with no consequences; the judgement is only a definition (at least a partial one); but with the latter this distinguishing mark must itself be distinct[25] so that we can have insight into its consequences, in order to attribute them to the subject by this means. For example, if I say **gold** is yellow, then I recognize only the gold by means of this predicate; but what follows from the gold being yellow? Nothing, because from yellow itself nothing follows (in so far as it is a merely clear, not a distinct, representation). On the other hand, if I say: 'A right-angled triangle is a triangle', then I do not define the subject by means of the predicate (because the definition of the subject is already contained in it), rather I mean | this: in the synthesis of a right-angled triangle I recognize the triangle as subject, i.e., as something that also has real consequences in itself outside this synthesis (for example, that its angles are equal to two right angles) so that I already attribute these consequences to the synthesis *a priori*, before I have any insight into what must follow from this new synthesis. The first kind of judgement does not extend our cognition and only the second kind can contribute something to this (through inference).

In the former kind of judgement the very same subject can possess different predicates at the same time; in other words, the subject is the whole [*Totum*] and the predicates are the different parts [*Partes*] of the synthesis. By contrast, in the latter kind only one predicate can be directly attributed to the subject; the others can be attributed only indirectly in

---

[25] TN. We have consistently used 'distinguishing mark' to translate '*Merkmal*', this gives rise to the possibility of 'an indistinct distinguishing mark' which might appear to introduce a contradiction not present in the original German. But in fact the issue here is of the distinctness of the mark in itself not of whether it is sufficiently distinct to distinguish that which it belongs to from other things. So there is no contradiction in yellow being a distinguishing mark of gold even though it is not in itself distinct.

that they are predicates of predicates. For example, 'triangle in general' is the direct predicate of 'right-angled triangle'; while 'shape' is in turn the direct predicate of this predicate, but is the indirect predicate of right-angled triangle, etc. In the former [kind of judgement] subject and predicate can be exchanged; in the latter they cannot. For example, I can say: 'gold is yellow'; and in this case by the subject 'gold', I understand all the other determinations besides the yellow colour. Again I can say: 'gold is exceptionally dense', and in this case by 'gold' I understand all the determinations except the exceptional density, consequently the yellow colour that was previously predicate is now subject, etc. But with the latter kind of judgement this is not permitted. I can certainly say: a right-angled triangle is a triangle, but not the reverse, etc.

40 *In a synthesis of intuition and concept* [*either the intuition or the concept can be subject or predicate*] ... Viewed as cause of the warming of the stone, the fire is a synthesis. The fire can be viewed as the subject and the concept of cause as its predicate (its determination) or the reverse, that is, cause can be viewed as the determinable (the subject) and fire as its determination (predicate).

41 *I do not know how it is possible that a thing is supposed be thought either in itself or through another thing* ... The concepts of subject and predicate are already determined as 'thinkability in itself' or 'thinkability through something else' [respectively], without relation to time-determinations. But then they do not possess a criterion by means of which we can recognize them as such and so they do not apply to things in themselves, where this criterion (time-determinations) is lacking. With *a priori* objects (like those of mathematics) we do not of course need this criterion because their thinkability in itself can be directly presented by means of the consequences derived from the concept. But things in themselves also lack this, because they lack the determining ground of these consequences.

42 *It follows that I am entitled to think a line as something given* [*without the relation-determination of being straight*] ... What is given [*das Gegebene*] must be possible even without what is thought [*das Gedachte*] because it is given before it is thought. Consequently, I can legitimately think the given as subject; but the **thing in itself** contains nothing given that can be taken as the subject of this thought.

201

43 *Apart from the fact that we have no insight into [einsehen] the possibility [of the mere form of synthetic judgement without intuitions, we can in any case only think an object by means of this form, but we cannot have cognition of it]* ... We can have insight into the possibility of analytic propositions *a priori* (i.e. prior to their actuality or application to particular cases) because their form (identity, contradiction) refers to a thing in general. So I already see in advance that I must maintain that any determined | thing is identical with itself because every thing in general must be identical with itself. By contrast, synthetic propositions do not possess any *a priori* principle like this because they refer to determined things and not to every thing in general, and consequently I can demonstrate their possibility only by actually using them. So I may meditate on the universal concept of thing in general as long as I like, but I will never be able to elicit from this that one thing should be the cause of another. And even if we assume this form is possible, we still cannot make use of it in intuition other than by means of a criterion. Now someone might think that we can also have insight into the possibility of synthetic propositions *a priori* because if I judge in a particular case that *a* is the cause of *b*, then this particular proposition is grounded in a universal proposition: i.e., whatever happens must have a cause (if it is to possess objective reality). So in this case too I can know in advance that *b* will have a cause as well. But we should bear in mind that there are determinations in particular judgements that are not contained in the universal judgement, | [e.g.] that *b* alone and nothing else can be the effect of *a*, not merely that something must follow it that stands in the relation of effect in general to *a*; and this I cannot determine *a priori*.

Chapter 5

44 *A right-angled triangle of a determinate size is certainly an* ens omni modo determinatum *[but is still not actual]* ... What if someone were to object that besides the magnitude and the determinations of the angle, still other determinations can be assumed? Then I ask: what determinations? The black colour used to draw the triangle is not one of its determinations, as I have already shown and it is determined just as little by the time and place of its representation. The reason is this: a determination is something that, when added to the determinable, provides a ground for new consequences (that the determinable did not have before); but the black colour, the time and place of the triangle, do not yield any new consequences, so they must be excluded from the list of determinations.

45 [*This concept is distinguished from the thing itself*] *only because of of its formal incompleteness* ... | That is, on the assumption that we can also state all its material determinations.

46 *The necessary is* [*opposed to all of these*] ... The necessary is a reciprocal synthesis, like, for example, the concept of relation. It is thus opposed to the merely possible, in so far as this is merely a one-sided synthesis, as well as to the actual, in so far as this is not a synthesis (of the understanding) at all. The possible is an object that consists of matter and form, whereas the actual is matter alone, and necessity is form alone.

47 *But the sufficient ground* [*is merely an idea of reason*] ... The sufficient ground for a thing is the complete concept of the way it arises, and although we can approach ever more closely to it, we cannot reach it, because to explain the way that something arises we must presuppose something else that has already arisen (in accordance with the famous axiom: *ex nihilo nihil fit*).[26]

48 *That a thing is equal to itself,* [*and that if two parallel lines are cut by a third, the corresponding angles are equal*] ... In other words, the reason why the angle opposite the base in a triangle | is one and the same as the middle angle on the line running parallel with the base is that a thing is equal to itself; and the reason why the other two angles of the triangle are equal to the other two angles of the line previously mentioned is that if two parallel lines are cut by a third, etc.

49 *Which concerns the existence of these objects* ... That is, the mode of existence. The universal judgement that the preceding determines the succeeding (which is a condition of experience in general) grounds [the claim] that if *a* and *b* exist, then their existence must be such that *a* must precede and *b* must follow. But the existence of these objects in themselves has, as I have already remarked, no ground.

50 *It has in fact no ground,* [*or no cause*] ... I have already remarked above that the universal proposition: everything has its ground, or its cause, cannot provide a ground for the particular proposition: *a* is the ground or

---

[26] TN. Nothing comes from nothing.

NOTES AND CLARIFICATIONS

cause of *b*. Consequently this particular proposition has no ground (at least | in relation to our consciousness). Particular analytic propositions (for example, that a triangle is identical with itself) gain legitimacy simply through the general proposition (that every thing is identical with itself). On the other hand, with synthetic propositions it is quite the reverse, namely the universal proposition gains its legitimacy because we could not have a particular proposition of this kind without it. Consequently, the universal contains only the ground of what is universal in the particular proposition; but what is particular in the particular proposition has no ground at all.[27]

Chapter 6

51 *We also make these forms themselves into objects of thought, and think reality and negation as if they were things in themselves that are given to us* ... | Reality and negation are categories derived from the logical forms of *affirmation* and *negation* [*Verneinung*]. However, logical forms are unities that refer to something manifold. But, someone might ask, what do logical reality and negation have in common with transcendental reality and negation that enables the latter to be derived from the former? For the transcendental reality and negation are not unities that refer to something manifold; they are rather the manifold itself, which can be intuited or thought through a unity. **Kant** (*Critique of Pure Reason* 143)[28] claims that reality is what corresponds to a sensation in general in the pure concepts of the understanding. That is to say (if I have otherwise understood him), [reality is] what must be found in every sensation in so far as it is sensation in general ([it is] not what is particular to each sensation). But what does this have in common with logical affirmation? For the logical affirmation signifies a form, and the transcendental affirmation signifies a content. Who will help me out of this embarrassment, *erit mihi magnus Apollo*![29]

---

[27] TN. The note that follows in the original text is in the wrong place: it does not refer to s.112 as the text indicates, but to s.122. We have repositioned it in the correct sequence of the notes so that s.394–96 will be interpolated into the translation at s.399.

[28] TN. A143/B182.

[29] TN. 'To me be great Apollo', i.e. who will help me (if even Kant cannot)? Virgil, *Eclogue* III, verse 104.

397 | 399

52 [*To posit the one is not merely to cancel the other,*] *but the one is instead a different positing from the other* ... | That is to say a real, but merely subjective, synthesis.

53 *As I have already shown, the* minimum *of transcendental reality is an idea of the understanding* ... For we may always assume it to be as small as we like, it must still be an intensive quantity, i.e., have a degree (see *Critique of Pure Reason*, p. 169).[30]

Chapter 7

54 [*Given sensible representations that are different (in terms of the forms of intuition) but*] *homogeneous* [*(in terms of their concept)*] ... If they are not homogeneous, i.e. if they are not only different with respect to the form but also with respect to the matter of intuition, then they cannot be subsumed by the concept of a continuous quantity, but only by the concept of number; in this case they are not in space as intuition but merely in it as concept (see Chapter 1).

55 *(2) Gathered together in a concept.*[31] *(3) Gathered together in an intuition* ... Here apperception precedes apprehension (this is not how it is with the connection of several | intuitions by means of the categories) because we must first compare them with one another, and then gain insight into their identity before we are justified in bringing them into a unity of apprehension.

56[32] *Intensive magnitude is the differential of extensive,* [*and the extensive is, in turn, the integral of the intensive*] ... That is, if an extensive magnitude is reduced to its differential, it can nevertheless be thought as a ratio [*Größenverhältnis*] of extensive magnitudes because of its intensive

---

[30] TN. Maimon's reference is to the 'Anticipations of Perception' in the first edition of the *Critique*, A169/B211: 'Accordingly every sensation, thus also every reality in appearance, however small it may be, has a degree, i.e. an intensive magnitude'.

[31] TN. '*Die Zusammensetzung in einem Begriff*'. The original passage in Chapter 7 has '*Die Zusammennehmung in einem Begriff*'. The difference in meaning is slight since the former translates literally as 'the composing or positing together in a concept' the latter as 'the taking together in a concept'.

[32] TN. In the original this note was printed after note 50 on original pages 394–96 above. We have moved it to its correct place in the sequence.

magnitude. To explain this, consider a triangle; now move one side in relation to the opposite angle so that it always remains parallel to itself; do this until the triangle becomes an infinitely small [triangle] (a differential). The extensive magnitude of the sides then completely disappears and is reduced to their differentials; but the relation of the sides always remains the same because it is not the relation of number to number with respect to one and the same unit, but the relation of unit to unit.[33] Consequently, the intensive magnitude (the quality of the quantum) is in this case the differential of the extensive quantities, and the extensive quantities are the integral of the intensive magnitude. Perhaps some will find it incomprehensible that the quality, abstracted from all extensive quantity, can nevertheless be thought in a relation of extensive quantities. So let us take a [right-angled] triangle abc whose adjacent and opposite sides ab, bc are equal to one another. Let us further assume that one side bc moves relative to the opposite angle bac in such a way that it always remains parallel with itself, until it becomes df which I assume to be infinitely small. Consequently ad and af also become infinitely small, as does the triangle as a whole. The relation of af to ad or df, always remains just the same, namely it is equal to $\sqrt{2}:1$. So, it is not a relation of number to number, since I have assumed both to be infinitely small, *omni dabili minora*;[34] and consequently it cannot be expressed by any number in relation to any unit, but only by the relation of one unit to another unit, i.e. this relation does not hold between the lines in so far as they are measurable, but merely in so far as they are determined by their quality (by their position). As a result, they are not extensive but intensive magnitudes; with intensive magnitudes, the representation of the parts does not make possible the representation of the whole, but the reverse; because they have no parts, their magnitude can only be grasped by comparing it [the magnitude] as a whole with other wholes, for example by comparing df with de.

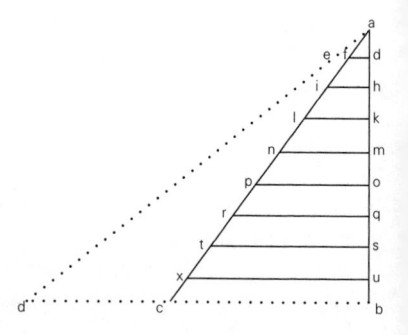

---

[33] TN. That is to say the relation of two different units to one another.
[34] TN. Smaller than any(thing) given. In this case: smaller than any given number.

Chapter 8

57 [*So this concept of the understanding is the imagination's guiding principle, and it must not lose sight of it if its procedure is to be legitimate; but if it does lose sight of it, then*] *it falls into fictions* ... The representation of empty space, for example, is of this kind: it arises when the imagination makes space transcendent, i.e. represents it as a thing in itself, instead of considering it in accordance with the understanding merely as a form or way of thinking things in relation to one another.

Chapter 9

58 *Logical truth* [*is the connection of objects of thought (concepts), according to the laws of the understanding*] ... I think it would not be out of place here for me to set down the essential points of my letter to Herr L in Berlin. (This gentleman is a wealthy man of upright character, a lover of the sciences, a promoter of what is good and noble, and someone who would certainly deserve to be made better known to the world, had his modesty not expressly forbade it). In I that letter I happened on the idea of comparing truth with coins. So I begin like this:

Wolff says:[35] truth is the agreement of our judgement with the object, and this is **logical truth**. To explain this he cites the following proposition as an example: 'A triangle (a three-sided figure) has three angles.' But I have already remarked elsewhere[36] that a logical object is simply the concept of a thing in general, i.e. something that is not determined by any conditions, whether *a posteriori* or *a priori*. So a logical proposition or a logical truth is simply one that can be predicated of a thing in general. A triangle is thus not a logical object because it is determined by means of particular *a priori* conditions; and the proposition: 'a triangle has three angles', is not a logical proposition, since it is not the predicate of a thing in general but of a determined object. What is more, this definition provides the truth merely in words, not in thought.[37] I For, if I say that a triangle has three angles, then in doing so I express something that I actually think, i.e. I speak truly, and the opposite would be false. But with for thought there is here no true

---

[35] TN. Logic. P. II, Cap. I. §505.
[36] TN. *Essay on Transcendental Philosophy*.
[37] TN. There is a mistake in the pagination of the original which here jumps from page 400 to page 405.

and false thought because I can think a triangle only with three angles, not with more angles. On the other hand, I hold this proposition, as well as all other synthetic propositions, to be a merely subjective truth, i.e. a necessary way **for me** to think a determined object. So such propositions are valid neither for an object in general nor for this determined object in relation to every thinking being in general. By contrast, the proposition 'A triangle is identical with itself', is an objective truth, for in it I think a triangle identical with itself, because not only I, but every thinking being in general, must think, not only a triangle, but every object, as identical with itself. Without this no thought is possible. So mathematical propositions are **objectively** true, but only on the presupposition of the objectivity of their principles (that these are possible), otherwise they are, like the principles themselves, only **subjectively true**. | But this does not detract from the legitimacy of their use, because they have a use and a truth merely for us. It follows that it cannot properly be said that a mathematical axiom is **objectively true**, but only that it is real; i.e. it is useful for the cognition of truth and in its application. And how could it be otherwise, because the principles of a thing are not the thing itself, for if they were, then the thing must already be presupposed before it has arisen. For example, the principles of an area are not areas, of a line are not lines, etc., so the principles of truth cannot already themselves be truths. Properly speaking, truth is not a proposition produced in accordance with the laws of thought; rather truth is the operation of thought itself and the proposition is produced from this. The proposition is merely the matter or stuff [*Stoff*] out of which the form becomes actual.

Now that I have made these preliminary points, let us see to what extent truth can be compared with a coin. A coin is either **ideal** or **real**; the ideal coin is coin properly understood, and means a universal standard by means of which the value of things | relative to one another is determined, but that in itself it has no value, and is a mere sign. On the other hand, the real coin also has (with respect to the matter it is made of) a value in itself as commodity, and in addition to this it also has a value as **sign** by virtue of its imprint [*Gepräge*]. Now, since the relation of things to one another can change, and the coin is supposed to determine the state of this relation at all times, it follows that if the material value of a real coin is identical to its imprinted value [*Wert des Gepräges*], then it completely ceases to be a coin, i.e. a universal standard, because it is then a commodity subject to change just as much as anything else, and consequently its value must itself be first determined by another standard that does not change. On the other hand, the more these two values differ from one another, the closer the **real** coin comes to the **ideal** coin, i.e. the more it becomes a coin, since an ideal coin is the surplus of the imprinted value over the real value, and this continues until this difference becomes a maximum, i.e. until it has only an ideal value and no real value. The ideal coin thus has an | advantage over the real coin with respect to its indirect use, namely as the standard of value; on the other hand the real has an advantage over the ideal with respect to its direct use, i.e. as something that has a value in itself.

Truth unites both advantages in itself: first of all it is the standard that determines the relation of things to one another; but in addition, this means that its fate is not to be an object that can itself be thought in relation to other things, but rather a mere form or way of thinking the relation of things to one another, and as such it is not subject to change, and this is how it can be compared with the merely ideal coin. Secondly, besides this, it also has a real value with respect to its direct use, namely as the perfection of a thinking being. The less pure a truth is, i.e. the more *a posteriori* concepts and propositions it must be grounded on, the less is it apt to be a universal standard of the objective value of all things in relation to one another; and in this it is like the real coin, where in order to determine the state of the relations things have to each other, | the state of the standard itself (which is also subject to change) must be taken into account; and since the latter must in turn be determined by something else that is in itself not subject to change and such a thing is nowhere to be found, so nothing can be determined in this way. As a result, pure reason alone can be used as a standard in determining the value of actions (their moral worth) relative to one another. If something else is mixed in with it (pleasure, perfection, and the like), then there is no universal unchanging standard because the value of this something is itself different for different subjects under different circumstances. I have thus arrived, although in my own way, at **Kant's** principle of morality; but I will save the further consideration of this matter for another occasion. For now, it is enough to remark that moral good is good only because it is true, i.e. when the particular maxim of actions is in agreement with a universal rule of reason.

Now that I have compared the truth to a coin from this side, I want to attempt | to do it again from another side; this will make it obvious both what the difference between symbolic and intuitive knowledge is, and what the advantage of the latter over the former is (as well as the

209

reverse). In the discovery [*Erfindung*] of truth an orderly trade takes place, for the unknown is produced from the known by substitution, i.e. through an exchange. Before the invention of the coin, trade consisted in a direct exchange of commodities for one another; but this was inconvenient because trade of this kind was very restricted, since it could only take place if each of the parties needed the commodities of the other and could do without their own; otherwise it could not take place. So people tried to get rid of this inconvenience by the introduction of money. By this means, trade became more extended and more general. In this way the first difficulty was overcome, but a new difficulty arose, namely that the value of the coin is only determined by its imprinted value, and as a result, it happened over time that (because of shortage of the raw material and the like) the imprinted value is now very different from | the real value of the coin. Because of this the universality of trade was restricted in another way, namely because such coins can be used only for internal but not external trade. This is how the situation now stands with regard to trade. Let us now see how it is with truth. As long as one remains with intuitive cognition, the discovery of truth takes place by means of a direct exchange, i.e. a direct substitution of thoughts for one another. This certainly has the advantage that we can always be sure of the reality of the thoughts; on the other hand, it has the inconvenience that using this method we cannot go far towards the discovery [*Erfindung*] of truth, particularly if it is well hidden. To overcome this difficulty, we make use of symbolic cognition, i.e. we first of all substitute signs for the things signified, and secondly we substitute for each of these signs a sign of the same value and so on, so that with each new formula a new truth arises. In this way we are in a position to discover the most hidden truth without much effort and, as it were, mechanically; But this gives rise to | a new difficulty, namely, we occasionally arrive at symbolic combinations or formulae that have no reality, i.e. that do not correspond to any real objects, for example the imaginary numbers, the tangent and cosine of a right angle and similar things in mathematics.

So symbolic cognition is certainly an excellent aid to the discovery [*Erfindung*] of truth, but one whose use requires great care; we must ask ourselves at every step we take, as politicians do, whether this ideal coin can also be realized. If we do not do this, then we arrive at the most peculiar ideas and will not be able to extricate ourselves from them. Mathematics has certainly achieved a lot through its new analysis, since it enables us to make discoveries that were almost impossible using the methods of the ancients; but it also leads careless mathematicians into difficulties unknown to the ancients, something the examples I have cited make clear.

So, like a coin, truth has two values. First, because truth in general is a determined form or a necessary way | of connecting concepts, it follows that with truth as well we can distinguish matter from form: concepts are the matter of truth, they are joined together in a proposition as subject and predicate, and only then become a truth. In themselves, concepts are not truths; rather they are mere realities (if they correspond to the object) or not realities (in the opposite case). Only the determined rule, i.e. the representation of their necessary connection, makes a proposition into a true proposition. So every truth or every proposition has two values: first, with respect to its matter, whether it is real; and then second with respect to its form as well. The latter is certainly always real with respect to thought alone (otherwise it is not a form); but in the relation of signs (of language) to what they designate they can also be not-real [*nicht-reell*]. This is how these two values can coexist, just as they do in a coin, as when we derive new propositions from real concepts and synthetic principles (these must be called real rather than true propositions, since they do not follow objectively in accordance with the universal grounds of thought in general, but only in accordance with subjective grounds unknown [*unbekannt*] to us; and this is why | I do not call them universal truths but merely real propositions, on account of their universality for us). But they can also be separated, as, for example, when we think the concept of a triangle, or this synthetic principle 'A triangle has three angles', etc. In the concept of 'triangle' and in the cited proposition there is merely a material value, but one that still does not possess a necessary *a priori* form; by contrast, if we think a triangle with two right angles, i.e. a concept that is not real, and derive certain consequences from this in accordance with the necessary form of thought, then we have a real form of thought, but without matter; we can therefore make no use of the proposition produced by this method, and yet by means of this operation we have really been thinking. And this is just how truth differs from the coin: for the coin, the form in itself, abstracted from matter, has no value, and hence can be used only as an agreed upon sign inside a country, not universally; while on the other hand, the matter keeps its value universally; for truth it is precisely the reverse. Form has a universal value, in so far as a real thought is always produced by its means; by contrast, | matter has a value only for us, but not for every thinking being in general.

211

Chapter 10

59 *According to the famous Delphic saying* ... I hope the reader will not think that I mean to attach the sense of my present investigation to this saying. I am well aware that this saying is moral, while the present investigation is metaphysical.

60 *There must be a thing at all times* ... Consequently my I must accompany all my times.[38]

61 *For example, the thought of a triangle is only possible, [because I relate the representation of three lines to that of space]* ... In other words: a thought requires a subjective unity as much as it does an objective unity (unity of consciousness and unity of the object). But the latter is a unity only in relation to the former, since there could certainly be thinking beings that think (but in another way) just what I think as a determination of something else (and thus as in a unity with it); and from this we see that objective unity itself presupposes subjective unity. |

62 *The materialist* ... All these partisans can and must be in agreement about the cognitive faculty. Their opinions differ only about the object that grounds the cognitive faculty. The materialist can (legitimately) claim only that the object (what grounds the given matter [*dem materiellen Gegebenen*] in representation) is what belongs to existence, or exists, outside representation. But he does not dare to determine this object (as to whether it is simple or manifold). The idealist, on the other hand, thinks himself entitled to determine the object to some degree, namely that it is not manifold, because the manifold can be thought as such only through a subjective unity, consequently it can be thought only as unity (which in this case is nothing more than the denial of being manifold), and it is still further determined by analogy with ourselves. The dualist cautiously opts for the middle path between these two extremes. Incidentally, I do not believe it necessary to note that I have not presented here what these men think, but merely what they could have a reason for thinking. |

---

[38] TN. '*Es muss zu allen Zeiten ein Ding geben ... Folglich auch zu allen meinen Zeiten mein Ich.*'

Short Overview of the Whole Work[39]

63 [419] *Sensation [is a modification of the cognitive faculty that is actualized within that faculty only passively]* ... For Kant, the given in representation cannot signify what has a cause outside the faculty of representation [*Vorstellungskraft*] because it is unthinkable that we can have cognition of the **thing in itself** (*noumenon*) as a cause outside the faculty of representation, since in this case the schema of time is lacking; we cannot even think it assertorically because the faculty of representation itself may be the cause of the representation just as well as the object outside it. So the given can only be something within representation whose cause is as unknown to us as the way it arises (*essentia realis*) in us, i.e. something we have merely an incomplete consciousness of. But this incompleteness of consciousness can be thought as going from a determined consciousness to complete **nothingness** through an infinite decreasing series of degrees. Consequently the merely given (what is present to the faculty of representation without any consciousness) is a mere idea of the limit of this series, which one can ever approach, but never reach (as with an irrational root).

64 [417] *Because the complete absence consciousness [= 0]* ... But I have already demonstrated on various occasions that activity is required for consciousness.

65 [417] *Intuition [is a modification of the cognitive faculty that is actualised within that faculty in part passively and in part actively]* ... The given in intuition (material) arises passively [*durchs Leiden*], but its ordering according to a form arises through activity [*durch Tätigkeit*].

66 [420] *Intuition [is a modification]* ... *Appearance [is an undetermined intuition, in so far as it is based on passivity]* ... For example, the representation of a **red colour** consists in the sensation of this particular sensible quality whose manifold is ordered according to the forms of intuition (time and space); so it is a determinate empirical intuition. On

---

[39] TN. Notes 63–72 were not printed in correct sequence in the original text. We have corrected this with the result that the page number references to the original in these notes jump around between pages 417–23. To help locate them in the original, we have inserted the page number at which it commences at the beginning of each of these notes.

the other hand, appearance is the concept of a sensible representation in general, abstracted from the red colour and from all other sensible representations.

67 [420] *The [absolutely] a priori* ... A priori cognition in general means cognition based on grounds (*cognitio philosophica*). The predicate is attributed to the particular subject because it was already attributed to the universal subject, which includes this particular subject. For example, I judge that the sum of the angles of a right-angled triangle of a given size is equal to two right angles. Why? Because I know in advance that the sum of the angles of a triangle in general must be equal to two right angles. The absolute *a priori* requires yet another condition, namely that the ultimate ground of the judgement or the universal judgement to which I reduce all particular judgements, is itself *a priori*. But this is not possible as long as the condition of the judgement is a particular determination of the subject (since it presupposes an infinite series). So the condition must be the universal concept of the thing in general. But the only judgement of this type is that of identity and contradiction, where the condition of judgment is not a determined object but a necessary form.

68 [417] *The axioms of mathematics* ... I mean the axioms that are proper to mathematics, such as, for example: 'a straight line is the shortest between two points', and so on; but I do not mean axioms that are used in mathematics merely because they are valid in general, such as, for example, 'the whole is equal to all of its parts taken together'. For a whole is (Baumgarten, *Metaphysik* §120) a one that is completely identical to many taken together, and the things that are taken together are identical to the one, are its parts; consequently, this axiom is based on the principle of contradiction, and is thus a priori in the strictest sense.

69 [421] *It is so used only in symbolic cognition* ... A contradiction can occur only between the signs of opposed forms (**being** and **not-being**), but it cannot occur between objects, or between objects and forms; so contradictions are used only in symbolic cognition (see the appendix on symbolic cognition). In symbolic cognition I can just as easily say that a triangle is possible (or that a space can be enclosed in three lines), as I can say that a triangle is not possible; neither claim is contradictory. On the other hand, in intuitive cognition I can maintain only the first of these claims. Why?

Because this is the way I actually think it. That is, this apodictic relation of the form to determinate objects (an apodictic relation that is a particular determination of the form) already presupposes the possibility of the form in itself (the absence of contradiction). If someone says 'a triangle must be possible before I actually think it because otherwise I could not think it', then I ask, 'what does it mean that it must be possible before I actually think it?' Presumably it means this: another thinking being, comparing me as something determinable with the triangle as determination, finds that **I**, determined by the modification **triangle**, am possible. But this in turn presupposes a third thinking being, and so on to infinity. The further along in this series a member comes, the more possibilities it thinks at once. For example, thinking being *a* just thinks space as possible in relation to three lines. But this supposes another thinking being, *b*, that besides thinking the triangle itself as possible, also thinks the first [thinking being] as possible in relation to it, and so on. Thus if someone demands that real possibility precede the thinking of an object, then this possibility is not to be found in any member of the series, not even in the last member (if we want to realize this idea) because the possibility of this last member certainly does not precede its actuality (see s.249).

70 [418] [*The absence of a contradiction*] *but not just in the combination of symbols, but in the object itself* ... That is to say, where those that are thought in a synthesis do not contradict one another in their concepts, but cancel out one another's consequences.

71 [423] [*For example, my judgement that a straight line is the shortest between two points,*] *can derive from my having always perceived it thus* ... That is, not in a pure, but in an empirical construction (whenever I drew a straight line on paper, I always found it to be the shortest). For what is the pure construction of a straight line be supposed to be, since we cannot give any definition of the straight line and consequently cannot specify any *a priori* rule for it to arise [*Entstehungsregel*]?

72 [418] *The proposition 'everything has its cause' possesses the same degree of self-evidence* [*Evidenz*] *as the proposition, 'a straight line ...'* ... That is, in itself, not merely as a condition of experience. Here I would like to state once and for all that I hold what Kant calls objective necessity (condition of an objective perception or experience) to be a merely subjective necessity; there are two reasons for this. 1) Suppose that a synthetic rule

in general were necessary within perceptions to assure their objective reality; even so, a determinate rule is not necessary for this. For example, we think the perceptions *a* and *b* by means of the form or rule of causality; but a different thinking being can think these very perceptions according to another rule, and so this rule is only subjective in relation to determined perceptions. 2) A synthetic rule is not at all necessary to assure objective reality for an unlimited understanding unaffected by sensibility. The latter thinks all possible objects according to their inner relations with one another, that is to say, according to the way that they arise out of one another, i.e. always according to an analytic rule; from this it follows that the forms or synthetic rules have objective necessity only for us (since we cannot make them analytic on account of our limitation), but not in themselves. |

73 [*We will find*] *that the expression, 'objective necessity'* [*is actually meaningless*] ... Objective necessity can be attributed only to the principle of contradiction (in so far as it signifies the necessary relation of a subject in general to an object in general), or to the categories (in so far as a real object in general can be thought in relation to our subject through them), but not to a proposition relating to a particular object. The former necessity is *a priori*, i.e. is attributed to the | particular object, because it must be attributed to an object in general. The latter, however, is merely *a posteriori*, on my definition.

74 *Then let us first assume* ... In a similar manner, Court Counsellor Kästner proves the proposition that every power of two is greater than its exponent by showing that if the claim is correct for a certain power it must also hold for the next higher power (see *Anfangsgründe Analysis endlicher Größen*, §45).

75 *The proposition,* $5 + 7 = 12$ ... The question could be posed: what is a determinate number? It is not an *a posteriori* object (something given) because it is merely a determinate way of thinking an object. It is not an *a priori* form because it is not a condition of an object. It is not an *a posteriori* form because this has no meaning at all, as each form can be nothing other than an *a priori* condition. What is it then?

76 *But this only proves that space is a universal concept* ... As far as I have been able to gather from Kant's theory, a form is thought) in this way: | it

is what, in the representation of an object, is grounded not in the object, but in the particular constitution [*besondere Beschaffenheit*] of the power of representation. But the question is: how is it recognized, or by what distinguishing marks can we tell whether any determination of representation is grounded in the object or merely in the faculty of representation? I have been able to find only these: 1) universality in relation to objects; 2) particularity in relation to the subject; and that they are both necessary. In other words, if I find a representation common to several objects, then from this I recognize that it is not a determination of the objects themselves (since this can only be what distinguishes one object from all others), but of our way of representing them. But this is merely a condition for recognizing form [as distinct] from matter, and the way of thinking of an object [as distinct] from the object itself (the given); but it is not a condition for recognizing what is grounded in a particular way of representing as opposed to what is proper to every way of representing in general in relation to the very same object. For example, matter (the given) is the very same in relation | to every thinking being it is given to; otherwise it would not be mere matter because the alteration that it would undergo in each of them would belong to form. Further, the material [*materielle*] difference between objects is a necessary condition for their perception as particular objects for every subject without distinction. From this it can be seen that the first distinguishing mark is only a *conditio sine qua non*, i.e. what is not proper to several objects cannot belong to the form (mode of representation) but only to matter (the given). However, it can belong to matter not only for a particular faculty of representation but also for any faculty of representation in general (either as the matter itself or as its condition). Space (and also time) is of this type. Space is not, like red, for example, the given in the object by means of which it is recognized and distinguished from all other objects; and the reason is that space is not a determination in the object, but a relation between several objects. So this is the first requirement: i.e. the distinguishing mark of a form in opposition to matter. But the second requirement or the distinguishing mark of subjectivity is missing in this case (and it is certainly of great importance for the Kantian theory). | So I maintain that space is definitely a form (since it cannot be discerned):[40] however, unlike **Kant**, I do not hold it to be a

---

[40] TN. '*nicht ausgemacht warden kann*'. This could mean either that space cannot be discerned (made out) or that it cannot be constructed (made up).

merely subjective form (necessary in relation to a particular kind of subject), but an objective form (necessary in relation to every subject in general). But I maintain this (according to my hypothesis) for space as a concept (of difference in general). By contrast, for space as intuition (the image of this difference), I hold space merely to be a universal concept rather than a form because in this case the second requirement (the distinguishing mark of subjectivity) is missing. So the difference between **Kant's** theory and mine is this: for **Kant**, space is merely a form of intuitions, whereas for me it is, as concept, a form of all objects in general and, as intuition, an image of this form. For Kant it is **nothing** in the object itself abstracted from our way of representing it; by contrast, for me it is always *something* in relation to any subject at all and certainly a form, but a form grounded in the object.

77 *For the following reason: in thinking I approach such a substance more and more closely ...* | It could certainly be objected that by thinking I do not approach ever closer to my subject, but to the transcendental subject; so what right do I have to determine my subject as substance? But we should bear in mind that when I judge that I am a human being, this does not mean that I am an indeterminate human being, but rather that I am a human being determined in an individual manner (without actually determining it). Consequently, the most universal predicate in the judgement does not in fact have a greater extension than the ultimate subject in the judgement, i.e. the object itself. So prior to the judgement my *I* was perceived to be determined as 'human being', for example, through *a*, i.e. at the furthest remove from the ultimate subject in the object. But by means of the judgement I think of myself as 'human being' by means of *x*, i.e. as determined through an unknown determination. So by means of the substitution of an unknown determination for the known (although it relates to the known), I have come closer not merely to a transcendental subject, but to my subject.

78 [*In the end all concepts must be reduced to one concept,*] *and all truths to a single truth ...* | With regard to the systematic sciences, everyone will surely agree with me. But the question remains, what kind of connection holds between the claim that air is elastic and the claim that the magnet attracts iron, and between the latter and the Pythagorean theorem for example? But what follows from this? Nothing other than that we do not understand this connection; the but the reason for this is that we are not

acquainted with objects themselves in their inner essence; once we do become acquainted with all the properties of air, of the magnet, etc. so that we are in a position to define these objects in their inner essence, then this connection will also be brought easily to light.

79 *However, I note [that at least this stranger cannot perceive any absolute alteration in me [considered] as his outer intuition]* ... The perception of an alteration in the object presupposes the perception of persistence in the subject viewed as object because otherwise the subject could never relate the changing determinations in the object to one another in a consciousness. But it also presupposes perception of persistence in the object because otherwise the subject could not view the different determinations of its self as different determinations of the object. Let us assume two thinking | beings, *A* and *B*. Identity of consciousness at different times (in relation to its time) must be attributed to each of them. Suppose someone says: perhaps the identity of *A*'s consciousness in relation to its time is itself alterable in the consciousness of *B* in relation to its own time. For example, at one time it has the determination, *a*, at another, the determination, *ae*. Then it must be assumed: 1) That *B*, as the object of these different representations, *a*, *ae*, must be one and the same as itself at different times because otherwise it would not relate these two different representations to itself as the very same subject, i.e. it would not even perceive a subjective alteration. 2) That *A*, as the object of *B* under these different determinations with respect to the latter (in relation to its time), must possess something (apart from these changing determinations) [that is] one and the same as itself, i.e., something persistent, because otherwise *B* would certainly have perception (subjective) but not experience (objective perception) of an alteration. The difference between *A* and *B* will then be merely this: that *A* would view itself (the subject of *a* and *ae*) as persistent, whereas *B* would not determine *A* as the | ultimate subject and consequently as persistent, but as something that in turn is determined through predicates; it must think the ultimate subject in *A* (even if not *A*) as being one and the same as itself, i.e. as persistent. So, to judge that the alteration in the identity of *A*'s consciousness has occurred not just subjectively in *B*, but objectively in *A*, the subjective identity of *B*'s consciousness is not sufficient; it must instead be viewed objectively, i.e. viewed with respect to a third [thing], *C*. But since the same goes for *C* as for *B*, it follows there is no subject at all that can think the alteration in *A* absolutely, without presupposing something persistent in it. But at the

219

same time the alteration of the relation, or the alteration of *A* in relation to the time of *B*, makes the alteration of *B* in relation to the time of *A* necessary because otherwise the time in both would have to be one and the same, i.e. objective, and this is contrary to our assumption.

My Ontology

80 *Does the principle of contradiction belong to logic or to metaphysics?* | I reply: it belongs to both at once. In logic it is expressed like this: the opposed forms of judgements (being and not being) cannot constitute a composite form (whatever the content may be, even if it is logical). But in metaphysics it is expressed like this: the very same logical object cannot be attributed by means of the very same form to two mutually exclusive contents (*a* and not-*a*, this would make the proposition at the same time affirmative and undetermined). There is no direct contradiction in this case because being *a* and being at the same time something different from *a*, for example *b*, do not contradict one another (realities exclude but do not contradict one another). But indirectly this proposition can be reduced to a contradiction because *a* must first be cancelled out in order to suppose something else *b* that is different from *a*; and gives rise to a logical contradiction. In addition, I note that this '**at the same time**' does not signify a time-determination (because logic has nothing to do with time-determinations), but merely the objective unity of consciousness.

Concluding Note

After what I have said so far, I believe I am now in a position to compare different | philosophical systems, both with regard to the legitimacy or illegitimacy of their claims and to their advancement or obstruction of the interest of reason.

1) The empiricists. They do not want to accept any *a priori* principle, either material or formal. To them, all our concepts (even the simplest) and (most universal) judgements (not even excluding the principle of contradiction) are abstracted by us *a posteriori* from sensible objects and the manifold relations that we perceive between them; and just as red, for example, is the abstractum[41] of a sensible thing, namely red colour, so for

---

[41] TN. Here and below 'abstractum' translates '*Abstraktum*', meaning the product of abstraction.

them, unity [*Einheit*] is the abstractum of something that is one [*eins*], and so on. According to them, all those things that we term intellectual are not real but merely logical objects that are only different ways of viewing things given to us with the things themselves. The empiricists are in fact irrefutable, for how are they supposed to be refuted? By showing that their thesis is inconsistent, i.e. contains a manifest contradiction? They do not want to accept the principle of contradiction. But they do not even deserve to be refuted because they assert | – nothing. I must admit that I can form no conception of this way of thinking. That any two lines intersecting in a circle must divide one another into parts that are in a proportion,[42] that however far the asymptote is drawn it can never touch the curve, and the like. In short, that a thing is not at the same time actual and not actual, possible and not possible, are only inductive claims [*Induktions-Sätze*]! With this thesis the interest of reason is quite lost because it leads to the total annihilation of reason itself. These gentlemen allow themselves no higher faculty [*grösseres Vermögen*] than a kind of instinct that they call *judicum practicum*[43] and the expectation of similar cases, something that the animals possess to an excellent degree. But enough of this!

2) The empirical dogmatists and rational sceptics. They assert that the objects of our cognition are given to us *a posteriori*, but that their forms are in us *a priori*. If neither we nor these forms existed, then the objects could nevertheless still exist (although in a different way from the way we think them). If these objects did not exist, then we could still exist (in a manner | unknown to us). Further, they assert that we have the ability [*Vermögen*] not only to **think** these forms in themselves as objects, but also to **recognize** them as forms in the objects. However this **cognition** does not occur through direct perception, but only by means of the perception of a schema or distinguishing mark in the objects, so that by means of the judgement that these forms belong to the objects, we attain consciousness of these forms themselves at the same time. The more general application of these forms to things in themselves (including those lacking this distinguishing mark) does not serve to determine something in the objects, but merely to provide reason with completeness

---

[42] TN. See Euclid, *The Elements*, Bk 3, Prop. 35. This is now known as the 'intersecting chords theorem': if two chords of a circle, *AB* and *CD*, intersect at point *E*, then $AE \times EB = CE \times ED$.

[43] TN. Practical judgement.

NOTES AND CLARIFICATIONS

and systematic unity. This is the Kantian system. It is not merely legitimate, but also furthers the interest of reason to the highest degree; because although it limits the use of reason by reference to this distinguishing mark, yet this mark is so constituted that it can cease only with reason itself (because it is an *a priori* form).

3) Rational dogmatists and empirical sceptics. They assert that both the forms and the objects of our cognition themselves are in us *a priori*, and that this faculty [*Vermögen*] does not consist merely in recognizing objects given to us by means of forms thought by us,[44] but also in producing the objects themselves by means of these forms. Sensible objects are confused representations of these objects of reason [*Vernunft-Objekten*]. If reason does use its forms of sensible objects (I mean synthetic objects, something that is dubious), then this does not take place directly, but by means of the objects of reason that they represent (no distinguishing mark is required to tell that these forms belong to the objects of reason because it is directly perceived). They therefore extend the use of reason further than the former. On the other hand, however, they doubt the fact itself, i.e. that reason possesses or uses these forms; they will only hear of a single form, namely that of identity and contradiction, to which they attribute objective reality. By contrast, they are certain that a merely subjective reality should be attributed to the other forms, but because of their universality in relation to us, these forms serve in exactly the same way as if they had objective reality, so that the interest of reason is not narrowed in any way. If I am asked: who are these rational dogmatists? then for the moment I can name no one but myself. But I believe that this is the Leibnizian system (if it is understood correctly).[45] But whether it be the Leibnizian system or not, what does it matter? I am not collecting opinions on it. **Mendelssohn** says somewhere: with regard to the truth, opinions must be weighed, not counted. If the Kantians are asked: do we in fact judge that certain forms belong to certain objects? they answer: certainly. If they are further asked: how do we recognize this? then they

---

[44] TN. '*Uns gegebene Objekte durch von uns gedachte Formen zu erkennen*'. The translation unfortunately introduces an ambiguity not present in the original, which means cognizing given objects through thought forms, not cognizing objects given through thought forms.

[45] TN. The implication is that the dominant 'Leibnizian-Wolffian' philosophy of Maimon's time is based on an incorrect understanding of Leibniz. Kant argues that Maimon's system is not Leibnizian in the letter in the Appendix.

answer: by an *a priori* distinguishing mark that refers necessarily to *a posteriori* objects. By contrast, if I am asked the first question, then I reply that I doubt it; but to the second question I reply that, supposing that the first question must be answered affirmatively, then this [recognition] could be accomplished even in the absence of such a subjective distinguishing mark by means of an objective one in the things themselves, so that we (according to our present condition) continually approach the mark (so that the judgement gains an ever greater degree of probability) | without ever being able to fully reach it (so that the complete certainty of the judgement is still withheld). But since I believe that I have sufficiently clarified this in the work itself, I do not wish to devote any more time to it here.

4) A system that is a composite of the foregoing:[46] those who favour this system assert that the objects are given to us *a posteriori*, but the forms of our cognition are given *a priori*, in such a way that these are in agreement with one another; however, they explain the possibility of this agreement in general as little as they explain how we attain certainty in the judgement of this agreement in particular cases. This is the system of most Wolffians: by positing objects in themselves and relating forms directly to them (not by means of [*vermittelst*] an *a priori* schema in the sensible objects, as in the former system,[47] nor by means of [*vermittelst*] a dissolution of the sensible objects into an infinite series, i.e. through a continual approach to the intellectual objects, as in the latter system), they interrupt the progress of reason, and check its interest. Consequently, this system cannot be upheld in any way.

Having thus compared these different systems with regard to the objective formal interest of reason in itself, I now want to compare them with regard to the subjective material interest of reason as well; this will explain why certain classes of thinking subjects | are more devoted to certain systems than to others (because of a subjective interest). This depends on ability, education and profession [*Lebensart*]. For those who cannot grasp it without great effort, a system that is harder to grasp than

---

[46] TN. From what follows it seems clear that Maimon means a composite of the latter two systems, the Kantian and the Maimonian systems, rather than of all three. He is no doubt being deliberately provocative to the Wolffians in describing their system as a combination of his own and Kant's, given that their system came first.

[47] TN. See previous note – by 'former system' Maimon evidently means the Kantian, by 'latter system' the Maimonian.

another must take second place to that other even though it furthers the objective interest of reason more than the other. The objective interest of reason lies with the former, but the subjective with the latter. Further, once someone's education and professional concerns [*Berufsgeshchäfte*] have accustomed them more to one way of thinking than another, then subjective reason will favour this way of thinking even if the other is more appropriate to the nature of objective reason, to say nothing of the material interest that a certain profession [*Lebensart*] can have in a certain system. Theologians, for example (when they also want to be philosophers), naturally find more subjective interest in the Wolffian system than in other systems. A system that holds the objects of their profession to be a mere idea (in the sense in which **Kant** and I define this word) will not please them. So they make their subjective limits into objective limits of reason itself, and in doing so bring its activity to an immediate halt, since reason's limit is in fact not the object, but the law of reason itself. Hence they can be reproached with righteous indignation: **Why, Moses and Aaron** (you theologians)**, do you disturb the people in its activity? Conduct your office dutifully!**[48] The politicians must stop at empiricism. They become queasy when they are asked the unexpected question, what is *salis populi*,[49] and what does it consist of? (even though this is the universally acknowledged principle of their science). Or, supposing they could agree on this principle, they would still think it ridiculous to proceed step by step following the rules of logic in applying it to particular cases. And it is the same with the jurists. They would find it very strange if, after they had explicated their Roman or canon law etc., they were asked the unexpected question: what is **right** [*Recht*] in general?, or if someone made the further demand that they should derive their deductions from firm principles according to the rules of logic. They must then not greatly favour a way of thinking that believes itself entitled to demand the latter, since no concept of right and law can be thought outside of **Kant's** formal principle. Physicians find themselves in a desperate situation in this regard. Their subjective interest requires them to endorse the system of the materialists because with

---

[48] TN. Exodus, Chapter 5, Verse 4. Maimon seems to have made his own translation from the Hebrew, at least it differs significantly from Luther's version. We have translated Maimon's version rather than quoting one of the standard English versions which differ somewhat in meaning.

[49] TN. The welfare or good of the people.

materialism they gain a wonderful opportunity to detail their anatomical and physiological knowledge[50] in explaining all vital functions | by mere physical mechanisms (on which commendable ground many do in fact declare themselves for materialism); but they find this brings with it the difficulty that this type of explanation presupposes a great deal of mathematical and mechanical knowledge that they may not always possess. On the other hand, they also find the very same interest in the opposite system (that of the spiritualists), namely in the assumption of an infinite wisdom and goodness that they likewise support with their anatomical and physiological knowledge. The difference consists merely in this: in the first case they apply this knowledge to the *causa efficiens*, and in the second to the *causa finalis*. What then is the philosophizing physician supposed to do? He either chooses a party according to time and circumstance, so becoming either a **La Mettrie** (who even seeks to explain sensation and thought by means of organization according to the laws of mechanics), or a **Stahl** (who even attributes all merely bodily functions to the soul and ascribes a complete insight into the composition of the body to it), or he does not join any party, but instead continually wavers between one side and the other. Naturally, educators do not especially relish the Kantian moral system; they prefer the system of perfection [*Vollkommenheitssystem*][51] that they modulate to their hearts' content according to time and circumstances and that allows them to treat the whole world as children, | whom they must educate and cultivate. So instead of leading their pupils to think and act for themselves, in accordance with free will and the laws of reason, they instead impress upon them a slavish imitation. But we are entitled to ask: who should be imitated? The good and wise; but who are they? Those who are held to be such by the good and wise: a truly pedagogical principle! – And it is the same with other professions. Incidentally, I hope that no intelligent reader will think that in describing these manifold subjective interests I ever had any particular person in mind, I know and even have as friends men of each of these professions, men who I highly esteem, and of whom I am certainly convinced that they put the universal interest of reason and humanity before that of their profession.

---

[50] TN. *Kenntnis*. From here to the end of the section 'knowledge' translates '*Kenntnis*'.
[51] TN. The Wolffian system, representing the anti-democratic *ancien regime* of government by one's betters.

It was not my intention here to present any facts, but merely to make such facts, should they ever occur, comprehensible from the state of things.

So according to Wolff's system reason sets out on conquests before it has investigated either its powers or its legitimate claims.[52] According to Kant's system, reason is brought back to knowledge of itself, and after it has investigated both its powers and its claims, it finds that these are adequate merely for securing its possession, but not for foreign conquests. According to my system (or non-system), on the other hand, while it is true that reason does not think of foreign conquests, but only of securing its legitimate possession, at the same time it finds that this possession is unlimited, so that it can never enjoy it all at once, but only little by little to infinity: these are, however, merely legitimate acquisitions and not at all violent conquests. Reason finds that both it and its mode of operation [*Wirkungsart*] are possible only on the presupposition of an infinite reason. The difference between these two kinds of reason (besides infinity) consists in this: infinite reason starts from the most universal and progresses (through determination) further and further towards the particular through nothing but infinite series (by this I do not mean starting out and progressing in time, but merely according to nature).[53] Each of the syntheses produced by reason in this manner constitutes a real object standing in a relation of subordination and coordination to all the others (as species and genus or as different species of one genus). By contrast, finite reason starts from the particular, and (by abstracting) always climbs towards the universal, something that does take place in time (the particular here means merely the lack of the universal, or of the common concept of different things; for the particular in the strictest sense can only occur after the attainment of the universal).[54] Finite

---

[52] TN. '*Sowohl ihre Kräfte als ihre rechtmäßigen Ansprüche*'. The same terms for powers and claims recur in the following sentence. The metaphors of possession and territory are taken from Kant's discussion of the limits of reason in 'On the ground of the distinction of all objects into *phenomena* and *noumena*', A235/B294ff.

[53] TN. '*Nicht ein Anfangen und Fortschreiten der Zeit, sondern bloss der Natur nach*'. Infinite reason is of course non-temporal and it is a Leibnizian doctrine that 'by nature' reason proceeds from the universal to the particular through progressive determination, it does not thereby approach the infinite but on the contrary is and begins in the absolute infinite.

[54] TN. The particular in the strict sense is presumably the completely determined individual known to infinite reason.

reason approaches ever closer to infinite reason to infinity. The idea of its complete attainment is the idea of their union. | It must therefore set itself no other limits, and it need have no fear of climbing too high, and of suffocating in the pure ethereal air (something that must of course happen without proper preparation) because it always acquires a constitution appropriate to the region. Shaftesbury rightly derided this idle fear. 'You know too, that in this academick philosophy, I am to present you with, there is a certain way of Questioning and Doubting which noway suites the Genius of our Age. Men love to take party instantly. They can't bear being kept in suspence, the Examination torments'em, they want to be rid of it, upon the easiest terms. 'Tis as if men fancy'd themselves drowning whenever they dare trust to the current of Reason. They seem hurrying away, they know not whither, and are ready to catch at the first twig. There they chuse afterwards to hang, tho ever so insecurely, rather than trust their strength to bear them above water. He who has got hold of an Hypothesis how slight soever is satisfy'd. He can presently answer every Objection, and with a few Terms of Art give an Account of every thing without trouble.'[55] Our Talmudists (who, from time to time, have certainly expressed thoughts worthy of a Plato) say, 'the students of wisdom find no rest, neither in this life nor yet in the life to come', to which they relate, in their own way, the words of the Psalmists: '**They go from strength to strength, to appear before the Almighty in Zion.**'[56]

---

[55] TN. Shaftesbury, *Characteristics of Men, Manners, Opinions, Times*, Vol. II, *The Moralists: A Philosophical Rhapsody*, p. 189.

[56] TN. Psalm 84, verse 7, translated from Maimon's German.

Appendix I
Letter from Maimon to Kant

Maimon to Kant, 7 April 1789[1]

|

Honourable sir!
Filled with the reverence owed to a man who has reformed philosophy (and hence every other science), it was only the love of truth that made me bold enough to approach you. Already destined by birth to live out the best years of my life in the forests of Lithuania, | deprived of every aid in acquiring knowledge of truth, I was finally fortunate enough to reach Berlin, though too late. Thanks to the support of a few noble-minded men I was here put in a position to apply myself to the sciences; and it was natural, I think, that in my eager desire to attain my highest goal, **the truth**, I should to some extent postpone the subordinate tasks of a linguistic ability, method, etc. For this reason it was a long time before I dared to reveal any of my thoughts to a public whose taste is today so demanding [*difficilen*], even though I had in particular read several systems of philosophy, thought them through, and from time to time found something new in them. Finally I had the good fortune to come across your immortal work, to study it, and to reconstruct my whole way of thinking in accordance with it. I have tried my utmost to draw out the final conclusions from this work, to imprint them on my memory, and to

---

[1] This letter is contained in Band XI (Briefe 1789–1794) of the Immanuel Kant, *Gesammelte Schriften* (Hrsg. von der Königlich-Preussischen Akademie der Wissenschaften zu Berlin, 1902), pp. 15–17 (Letter No. 352 [330]).

seek out the traces of its principal train of thought [*Ideenganges*], in order, so to speak, to enter into the mind of the author. With this goal in mind I wrote down my conclusions, in so far as I was able to make them comprehensible, and added a few comments that bear principally upon the following points.

1) The distinction that you make between analytic and synthetic propositions, and the reality of the latter.
2) The question *quid juris?* The importance of this question makes it worthy of a **Kant**; and if it is given the scope that you yourself give it, it demands: How can something *a priori* apply [*applicieren*] with certainty to something *a posteriori*? In this case the answer or *deduction* that you give us in your writings is completely satisfying, as [only] the answer of a Kant can be. But if the scope of the question is enlarged, it demands: How can an *a priori* concept apply to an intuition even to an *a priori* intuition? Now the question must await the master once again before it is satisfactorily answered.
3) A newly identified kind of *idea*, that I call *ideas* of the understanding, indicating [*hindeuten*] **material totality**, just as the **ideas of reason** identified by yourself indicate | **formal totality**. I think I have thereby opened up a new approach to answering the aforementioned question, *quid juris?*
4) The question *quid facti?* You seem to have merely touched upon this; but because of Hume's doubt it seems to me important to answer it satisfactorily.

These remarks are a summary of the content of the manuscript that I dare to set before you. My kind friends have already urged me for a long time to publish this manuscript, but I did not want to agree to their wish without first subjecting it to your judgement, which is priceless to me. If a Kant finds my endeavour not completely worthless, then he will certainly not despise someone who approaches him respectfully. He will reply to him, instruct him where he errs, commend him if he finds something worthy of this, and so make him doubly happy.

Your wholly devoted servant and admirer, Salomon Maymon
Berlin the 7th April 1789.

Appendix II
Letter from Kant to Herz

Kant to Herz, Königsberg, 26 May 1789[1]

Dearest friend, I receive all your letters with genuine delight. Your noble feeling of gratitude for the small contribution that I was able to make to the development of your exceptional natural talents sets you apart from most of my audience; and what can be more consoling to someone when he is close to leaving this world than to see that he has not lived in vain because he has formed some, if only a few, into good human beings.

But what are you thinking, dearest friend, when you send a package of the most subtle investigations, not only to read through, but also to think through, to me, in my 66th year still burdened by the extensive task of completing my plan (in part by delivering the final part of the critique, namely that of **judgement**, which should come out soon; and in part by working out a **system** of metaphysics that conforms to those critical demands, one of nature as well as of morals), a task that is continually interrupted by many letters demanding special explanations of certain points;[2] and on top of all this, my ever worsening health. I had already half resolved to send the manuscript straight back to you with the well-justified apology I mentioned; but just a glance at it was enough to make

---

[1] TN. This letter is contained in Band XI (Briefe 1789–1794) of the Immanuel Kant, *Gesammelte Schriften* (Hrsg. von der Königlich-Preussischen Akademie der Wissenschaften zu Berlin, 1902), pp. 48–55 (Letter No. 362 [340]).

[2] TN. At this time Kant is involved in a protracted correspondence with Reinhold, helping him to write an article for the *Allgemeine Literatur Zeitung* responding to Eberhard's attack on the critical philosophy in recent issues of the latter's *Philosophisches Magazin*.

me recognize its excellence, and not only that none of my opponents has understood me and the principle question as well as Mr **Maimon**, but also that only a few people possess such an acute mind for such profound investigations [as he does]; and this persuaded me to reserve his manuscript for a few moments of leisure; only now have I obtained these, and only enough to go through the first two chapters,[3] which I can only discuss briefly.

Please communicate the following ideas [*diesen Begrif*] to Mr **Maimon**. I assume it goes without saying that they are not written for publication.

If I have correctly grasped the meaning [*Sinn*] of his work, he sets out to prove that if the understanding is to have a law-giving relation to sensible intuition (not merely to empirical but also to *a priori* intuition), then the understanding must itself be the originator [*Urheber*] not only of sensible forms but also of their matter, i.e. of objects; otherwise the *quid juris?* could not be answered satisfactorily, whereas it can be answered according to Leibnizian-Wolffian principles, if these are understood to state that sensibility is not specifically different from the understanding, but rather belongs to the understanding as cognition of the world [*Welterkentnis*], and differs from it only in degree of consciousness: in the former mode of representation [*Vorstellungsart*] [sensibility], this degree is infinitely small, and in the latter [understanding], it possesses a given (finite) quantity. He seeks further to demonstrate that *a priori* synthesis can possess objective validity only because the divine understanding, of which our understanding is only a part (or in his words 'is one and the same as, although only in a limited way'),[4] i.e. is itself | the originator [*Urheber*] of the forms and of the possibility of the things of the world (in themselves).

But I very much doubt that this was Leibniz's or Wolff's meaning, or whether it can really be inferred from their definitions of sensibility as opposed to the understanding; and it would be difficult for any man who knows their doctrines to agree that they assume a Spinozism, for Mr **Maimon's** way of presenting things [*Vorstellungsart*] is in fact one and the same as Spinoza's; and if this is conceded [*ex concessis*] it could serve very well to refute the Leibnizians.

---

[3] TN. Kant in fact discusses material from the first *three* chapters of the published version of the *Essay*.
[4] TN. See Chapter 2, s.65.

APPENDIX II

Mr **Maimon's** theory is basically that there is an understanding (and indeed a human understanding) that is not merely a faculty for thinking (as our understanding is and perhaps those of all created beings are) but properly a faculty for intuiting; for this faculty, thinking is only a way of bringing the manifold of intuition (that is obscure only because of our limitations) into a clear consciousness. By contrast, I attribute to the understanding, as to a special faculty, the **concept of an object** in general (which is not to be found even in the clearest consciousness of our intuition), that is to say, the synthetic unity of apperception; and it is only by this means that the manifold of intuition (after all, I may have a **particular** consciousness of **each** [part] of this)[5] is brought to the representation of an object in general in a unified consciousness (whose concept is now determined by means of that manifold).

Now Mr **Maimon** asks: How do I explain the possibility of harmony [*Zusammenstimmung*] between *a priori* intuitions and my *a priori* concepts if they have a specifically different origin; although this harmony is given as a *factum*, its legitimacy or the necessity of the agreement [*Übereinstimmung*] of two such heterogeneous kinds of representation cannot be made comprehensible; and the reverse: how can I prescribe the law to nature (i.e. for objects themselves) using my concepts of the understanding (for example my concept of cause) when their possibility in itself is merely problematic; and finally: how can I prove the necessity of these functions of the understanding when their existence in the understanding is again merely a fact (since their necessity must certainly be presupposed if we are to subject things, no matter how they appear to us, to these functions).

To which I reply: all this happens in relation to an experiential cognition [*Erfahrungs-Erkentnis*] that is possible for us only under these conditions, and so from this point of view it is subjective; but at the same time it is objectively valid because the objects [of cognition] are not things in themselves but mere appearances so that the form in which they are given is also dependent on us (according, on the one hand, to what is subjective in these objects, i.e. what is specific to our type of intuition [*Anschauungsart*]; and on the other hand, to the unification of the manifold in one consciousness, i.e. to the thought and cognition of these

---

[5] TN. '*deren jedes ich mir besonders immerhin bewust seyn mag*'. A more literal translation is 'I may after all be particularly conscious of each [part]'. The given translation assumes that Kant is here positing the possibility of many particular consciousnesses which will then be synthesized into a single consciousness.

APPENDIX II

objects, which depends on our understanding); as a result, we can have experience of objects only under these conditions, and if intuitions (objects as appearances) were not in harmony with these conditions [*nicht zusammen stimmeten*], they would be nothing for us, i.e. not objects of **cognition** at all, not of [our cognition of] ourselves nor of [our cognition of] other things.

In this way it is easy to show that if we are able to make synthetic *a priori* judgements, then these judgements are only about objects of intuition as mere appearances, and even if we were capable of intellectual intuition (e.g. if the infinitely small elements of intuition were noumena), then such judgements could not achieve necessity (according to the nature of our understanding in which such concepts as necessity are to be found) because an [intellectual] intuition could only ever be a mere perception, for example, that in a triangle two sides taken together are greater than the third; it could not be [any cognition] that this property must necessarily belong to it. But how such a sensible intuition (as time and space), a form of our sensibility is possible,[6] or such functions of the understanding as those which logic develops out of it are possible, or how it happens that one form is in harmony with another in a possible cognition, [all] this is absolutely impossible for us to explain any further, because to do so we would need another kind of intuition than the one we have and another understanding so that we could compare our understanding to it and moreover, an understanding that could present things determined in themselves to each of us. But we can judge all understanding only by means of our understanding and likewise all intuition only by means of our intuition. And in any case it is not necessary to answer this question. For if we can demonstrate that in **our cognition** of things experience is possible only under those conditions, then it follows not only that all other | concepts of things (that are not so conditioned) are empty for us and completely unable to serve any cognition, but also that no sense *data*[7] for a possible cognition could ever represent objects without these conditions, nor indeed ever attain that

---

[6] TN. '*Wie aber eine solche sinnliche Anschauung (als Raum und Zeit) Form unserer Sinnlichkeit oder solche Functionen des Verstandes ... selbst möglich sey*'. This is expressed over-concisely, but in light of the fact that for Kant space and time are both forms of our sensibility and themselves sensible intuitions (albeit pure ones), 'sensible intuition' and 'form of our sensibility' probably both refer to space and time.

[7] TN. 'data [in Latin] der Sinne'. Kant is using the Latin word for 'what is given'.

233

APPENDIX II

unity of consciousness that is required for cognition of myself (as object of inner sense). I would not even ever be able to know that I had these sense *data*, consequently **for me** as a cognizing being they would be absolutely nothing. They could (if I imagine myself as an animal) still carry on their play in a rule-governed way [*regelmäßig*], as representations that would be connected according to an empirical law of association, even influencing my faculties of feeling and desire, yet unaware of my existence [*meines Daseins unbewust*] (assuming that I am conscious of each individual representation, but not of their relation to the unity of representation of their object, by means of the synthetic unity of their apperception), without me ever having any cognition of anything, not even of my own state. It is difficult to guess at the thoughts that a profound thinker may have hesitated over and that he himself could not make altogether clear; all the same I am quite convinced that Leibniz with his pre-determined harmony (which he made very general, as did Baumgarten after him in his cosmology) did not have in mind the harmony of two different beings [*Wesen*], namely, sensible and intellectual beings [*Sinnen und Verstandeswesen*], but rather the harmony of two faculties belonging to one and the same being in which sensibility and understanding harmonize in an experiential cognition. If we wanted to make a judgement about the origin of these faculties (although such an investigation lies completely beyond the limits of human reason), we can provide no further ground than our divine creator [*Urheber*]; but once they are given we can completely account for our right [*Befugnis*] to judge *a priori* by means of them (i.e. the *quid juris?*).

I must be satisfied with what I have said, and because of the shortness of my time cannot go into details. I only remark that it is not necessary with Mr **Maimon** to admit **ideas of the understanding**. In the concept of a circular line[8] nothing more is thought than that **all** straight lines

---

[8] TN. '*einer Cirkellinie*'. In geometry 'circle' can refer either to the line that describes the circumference (a circle as opposed to a parabola or hyperbola) or to the plane figure delimited by this line (a circle as opposed to a triangle or square). Kant removes the ambiguity in favour of the former sense by using the phrase 'circular line', Maimon uses 'circle' in both senses but explicitly defines 'circle' in the latter sense (as 'a figure delimited by a line') in Chapter 2, s.38. This difference of course matters when determining what is required for a complete concept of a circle, which is to say a concept from which all the properties of the circle follow. For example, the formula for its area can be obtained by integration, but for Maimon this involves thinking of the area as the sum of an infinite number of lines, and only a 'materially complete' concept of the circle includes this idea.

drawn from it to a single point (the centre) are equal: this is a merely logical function of the | universality of the judgement in which the concept of a line constitutes the subject and refers merely to **each** [*eine jede*] of the lines, not to the **totality** [*das All*] of the lines that can be described on a plane to a given point; if it did not, then every line would with equal right be an idea of the understanding, because they all contain lines (as parts) that can be thought between any two arbitrary [*nur denkbaren*] points in them, whose number equally goes to infinity. That this line can be divided to infinity is not an idea, because it signifies only a progressive division that is certainly not limited by the magnitude of the line, but this infinite division regarded in its totality and thus as completed, is an idea of reason, an idea of an absolute totality of conditions (of combination), which is postulated [*gefodert*] in a sensible object; but this is impossible because the unconditioned is not to be found in appearances.

In addition, prior to the practical proposition: 'to describe a circle by moving a straight line around a fixed point', the possibility of a circle is not merely **problematic**; rather the possibility is **given** in the definition of the circle; this is because it is constructed by means of the definition itself, i.e. presented in intuition, not indeed on paper (in empirical intuition) but in the imagination (*a priori*). For I can always draw a circle freehand with chalk on the board and put a point in it, and I can just as well demonstrate all the properties of the circle in this circle, presupposing the (so called) nominal definition, which is in fact real, even if this circle does not coincide with the line described by rotating a straight line around a fixed point. I assume that the points of the circumference are at an equal distance from the centre. The proposition: 'to describe a circle' is a practical corollary outside the definition (or a so called postulate), and it certainly could not be postulated [*gefodert*] if the possibility, and indeed

---

[9] TN. This paragraph concerns the discussion of the difference between the nominal and real definitions of the circle in Chapter 2, s.39, s.50. Kant here shows that he rejects an important tenet of the classical axiomatic geometry described by Aristotle in the *Posterior Analytics* and realized in Euclid's *Elements*. This approach insists that a definition is only nominal and as such establishes neither the existence of what is defined, nor the possibility of that existence. Its possibility must either be postulated (Euclid simply postulates the possibility of straight lines and circles) or proved through construction (e.g. the first theorem that Euclid proves is that of the possibility of an equilateral triangle which he constructs from circles and straight lines – see Bk 1, Proposition 1). Leibniz also insisted on the importance of this distinction, demonstrating it with the example of the regular decahedron – easily defined but nevertheless impossible, and

the mode of possibility as well, were not already given in the definition.[9]

As for the definition of a straight line, this cannot be done by means of the identity of direction of all its parts because the concept of direction (as that of a **straight line**, through which movement is | distinguished **without regard to its magnitude**) already presupposes that concept.[10] But these are trifles.

Mr **Maimon**'s work contains besides this so many acute remarks that he could have published it at any time and created a favourable impression, and this would not have offended me in the least, even though he takes a completely different path than me; for he is of one mind with me as to the necessity of a reform in establishing the principles of metaphysics, and few are interested in being convinced of this necessity. There is, dear friend, just one request that I cannot agree to: the publication of this work with an accompanying commendation from me – since it is in fact for the most part directed **against me**. So that is my judgement, if this work is to be published. But if you want my advice as to whether to publish it as it stands, then I recommend that since Mr **Maimon** is presumably not indifferent to being completely understood and if he has the time before approaching a publisher, then he might apply it to delivering a whole system [*ein Ganzes*]. This would clearly show not only the way he thinks of the principles of *a priori* knowledge, but also the implications of his system for the solution of the problems of pure reason (after all, this is the most essential of the goals of metaphysics). Here the antinomies of pure reason can provide a good touchstone, and may convince him of the following: that human understanding is not of the same species as divine understanding so that it can be taken to differ from it only by limitation, i.e. in degree – that unlike divine understanding, human understanding must be treated as a faculty of thinking, not of **intuiting**, and must always have a completely different faculty (or receptivity) of intuition at its side, or better as its matter, in order to

cont.

warned of the danger of drawing inferences from mere definitions which might contain unseen contradictions (see the discussion in Heath's introduction to his translation of the *Elements*, pp. 117–20 and pp.143–46). Kant is thus setting himself against a long tradition in advocating the making of deductions from the mere definition of a circle and in claiming that this definition already involves the possibility of presenting the circle in pure intuition.

[10] TN. Maimon provisionally adopts this definition derived from Wolff's definition in Chapter 2, s.65.

produce cognition; and that, because intuition merely provides us with appearances and the thing itself [*die Sache selbst*] is a mere concept of reason, the antinomies, arising entirely from the confusion of the two, can never be resolved unless the possibility of synthetic *a priori* propositions is deduced according to my principles.

I remain ever your true servant and friend
I Kant

Appendix III
Maimon's Article from the *Berlin Journal for Enlightenment*

'Herr Maimon's reply to the previous article', *Berlinisches Journal für Aufklärung* (1790), Bd. IX/I, 52–80

Most worthy friend,

I have received your article of the ... In it you express the wish that I explain the plan of the work I sent you more precisely, and put the reader in no doubt as to which faction [*Partei*] I belong to, because you think I have failed to do this in a precise enough fashion in the work itself. But to what end? In this case the factions cannot be exactly determined and philosophical sects cannot be brought under definite classes like objects of natural history. However, because this is what you want, and because you believe that this will contribute to a better understanding and overview of the whole work, I will do as you say.

I maintain that the results of the *Critique of Pure Reason* controverting the dogmatists are irrefutable, and hence that the question: 'Is metaphysics possible?' (in the sense that Kant understands it, that is, as a science of things in themselves) must be answered with a 'No'. But at the same time I maintain that this [Kantian] system is insufficient in two respects. In the first place it is insufficient to overturn all dogmatism as such; this follows from my demonstration that metaphysics, understood not as the science of things in themselves (these cannot be thought at all), but merely as the science of the limits of appearances (ideas), is not only possible, but is in fact necessary, because no cognition of any object at all would be possible without it; cognition of the objects of appearance necessarily leads us to these ideas that comprise the proper objects of complete [or perfect] thought [*die eigentlichen Objekte des vollständigen Denkens*].

So I agree with Kant that the concepts of metaphysics are not real objects of experience but merely ideas that one can approach ever closer to in experience; but at the same time I maintain that ideas are not the proper objects just of metaphysics, but of any science that deserves the name. In the second place, this system is insufficient to prevent all further dogmatism. I will explain more closely the grounds for these claims.

First, I differ from Kant on the difference between the **thing in itself** and the **concept or representation of a thing**. | According to Kant, the thing in itself is what the concept or representation refers to outside our cognitive faculty.[1] By contrast, I claim that the thing in itself (understood in this way) is an empty and completely meaningless word because we are unable either to demonstrate its existence or to form any concept of it. For me, things in themselves and concepts or representations of things are objectively one and the very same thing: they differ only subjectively, i.e. in relation to the completeness of our cognition. For example, a triangle, considered in itself, is both a thing (object of thought) and a concept of a thing (of a general distinguishing mark [*allgemeines Merkmal*]), but it is a concept in relation to this thing in itself, and so on. What belongs to the concept of a thing necessarily belongs to the thing itself; but what belongs to the thing itself belongs to its concept only to the extent that the concept is identical with it. A regular polygon is a concept | in relation to the circle (in which or around which it is described); on the other hand, the circle is the thing in itself in relation to the polygon. I can assert of the polygon that I can identify two points (that are the limits of any side of the polygon) such that the straight lines drawn from them and intersecting at the centre are equal to each other,[2] and this is also true of the circle. On the other hand, it is asserted of the circle that all lines drawn from the centre to the circumference are equal; but this can only

---

[1] TN. '*Außer unserm Erkenntnisvermögen*'. This could also be translated as 'beyond our power of knowing'.

[2] TN. '*Daß man darin gewisse zwo Punkte (die irgend eine Seite desselben begrenzen, und sich in dessen Mittelpunkt einander scheiden) von der Art, daß sie einander gleich sind denken kann*'. The German text is elliptical so some words have been interpolated in the translation to convey Maimon's meaning which seems clear.

be true of the polygon to the extent that it is identical to the circle (in the points they have in common [*in ihren Vereinigungspunkten*]), and similarly in other cases. So the **thing in itself** is an idea of reason provided by reason itself to solve a **universal antinomy of thought in general**. For thought in general comprises the relation of a form (rule of the understanding) to a matter (the given subsumed under it). Without matter we cannot achieve consciousness of the form I so that matter is a necessary condition of thought, i.e. really thinking a form or rule of the understanding requires a given matter that it refers to; by contrast, what is required for completeness in the thought of an object is that nothing in it should be given and everything thought. We cannot reject either of these requirements as illegitimate, so we must satisfy both by making our thought ever more complete, a process in which matter approaches ever closer to form to infinity, and this is the solution of the antinomy.

Secondly, the principle question that the *Critique of Pure Reason* raised is: 'How are synthetic *a priori* propositions possible?' In the sense that he attaches to it, Kant also resolves this question satisfactorily. On the other hand, I think I am justified in posing this question in a stricter sense, whereby Kant's solution becomes unsatisfactory. I That is to say, for Kant, a cognition is *a priori* if both its matter and its form have their ground in the faculty of cognition itself, without considering the possibility that the connection of form and matter might already be made comprehensible by another cognition prior to their arising. So when Kant divides this principle question into its subordinate parts and asks, for example, 'how are synthetic *a priori* propositions in mathematics possible?' then his meaning is merely, 'how do they attain existence in our cognition?' to which the answer: 'through an *a priori* construction (from the cognitive faculty itself)'[3] is completely satisfactory. For me, on the other hand, this question has the following meaning: their construction certainly convinces us entirely both of the existence of mathematical synthetic *a priori* propositions and of the nature of this existence, but the question is: I 'How are we to comprehend this existence in us *a priori* (from a preceding cognition)?' For example, the concept of an equilateral triangle does not exist merely in the actual construction (in so far as we construct a triangle in general, and think in addition [*hinzudenkt*] the possibility of the

---

[3] TN. '*Aus Vermögen unsrer Erkenntnis selbst*'. This could also be translated as 'from the power of our cognition itself'.

equality of the sides); rather, as Euclid (Prop I) teaches us, we are already convinced of its reality before its actual construction, and it is by means of this that its construction is not only accomplished but is even comprehensible.[4] In the same way, every analytic proposition is already comprehensible from discursive cognition prior to the construction of the concept. By contrast, the truth of mathematical axioms is imposed on us, without being in any way made comprehensible, and this comprises the formal incompleteness of our cognition with respect to them. But our cognition also possesses an inescapable material incompleteness, namely when the construction cannot fully comply with the conditions of the concept (because the concept stretches to infinity). | This gives rise to an antinomy: on the one hand, reason commands us to attribute reality to the concept only in so far as it is constructible because the reality of what is not constructible is merely problematic. But on the other hand, reason demands that the proposition should hold only for the complete concept as it is thought in the understanding, and not for the incomplete concept as it is constructed by the imagination!

The second subordinate question is: '**How is pure natural science possible?**' According to Kant, its meaning is this: 'How can the understanding prescribe *a priori* laws for things outside [of] it?' According to him, the answer to the question is this: there is no way that the understanding can prescribe laws for things in themselves outside it, it merely prescribes laws for things in so far as they are intuited by sensibility and thought by the understanding. The laws of the understanding are conditions of the thought of an | object in general. They must

---

[4] TN. Maimon's reference is to the proof of the possibility of an equilateral triangle in Book I, Proposition I of Euclid's *Elements*. *Prima facie*, the claim that 'Euclid teaches that we are convinced of its reality before its construction' is simply false. For Euclid construction is necessary precisely because we *cannot* know that something is possible prior to constructing it. In this case Euclid proves the existence of equilateral triangles by drawing two intersecting congruent circles whose centres are on each other's circumferences, this means that the line connecting their centres is a radius of each, and the lines from their point of intersection to the centres of each are also radii, so that the triangle constructed from these three lines (i.e. radii) must be equilateral. So why does Maimon make this claim of Euclid? Apparently on the understanding that construction is not this whole process but just the final drawing of the radii that completes it. On this heterodox understanding of construction it is true to say that we comprehend the possibility of the triangle from thinking the arrangement of the circles prior to actually drawing it (constructing it), and hence its actual construction is redundant.

therefore be valid for all objects *a priori*. So this is how synthetic propositions concerning nature are possible *a priori*. The foundations of these laws are the familiar logical forms or the [different] kinds of relation of one object to another. Next come the categories or the particular determination of these forms with respect to the objects they are brought into relation with and hence acquire their reality. This particular determination must be found not in the objects themselves *a posteriori*, but in something *a priori* that refers to the *a posteriori* object. And because this determination is not in the logical form itself, it can only be found in the *a priori* forms of sensibility, etc. All of which must be familiar to you from the *Critique of Pure Reason*.[5]

Again at this point, new deficiencies [in Kant's argument] are visible. First, I think a distinction needs to be made between the genuine **logical forms** | and what are passed off as such forms in the **logic books**. Let me explain this using the example of the form of the hypothetical proposition: 'if a thing *a* is posited, then another thing *b* must be posited'. In itself, this form is merely problematic, and so can attain reality only in actual application [*Gebrauch*]. If its application is unproven, then the form lacks any reality. David Hume denies that this form has any application, i.e. he denies any application for the concept of cause, or the judgement: 'if a thing *b* is given, another thing *a* must be given so that *b* follows from *a* according to a rule'; he does this by showing that this form (in relation to determinate objects) is not a judgement of the understanding, but merely a consequence of an association in the imagination; and I think he is right to judge it like this because a judgement of the understanding does not arise gradually, and is not dependent on habit, as is the case with this judgement. Savages ignorant of the use of fire will certainly not make the judgement: 'the fire warms (makes warm, is cause of the warming of) the stone' the very first time they perceive a fire | and the subsequent warming of a stone; but after they have perceived the one appearance follow the other several times, they will connect them in their imagination in the order they were perceived in, so that if one of these appearances comes before them, then they will imagine the other in the order they have frequently been perceived in. As a result, there is no objective *a priori* necessity at all in this case, but only a subjective necessity according to an empirical law. Kant has indeed proved that we

---

[5] See 'On the schematism of the pure concepts of the understanding', A137/B176.

cannot possess any concept of an object in general (as in this case for example of something arising [*das Entstehung eines Dings*]), unless the faculty of judgement [*Urteilsvermögen*] determines the logical form in a judgement (for itself this logical form is undetermined with respect to the object). But if, with David Hume, I maintain that this is not a judgement of the understanding, then I also deny | the very fact that is dependent on it, since I claim that, if we should judge that a thing *b* arises [*entstehet*] [from *a*], we only do so by judging that it follows *a* according to a rule (that *a* must constantly precede and *b* follow); but because this is not a judgement of the understanding (we term the way we have become used to things following one another 'actual experience', but others call it a mere play of the imagination), all that Kant has proved is that these two things presuppose one another reciprocally, i.e., in order to think something as actually arising [*ein wirkliches Entstehen*], we must think the thing that is coming into being [*das zuentstehende Ding*] with respect to another thing in a rule-governed sequence, and also the reverse; and no one would dispute this. However, what is in question here is not the logical relation of these thoughts, but their real use; and this is just what cannot be admitted. And so, since the concept of cause has no reality in relation to determinate objects of experience, | it follows that the concept of cause in general, as an abstraction from this, has no reality.

Suppose someone objects: let us concede that the uniformity of the perceptions is the ground of this judgement of habit; but what then is the ground of this uniformity itself? Then I reply: this is no more of a problem for this theory than it is for Kant's. Kant certainly says that there must be an *a priori* rule determining perceptions that are related to one another, because otherwise the imagination would find no matter to act on. As a result, the order of the things in relation to one another is determined *a priori*. But I have to confess that I cannot see the strength of this argument. Suppose that there was no unalterable order of the perceptions, and at the same time no unalterable disorder, then the imagination would still always have enough matter to be effective. This is because its effectiveness does not presuppose an unalterable succession of determinate perceptions, but simply | an often repeated one, such that the degree of its effectiveness is determined by the degree of this repetition. It follows according to this way of presenting things that the concept of cause is not a category, but an idea: we can approach it ever more closely in practice [*Gebrauch*], but we can never reach it. The more often we have seen determinate perceptions succeed one another, the more precisely

APPENDIX III

they are connected to one another in our imagination, so that the subjective necessity of this succession approaches ever closer to the objective succession, but without ever being able to reach it. And it is the same with all the remaining categories.

Now that I have shown the difficulties with Kant's theory, I will now strike off on a somewhat different path, by means of which I think these difficulties can be, if not completely overcome, at least considerably reduced.

The universal antinomy of thought in general obviously contains its own solution in itself, and it is the following: reason demands that what is given in an object must be treated not as something that is in its nature unalterable, but unalterable merely as a consequence of the limitation of our faculty of thought. As a result, reason commands us to **progress to** infinity, so that what is thought ever increases and on the other hand what is given becomes infinitely small. The question here is not how far we can go in this, but simply: what point of view we must consider the object from, in order to be able to judge correctly about it. But this [point of view] is nothing other than the idea of the most-complete-of-all [*allervollkommensten*] faculty of thought, to which we must approach ever closer to infinity.

Since **the mathematical antinomy** has a similar origin to the universal antinomy, it will be resolved in a similar way. I will explain this.

There are two kinds of construction, namely an **object-construction** and a **schema-construction**, i.e. either the object itself (corresponding fully to its conditions in the understanding) is presented in the pure imagination *a priori*; or it can be presented not as corresponding fully to its conditions *a priori* but rather merely by means of an empirical construction.

If the equation of a circle is expressed algebraically, and an arbitrary number of points are determined that satisfy the equation, then a circle is constructed *a priori*; but by this method only a few points in the circle are constructed (the *loci geometrici* of this formula) and not the circle itself as a continuous magnitude, as a single line; to construct the circle as a single line, the points must be joined up by means of straight lines. But then this construction does not fully agree with its corresponding concept because it conforms to the latter only in its determined points. On the other hand, if a circle is described by moving a line about one of its endpoints, then the construction will fully correspond with the concept. I think this is also the reason why the ancient geometers up to Descartes termed curved

APPENDIX III

lines (other than the circle) 'mechanical', terming only the straight line and the circle 'geometrical', and were reluctant to give the former lines a place in their geometry. Descartes puzzled over this not a little, and was of the opinion that they had no reason for this. For, he says, if the curved lines were supposed to be termed 'mechanical' because a machine was required to describe them, then on this ground even the straight line and the circle would have had to be excluded from their geometry because machines must also be used to describe circles and draw lines. By contrast, Descartes believed that whatever permits exact specification [*genau angeben*] may be correctly termed 'geometrical', and that this applies to every line determined either by one continuous movement or by several successive movements.[6]

However, it seems that this great man did not notice that there are two criteria for a geometrical line, first it must be a line, i.e., a continuous quantity, or else it does not belong to geometry. Second it must be in some way measurable [*ausmeßbar*],[7] i.e. be a geometrical line. If a curved line is to be constructed by means of its equation, then this can only happen by determining some points, such that lines drawn from them to intersect the diameter stand to the section of the diameter[8] in the relation

---

[6] 'I am surprised, however, that they did not go further, and distinguish between different degrees of these more complex curves, nor do I see why they called the latter mechanical rather than geometrical. If we say that they are called mechanical because some sort of instrument has been used to describe them, then we must, to be consistent, reject circles and straight lines, since these cannot be described on paper without the use of compasses and a ruler, which may also be termed instruments. [...] Nevertheless, it seems very clear to me that if we make the usual assumption that geometry is precise and exact, while mechanics is not; and if we think of geometry as the science which furnishes a general knowledge of the measurement of all bodies, then we have no more right to exclude the more complex [*composés*] curves than the simpler ones, provided they can be conceived of as described by a continuous motion or by several successive motions, each motion being completely determined by those which precede; for in this way an exact knowledge of the measure of each is always obtainable.' (Maimon's footnote provided the original French text for which we have substituted this English translation, slightly modified from Descartes, *The Geometry*, trans. Smith and Latham (New York: Dover Publications, 2003), Bk II, paragraphs 1, 2).

[7] TN. The passage from Descartes quoted in the previous footnote suggests the sense in which 'measurable' is being used.

[8] TN. Maimon is referring to the relation of the coordinates of a point on the line. In the case of a circle with centre at the origin and a diameter drawn along the x-axis, the y-coordinate of the point is the length of the line dropped perpendicularly from it to the diameter, and the x-coordinate the length of the section of this diameter from the origin to the point of intersection with this line.

APPENDIX III

expressed by the equation. So in this case only these points and not the curved line itself are measurable. Consequently, I think the ancient geometers were right not to want to call such lines geometrical lines: although they are indeed (in the constructed points) **geometrical**, they are not **lines**; if they are to be so, then the connecting straight lines between these points must be added to the simple construction of the points; but this is no longer geometrical because the points that fall on these straight lines, can no longer be determined by the equation. So in this case reason demands that we increase the number of points to infinity so that this construction approaches ever closer to its concept, and only when this is fully accomplished do we get a real object *a priori*, which otherwise is impossible. For example, if the concept of a circle is determined by its equation, then its construction cannot completely conform to the latter. But if the concept is determined as in ordinary geometry (a line whose points are an equal distance from a given point) and it is constructed in the usual way through the movement of a line around one of its endpoints, then this construction is certainly complete, but it is not complete *a priori* because the concept of movement is itself *a posteriori*. As a result, the only way of constructing a concept completely *a priori* is a *progressus in infinitum*, as I have already shown.

I come now to the third subdivision of the principal question, namely: how is **natural science** *a priori* possible? Kant's explanation of this is the following: natural science contains synthetic *a priori* propositions (every effect must have a cause, etc.); how then is it possible that the understanding can prescribe *a priori* laws for *a posteriori* nature (i.e. that nature must conform to its propositions *a priori*)? And because I think I have found difficulties in Kant's solution to this problem, I find myself forced to venture a solution of my own. In the first place, I maintain, with Kant, that time and space are *a priori* forms of sensibility, and that they contain nothing that is in sensible objects themselves, but are merely our way of being affected [*affiziert*] by them. Secondly, I maintain that the logical forms of thought, presuming that they have reality, cannot be used of things in themselves (in so far as these are totally unknown) but merely of their appearances in us so that their absolute totality cannot be used constitutively but only regulatively. So much against metaphysical dogmatism. But I also join my sceptical friend David Hume in maintaining (in opposition to critical dogmatism) that these logical forms of thought do not have any direct application to sensible natural objects (in so far as their pseudo-use [*Quasigebrauch*] of natural objects can be explained on psychological grounds drawn from experience), but can attain their objective reality only by means of a complete induction | (that we can approach ever closer to, but never achieve): by this means their subjective reality approaches ever closer to objective reality, until they are united. Now I want to explain in more detail how this procedure of the doctrine of nature is the same as that of mathematics, and that it is legitimate in both in the same way.

Mathematics contains nothing but synthetic *a priori* propositions, i.e. rules of the understanding that are given with the construction of the objects themselves, or more precisely: the faculty of cognition produces objects in conformity with these rules. So the rules first acquire their reality through the objects themselves being present. Prior to the existence of these objects in the mind, we cannot know which rules they have to be subsumed under after they arise. Here it is not the same as in the case of the analytical principle 'A thing cannot at the same time be and not be', where we can already assert something with certainty prior to the construction of | a determinate object (a triangle for example), namely that it cannot be the same and not the same. In this respect, the synthetic *a priori* propositions do not possess any advantage over synthetic *a posteriori* propositions, the difference lies only in the fact that in the *a priori* propositions the object itself is produced *a priori* by the faculty of cognition as their matter, whereas in the *a posteriori* propositions it is given *a posteriori* by something else; but the judgements themselves, as forms or ways of thinking these objects, are in both cases *a posteriori*. The understanding prescribes a rule for the productive imagination to produce a space enclosed by three lines;[9] the imagination obeys and constructs a triangle but sees that at the same time three angles are forced on it, something the understanding certainly did not ask for. At this point the understanding becomes cunning: it learns to see into [*einsehen*] the previously unknown connection between three sides and three angles, although its ground is still | unknown to it. It thus makes a virtue out of a necessity, adopting an imperious manner and saying: 'a triangle must have three angles', as if it were itself the law-giver here, when in fact it has to obey a completely unknown law-giver. As a result, we are entitled to doubt the objective necessity of this proposition: perhaps some thinking being, or I myself under certain

---

[9] TN. Correcting the original which read: 'a space enclosed by two lines'.

circumstances, can construct a triangle with more angles or fewer angles, since in itself this does not involve a contradiction.[10] So the necessity of this proposition is merely subjective, but it can have different degrees up to the very highest degree where (as an idea) it attains objective necessity: the whole advantage of objective necessity (whose opposite involves a contradiction) lies merely in our conviction that it cannot be different in any other construction, no matter what the circumstances. So if I am convinced by means of a complete induction that in a construction a triangle can only have three angles (in so far as I have constructed the triangle under all possible circumstances and other thinking beings have also constructed it under all these circumstances, (assuming this to be possible) and found this to be true) then it would be as good as if I were convinced by the principle of contradiction. But this induction can never be complete so that subjective necessity can approach ever closer to objective necessity but never completely attain it. It is the same with our judgements about natural objects. I notice that fire is warm (that the sensation of warmth arises in me after the representation of the firelight or some other property of fire); this is merely what Kant calls a perceptual judgement and according to me it cannot be turned into an experiential judgement by means of any direct operation of the understanding as Kant claims. If I notice this again and again, so that these two appearances are ever more strongly connected in me, then at last (through a complete induction) this subjective connection reaches its highest degree, and becomes equivalent to the objective.

Concerning the final question,[11] namely: **How is metaphysics possible?** we must first determine what is meant by 'metaphysics'. I think I am in agreement with Kant as to the definition of metaphysics,

---

[10] TN. The German word *'Dreieck'* as much as the English 'triangle' connotes three angles, but Maimon is basing his argument on the definition he gave of triangle above, viz. a space enclosed by three lines.

[11] TN. The principle question, 'how are synthetic *a priori* propositions possible' divides into three subordinate questions, viz. 'how are such propositions possible in mathematics?', 'how are they possible in natural science?' and finally 'how are they possible in metaphysics?'. These are the questions 'how is mathematics possible?', 'how is natural science possible?', 'how is metaphysics possible?' as interpreted by the Kantian philosophy. This series of questions corresponds to the chapter headings in Kant's *Prolegomena to any Future Metaphysics*.

namely, metaphysics is the science of things in themselves.[12] I differ from Kant only in this: according to him things in themselves are the substrata of their appearances in us, and are quite heterogeneous with these appearances so that this question must remain unresolved in so far as we have no available means of cognition of things in themselves abstracted from the way they affect us. According to me, on the other hand, cognition of things in themselves is nothing other than the complete cognition of appearances. Metaphysics is thus not a science of something outside appearance, but merely of the limits (ideas) of appearances themselves, or of the final members of their series. Now these are indeed impossible as objects of our cognition, but they are so closely connected to the objects that without them no complete cognition of the objects themselves is possible. We approach ever closer to cognition of them according to the degree of completeness of our cognition of appearances. But since I think I have expounded all this at length in the *Essay* itself, and here I only wanted to determine the principle points in accordance with your request, I will now break off, and remain your most eager friend.

S. Maimon

---

[12] TN. It is somewhat misleading to describe this as Kant's definition of metaphysics. For Kant metaphysics so defined is indeed an illusory science, but the project of the *Critique* is not only to demonstrate the impossibility of such metaphysics (knowledge of things in themselves), but also to establish a well-founded scientific metaphysics consisting of *a priori* knowledge of the conditions of all possible objects of experience, and hence to give a positive explanations of how metaphysics is possible. See A841/B869f.

Appendix IV
Newton's *Introduction to the Quadrature of Curves*[1]

I don't here consider Mathematical Quantities as composed of Parts *extreamly small*, but as *generated by a continual motion*. Lines are described, and by describing are generated, not by any apposition of Parts, but by a continual motion of Points. Surfaces are generated by the motion of Lines, Solids by the motion of Surfaces, Angles by the Rotation of their Legs, Time by a continual flux, and so in the rest. These Geneses are founded upon Nature, and are every Day seen in the motion of Bodies.

And after this manner the Ancients by carrying moveable right Lines along immoveable ones in a Normal Position or Situation, have taught us the Geneses of Rectangles.

Therefore considering that Quantities, encreasing in equal times, and generated by this encreasing, are greater or less, according as their Velocity by which they encrease, and are generated, is greater or less; I endeavoured after a Method of determining the Quantities from the Velocities of their Motions or Increments, by which they are generated; and by calling the Velocities of the Motions, or of the Augments, by the Name of *Fluxions*, and the generated Quantities *Fluents*, I (in the years 1665 and 1666) did, by degrees, light upon the Method of Fluxions, which I here make use of in the *Quadrature of Curves*.

---

[1] This is an extract from the first paragraphs of the text; it is John Harris's translation of Newton's 1704 Latin original, and was published in *Lexicon Technicum*, vol 2 (London, 1710).

APPENDIX IV

Fluxions are very nearly as the Augments of the Fluents, generated in equal, but infinitely small parts of Time; and to speak exactly, are in the *Prime Ratio* of the nascent Augments: but they may be expounded by any Lines that are proportional to 'em. As if the *Areas ABC, ABDG* be described by the Ordinates *BC, BD*, moving with an uniform motion along the Base *AB*, the Fluxions of these *Areas* will be to one another as the describent Ordinates *BC* and *BD*, and may be expounded by those Ordinates; for those Ordinates are in the same Proportion as the Nascent Augments of the Areas.

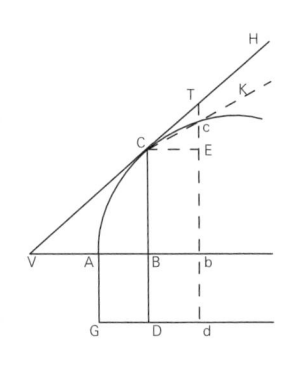

N.B. Maimon's example from Chapter 2 (which is expressed in Leibnizian rather than Newtonian notation) can be mapped onto this diagram using the following key:

subtangent = VB   y = BC (fluent)

Δx = CE (augment of fluent AB)

Δy = Ec (augment of fluent BC)

dx = fluxion of AB   dy = fluxion of BC

Let the Ordinate *BC* move out of its place *BC* into any new one *bc*: Compleat the Parallelogram *BCEb*, and let the Right Line *VTH* be drawn which may touch the Curve *C* and meet *bc* and *BA* produced in *T* and *V*; and then the just now generated Augments of the Abscissa *AB*, the Ordinate *BC*, and the Curve Line *ACc*, will be *Bb*, *Ec* and *Cc*; and the Side of the Triangle *CET*, are in the *Prime Ratio* of these Nascent Augments, and therefore the Fluxions of *AB*, *BC* and *AC* are as the Sides *CE*, *ET* and *CT* of the Triangle *CET*, and may be expounded by those Sides, or which is much at one, by the Sides of the Triangle *VBC* similar to it.

'Tis the same thing if the Fluxions be taken in the *ultimate Ratio* of the Evanescent Parts. Draw the Right Line *Cc*, and produce the same to *K*. Let the Ordinate *bc* return into its former place *BC*, and the points *C* and *c* coming together, the Right Line *CK* co-incides with the Tangent *CH*, and the Evanescent Triangle *CEc* in its ultimate form becomes similar to the Triangle *CET*, and its Evanescent Sides *CE*, *Ec* and *Cc* will be ultimately to one another as are *CE*, *ET* and *CT* the Sides of the other Triangle *CET*, and therefore the Fluxions of the Lines *AB*, *BC* and *AC* are in the same *Ratio*. If

APPENDIX IV

the Points *C* and *c* be at any small distance from one another, then will *CK* be at a small distance from the Tangent *CH*. As soon as the Right Line *CK* coincides with the Tangent *CH*, and the ultimate Ratio's of the Lines *CE*, *Ec* and *Cd* be found, the Points *C* and *c* ought to come together and exactly to coincide. For errours, tho' never so small, are not to be neglected in Mathematicks. [...][2]

By like ways of arguing, and by the method of Prime and Ultimate Ratio's, may be gathered the Fluxions of Lines, whether Right or Crooked in all cases whatsoever, as also the Fluxions of Surfaces, Angles and other Quantities. In Finite Quantities so to frame a Calculus, and thus to investigate the Prime and Ultimate Ratio's of Nascent or Evanescent Finite Quantities, is agreeable to the Geometry of the Ancients; and I was willing to shew, that in the Method of Fluxions there's no need of introducing Figures infinitely small into Geometry. For this Analysis may be performed in any Figures whatsoever, whether finite or infinitely small, so they are but imagined to be similar to the Evanescent Figures; as also in Figures which may be reckoned as infinitely small, if you do but proceed cautiously.

---

[2] The way that Maimon expresses a similar point in Chapter 2 is that for finite dx and dy (i.e. Δx: Δy) subtangent:y:y $\neq$ dx:dy, but tends to this ratio as c approaches C, at which point subtangent:y = dx:dy. Since in any construction the quantities must be shown as finite (i.e. triangle CEc must be finite) it follows that in any construction the equation is false (because in any construction triangle CEc is not similar to triangle VBC).

Glossary of Philosophical Terms and their Translations

English	Maimon's German
accompaniment	Begleitung (f)
to be acquainted	kennen (see Note on the Translation)
act	Handlung (f)
action	Handlung (f), Handeln (n) (see Note on the Translation)
activity	Thätigkeit (f)
actual	wirklich
advantage	Vorteil (m)
agreement	Übereinstimmung
alteration	Veränderung (f)
appearance	Erscheinung (f)
arising	Entstehung (f)
attraction	Anziehung (f)
to attribute (to)	beilegen, zukommen
to belong (to)	zukommen
to cancel	heben
to cancel out	aufheben
cause	Ursache (f)
change	Wechsel (m)
claim	Satz (m)
cognition	Erkenntnis (f) (see Note on the Translation)
cognitive faculty	Erkenntnisvermögen (n)

GLOSSARY

to cognize	erkennen
collision	Stoss (m)
to come before	vorhergehen
to come first	vorhergehen
comparison	Vergleichung (f)
completeness	Vollständigkeit (f)
composed	zusammengesetzt
composite	zusammengesetzt
to comprehend	begriffen
comprehensible	begreiflich
comprehension	Intension (f)
conceivable	begreiflich
concept	Begriff (m)
condition	Bedingung (f)
connection	Verbindung (f), Zusammenhang (f) (see Note on the Translation)
consciousness	Bewusstsein (n)
consequence	Folge (f) (see Note on the Translation)
consequent (as opposed to antecedent of a hypothetical statement; see Folge)	Konsequenz (f)
to consider	betrachten
consideration	Rücksicht (f)
constantly	beständig
constituent part	Bestandteil (m/n)
constitution	Beschaffenheit (f)
continual(ly)	beständig
continuity	Stetigkeit (f)
correspondence	Übereinstimmung (f)
delimited space	beschränkter Raum
to designate	bezeichnen (see Note on the Translation)
determination	Bestimmung (f) (see Note on the Translation)
difference	Verschiedenheit (f)
doctrine of nature	Naturlehre (f)
domain	Umfang (m)
direct	unmittelbar
discovery	Erfindung (f) (see Note on the Translation)
distinct	deutlich

GLOSSARY

distinguishing mark	Merkmal (n)
effect	Wirkung (f)
effecting	Wirken (n)
to eliminate	heben
experience	Erfahrung (f)
experiential concept	Erfahrungsbegriff (m)
experiential claims	Erfahrungssätze (m)
experiential propositions	Erfahrungssätze (m)
extension	Ausdehnung (f)
extent	Umfang (m)
faculty	Vermögen (n)
faculty of cognition	Erkenntnisvermögen (n)
faculty of fictions	Erdichtungsvermögen (n)
to be familiar with	kennen
gathering (together)	Zusammennehmung (f)
general (in comparative contexts)	allgemein
to grasp	begriffen
ground	Grund (n)
guiding principle	Richtschnur (f)
to have cognition of	erkennen
heat	Wärme (f)
heterogeneous	ungleichartig, verschiedenartig (see Note on the Translation)
homogeneous	einartig, gleichartig (see Note on the Translation)
human being	Mensch (m)
idea	Idee (f)
identical	einerlei
identity	Einerleiheit (f)
image	Bild (n)
imagination	Einbildungskraft (f)
immediately	unmittelbar
inability	Unvermögen (n)
indeterminate	unbestimmt (see Note on the Translation)
indirect	mittelbar
individual (intuition)	einzeln
intuition	Anschauung (f)
invention	Erfindung (f) (see Note on the Translation)

GLOSSARY

judgement	Urteil (n)
kind	Art (f)
kind of cognition	Erkenntnisart (f) (see Note on the Translation)
lawful	gesetzmäßig
legitimate	gesetzmäßig
limit	Gränze (f)
limit concept	Gränzbegrif[f] (m)
limitation	Einschränkung (f)
loss	Verlust (m)
magnitude	Größe (f)
(the) manifold	Mannigfaltige (n)
matter	Materie (f), Stoff (m)
merely	bloß
mind	Gemüth (n)
mode	Art (f)
mode of operation	Wirkungsart (f)
motion	Bewegung (f)
movement	Bewegung (f)
natural event	Naturbegebenheit (f)
negation	Negation (f), Verneinung (f)
to notice	bemerken
object	Gegenstand (m), Objekt (n) (see Note on the Translation)
oblique	schief
to observe	bemerken
one and the same (as)	einerlei
one-sided	einseitig (see reciprocal)
particular	besondere
passive(ly)	leidend (see Note on the Translation)
passivity	Leiden (n)
permanence	Beharrlichkeit (f)
persistence	Beharrlichkeit (f)
persistent	beharrlich
person	Mensch (m)
plurality	Vielheit (f)
to posit	setzen
power of judgement	Beurtheilungskraft (f)
power of representation	Vorstellungskraft (f)
powerlessness	Unvermögen

GLOSSARY

to precede	vorhergehen
to present	darstellen
presentation	Darstellung (f)
principle of contradiction	Satz des Widerspruchs
principle of identity	Satz der Identität
probability	Wahrscheinlichkeit (f)
procedure	Verfahren (n)
proposition	Satz (m)
quality	Beschaffenheit (f)
reaction	Gegenwirkung (f)
real	reell
reason	Grund (n), Vernunft (f)
reception	Aufnahme (f)
reciprocal	wechselseitig
to recogize	erkennen
relation	Verhältnis (n) (see Note on the Translation)
relational concept	Beziehungsbegriff (m), Verhältnisbegrif[f] (m)
representation	Vorstellung (f)
rule by which [something] arises	Entstehungsregel (f)
rule of arising	Entstehungsregel (f)
sensation	Empfindung (f)
senses (the)	Sinne (m pl)
sequence	Folge (f) (see Note on the Translation)
sign	Zeichen (n)
simplicity	Einfachheit (f)
single	einzig
singular (proposition)	einzeln
special	besondere
species	Art (f)
spontaneous	freiwillig
standard	Maßstab (n)
succession	Folge (f), Sukzession (f) (see Note on the Translation)
sum total	Inbegriff (m)
to suppose	setzen
temporal sequence	Zeitfolge (f)
term	Glied (n)
time-determination	Zeitbestimmung (f)

GLOSSARY

thinking	Denken (n)
thought	Denken (n)
totality	Allheit (f), Totalität (f)
to treat	betrachten
type	Art (f)
type of cognition	Erkenntnisart (f) (see Note on the Translation)
ultimate	letzte
understanding	Verstand (m)
undetermined	unbestimmt (see Note on the Translation)
unit, unity	Einheit (f)
universal	allgemein
unlimited	uneingeschränkt
velocity	Geschwindigkeit (f)
to view	betrachten
way of arising	Entstehungsart (f) (see Note on the Translation)
way that (something) arises	Entstehungsart (f) (see Note on the Translation)
world-whole	Weltganze (n)

Bibliography

Primary Texts by Maimon

A comprehensive bibliography of works by Maimon can be found in Freudenthal (2003).

Maimon, S., *Giva'at ha-Moreh*, ed. S.H. Bergmann and N. Rotherstreich (Jerusalem: Israeli Academy of Science, 1965) [*The Hills of the Master*, Maimon's Hebrew commentary on Maimonides' *Guide for the Perplexed*].

Maimon, S., *Gesammelte Werke*, ed. V. Verra, 7 vols (Hildsheim: Olms, 1965–76).

Maimon, S., *Salomon Maimons Lebensgeschichte*, ed. Zwi Batscha (Frankfurt: Insel Verlag, 1984).

Maimon, S., *Versuch über die Transzendentalphilosophie*, ed. F. Ehrensperger (Hamburg: Felix Meiner Verlag, 2004).

Maimon's Works in Translation

Maimon, S., *Essai sur la Philosophie Transcendentale*, trans. J-B. Scherrer (Paris: Librairie Philosophique J. Vrin, 1989).

Maimon, S., 'Letters of Philaletes to Aenesidemus', in trans. and ed. G. di Giovanni and ed. H.S. Harris, *Between Kant and Hegel: Texts in the Development of Post-Kantian Idealism* (Indianapolis, IN: Hackett, 2001).

Maimon, S., *The Autobiography of Solomon Maimon*, trans. J. C. Murray (Chicago: University of Illinois Press, 2001).

Maimon, S., 'Essay on Transcendental Philosophy: A Short Overview of the Whole Work', trans. H. Somers-Hall and M. Reglitz, in *Pli: The Warwick Journal of Philosophy* 19 (2008), pp. 127–65.

Selected Secondary Literature

See Ehrensperger (2004) for a more comprehensive list.

Monographs

Atlas, S., *From Critical to Speculative Idealism: The Philosophy of Solomon Maimon* (The Hague: Nijhoff, 1964).

Bergman, S. H., *The Philosophy of Salomon Maimon*, trans. N. J. Jacobs (Jerusalem: The Magnes Press, 1967).

Bransen, J., *The Antinomy of Thought: Maimonian Skepticism and the Relation between Thoughts and Objects* (Dordrecht: Kluwer, 1991).

Buzaglo, M., *Solomon Maimon: Monism, Skepticism and Mathematics* (Pittsburgh, PA: Pittsburgh University Press, 2002).

Guéroult, M., *La Philosophie Transcendentale de Salomon Maimon* (Paris: Societe d'edition, 1930).

Kuntze, F., *Die Philosophie Salomon Maimons* (Heidelberg 1912).

Socher, A. P., *The Radical Enlightenment of Solomon Maimon: Judaism, Heresy, and Philosophy* (Palo Alto, CA: Stanford University Press, 2006).

Collections of articles on Maimon

Freudenthal, G., ed., *Salomon Maimon: Rational Dogmatist, Empirical Skeptic* (Dordrecht: Kluwer, 2003) [Papers from an international conference on Maimon held in Tel Aviv and Jerusalem].

Articles on Maimon

Atlas, S., 'Solomon Maimon's Treatment of the Problem of Antinomies and its Relation to Maimonides, *Hebrew Union College Annual* 21 (1948), pp. 105–53.

Atlas, S., 'Maimon and Maimonides', *Hebrew Union College Annual*, 23.1 (1950–51), pp. 517–47.

Atlas, S., 'Solomon Maimon: The Man and his Thought. On the Occasion of the 150th Anniversary of his Death', *Historia Judaica*, 13.2 (1951), pp. 109–20.

Altas, S., 'Solomon Maimon's Doctrine of Infinite Reason and its Historical Relations', *Journal of the History of Ideas*, 13. 1 (1952), pp. 68–187.

Altas, S., 'Solomon Maimon's Philosophy of Language Critically Examined', *Hebrew Union College Annual*, 28 (1957), pp. 235–88.

Altas, S., 'Solomon Maimon and Spinoza', *Hebrew Union College Annual*, 30 (1959), pp. 233–85.

di Giovanni, G., 'The Facts of Consciousness', in *Between Kant and Hegel. Texts in the Development of Post-Kantian Idealism*, ed. G. di Giovanni and H.S. Harris (Albany, NY: Hackett Publishing Co. 1985), pp. 32–36.

Franks, P., 'All or nothing: systematicity and nihilism in Jacobi, Reinhold, and Maimon', in *The Cambridge Companion to German Idealism*, ed. K. Ameriks (Cambridge: Cambridge University Press, 2000), pp. 95–116.

Franks, P., 'Does post-Kantian Skepticism Exist?' in *Internationales Jahrbuch des Deutschen Idealismus/International Yearbook of German Idealism: Konzepte der Rationalität/Concepts of Rationality*, ed. K. Ameriks and J. Stolzenberg (New York: de Gruyter, 2003), pp. 141–63.

Freudenthal, G., 'Maimon's Subversion of Kant's *Critique of Pure Reason*: There are no Synthetic *a priori* Judgments in Physics. Preprint 170 of the Max Planck Institute for the History of Science (Berlin 2001).

Horstmann, R. P., 'Maimon's Criticism of Reinhold's "Satz des Bewußtseins"', *Proceedings of the Third International Kant Congress* (1972), pp. 330–38.

Jacobs, N. J.,'Maimon's Theory of the Imagination', *Scripta Hierosolymitana*, 6 (1960), pp. 249–67.

Lachterman, D., 'Mathematical Construction, Symbolic Cognition and the Infinite Intellect: Reflections on Maimon and Maimonides', *Journal of the History of Philosophy*, 30 (1992), pp. 497–522.

Melamed, Y. 'Salomon Maimon and the Rise of Spinozism in German Idealism', *Journal of the History of Philosophy*, 42 (2004), pp. 67–96.

Nacht-Eladi, S., 'Aristotle's Doctrine of the Differentia Specifica and Maimon's Law of Determinability', *Scripta Hierosolymitana*, 6 (1960), pp. 222–48.

Thielke, P., 'Getting Maimon's Goad: Discursivity, Skepticism, and Fichte's Idealism', *Journal of the History of Philosophy*, 39.1, (2001), pp. 101–34.

Books containing substantial discussion of Maimon's philosophy

Beiser, F. C., *The Fate of Reason – German Philosophy from Kant to Fichte* (Cambridge, MA: Harvard University Press, 1987), pp. 285–323.

Beiser, F. C., *German Idealism: The Struggle against Subjectivism, 1781–1801* (Cambridge MA: Harvard University Press, 2002), pp. 240–60.

BIBLIOGRAPHY

Deleuze, G., *Difference & Repetition*, trans. P. Patton (London: Athlone Press, 1994), Ch. 4, 'Ideas and the Synthesis of Difference'.

Franks, P., *All or Nothing: Systematicity, Transcendental Arguments, and Skepticism in German Idealism* (Cambridge, MA: Harvard University Press, 2005).

Index

The scope of the index is restricted to the translations of the texts of the original edition of the *Essay* and does not cover the 'Introduction to the Translation' or the appendices. The numbers refer to the page numbers of the original edition, which can be found at the top of the pages of this translation. References to the 'Notes & Clarifications' *also* include the note number, preceded by the symbol '#'; references to footnotes include the note number preceded by 'n.'. Some terms, such as 'consciousness' and '*a priori*', which occur very frequently in the text, have been omitted or have only subheadings specifying important occurrences of the term.

$\sqrt{2}$, root of 2 58, 361 #25
$\sqrt{}$-a 59, 361 #25
0.1, 0.01, etc., considered as units 350 #15
10, 100, considered as units 350 #15
10, 100, 1000, objects of intuitive or symbolic cognition 273
1000, and 1000-sided polygon 272
$7 + 5 = 12$ or $5 + 7 = 12$, as an example of synthetic *a priori* proposition 178, 180, 424 #75

'A is A' 3, 52
a priori, see also $7 + 5 = 12$, opposition definition 179, 184, 424 #73
Aaron 440
abstraction 88, 121–2, 194, 205, 257, 310, 373–4 #31
abstractum 433
accident [*Accidenz*] 4, 24, 95–6, 116, 136–7, 143–4, 185, 189, 215, 259–61, 299–300, 305, 320, 348–9 #14, 363 #26
act [*Handlung*] 29, 117, 381 #39
action [*Wirkung*] 31, 222–3
activity [*Thätigkeit*] 20, 29, 170, 417 #64, 417 #65, 439–40
actual, the [*Wirkliche*] 99, 101–5, 238, 249, 392 #46
actuality [*Wirklichkeit*] 46, 102–3, 122, 171, 189, 204, 247–51, 308, 358 #19, 389 #43, 421 #69
 definition 102, 249
acumen versus wit 309
Adam 307
Adelung, Johann Christoph (1732–1806) 321
affirmation [*Bejahung*] 113, 115–17, 254–5, 381 #39, 396–7 #51
 logical 397 #51
agreement [*Übereinstimmung*] 400 #58, 409 #58, 439

INDEX

Ahriman, Zoroastrian spirit 302
air 46–7, 240, 371 #30, 429 #78, 444
alchemist 339 #3
algebra, algebraic 86 n.1, 241, 275, 277–80, 323
Alpine mouse, a machine 280
alteration [*Veränderung*] 50 n.24, 124–6, 137, 211, 215–16, 223–5, 229–30, 254–5, 261–2, 308, 349 #14, 426 #76, 429–31 #79, *see also* change
  absolute 211, 429 #79
analogy, *per analogiam* 40 n.16, 141, 160, 184, 201–2, 294, 416 #62
analysis, mathematical 279, 281, 412 #58, *see also* calculus
analytic, analytically 4, 43, 55, 61, 65 n.32, 66–8, 93, 106–7, 172, 178, 181, 199, 253, 280, 360 #22, 368 #28, 389 #43, 394 #50, 418 #72
anatomical knowledge 440–1
ancients, mathematical methods of, *see* method
angle 79, 149, 165, 245, 286–91, 311, 326, 351–3 #15, 369–70 #29, 378–9 #36, 380 #38, 391 #44, 392 #48, 394–5 #56, 412 #58
animal 94, 194, 253, 295, 297, 309, 320, 380–6 #39
antecedent 52, 108, 217, 240, 260, 262
antinomy of pure reason, *see* reason
apart, being-apart of objects in space [*Auseinandersein*] 17–18, 21, 25, *see also* separateness
apodictic 51, 54, 59, 61, 93, 180, 184–5, 253, 421 #69,
Apollo 397 #51
apostrophe, example of a trope 316
appearance(s) [*Erscheinung*] 72, 128, 140, 142, 152, 182, 187, 192–3, 201, 239, 363 #26, 420 #66,
  definition 168,
appellativa, nomina appellativa 319
apperception [*Apperzeption*] 211 n.29, 398 #55,
  unity of 377 #34

apple 307
apprehension [*Apprehension*] 35, 160, 187–8, 210, 360 #23, 398 #55
arising [*Entstehen, Entspringen* and cognates] 7, 19, 30, 41, 44, 62, 66, 73, 157, 203, 209, 266, 278, 282, 285, 289, 294, 301, 305, 317–8, 326, 327, 382 #39
  of antinomies 227, 229
  of concept(s) 48–9, 85–6, 118, 252, 301
  of cause 94
  of human being 94, 380 #39
  of line 36
  of consciousness 29–30, 81
  of difference 343 #7
  of the given 203, 417 #65, 419 #63
  of form and matter 13, 63, 115, 417 #65
  of intuition(s) 32, 49, 196, 356 #15
  of line(s) 70, 289
  of number(s) 361 #25
  of large numbers 272–3
  of object(s) 32ff, 106, 118, 132, 188, 256, 277, 418 #63
  of mathematics 19
  of relations 33
  of representations of space and time 19, 22, 25, 57, 136, 188, 399 #57
  rule of [*Entstehungsregel*] 33, 49, 277, 424 #73
  of synthesis 88–9, 143, 385 #39
  of thing(s) 257, 406 #58
  of triangle(s) 19, 34, 66, 274–5, 356–7 #16, 367–8 #28
  way of [*Entstehungsart*] 36, 58, 82, 101, 171, 249, 274
  as sufficient ground 392 #47
Aristotle (384–322 BC) 31, 232, 299, 362 #26
arithmetic 22, 69, 169, 323, 350 #15, 354 #15, 356 #15
ars characteristica combinatoria 323, *see also characteristic universalis*
art, artists 280–1, 370 #29
assertoric judgements, concepts or propositions, *see* judgement

264

association [*Association*]
  law of association, association of ideas, association of perceptions 4, 20, 26, 73, 141, 216–17, 268, 269 n.4,
  of words 278–9, 304
asymptote, of a curve 79, 100, 274, 329, 373 #31, 375 #33, 434
atheist(s) 208, 285
attraction, gravitational 222
axiom(s) 66, 148–9, 169, 174, 176, 184–5, 199, 277, 324, 392 #47, 406 #58, 417 #68
  of mathematics 169, 176, 184, 277, 406 #58, 417 #68
  real, not true 406 #58

ball, example of a falling body 222
bank, of a river, example of relative motion 158, 346 #9
Baumgarten, Alexander Gottlieb (1714–1762) 111, 239, 268, 270, 345 #9, 417 #68
being-apart [*Auseinandersein*] 17–18, 21, 25, *see also* separateness
Bendavid (or Ben David), Lazarus (1762–1832) 275–6, 291–2
Berlin blue (or Prussian blue, a synthesized pigment) 339 #3
best world, creation of the 200
black circle, black triangle, not true concepts 124, 146–7, 391 #44
blind,
  how those born blind distinguish colours 58, 201
bloodhound
  the discoverer compared to 370 #29
body [*Körper*]
  colour of, *see* colour
  movement or motion of 129 n.5, 220–4, 211, 229–30, 232, 255, 290, 328
    accelerated movement or motion of 30, 221–2
    falling, *see* ball
    as opposed to mental movement 141, 306–8, 310
  object and its properties 5, 7, 92–3, 100, 127, 185, 343 #7, 346 #9, *see also* impenetrability, weight, hardness
  organized 193
  as opposed to soul 62–3, 362 #26, 442, *see also* de commercio animi et corporis
Burnet, James, *see* Monboddo, Lord

cabin, example of relative motion of a ship 157
calculus, *see also* analysis, mathematical algebraic/mathematical/philosophical calculus 280–2, 286–7, 327
  infinitesimal 22, 27 n.1, 274
  integral 122, 196, 206, 394–5 #56
  mathematical 281
Cartesian, *see also* Descartes, René 1
category [*Kategorie*], categories, pure concepts of the understanding 23–4, 27, 31, 43–5, 47, 69, 71, 81, 110, 130, 135, 156, 183, 189, 214–15, 217, 226, 261, 277, 299, 329, 348 #14, 355 #15, 397 #51, 399 #56, 423 #73
  definition of, is independent of intuition 189
  legitimate use of 47, 51–2, 54, 364 #26, 435
cause [*Ursache*], *see also* fire, genetic concept of 23, 37–8, 40–2, 46, 51–2, 54–5, 57, 64, 71, 73–4, 80, 81, 83, 86, 94, 99, 107–9, 114, 116, 125, 129, 138, 140–1, 174, 187, 189, 192, 203, 213–15, 218–26, 241, 243, 247, 254, 260–1, 286, 305, 310, 321, 330, 337 #2, 356 #15, 359 #21, 372 #30, 377 #34, 388, #40, 390 #43, 393 #50, 418 #72, 419 #63,
  definition 37
  infinite chain of, infinite dignity of 81
  origin of concepts of cause and effect 220

INDEX

causality [*Kausalität*]
  category of 370 #30
  form or rule of 418 #72
  law of 200, 262, *see also* causation, principle of
causation, principle of [*Satz von Ursache*] 371–2 #30, *see also* law of causality
causa efficiens, causa finalis [efficient cause, final cause] 441
change [*Wechsel*] 17, 124–6, 138, 157, 307–8, 407–9 #58, *see also* alteration
characteristica universalis, Leibniz's universal characteristic, *see also ars characteristica combinatoria* 327–8
cherry, red cherry not a trope 307
child, children 74, 139, 441
chord, *see* circle
circle
  arbitrary arc of 165, 235
  concept of 38–9, 42–3. 47, 50–1, 56, 75–8, 105–6, 124, 147, 171, 190, 231–6, 257, 274, 276, 378 #35, 381–3 #39, 434
  chord of 234–6
  circumference of 50, 78, 149, 171, 231, 234–6, 382 #39
  definition of 77–8
citizen, of an intelligible world 338
clay, receives impression of falling ball 222
clear, contrasted with distinct 70, 296–7, 344 #9, 384 #39, 386 #39
clock, perception of time by means of 22, 134
coexistence [*Zugleichsein*], determination of time or space 36, 92, 100, 308, *see also* simultaneity
'cogito ergo sum' 1
cognition [*Erkenntnis*]
  subjective order of cognition, as opposed to objective 81, 376 #34
  sources of 63
  symbolic 73, 88, 170, 265–73, 276–9, 285, 410–12 #58, 421 #69
  definition 267–8, 270–1, 276, 285
cognitive faculty [*Erkenntnisvermögen*], *see* faculty
coin, compared with truth 406–14 #58
cold, has intensive magnitude 122
colour, *see also* Prussian Blue, green, red, yellow, blind, body, quality
  actual 360 #24
  perception and representation of 13, 27, 58, 82, 201, 340 #5, 342 #5, 420 #66, 433
  property of a body 15, 92, 102–4, 146, 283–4, 360–1 #24, 388 #39, 391 #44, 433
combination [*Verbindung*]
  in symbols as opposed to in things themselves 171, 412 #58, 418 #70
  of matter and form 247
  of sounds constitutes language 294
commercio animi et corporis [community or interaction of mind and body] 141, 362 #26, *see also* community
commodity 407 #58
communia [common properties] 250
community [*Gemeinschaft*], Kantian category, community of soul and body 62
complementum possibilitatis [complement or completion of possibility] 365 #27
completeness [*Vollständigkeit*], of a concept 9, 64–5, 75, 78–80, 103–4, 183, 195, 210, 250, 347 #11, 348 #12, 373 #31, 391–2 #45, 419 #63, 435, *see also* perfection
composite as opposed to simple 295–301, 330, 432 #80, 438
comprehension, *see* concept
concept [*Begrif*], *see also* category
  absolute 37, 85–6, 94 n.5, 124
  abstract 86–7, 91, 265, 378–9 #36
  arbitrarily assumed 39–40, 43, 46–7

concept, *cont.*
  produced, as opposed to spontaneously produced or passively given 20, 317
  arbitrary 317
  comprehension of, as opposed to extension of 382 #39
  disjunctive, *see* judgement
  empirical 179, *see also* gold
    construction of 272, 374 #31, 423 #72
    dogmatists and 434
    'I' and 202
    intuition, and the empirical *in* intuition 26, 202, 204–5, 420 #66
    psychology and 159
    realism and 162
    sceptics and 436
  limit 76, 192, 352 #15, 373 #31
  logical 185
  material as opposed to formal completeness of 75, 79–80, 103–4, 373 #31
  mathematical 42, 49, 56, 77–8, 285
  real, as opposed to symbolic 88, 386 #39, 413–4 #58
  of reflection 68, 89, 129–30, 133, 213–14
  relational 56, 59, 69, 86, 99, 110, 112–5, 124, 343 #6
  symbolic, *see* symbolic
concrete [*Konkretion, konkret*], as opposed to abstract 257, 310–11
confused [*verworrene*], as opposed to distinct representations etc. 160, 297, 436
connection or relation [*Verhältnis* or *Beziehung*]
  contingent as opposed to necessary 5, 36, 129, 150, 187–9, 200–1, 206, 219, 268, 284, 289, 305
  natural as opposed to arbitrary 284
  real connection between subject and predicate 145–6
consequence(s) [*Folge*], of a concept or proposition 20, 35, 61, 78, 88–92, 98, 148–50, 200, 242–5, 250–1, 258, 281, 330, 371–3 #30, 414 #58, 418 #70
consequent [*Konsequent*], as opposed to antecedent 52, 108, 217, 240, 260, 262, 382 #39
construction, mathematical, geometrical 2, 6–7, 34–5, 42, 54, 79, 103, 165, 176–7, 272, 275–6, 280, 326, 356 #15, 374 #31
  empirical 358 #19
  pure 358 #19, 423, #71
consume, example of word with two meanings 309
continuity [*Stetigkeit*], of time and space 136, 139–42
  principle of 139, 142
contradiction, principle of 4, 57, 60, 71, 146, 150, 169, 172, 175, 178, 184, 241, 359 #22, 417 #68, 423 #73, 431 #80, 433
  as criterion of truth 146
  logical 432 #80
coordination, as opposed to subordination 321, 443
copula 114, 252, 255–6, 382 #39, ambiguity of 382 #39
copy, as opposed to original 134, 181
correspondence [*Übereinstimmung*]
  between intuitions and concepts 54–5
  between sign and designated thing 252
  of concepts 253
cosine 287–8, 351–3 #15, 412 #58
cosmological proof of existence of God 200
creator 283
curve, curved line 35, 65, 79, 100, 257, 274, 279, 329, 373–4 #31, 375 #33, 381–3 #39, *see also* asymptote, parabola, line
  directrix of 40

darkness, *see* light
decreasing, infinite series 351 #15, 419 #63, *see also* diminishing

deduction, transcendental, of the categories 52, 54–5, 186, 440
definitio nominalis, definitio realis, see definition, real as opposed to nominal
definition [*Erklärung, Definition*]
  infinite series of predicates not a definition 191
  of pure 34, 359 #22
  pure *a priori* judgements are definitions 107
  real vs nominal 36, 50, 200, 303, 340 #5
  of a thing in a truly philosophical language 319, 325–6
delimited, *see* figure
Delphic saying 155, 415 #59
Descartes, René (1596–1650) 362 #26, *see also* Cartesian
designation, signs designate [*bezeichnen*] things 252, 267–8, 279, 293, 296–306, 312, 315, 320–3, 340–2 #5, 352 #15, 413 #58
determinable, the [*Bestimmbares*], and its determinations 3, 20, 21, 41, 56, 84, 91, 94, 98–9, 102, 110, 124–7, 140–5, 151, 194, 243–7, 258–60, 269, 286, 305, 345 #9, 352 #15, 359 #20, 388 #40, 391 #44, 421 #69
  definition of 379 #37, 385 #39
  law of 21, 260
determinability [*Bestimmbarkeit*] 258
  law of the determinable and the determination 21, 260
determination [*Bestimmung*]
  absolute 194
  arbitrary 40, 137
  definition 379 #37, 385 #39
  infinite determination required for individuation 257, 349 #15
  inner 70, 309
  material, as opposed to formal 52, 128, 392 #45
  outer 70, 307
  time-determination 214, 241, 315, 348 #14, 388–9 #41, 432 #80

dictionary, philosophical 296, 330–1
Diderot, Denis (1713–1784) 280
difference [*Verschiedenheit*], concept of 16, 18–19, 29, 32, 56–7, 64, 68, 85, 88–9, 110–12, 127, 129–33, 135–9, 146–50, 159, 163, 179–82, 186, 210, 213, 216–7, 256, 260, 307, 309, 343–4 #7, 344–7 #9, 347 #11, 374 #32, 407 #58, 426–7 #76, 430 #79
  Baumgarten's definition of 111, 344–5 #9
  material 426 #76
differential 21, 28–9, 31–3, 35, 112, 122, 196, 206, 217, 274, 276, 290–1, 352 #15, 355–6 #15, 373 #31, 394–5 #56, *see also* element of intuition
  quality of, *see* quality
diminishing to infinity 168, *see also* decreasing
direction, *see* line
directrix, *see* curve
discovery, scientific, and discovery of truth 324, 327, 330, 339 #3, 353–4 #15, 410–12 #58
disjunctive judgement, proposition or concept, *see* judgement
dispositions [*Anlagen*], innate ideas are not mere dispositions 46
distinct [*deutlich*], contrasted with distinct and opposed to confused 64, 70, 297,311, 344 #9, 384–6 #39
divisibility, of space and time, infinite 30, 235–7, 284, 288, 350 #15, 353 #15, 375 #32
division 301, 375 #32
  actual 231
doctrine of nature 3–4, 140, 174, 240, 337
dogmatists, empirical, rational 434, 436–7
dream, dreams 83, 327, 372 #30
drives [*Triebe*], human 1
dualism, dualist 155, 160, 164, 416 #62
duration 136, 290, 352–3 #15

dx, dy 32, 35, 292

Ecclesiast, the (c.250 BC) 339 #3
education 439
effect 24, 37–8, 40–2, 46, 54, 57, 81, 86, 99, 107, 114, 125, 137, 189, 200, 202–3, 214–5, 218–25, 241, 243, 260, 262, 290, 305, 321, 330, 337 #2, 356 #15, 373 #30, 391 #43
element of intuition 9, 24, 35, 112, 192–3, 196, 355–6 #15, *see also* differential
  finite, made up of infinite elements 236
  axioms the elements of truth 148
  unity an element of plurality 252
empirical concept, *see* concept
empiricism, empiricists 433, 440
endpoint, *see* line
ens imaginarium [imaginary entity] 19
ens logicum [logical entity] 192
ens omni modo determinatum [completely determined entity] 101–2, 391 #44
ens reale [real entity]192
ens realissimum [most real entity] 207
essence [*Wesen*] 21, 61, 72, 103–4, 161, 201, 250, 254, 258, 286, 288, 290, 300, 338–9 #3, 367 #27, 376 #34, 429 #78
  inner 103, 429 #78
essentia nominalis, realis [nominal, real essence] 38–9, 419 #63
existence 1, 65, 97, 107–8, 135, 160–3, 188, 196, 199–204, 219–20, 224–5, 252–4, 309, 338–9 #3, 350 #15, 365 #27, 393 #49, 416 #62
experience [*Erfahrung*]
  actual 186
  experiential propositions 4–5, 39, 73, 186, 192, 336 #2, 358–9 #20
  experiential concepts, *see* concepts, empirical; *see also* gold
  law of 45
  outer, *see* outer
extension [*Ausdehnung*]
  property of bodies 15, 28, 92, 161
  of a concept and as opposed to comprehension or intension 382 #39, 428 #77
extensive magnitude, *see* magnitude

faculty [*Vermögen*]
  for determining real objects through thinking 206, *see also* understanding
  of cognition [*Erkenntnisvermögen*] 12–13, 168, 207, 305, 340–1 #5, 416 #62, 417 #65, 419 #63, 436
    absolute 207
    limited 349 -50 #15
    unlimited 377 #34
  of fictions [*Erdichtungsvermögen*], 19, 20, *see also* imagination
  of intuition(s) 8, 34, 206–7
  of judgement [*Beurteilungsvermögung*] 53–4
  of practical judgement 434
  of representation 161, 419 #63, 425–6 #76
  of rules 7, *see also* understanding
  of thought 2, 29, 116, 156, 206–7, 257, 286
false, falsity 145–50, 252, 282, 405 #58
father, cause of son 140
fictional, the merely possible 103
fictions [*Erdichtungen*] 19, 134, 399 #57
  the imagination as faculty of fictions 19
figure
  delimited space 19, 39, 43, 47, 50, 66, 69, 92, 127, 181, 234, 244–5, 276, 311, 370 #29, 400 #58
  of speech 316
final end [*Endzweck*] 292, 297–8
fine arts 293
fire, as cause of warming 5, 7, 72–4, 102, 140, 247, 309, 356 #15, 388 #40
flower 307–8
flowing [*fließend*]
  we can only think objects as flowing 33–4
  body or speech 308

INDEX

forcefulness [*Stärke*], of representations 103
force [*Kraft*], concept of 330
form
function
  mathematical 35, 290, 354 #15, 373 #31
  logical 113, 125, 183

Galileo (1564–1642) 232
gaps, experience constructed by filling in gaps in our perceptions 140
genetic explanation or definition of a concept 58
genius 279, 294, 369 #29, 444
genus, classification by genus and species 77, 317–18, 320, 322, 443
geometry 22, 69, 275–6, 280
  geometric figures 276
  geometric series 77
geometrical, *see also* magnitude
  proposition, principle, theorem 180, 274, 369 #29
  learning 281
German, Germany 10, 280, 314, 321
giant, child suddenly turning into 139
given, the 21, 48, 63, 99, 131, 199, 200, 201, 248, 251, 271, 385 #39, 389 #42, 416 #62, 417 #65, 419 #63, 425–6 #76
God 196, 199–200, 206–7
  definition 196, 200
gold, example of an experiential concept 15, 102–5, 161, 283, 339 #3, 386–8 #39
good spirit, *see* Ormuzd
good, goodness, moral good 409 #58 441, 442
grammar, universal vs particular 296–7
grammarians 319
Greek language 330
green, perception of or property of a body 32, 41, 44, 103, 131–2, 181, 216, 260
ground [*Grund*], *see also* sufficient reason
  definition of 242
  real as opposed to ideal 135, 171
  ultimate 420 #67

haptic 201
hardness, property of a body 92, 102, 161
heat
  has intensive magnitude 122–3
  as cause: expands air, melts water 46–7, 129, 240
heathen mythology 294
Hebrew 309, 319
heterogeneous [*ungleichartig/verschiedenartig*]
  heterogeneity of objects of intuition 15, 54, 179, 346–7 #9
  heterogeneity of intuitions and concepts 63–4, 365 #27
  heterogeneity of inner and outer perceptions 159–60
  use of one expression for heterogeneous things 303, 306, 313–4
hexagon 233–4
history 154, 306, 319–20
hochel, Hebrew word meaning to consume 309
homogeneous [*einartig, gleichartig*]
  sensible representations 30, 81, 120–1, 346–7 #9, 360 #23, 398 #54
Horace (65–8 BC) 322, 367 #27
hot and cold as mutually exclusive determinations 138
house, Kant's example of successive representation 188
human being [*Mensch*] 94, 193–4, 253, 380 #39, 386 #39, 428 #77, *see also* man
human soul 207
development, historical 306
humanity, interest of 442
Hume, David (1711–1776) 9, 72–3, 215, 371 #30
Hurons, Canadian people 301
hyperbole, example of trope 276, 316
hypotenuse 243
  definition 326

INDEX

hypothetical judgement, proposition or concept, *see* judgement
positing of principles 359 #22

I, the 157, 163, 193–4, 202, 208–10
idea [*Idee*], of reason, of the understanding 8, 64–5, 75–7, 80–1, 99, 102, 106, 118, 163–5, 168, 192, 194, 196, 198, 200, 226, 228, 237–8, 248, 251, 266, 327–9, 347 #11, 350–1 #15, 365–6 #27, 374 #32, 375–6 #33, 392 #47, 398 #53, 419 #63, 421 #69, 439, 443
ideal coin, as opposed to real 406–8 #58, 412 #58
idealism, idealist 155, 159–60, 162–4, 202–5, 208, 416 #62
illusion 202, 363 #26
image [*Bild*] 69–70, 179, 182, 202, 346 #15, 427 #76
imagination, the [*Einbildungskraft*] 19–20, 27, 30–2, 36, 45, 80, 82, 92, 100, 102–5, 127, 129, 133–5, 161, 268, 302, 348 #12, 357 #16 357 #17, 360 #23, 399 #57
impenetrability, property of a body 15, 92, 161
impossible, the 98, 104–5
impulse 222
individual [*Individuum*], an
possibility of thinking 77
not determined by transcendental I 156
individual judgement, proposition or concept, *see* judgement
individuality of things in themselves, beyond our grasp 257
induction 5, 92, 336 #2, 342 #5
inference 203, 277, 346 #9, 387 #39
infinite, the
is a mere idea 237–8, 274, 328
real as opposed to symbolic infinite 353 #15
infinite
approximation 329, *see also* infinity, approach to

distance 289
series 77, 164–5, 191, 201, 228–9, 419–20 #63, 438, 443
infinitely
decreasing consciousness 351 #15
small 82, 217, 231, 235–7, 287–8, 291, 351–5 #15, 394–6 #56
large 287, 291, 353 #15
long 289
infinity 197
actual 236–7
approach to 76, 102, 164, 193, 329, 443
progress to infinity, *ad infinitum* 11, 207, 228, 230, 248, 254–5, 265, 273, 421 #69, 443
of the quantum 288
mathematical, as opposed to actual 236, 275
of space 182
theory of infinity in mathematics 227, 275
innate, all concepts of the understanding are 44
inner, the thing in itself 69
ground 61, 92, 103
sense 194
instant 236, 290, *see also* point in time
instinct, in mathematics 369 #29
empiricists reduce reason to instinct 433
intellectual
representations, succeed sensible representations 306
things 204, 433, 438, *see also* noumena
world 207
intelligible world, intelligible objects 338–9 #3
intensive magnitude, *see* magnitude
interaction of mind and body, *see commercio animi et corporis*
interest
material 438–9
objective or subjective 439–40, 442
of reason, *see* reason
intuition(s) [*Anschauung*]
actual 207

271

INDEX

intuition(s), *cont.*
individual 29–30, 121, 131–2, 283
quality of, *see* quality
outer, *see* outer
reduction to their elements, *see* reduction
invention [*Erfindung*] 70, 283, 309, 317, 324, 326, 328, 353 #15, 360 #29, 370 #30, 410 #58
irrational magnitude, *see* magnitude
root 77, 164, 229, 361 #25, 374 #31, 374 #32, 419 #63
animals, the 265

Jourdain 316
judgement [*Urteil*], *see also* faculty of judgement, power of judgement
assertoric 47, 50–1, 93, 184–5, 419 #63
disjunctive 45, 84, 86, 98, 126, 150, 226, 380 #38
hypothetical 23, 39–41, 51–2, 71–2, 94, 108, 150, 174, 183–4, 213, 217–8, 226, 240, 260, 262, 324, 337 #2
individual 180, 242
universal 106, 109, 242, 390 #43, 393 #49, 420 #67
judicum practicum [practical judgement] 434

Kästner, Abraham Gotthelf (1719–1800) 232, 234, 236, 279, 287, 424 #74
Klopstock, Friedrich Gottlieb (1724–1803) 370

La Mettrie, Julien Offray de (1709–1751) 441
language(s) 264, 267, 293–332, 381–2 #39, 413 #58, *see also* Greek, parts of speech
actual languages 297–99, 301–2
ideal language 298, 301, 328
mechanics of, *see* mechanics
origin of 294
sounds of 147–8, 294, 298

last thing [*Zuletzt*], = the true I 194
Latin 330
law
canon 440
moral, Kant 440
objective 21
subjective 127
of identity or relation 100
of mechanics 441
of my mode of representation 127
for the application of a priori concepts to experience 51
left and right as different determinations of space 121, 343 #6
Leibniz, Gottfried Wilhelm (1746–1716) 323–5, 327, 330, 362 #26
Leibnizian
philosopher 136, 208
system 206, 437
Leibnizian-Wolffian 63–4, 248–9
Lessing, Gotthold Ephraim (1729–1781) 329
light rays 202
light and darkness 321
limit [*Gränze*] 43, 50, 186–7, 194, 257, 266, 306, 339 #3, 349 #15, 374 #32, 419 #63, 439, 444
line(s), *see also* curve, straight line
crooked as opposed to straight 99 252
direction of 49, 65, 70, 79, 95, 245, 314
endpoint 39, 43, 51, 75, 79, 106, 235
measurable, a geometrical line must be measurable 396 #56
quality of, *see* quality
parallel 107, 232–4, 274, 287, 289, 351 #15, 368 #29, 392–3 #48, 394–5 #56
Locke, John (1632–1704) 295, 310
logic 3–4, 8, 41, 71–2, 74, 85, 115, 185, 210, 240, 259, 299, 305, 316, 330, 336 #2, 381 #39, 431–2 #80, 440
general versus transcendental 85
logical form 23–4, 118, 215, 329, 331, 397 #51

logic, *cont.*
  logical functions 113, 125, 183
  logical object, *see* object, logical
  logical reality, *see* reality
  logical truth, *see* truth
logicians 178, 317
Lucretius (c.99-c.55 BC) 370 #29

machines, mechanical calculation 279–80, 282
magnet 5, 429 #78
magnitude [*Größe*] 22, 34, 65, 68–9, 111, 113–14, 120–3, 176–7, 182, 196, 221, 235, 241, 258, 276, 290–2, 350–6 #15, 357 #17, 373 #31, 374 #32, 391 #44, 394–6 #56,
  definition of 113
  extensive 22, 27, 120–2, 394–5 #56
  geometrical 374 #32
  infinite 182
  infinitely small 354 #15
  intensive 27, 120–2, 290, 394–6 #56, 398 #53, *see also* cold, heat
  irrational 354 #15
  smaller and greater, ingredients of magnitude 113–14
man [*Mensch*] 320, 322, *see also* human being
manifold, the [*Mannigfältiges*] 13–21, 24, 31, 33, 35, 37, 55, 57, 75, 80–1, 112, 130–2, 153, 159–61, 187, 191, 215–16, 249, 256, 259, 271, 283–4, 343 #6, 360 #23, 397 #65, 416 #62
materialism, materialist(s) 155, 159, 163, 208, 302, 416 #62, 417 #65. 440–1
materialiter, materially, as opposed to *formaliter* 41, 58, 99–100, 128, 133, 146, 169, 174
material
  the material, the real 121, 190, 202
  raw material 410 #58
  completeness or totality of a concept, *see* concept
  lack 59
  things 306
mathematical
  invention 370 #29
  propositions 57, 61, 152, 405 #58
mathematics 2, 19, 59–61, 96, 106, 173–4, 178, 183, 185, 189, 227, 229, 237, 283, 329, 330, 335 #1, 337 #2, 248 #12, 355 #15, 363 #26, 373 #31 389 #41, 412 #58, 417 #68
  invention of a new 150
matter [*Materie, Stoff*] 2, 10, 12–14, 37, 43, 48–52, 60–6, 74, 76, 81–2, 113, 115, 117, 128, 133, 135, 139, 147, 160–4, 168, 201, 203–5, 213, 223, 247, 252, 271, 296, 309, 335 #1, 336–7 #2, 338 #3, 340–1 #5, 362 #26, 376 #34, 392 #46, 398 #54, 406–7 #58, 413–15 #58, 416 #62, 425–6 #76, 437
  contingent 99
  definition of matter and form of cognition 340 #5
  essential 99
  real as opposed to imagined 135, 413 #58
maxim of actions, in agreement with universal rule of reason 409 #58
maximum
  of difference 407 #58
  of identity, = minimum of difference 213, 218, 220, 372 #30
  in thinking 2
mechanics 232
  of language 315
  laws of mechanics 441
  mechanical action, not based in understanding 281, 411 #58
  mechanical knowledge, knowledge of mechanics 441
Mendelssohn, Moses (1729–1786) 329, 437
metaphysical, this investigation metaphysical not moral 415 #59
  proposition 360 #24
  truth, *see* truth

metaphysical, *cont.*
  metaphysically infinitely small 355 #15
metaphysics 9, 174, 195–6, 227, 240–1, 335 #2, 431–2 #80
method 51, 165, 285, 325, 365 #27, 369 #29, 411 #58, 414 #58
  mathematical methods of the ancients 279, 285, 412 #58
methodus indivisibilium [method of indivisibles] 274, *see also* calculus
mind, the [*Gemüth*] 81, 133, 168, 269, 306, 308, 316, 338 #3, 381–4 #39, 390 #43
minimal mutual exclusion of determinations, condition of experience 138
moderns 279
modification(s) [*Modifikation*] 62, 159–61, 163–5, 168, 202, 223, 251–3, 261, 308, 340 #4, 417 #65, 419 #63, 420 #66, 421 #69
  inner 223, 308
  outer 308
Monadology 27 n.1
Monboddo, Lord [James Burnet] (1714–1799) 317
moral worth of actions 409 #58
morality 150, 302, 409 #58
moral good 409 #58
moral as opposed to metaphysical 415 #59
moral system, Kantian 441
Moses 440
motion, *see* movement
movement [*Bewegung*] 17, 19, 22, 30, 36, 39, 42, 51, 106, 141, 188, 220–2, 225–6, 230, 229–31, 290, 292, 306–8, 310, 328, *see also* rest
  absolute 19, 230
  accelerated 30, 221–2
  actual 188
  of body, *see* body
  relative 220, 347 #11, 397 #55
    arbitrary choice in 226, 232
    examples of, *see* bank, cabin, ship, stream

music, musicians 280

natural
  sciences 173
  events 184
  history 320
  laws, *see* nature, law of
  philosophical language 318–9
  ability 280
nature
  doctrine of 3–4, 140, 174, 240, 337 #2
  law of 31, 129 222, 363–4 #26
  inner 318
necessity 64, 72–74, 91, 128–9, 171, 173–5, 180, 184–7, 200, 215, 247, 252–4, 295, 330, 342 #5, 360 #22, 370 #30, 392 #46, 418 #72, 423 #73
  inner 235
  logical, as opposed to real 200, 254
  outer 253
  real 254
negation 17, 110, 113–18, 142, 197, 255–7, 365 #27, 394 #51, 397 #51
  logical 110, 113, 115, 117, 255–7
  material 257
Newton, Isaac (1643–1727) 328, 369–70 #29
Newtonian law of nature 31
nihil negativum / nihil privativum [negative nothing, privative nothing] 291
nomina propria [proper name] 319
nomina substantiva [substantive] 323
nominal definition, *see* definition
non-system, Maimon's 443
not-being 421 #59
nothing
  nothingness of consciousness 419 #63
  formally and materially nothing 98–9, 105, 241
  the infinitely small is not nothing 352 #15
  irrational root is not nothing 374 #32

274

nothing, *cont.*
  kinds of 286–91
  nothing is identical with nothing 259
  as opposed to something 115, 321
noumena 32, 97, 209, 362 #26, 419 #63, *see also* intellectual things, thing in itself
number(s) 22, 58, 75–7, 105, 111, 165, 190, 197, 227–9, 235–6, 244–5, 272–3, 275, 288, 291, 294, 312–3, 324, 329, 350 #15, 361 #25, 374–5 #32, 395–6 #56, 398 #54, 424 #75, *see also* arising
  infinite 75, 105, 111, 228, 235–6, 274, 375 #32, 381 #39
  natural, complete series of 227, 288
  whole 229, 374 #32

object [*Gegenstand, Objekt*]
  actual 188
  object in general 206
  geometrical, definition of 276
  logical, as opposed to real 190–1, 212, 241, 336–7 #2, 400 #58, 432 # 80, 433, *see also* object in general, *objectum logicum*
  real 31, 72, 162, 164, 190, 192–3, 196, 206, 212, 228, 241, 250, 259, 272, 286, 289, 336–7 #2, 345 #9, 359 #20, 360–1 #24, 365 #27, 373 #31, 412 #58, 423 #73, 433, 443
  symbolic, *see* symbolic
objective order of cognition 82, 377 #34
objectum logicum [logical object] 151, 206, 286, 345 #9, *see also* object
objectum reale [real object] 251, 286, *see also* object
omni dabili majus, omni dabili minor/ minus [greater than, less than any given] 231, 288, 353 #15, 396 #56
ontological definition of God 196
ontology 239–40
opposition, *a priori* concept 56, 85, 90, 110, 113–15, 117, 139, 255–6, 305, 344–5 #9, 426 #76
  logical 115
organs, sense organs 381 #39
origin
  of synthetic propositions 9
  of synonyms 312
original meaning 303, 306, 309, 313–4
original, as opposed to copy 78, 134–5, 181
Ormuzd, Zoroastrian spirit 302
outer
  the, relation to other things 69
  sensation, perception, experience, intuition 141, 159–60, 179, 210–11, 429 #79

painters 280
parabola, parabolic line 257, 276, 382–3 #39
paradox 70
paralogisms, Kantian 208–9
partes orationis [parts of speech] 298–9, 301, 321
  quality of, *see* quality
parts of speech, *see partes orationis*
passive(ly) [*leidend*] 13, 20, 29, 168, 203, 417 #65, 419 #63
perception(s) [*Wahrnehmung*]
  actual 372 #30
  inner 259–60
  outer, *see* outer
perfection [*Vollkommenheit*], *see also* completeness 297–8, 329, 408–9 #58, 441
  highest degree of 239
perimeter, of a polygon 233
persistence [*Beharrlichkeit*] 157, 210, 429 #79
personality, identity of consciousness at different times 156, 166, 210
personification, example of trope 316
phenomena, vs noumena 32
philosophy 2–5, 8, 62, 259, 296–7, 299, 320, 330, 335–7 #2, 346 #9, 363–4 #26, 444
physicians 440
physiological knowledge 440–1

INDEX

place, in space 17, 19, 90, 140, 344 #8, 347 #11, 391 #44
  absolute 19
Plato (427–347 BC) 444
pleasure 280, 409 #58
Ploucquet, Gottfried (1716–1790) 327, 380–4 #39
plurality [*Vielheit*] 15, 67, 76, 120–3, 198, 251–2, 258, 356 #15
  arbitrary 21, 348 #13
  inner 122–3, 252
  outer 252
poetry
  as opposed to prose 304, 315, 370 #29
point
  differentials of sensation as physical points 28, 82–3
  mathematical, as opposed to physical 28
  is an extended point possible? 171
  no pure intuition of space or time can arise from adding points together 25
  in time 17, 24–5, 83, 136
politicians 339 #3, 412 #58, 440
polygon 233–6, 245, 272, 274
possible, possibility
  arbitrary 172
  definition 250
  real 421 #69
postulates, in Euclid 66
power [*Kraft*]
  of judgement 71, 129, *see also* faculty of judgement
  of representation 117–19, 162–3, 425 #76
  of invention 70, 368 #29
practical judgement, *see judicum practicum*
principium exclusi tertii [principle of excluded middle] 71
principle [*Satz*]
  of continuity 139, 142
  of contradiction 4, 57, 68, 71, 146, 150, 169, 172, 175, 178, 184, 241, 359 #22, 417 #68, 423 #73, 431 #80, 433
  of determination or determinability, *see* law of the determinable and the determination
  of identity 61, 58, 150, 170
  material as opposed to formal *a priori* principle [Princip] 433
probability [*Wahrscheinlichkeit*] 61, 173, 437
  highest degree of 61
problematic, judgements, concepts etc. 46, 48, 50, 58, 98, 105, 146, 151, 184, 253, 360–1 #24
production [*Hervorbringung*]
  of an intuition 246
  of objects 19, 58, 68
profession 439, 442
progressum in infinitum [infinite regress] 11
pronomen demonstrativum [demonstrative pronoun] 322
  relativum [relative pronoun] 322
proportion [*Größenverhältnis*], *see* ratio
prose, as opposed to poetry 303–4, 306, 315–17
Prussian blue, *see* Berlin blue
Psalmists 444
psychologia rationalis [rational psychology] 155, 158
Pythagorean theorem 429 #78

quadrilateral 311
quality
  of intuitions and differentials as opposed to quantity 15, 23, 27–8, 291, 355 #15, 395 #56
  of a line as opposed to quantity 177, 396 #56
  of parts of speech 298
  colour as sensible quality 420 #66
quantity [*Quantität*] 23, 27, 82, 268, 290–2, 355 #15, 383 #39, 395 #56, 398 #53, 398 #54, *see also* magnitude
quantum 288, 290–2, 351 #15, 395 #56
quid facti? [question of fact] 9, 27, 70, 129

quid juris? [question of right] 9, 27, 32, 41, 48, 51, 55, 59–62, 72, 82, 112, 128, 135, 187, 192, 209, 212–13, 355 #15, 362–4 #26
quid rationis? [question of reason] 364 #26
ratio [*Zahlen-Verhältnis, Größenverhältnis*] 34–5, 190, 394 #56, *see also* proportion, reason
reaction, in dynamics 224
real, the [*reale, reelle*], something real 21, 121, 142, 159, 171, 210, 286
  ideas, though they cannot be presented in intuition, are real 328–9
real
  a priori 363 #26
  axioms of mathematics real, not true, *see* axiom
  artist, as opposed to fake 281
  coin, as opposed to ideal 406–8 #58
  concept, as opposed to symbolic, *see* concept
  consequences 385–7 #39
  real as opposed to nominal definition, *see* definition
  form 413–4 #58
  infinitely small 353–5 #15
  matter, as opposed to imagined, *see* matter
  most real being 199
  necessity, as opposed to logical, *see* necessity
  object(s), *see* object
  possibility, *see* possibility
  proposition, as opposed to not real 149–50, 413–4 #58
  relation, *see* relation
  synthesis, as opposed to symbolic, *see* synthesis
  thought, *see* thought
reality [*Realität*], a priori concept, correlate of negation 110, 113–19, 255–7, 394 #51, 397 #51
  degree of 23, 88, 101, 165, 398 #53

  logical 115, 117, 255–6
  material 257
  objective, of a concept or a synthesis or a judgement 39, 41, 46, 48–51, 62, 71–2, 74, 99, 130, 151, 153, 179, 182–3, 185–7, 190, 197–9, 212, 215, 247, 261, 265, 271, 275, 328, 336–7 #2, 354 #15, 365–7 #27, 372 #30, 390 #43, 398 #53, 411–2 #58, 418 #72, 436–7
realities 196–200
God contains all possible realities 196
reason [*Vernunft*], *see also* maxim of actions
  annihilation of 434
  antinomy of pure reason 226–31, 237–8
  claims and possessions of 442–3
  faculty of 32, 75, 77, 80–3, 106, 118, 150, 187, 226–30, 237, 257, 265, 285, 302, 348 #12, 355 #15, 359 #22, 364 #26, 367 #27, 373–4 #31, 374 #32, 376 #33, 377 #34, 392 #47, 409 #58, 433–9, 442–4
  idea of, *see* idea of reason and understanding
  infinite 443
  interest of 150, 433–5, 437–9, 442
  law of 439, 442
  reduction to instinct, *see* instinct
  of sides, i.e. ratio 369 #29
reception [*Aufnahme*], of sense perceptions 29
reciprocal 37, 47, 107, 124–5, 190, 212–13, 262, 300, 314, 392 #46
red 13, 27, 32, 41, 44, 67, 82–3, 92–3, 121, 131–2, 181, 307, 340–2 #5, 426 #76, 433, *see also* colour
reduction
  of intuitions to their elements 9
  of reason to instinct, *see* instinct
reflection, concepts of, *see* concept
regress to infinity 248
relation [*Verhältnis, Beziehung*] 17–18, 21, 23–5, 31–8, 42, 44, 47, 54, 57, 59–60, 64–70, 76–8, 89, 95,

277

relation, *cont.*
100–2, 105, 107, 112–14, 116–121, 125–6, 131, 134, 136, 142, 145, 147, 150, 156–8, 160–2, 169–70, 179–83, 185–7, 189–91, 193, 196, 201–207, 211–15, 217–20, 222–5, 229–30, 240–1, 244, 247–8, 250–62, 268, 270, 273, 277, 285–6, 290, 298, 300–1, 305, 307–8, 313, 315–16, 321, 323, 325, 327, 336–7 #2, 340–2 #5, 344 #8, 346 #9, 349 #15, 354–6 #15, 359 #20, 364 #26, 372–3 #30, 373 #31, 378 #35, 383 #39, 388 #41, 391 #43, 392 #46, 395–6 #56, 399 #57, 405 #58, 407–8 #58, 413 #58, 415 #61, 418 #72, 421 #69, 423 #73, 425–6 #76, 431 #79, 433, 443

inner 95, 213–4, 217, 262, 307, 418 #72

logical 116

outer 95, 213, 262

real 214, 355–6 #15

relation-determination 97, 389 #42

relational concept, *see* concept

re-membrance [*Widererrinerung*] 94

repetition [*Wiederholung*] 80

representation(s) [*Vorstellung*] 18, 22–3, 25, 27–31, 44–6, 57, 62, 64, 80–83, 96, 103, 117–21, 124, 127, 132–6, 141, 157–63, 165–6, 169–72, 175, 179–80, 182, 188, 193, 195, 202–4, 208–10, 216, 229, 238, 248, 260, 267–70, 277, 283, 293, 295–7, 305, 342 #5, 344 #9, 346 #9, 348 #11, 349 #15, 365 #27, 377 #34, 386 #39, 391 #44, 396 #56, 398 #54, 399 #57, 413 #58, 415 #61, 416 #62, 419 #63, 420 #66, 425–6 #76, 430 #79, 436

obscure as opposed to clear 269 n.11, 296

individual 29–30, 121, 131–2, 283, *see also*, intuition

reproduction [*Reproduktion*]
in intuition of succession 26, 216, 268–9, 278, 372 #30

involved in any representation 349 #15

rest [*Ruhe*], absolute or relative, as opposed to motion 158, 224–6, 328, 444

riddle, of existence of transcendental object 161

right, and left as different representations of space 121, 343 #6

right, legal 64, 135, 428 #77, 440

right-angled triangle, *see* triangle

rolling, paradox of the wheel 231–6

Roman law 440

rotation, *see* rolling

rule
the understanding is the faculty of rules 7

conforming with a rule as opposed to comprehending it 20, 35

salis populi [welfare of the people] 440

Satan 302

sceptics 434, 438

schema 27, 121, 126, 133, 156, 179, 275–6, 328, 346–7 #9, 365–6 #27, 419 #63, 435, 438

scholastic professor 362 #26

science(s) [*Wissenschaft*] 2–3, 8–9, 154, 173–5, 183–4, 189, 196, 227, 239–40, 266, 275, 330, 399 #58, 429 #78, 440

natural science 173

self 56, 210, 429 #79

self-contradiction, self-contradictory 29, 105, 152

self-evidence, self-evident [*Evidenz*] 174, 178, 227, 242, 275, 348 #12, 418 #72

self-identical 83, 89, 96, 136–8

sensation [*Empfindung*] 21, 141, 168, 170, 179, 205, 340 #4, 397 #51, 419 #63, 420 #66, 441

outer, *see* outer

INDEX

sense, inner, outer 82, 194, *see also* sensibility

senses, the [*Sinne*] 174, 207

sense organs 381 #39

sensibility [*Sinnlichkeit*], faculty 12, 14–15, 27, 31, 36, 56, 63, 81–2, 96, 127, 133, 135–6, 157, 182–3, 191, 227, 237, 340 #4, 347 #9, 348 #12, 376–7 #34, 418 #72

law of 227

separate, separateness [*Auseinandersein*] 17, 24, 25, 88, *see also* being-apart

sequence, temporal 54, 64, 125–8, 135–6, 142, 158, 183, 187–8, 216–18, 220, 228, 261, 268, 308, 370 #30, 372 #30, *see also* succession

series [*Reihe*] 77, 135, 164–6, 191, 193, 195, 201, 209, 227–9, 248, 304, 374 #32, 419 #63, 420 #67, 421 #69, 438, 443

Shaftesbury [Anthony Ashley-Cooper, 3rd Earl of] (1671–1713) 444

shape [*Figur*] 147, 222, 274, 283–4, 341 #5, 387 #39, *see also* figure

ship, example of relative motion 157–8, 188–9

Sibyl 367 #27

sign [*Zeichen*] 145–7, 252, 266–73, 277–8, 281, 284–5, 287, 292–302, 315, 319, 324, 342 #5, 382–3 #39, 407 #58, 411 #58, 413–14 #58, *see also* correspondence, designation, symbol

natural as opposed to arbitrary 268, 277–8, 293–5

similarity [*Aehnlichkeit*] 70, 139, 304, 313, 325

simple, simplicity 156, 165, 174, 195, 208–9, 295, 330, 433

simultaneous, simultaneity [*Zugleichsein*] 17–8, 25, 92, 141–2, 188, 224, 230, 262, 344 #8, 373 #30, *see also* coexistence

sine, trigonometry 165, 228, 352 #15

small, infinitely 82, 137, 139, 217, 231, 235–7, 287–8, 291, 351–5 #15, 394–6 #56, 398 #53

smaller and greater, *see* magnitude

'snow is white', synthetic *a posteriori* proposition 4

snow, snowfall 371 #30

soul [*Seele*] 62–3, 141, 166, 174, 207, 209, 293, 339 #3, 362 #25, 441

space [*Raum*] 4, 12, 14–26, 30, 32, 36, 47, 55, 57, 60, 64, 804, 92, 96, 100, 103, 105, 112–13, 121, 127, 133–6, 157, 159–62, 169, 174, 178–82, 185, 198, 202–5, 229, 231, 237–8, 247–9, 271, 284, 290–2, 308, 315, 335 #1, 337 #2, 341–2 #5, 343 #6, 344 #8, 346–7 #9, 347 #10, 347 #11, 348 #13, 354 #15, 398 #54, 399 #57, 415 #61, 420 #66, 421 #69, 424–7 #76, *see also* right

speciosa generalis, see ars characteristica combinatoria

Spinoza, Baruch (1632–1677)

Spinozans 208

spontaneity, spontaneous [*freiwillig*] 20–1, 168, 203, 246

square 78, 105, 147, 377 #35

square sphere or circle 105, 147

Stahl. Georg Ernst (1660–1734) 441

stone

warmed by fire 72, 74, 141, 247, 388 #40

'the stone is round' 384 #39

stove, warms the room 371 #30

straight line

concept of 49, 79, 95–7, 99, 101, 125, 169, 191, 198, 246, 252, 257, 286, 389 #42

shortest between two points 6, 19, 43, 54, 59, 61, 65–6, 68–70, 80, 100, 106, 108, 169–70, 173–4, 176–8, 181, 183–4, 242–3, 253, 358 #19, 417 #68, 418 #72, 423 #71

Wolff's definition of 65, 68, 70, 358 #19, 358 #19, 423 #72

279

INDEX

stream, as example of relative motion 189
subject [*Subjekt*]
  of thought, of representations, transcendental etc. 115–16, 119, 129, 131, 141, 146, 155,165, 193–4, 202, 208, 226, 268, 270, 423 #73, 425–7 #76, 428 #77, 429–31 #79
    absolute 208
    as opposed to predicate 4–6, 39–40, 45, 55, 61, 71–2, 84–88, 92–3, 95–102, 106, 109, 113–16, 124, 142, 145–7, 159, 176, 178, 185, 189, 191, 193, 214, 240–1, 247–8, 252–3, 259, 284, 308, 322, 330, 377–8 #35, 379 #36, 379 #37, 380 #38, 381–8 #39, 388 #40, 388 #41, 389 #42, 413 #58, 420 #67
  thinking subject 85, 107, 438
  subjective order of cognition, *see* cognition
  ultimate subject 193, 226, 428 #77, 431 #79
subjectum logicum, *subjectum reale* [logical subject, real subject] 300–1
sublime [*erhaben*] idea 65
subordination, as opposed to coordination 321, 443
substance [*Substanz*], category of 4, 24, 57, 83, 95–6, 116, 126, 136–7, 143–4, 156, 158, 165, 185, 189, 193, 208–9, 215, 259, 260, 286, 299–300, 305, 321, 330, 348–9 #14, 363 #26, 377 #34, 427–8 #77
substrate 159, 162
substratum 99
subtangent 35
succession, temporal 17–18, 21, 30, 36, 54, 64, 71–3, 80, 83, 125, 128–9, 137–8, 140–1, 187–8, 217, 219, 228, 241, 260–2, 370–3 #30, *see also* sequence
  arbitrary 127, 141, 188
  infinite 228

sufficient reason [*zureichender Grund*] 106, 294, 392 #47
Sulzer, Johann Georg (1720–1779) 303 n.12
sum total of possible realities 199, 207
suum cuique [to each his own] 281
'sweet line', cannot be thought 93
syllogism 106, 226, 328
symbol 58, 171, 277, 418 #70
  arbitrary as opposed to natural 277–8, 291, 293–5, *see also* sign
  symbolic concept, *see* symbolic concept
  symbolic cognition, *see* cognition
symbolic concept or object or synthesis as opposed to intuitive 48–50, 69, 100, 171, 289, 351–3 #15
symbolism 266
  mathematical 284
synthesis [*Synthesis*] 21–2, 31, 49–50, 58, 84–6, 88–93, 95, 98–105, 107, 124–7, 138, 143, 145, 154, 161–2, 182, 189, 191, 194, 198–100, 215, 219, 243, 246, 252, 259, 272, 283–4, 314, 348 #13, 349 #15, 377–8 #35, 378–9 #36, 379 #37, 384–6 #39, 388 #40, 392 #46, 398 #52, 418 #70
  arbitrary 22, 99, 101, 103, 105, 143, 284of the imagination 20, 80, 92, 103, 105, 161
  of the faculty of fictions 20
  of the understanding 93, 100, 104, 124
  one-sided 37, 98–9, 124–5, 392 #46
  reciprocal 99, 124, *see also* reciprocal
  real 89–90, 105, 200, 284, 398 #52
  symbolic, *see* symbolic concept
system 10, 63–4, 206, 227, 266, 282–3, 299, 302, 320, 324, 329, 338–9, 350 #15, 433, 435, 437–443

table, Kant's table of categories 183
'table square', impossible synthesis 377–8 #35
Talmudists 444
theists 208

INDEX

theologians 439, 440
things in themselves 96, 108, 113, 204, 255, 257, 343 #7, 389 #41, 394 #51, 435, *see also* noumena
thinkability 61, 77, 107, 194, 247, 376 #34, 388–9 #41
thinking being 1–2
  individual 305
  infinite 182–3
thinking/thought [*Denken*]
  law of 149, 207, 406 #58
  real 89–90, 105, 200, 284, 398 #52
thousand, *see* 1000
time [*Zeit*] 4, 8–9, 12–19, 21–26, 30, 36–8, 42, 45, 48, 52–3, 55–7, 60, 64, 70, 72, 80–1, 83, 85, 90, 92, 94, 96–7, 99–100, 103–5, 111–13, 115, 117, 121–2, 124–7, 133–9, 141–4, 146, 156–60, 163–6, 169, 182, 185, 190, 202, 204–5, 209–11, 214, 228–9, 231–3, 235–7, 247–9, 251, 258, 268, 271, 284, 290–2, 301, 307–8, 314, 319, 335 #1, 337 #2, 342 #5, 343 #6, 343 #7, 344 #8, 347 #9, 348 #13, 349 #14, 350 #15, 354 #15, 376 #34, 380 #38, 387 #39, 391 #44, 415 #60, 419 #63, 420 #66, 426 #76, 430 #79, 432 #80, 443
time-determination, *see* determination
totality 76–7, 80–1, 83, 328, 367 #27, 376 #33
  absolute 367 #27
  infinite 77, 80
tangent, trigonometric 287, 289, 291, 412 #58
town, example of a trope 315
transcendent, illegitimate use of concept of space 134–5, 179, 182, 399 #57
transcendental philosophy 3, 5, 8, 259, 299, 330, 363–4 #26
  idealism 162, 202
  subject 202, 428 #77
triangle, mathematical example 19, 21, 34, 44–5, 47, 66, 84, 93, 100–1, 103–4, 106–7, 118, 122, 125–6, 129, 132–3, 145–7, 149, 157, 161, 171, 198, 243–51, 271, 274–5, 284, 288, 326, 356 #16, 367–8 #28, 369–70 #29, 378 #35, 386–8 #39, 391 #44, 392–3 #48, 394 #50, 394–5 #56, 400 #58, 405 #58, 414 #58, 420 #67, 421 #69
  Wolff's definition 400 #58
  oblique-angled 45, 84, 125–6, 248–9, 311, 370 #29
  obtuse-angled 21, 122
  right-angled 21, 45, 84, 93, 101, 103, 118, 122, 125–6, 145, 161, 198, 243, 248, 251, 288, 311, 326, 386–8 #39, 391 #44, 395 #56, 420 #67
trinity, of God, world and human soul 206
tropes 303–7, 313–6
truth [*Wahrheit*] 1, 10, 60, 70, 167, 252, 282, 285, 301, 339, 383 #39, 406 #58, 437, *see also* principle of contradiction
  compared to coins 400ff #58
  elements of 148
  logical 145ff, 399–400 #58
    defined 148, 150
  objective 145ff, 151–4, 405–6 #58
  principles of 406 #58
  products of 148
  of representation 210
  subjective 145ff, 151–4, 405–6 #58
  truths 9, 148, 153, 198, 304, 326, 339, 406 #58 428–9 #78
    mathematical 190
    metaphysical 150\
    new 265, 326, 353 #15, 411 #58

unconditioned, the 201, 226, 347 #11
understanding, faculty of the [*Verstand*] 2, 7, 9, 12–14, 19–21, 23, 27, 31–5, 37–39, 41, 44–5, 48–50, 52–4, 56, 59, 62–5, 68–9, 73, 75–6, 78–83, 92–3, 97, 100, 102–6, 112, 114, 118, 124, 128,

INDEX

understanding, faculty of the, *cont.*
130–1, 133–6, 148–9, 152, 170, 172, 181–3, 189–93, 195, 206–7, 212–3, 217, 227–8, 248–51, 256, 271, 278, 282–3, 285, 310, 317, 336 #2, 338 #3, 340 #4, 342 #5, 348 #12, 349 #15, 355–6 #15, 356–7 #16, 357 #17, 359 #20, 360 #22, 361 #24, 365–7 #37, 373 #31, 374 #32, 375–6 #33, 376–7 #34, 385–6 #39, 392 #46, 397 #51, 399 #57, 399 #58, 418 #72
an absolute understanding 227–8
human understanding limited 207, 227, 365 #27, 418 #72
an infinite understanding 64, 93, 100, 181, 195, 207, 248–51, 289, 365–6 #27 376 #33
law of 148, 227, 399 #58
uniform [*einförmig*] intuition 18
unit, unity 21–2, 34, 273, 348 #13, 350 #15, 354 #15, 374–5 #32, 395–6 #56
absolute 24, 258, 273, 327, 350 #15, 353–4 #15
arbitrary 21, 29 n.2, 34
inner 122, 252
outer 252
universal grammar 296
universalization 164

value [*Werth*]
material 407 #58, 414 #58
real as opposed to ideal 407–8 #58, 411 #58
standard of value 406–9 #58
validity [*Gültigkeit*]
objective 16, 186, 229
velocity 30–1, 231, 290–2
volatile 308–9

water
difference of two drops 120
alters from fluid to solid 127, 129
alters from cold to warm 137–8
homogeneous in intuition 134, 346 #9
weight, determination of a body 92, 102–4, 203, 283–4, 343 #7
wheel, paradox of 230ff
whole 22, 65, 70, 140, 149, 162, 243, 248, 258, 261, 288, 305, 308, 375 #32, 387 #39, 396 #56, 417 #65, *see also* world-whole
definition 258
Wieland, Christoph Martin (1733–1813) 329
Wilkins, John [Bishop of Chester] (1614–1672) 317
wine, takes shape of its vessel 341 #5
wisdom [*Weisheit*], infinite 441
students of 444
wit 279, 309–11
Wolff, Christian Freiherr von (1679–1754) 65, 267, 270, 324, 400 #58, 442
Wolffian(s) 68, 70, 239, 438–9, *see also* Leibnizian-Wolffian
world 62, 200, 207, 338–9
world-whole [*Weltganze*] 227

yellow, property of gold 15, 102, 104, 283–4, 386–8 #39, *see also* colour

Zion 444

282